Magnus Felix Ennodius

RECENTIORES: LATER LATIN TEXTS AND CONTEXTS
James J. O'Donnell, Series Editor

Magnus Felix Ennodius

A Gentleman of the Church

S. A. H. Kennell

Ann Arbor

THE UNIVERSITY OF MICHIGAN PRESS

2003   2002   2001   2000   4   3   2   1

A CIP catalog record for this book is available from the British Library.

Library of Congress Cataloging-in-Publication Data

Kennell, S. A. H., 1959–
    Magnus Felix Ennodius : a gentleman of the church / S. A. H. Kennell.
        p.   cm. — (Recentiores)
    Includes bibliographical references and index.
    ISBN 0-472-10917-0 (alk. paper)
        1. Ennodius, Magnus Felix, Saint, 474–521.   I. Title.   II. Series.
    BR65.E456 K46 2000
    270.2'092—dc21   00-08542

Epigraph from Robertson Davies, *Murther & Walking Spirits.* Reprinted by permission of Curtis, Brown, Ltd. Used by permission of Viking Penguin, a division of Penguin Putnam Inc. and by McClelland & Stewart Inc. *The Canadian Publishers.*

Dis Manibus

Brocky . . . is no philosopher, and certainly no theologian, but is he not the better for that? He is open to contradiction on just about every point in his reflections that I have overheard, and seen projected on the screen that is the correlative of his mind. He is really not much more than a boy, and loaded as he is with Eng-Lang-and-Lit he has had small experience of life, although this war is maturing him rapidly and roughly. But I like him—love him, indeed—as I never did when I knew him simply as my father. He is not the slave of his intellect; he has a heart and—what am I saying—a soul.

—Robertson Davies, *Murther & Walking Spirits*

Acknowledgments

Many have contributed over the years to the development of this book. At the University of Toronto I thank Chris McDonough, John Magee, Elaine Fantham, Fr. Leonard Boyle, and especially Tim Barnes; their scholarship continues to instruct and inspire. Elsewhere, I exchanged ideas (often quite energetically) with Peter Brown, Judith Herrin, Robert Benson, Glen Bowersock, Giles Constable, John Van Engen, Tomas Hägg, Anthony Cutler, Franz-Georg and Marie-Louise Maier, Michael Roberts, and Christian Rohr. I also thank the Interlibrary Loan office staff at Memorial University of Newfoundland's Queen Elizabeth II Library and the Historical and Social Science Library of the Institute for Advanced Study for fulfilling many a challenging request. The kindness of Gilbert Dagron and Marguerite Debae facilitated library access in France and Belgium. Through the good offices of an anonymous priest of Pavia, I was able to inspect Ennodius' epitaph. Enrico Galbiati, Beat Näf, and Eckhard Wirbelauer generously provided me with offprints and books. Finally, I owe lasting gratitude to Jim O'Donnell, the editor of *Recentiores;* the press's three anonymous readers, for their long-suffering discernment; and the editorial team led by the extraordinary Ellen Bauerle. Deserving of recognition *hors categorie* is my husband, Nigel, to whom this work owes both form and being.

Contents

Abbreviations

For reasons of economy all works are cited by short title (full references in the bibliography), according to the conventions of *L'Anneé Philologique* and the *Oxford Classical Dictionary* (3d ed., Oxford University Press, 1996), supplemented by the following items.

BEFAR   Bibliothèque des Écoles Françaises d'Athènes et de Rome

CJ   *Codex Justinianus,* ed. P. Krüger (Berlin, 1906)

CTh   *Codex Theodosianus,* ed. T. Mommsen and P. Meyer (Berlin, 1905)

Hartel   *Magni Felicis Ennodii Opera,* ed. G. Hartel, *CSEL* 6 (Vienna, 1882)

LP   *Liber Pontificalis,* ed. T. Mommsen (Berlin, 1898)

PL   *Patrologia Latina,* ed. J.-P. Migne (Paris, 1844–64)

TRE   *Theologische Realenzyklopädie*

Vogel   *Magni Felicis Ennodi Opera,* ed. F. Vogel, *MGH AA* 7 (Berlin, 1885)

Introduction

Magnus Felix Ennodius (474–521), deacon of Milan and later bishop of Ticinum (Pavia), has never been considered a great man of literature or history. Compared to his more esteemed contemporaries Boethius and Cassiodorus, he receives very short shrift. More than four centuries of scholars have exploited Ennodius' generically diverse and pervasively rhetorical corpus of writings, especially the *Panegyric* of King Theoderic and the *Life* of St. Epifanius, quarrying them for information about politics, religion, and education in Ostrogothic Italy. The recent growth of interest in Late Antiquity and the Early Middle Ages has increased the rate at which people are consulting Ennodius' works. The references to secular and ecclesiastical notables they contain, highlighting the eminence of Ennodius' family connections and official acquaintances, give them prosopographical value.[1] Their allusions to buildings, art objects, current events, and educational practice also attract researchers.[2] Ennodius' intricately unclassical Latin appeals to philologists.[3]

Despite, or perhaps because of, this upsurge in interest, some may ask if we really need an entire book devoted to a writer regarded as either a passable source of historical information or a third-rate hack? Yes, we

---

1. Fertig, *Magnus Felix Ennodius;* Hasenstab, *Studien zu Ennodius;* Sundwall, *Abhandlungen;* Stroheker, *Der senatorische Adel;* Näf, *Senatorisches Standesbewusstsein.*
2. Léglise, "Saint Ennodius et la haute éducation littéraire"; Schanz-Hosius, 131–48; Mochi Onory, *Vescovi e città;* Caspar, *Geschichte,* 2; Townsend and Wyatt, "Ennodius and Pope Symmachus, I–II"; Marrou, *History of Education,* 284–91; Ensslin, *Theoderich der Grosse;* Norden, *Die antike Kunstprosa,* 631–56; Fontaine, "Ennodius"; Navarra, "Contributo storico di Ennodio"; Riché, *Education and Culture;* Wolfram, *History;* Moorhead, *Theoderic;* Ward-Perkins, *From Classical Antiquity;* Picard, "Ce que les textes nous apprennent"; Heather, *Goths,* esp. 216–48.
3. Dubois, *La latinité;* Fougnies, *Een Studie over de clausulen;* Fini, "Le fonti delle *dictiones.*"

do—precisely because Ennodius is *not* a towering intellect of timeless importance but an articulate human being fully engaged with his physical and emotional environment. The corpus of Ennodius' works offers an entree into the literary culture and wider society of that intensely self-conscious, self-inventing period between Classical Antiquity and the Middle Ages whose dichotomies and concords intersect categories both temporal and conceptual. The fact that this book's title calls him a gentleman distinguishes him as a person who knew how to behave in polite company. Reflecting a concern for the individual audience, the works assume a variety of literary forms realized in vocabulary appropriate to the particular circumstance. The fact that Ennodius was also a Catholic clergyman increases the interest of what he wrote, because we can gain a better sense of the complexities of the spiritual life in early-sixth-century Italy. For Ennodius Theoderician *civilitas* (civility) was no mere political catch phrase but an integral principle of truly humane life, indispensable to holy men and masterful rulers alike.

Why have these things not been said before? I believe the problem is largely one of perception. When people look at Ennodius' writings, they tend to see only the editorial scheme established by the Jesuit Jacques Sirmond in 1611: nine books of letters, ten *opuscula miscella,* four sorts of *dictiones* (declamatory pieces), and two books of poetry. Even when they are aware that the actual manuscripts exhibit an intermingling of genres inherited from the chronological registers into which Ennodius originally had his compositions copied, readers find Sirmond's nice generic classifications a more congenial guide to assessing the corpus's literary nature and merit than the stream-of-consciousness format in which the author himself left it, for good or ill. Misconceptions inevitably abound.[4]

I therefore invite you to join me in reaching out toward what Ennodius wrote in its material context, textually and archaeologically. On one hand, we do need to come to grips with the cheek-by-jowl alternation of prose and poetry, oratory and epistle characteristic of his copybook corpus. By doing so, we can see that certain phrases or motifs recur in a variety of genres and situations; the variations on themes of kinship and devotion are particularly arresting, cropping up not only in connection with Ennodius' own natural family but also among the fictional relationships of the epi-

---

4. Brunhölzl, *Geschichte der lateinischen Literatur des Mittelalters* 1, 25–66, cf. 150, contains no references to Ennodius. Cf. Magani, *Ennodio* 3, 233–53, 432–33; Schanz-Hosius, esp. 136–37, 143–48; Rohr, *Theoderich-Panegyricus,* 15, 26; Fuhrmann, *Rom in der Spätantike,* 333–36; Reydellet, "Ennodio"; McHugh, "Ennodius."

grams and *dictiones* as well as in transcendent spiritual affinities. On the other hand, comprehending the material context also means allowing for the real things that inspired Ennodius' reactions—buildings, people, legal documents, marvels of technology.[5] In rhetoric appropriateness is paramount; we need simultaneously to see and to look past this value in examining the corpus as not only a quasi-autonomous verbal construction but also a response to and representation of the real world.[6] The secret of understanding Ennodius, I have found, is that, though his luxuriant Latin is far removed from the severity of Cicero and Vergil, most of our difficulty in following his trains of thought comes not because the works are fraught with intellectual abstractions but because they convey highly topical material with exquisite elegance.[7]

As I read and reread Ennodius, a great many questions arose. Some I have tried to articulate and answer here. But this book has no pretensions to be the last word about things Ennodian; many other questions remain to be raised and resolved in the future. For now I hope I have succeeded in transforming Magnus Felix Ennodius from an oddity of the specialist literature into a subject of legitimate discourse as author and historical personality.

Please note that, because of my views regarding the effect of Sirmond's book and opus numbers, all citations of the text of Ennodius follow the numeration and pagination (though not always the punctuation and capitalization) of Vogel's *MGH AA* 7 (1885). I provide a *comparatio numerorum* at the end of the book. All translations, with their concomitant errors and infelicities, are my own.

---

5. Prown, "Material/Culture."

6. Cf. Kushner, "Articulation historique"; Tilley, *Reading Material Culture,* 3–81, 281–347.

7. Including more Vergilian and Scriptural allusion than has been realized; cf. Stock, *Listening for the Text,* 52–74; Kibedi Varga, "Rhétorique et production du texte."

CHAPTER 1

Looking for Ennodius

Magnus Felix Ennodius, the tenth bishop of Ticinum (modern Pavia, southwest of Milan), died on 17 July 521. His still-extant epitaph provides this information, which is one of the few things about his life we can say with any confidence. His career in the Church was fairly distinguished, with the leadership of two papal embassies to Constantinople in 515 and 517 its high point. Ennodius is known today, however, for having left an intensely rhetorical trove of letters, poems, oratorical pieces, saints' lives, and controversial literature composed during his pre-episcopal years.[1] Once he became bishop of Ticinum in 513, Ennodius undoubtedly continued to write, but everything from that last period is lost, including his correspondence with Rome concerning relations with Constantinople. His old see has preserved his name and fame for a slightly different reason: sanctity. Despite the lack of documentation—the only evidence for his episcopal activities is some correspondence to and about him, his still-extant metrical epitaph, and a sprinkling of references to him in a fourteenth-century description of Pavia—local pious tradition calls him a saint who brought about ecclesiastical unity by defending orthodox belief and the primacy of Rome.[2]

Who was Magnus Felix Ennodius? Ennodius the *littérateur* has yet to be integrated with the Ennodius of hallowed tradition, although the latter is ironically responsible for the former's survival. Their allusiveness by turns exhibitionistic and self-concealing, Ennodius' writings boast neither

---

1. Nearly all from the years 503–13. Unless noted, all dates derive from Sundwall, *Abhandlungen*. Tenth bishop: Lanzoni, *Le diocesi*, 989; Picard, *Le souvenir*, 198–209, 746.

2. Papal letters: Thiel, *Epistolae Romanorum Pontificum;* Guenther, *Epistulae Imperatorum Pontificum*. Avitus, *Ep.* 41, 42 (*MGH AA* 6.2, 69–72). Epitaph: *CIL* 5.2, 6464 (*ILS* 2952); Merkel, "L'epitafio"; *Acta Sanctorum* 4 (*XVI Kal. Aug.*): 271–76; Gianani, *Opicino de Canistris.*

lofty intellectualism nor heroic piety. Moreover, much like the correspondence of Symmachus, whose ethos and diction evidently inspired Ennodius, they were composed for specific audiences on particular occasions,
which often makes it rather difficult for anyone other than his contemporaries to deduce anything of his life beyond a lively zeal for the social rituals of rhetorical discourse.[3] Their Latinity is so emphatically literate, so
syntactically complex yet grammatically correct as to confound casual
perusings for topical allusions or intellectual gems.

How, then, are we to approach the historical Ennodius? For an outline
of his life the end presents no problem, but the beginning and early years
do. Only one of his writings gives a few clues: Vogel's #438, the confessional work widely (though erroneously) known as the *Eucharisticon*. In
this most obviously autobiographical creation, written in mid-511 while he
was recovering from a grave illness, Ennodius examines his life, offering
his errors and weaknesses up to God. Chronology is emphatically not a
priority in a document so inward gazing; still, it sometimes mentions
events in the outer world. From them, scholars have attempted to extrap-
olate three key dates in Ennodius' life: his birth, the period within which he
became betrothed if not actually married, and when he was elevated to the
diaconate. Orphaned while still a child, Ennodius was sent, most likely
from Arles, to live with an aunt in Ticinum who, fortunately for scholars,
died at a crucial historical moment. The passage that records her death is
the single pivot on which all modern discussions of Ennodius' birth incon-
clusively turn; it can also serve as our introduction to his tantalizingly allusive style. Looking back over the providentially guided events of his life, he
writes,

> *tempore quo Italiam optatissimus Theoderici regis resuscitavit*
> *ingressus, cum omnia ab inimicis eius inexplicabili clade vastarentur et,*
> *quod superesset gladiis, fames necaret, cum excelsa montium castro-*
> *rumque arces penuria perrumperet et in culminibus locatos armis saev-*
> *ior egestas obsideret, ego annorum ferme sedecim amitae, quae me*
> *aluerat, ea tempestate solacio privatus sum.*[4]

At the time when the most longed-for entrance of King Theoderic
revived Italy, when all things were being laid waste by his foes with
unbounded destruction and famine slew what survived the swords,

3. Matthews, "The Letters of Symmachus"; Bruggisser, *Symmaque,* 3–15, 411–39.
4. #438.20.

when poverty was breaking down the lofty bulwarks of the mountain camps and want, crueler than weapons, besieged those stationed on the peaks, I (aged about sixteen) was at that time robbed of the succor of the aunt who had nurtured me.

With that enigmatic *annorum ferme sedecim,* Ennodius generated a spectrum of opinions concerning the year of birth. The compromise of 473/4 has its following, whereas the appearance of precision lends 473 and 474 a certain charm.[5] Late summer 489 is the moment when Theoderic is known to have arrived in Italy and hostilities began in earnest, as Ennodius himself was undoubtedly aware; 473 would be the corresponding birth year. In terms of the unfolding political and economic circumstances Ennodius emotively renders here, however, his aunt may very well have died in the first half of 490, when Ticinum, Milan, and indeed all Liguria were ravaged by the struggle with Odoacer and the opportunistic rampagings of the Burgundians.[6] If we take Ennodius' indefinite "about" (*ferme*) in the sense of approaching the age indicated—"going on sixteen," so to speak—we obtain a birthdate of 474 by going back from 490. The impreciseness of expression may be due to a desire to stress his youth at that moment of utter bereavement, if his object is simple pathos. On the other hand, statistical data are irrelevant to episodes meant to illustrate spiritual development; the document that contains this passage is consistently vague regarding events that occurred over a period of several years two decades before Ennodius wrote.[7]

Having sampled some of the difficulties inherent in using #438, we can turn to the other two tentatively datable events in Ennodius' life: his betrothal (or, as I argue, marriage) and his elevation to the diaconate. The majority of the works we have from his pen were written while he was a deacon (*diaconus, levita*), and the ideal and reality of that office within the scheme of holy orders is easier to assess than his brief allusion to matri-

---

5. For 473/4: Schanz-Hosius, 131; Stroheker, *Der senatorische Adel,* 166 (112); Fontaine, "Ennodius," 399–400; Cesa, *Ennodio,* 8 n. 5; Reydellet, "Ennodio," 689; Rohr, *Theoderich-Panegyricus,* 2–3. For 473: Fertig, 11; Hartel, 620; Magani, *Ennodio* 1.20. For 474: Ferrai, "Il matrimonio," 950; Vogel, ii; Dubois, *La latinité,* 5; Navarra, *Ennodio,* 7, 17; Galbiati-Poma-Alfonsi, *Magno Felice Ennodio,* 4, 11; Reydellet, *La royauté,* 141.

6. #80.111–17, 138–41 (*Vita Epifani*); Wolfram, *History,* 281. Cf. Ruggini, "Ticinum," 295–97.

7. The ages at which Ennodius became a deacon and later a bishop agree broadly with the implied time frame. Classical Roman age terminology: Sumner, "Germanicus and Drusus Caesar."

monial entanglements.[8] That relationship took place before he entered the Church, however, so we must consider the little he says about it before proceeding to what we can gather of his ecclesiastical career.

After Ennodius' aunt died, the narrative of his spiritual journey in #438 tells us that the helping hand of divine providence furnished a family both wealthy and pious who took him under their wing. He soon became betrothed to their daughter. The reading of the earliest manuscript states, *poposci in matrimonio cuiusdam nobilissimae et tibi bene compertae parvulam filiolam, protinus... exceptus:* "I asked for the hand of the dear little daughter of a certain very noble woman, and one well known to you, and was accepted straightaway."[9] Ennodius experienced worldly good fortune as a result of this alliance, causing him temporarily to forget God's will, but cautionary hardships soon intervened, so that Victor, the Milanese saint who was Ennodius' heavenly patron, eased his transition to the clergy by having "the woman who was about to go under the yoke with me in the equality of marriage share the seemliness of the religious life with me (*suffragator meus emeruit quam poposci, ut illa, quae mecum matrimonii habuit parilitate subiugari, religiosae mecum habitudinis decora partiretur*)."[10] This reading saves Ennodius from impending matrimony by making his betrothed willing to enter religion as well. All the other manuscripts, however, indicate consummated marriage with the phrase *illa, quae mecum matrimonii habuit parilitatem, religiosae mecum habitudinis decora partiretur,* which states that Victor caused "the woman who had equality of marriage with me to share the seemliness of the religious life with me." Taken in concert with three letters concerning a woman named Speciosa, whom we will meet properly in chapter 4, this reading disposes me to believe that Ennodius was in fact married before another reversal of fortune induced him to heed the call to the religious life.[11]

After trying his hand at affluent domesticity, how did Ennodius then rise to the diaconate, the *officium levitarum?* Also, what did that office entail, and where might it lead? While somewhat obscure, the early steps of Ennodius' ecclesiatical career are not altogether invisible or unparalleled. To trace them, however, we need to put aside schematic modern notions of

---

8. The equation *levita-diaconus,* present in Ambrose (e.g., *de mys.* 2.6; *CSEL* 73.90), is fully accepted by Ennodius (#80.20); cf. *TLL* 5.1, 943–44, s.v. *diaconus;* and Klauser, "Diakon."

9. #438.21, following the Brussels manuscript.

10. #438.27.

11. Ferrai ("Il matrimonio," 955) argued for a fully consummated five-year marriage on the basis of the later manuscripts' reading of #438.27. Speciosa: #35–36 and #48.

organization. The homogenizing model of Rome, which began to assert its primacy during the fifth century, tends to color the way holy orders in the Latin West between Ambrose of Milan and Caesarius of Arles are understood. The precepts set out by several bishops of Rome in letters of instruction regarding ordinations have some relevance to Ennodius' situation but should be applied with considerable discretion, as we will see; conciliar and synodical documents from Gaul, on the other hand, give an idea of actual practices and exigencies outside the paradigmatic domain of Rome.

For establishing Ennodius' path through the lower orders, our focus will be on the metropolitan area of Milan in the fifth century, avoiding extraneous comparanda as far as possible. The starting point is thus Ennodius' *Life of Epifanius,* because it describes the ecclesiastical cursus followed by the sainted bishop who brought him into the service of the Church and indicates the practice of the see to which Ennodius himself eventually succeeded.

Epifanius' hagiographer shows him fulfilling the duties connected with at least two clerical grades in addition to the diaconate before he was made bishop of Ticinum. When he was "about seven," already precocious in his sanctity at an age that had long marked entry into the classical education system, Epifanius began his ecclesiastical career by undertaking the office of lector, a first step congruent with his early vocation.[12] That office's fundamental duty was the reading of Scripture and of the Psalms; as the lectorate is explicitly attested in both Milan and Rome by the later fourth century, its validity as a clerical grade is unquestionable, as is its relevance to Ennodius' situation.[13]

Epifanius' swift mastery of "the notational signs for writing and the various symbols encompassing a multitude of words" soon revealed his intellectual and spiritual gifts, so he was assigned to the corps of the *exceptores.*[14] These were the stenographers, essential to any bureaucracy, whose property was the gathering and promulgation of information; originally skilled private slaves and functionaries in Imperial service, they became an

---

12. #80.8: *orditus annorum ferme octo; ferme* may mean "going on eight" (cf. #438), as the context is not restrictive.

13. Leclercq, "Notaire." Amb. *de exc. frat.* 1.61 (*PL* 16.1366) and *Ep.* 70.25 (*PL* 16.1241); cf. Siric. *Ep.* 1.9 (*PL* 13.1142).

14. #80.9: *notarum in scribendo conpendia et figuras varias verborum multitudinem conprehendentes brevi adsecutus in exceptorum numero dedicatus enituit.*

equally indispensable adjunct to ecclesiatical scholarship and administration soon after Christianity was legalized.[15] These secretarial personnel may have constituted an order in themselves, or simply comprised a subset within the recognized orders in the hierarchy. Ennodius' other mention of *exceptores,* also in a hagiographical connection, tends to support the former possibility but does not quite settle the question. In the *Life of Blessed Antony,* he states that Bishop Constantius commanded Antony "to begin his career in the service of heaven among the *exceptores* of the Church," indicating that, at least in mid-fifth-century Liguria and Noricum, trained note-taking in an ecclesiastical setting was the core of one of the minor orders.[16] This practice appears to hold true later in the century for Lucania and Bruttium as well, though that evidence comes in the form of a directive from Rome, a see that pragmatically linked religious vocation and bureaucratic service.[17] Consequently, we can assume Ennodius himself either began his career among the *exceptores* or was soon promoted to that rank, since his education would already have prepared him for the work.

Returning to the example of Epifanius, the next level of his ascent through holy orders is said to have been the subdiaconate, to which he was raised in his eighteenth year; the name itself signifies that this office existed to complement the ministry of the deacons, whose number is generally assumed to have been seven or fewer in every diocese.[18] While some men might remain subdeacons for the rest of their careers, as for example Ennodius' friend Arator, who entered the Roman clergy after decades in public life, Epifanius spent only two years at this rank and became a deacon at the tender age of twenty.[19]

Before treading the firmer ground of the diaconate, we should briefly

---

15. Jer. *Comm. in Ep. ad Gal.* 3, *praef.; Gesta Conc. Aquil.* 34, 43. Teitler, *Notarii and Exceptores,* 38–53: *exceptor* and *notarius* (the latter more common) appear interchangeably in ecclesiastical contexts.

16. #240.10: *eum inter ecclesiasticos exceptores caelestem militiam iussit ordiri.* Magistretti (*La liturgia,* 38–41), assimilating *exceptores/notarii* to the Roman acolytes and subdeacons not found in Ambrose's Milan, supplemented his account with the *Ordo Romanus* and the Gallic *Statuta Ecclesiae Antiqua,* not with Ennodius. Cf. Monachino, *S. Ambrogio,* 22–24; Cesa, *Ennodio,* 126.

17. Gelas. *Ep.* 14.2, an accelerated scheme for filling ecclesiastical vacancies. Roman pragmatism: Faivre, *Naissance,* 338, cf. 358–59, 378.

18. #80.18. The number: *Acts* 6.1–6. Cf. Gaudemet, *L'église,* 102–5; Faivre, *Naissance,* 62–66.

19. Hillier, *Arator,* 5–12. Epifanius: #80.20, 26.

examine the wider context of these preliminary orders and their relevance
to the duties Ennodius would have had. First of all, the so-called minor
orders are distinguished from the major triad of deacon, priest, and bishop
by their post-Apostolic origins; even the lectorate and the subdiaconate
are not attested anywhere until the beginning of the third century, and not
until the century and a half after Nicaea (325) did Rome's standardizing
influence spread throughout the West.[20] Nevertheless, the supposedly
canonical Roman schema laid out in a letter of Pope Siricius (384–98) to a
Spanish bishop—lector, (exorcist), acolyte, subdeacon, deacon, and so
on—is not visible in Liguria, Gaul, or Africa.[21] Neither is it identical with
the sequence of lector, exorcist, acolyte, subdeacon, "keeper of the martyrs" (custos martyrum), deacon, and priest ascribed to Pope Silvester
(314–35) by the sixth-century recension of the Liber Pontificalis.[22]

The lesser orders are also differentiated by two procedural characteristics. The first lies in what the minor clergy did not do. Unlike the major
orders, they had no essential liturgical function although they might be
present at the administration of the sacraments; the increased importance
of the subdiaconate as a sort of intermediary between the lower orders and
the sacramental clergy, however, emerges in canons of sixth-century Gallic councils.[23] The second is the way in which they were created and how
they were to live. They were ordained not by the laying-on of hands but by
being entrusted with the objects appropriate to their office.[24] Also, from
the evidence nearer to Ennodius' time, it becomes apparent that the minor
orders, in spite of their nonsacramental ordination and ministry, were
bound to celibacy as members of a clerical hierarchy increasingly distinct
from the laity; this development fell especially hard on the subdeacons
because of their more frequent presence at the altar substituting for or

---

20. Explicitly mentioned only in the *Apostolic Tradition,* Tertullian, and Origen, though
intimated somewhat earlier: Faivre, *Naissance,* 58–66. Cf. Gaudemet, *L'église,* 104; Piétri,
Roma Christiana, 887–1068, 1245–75.

21. Rome: Siric. *Ep.* 1.8–10 (*PL* 13.1142–43), cf. Zos. *Ep.* 8.3 (*PL* 20.672–73). Gaul: *Stat.
Eccl. Antiq.* 93–98 (*CCSL* 148), (subdeacon, acolyte, exorcist, lector, porter, psalmist);
Munier, *Les Statuta,* 162–87. Liguria: Magistretti, *La liturgia,* 27–39, borrows *ostiarii* from a
ninth-century synod; but cf. Monachino, *S. Ambrogio,* 21–24; and Faivre, *Naissance,* 242–58.

22. Duchesne, *Liber Pontificalis* 1, 171–72 (notes: 190–91); Wirbelauer, *Zwei Päpste,*
142–47.

23. Monachino, *S. Ambrogio,* 26, emphasizes the higher clergy's pastoral mission. Gallic
councils: Arles 5 (554), can. 4; Mâcon 2 (585), can. 10; Narbo (589), can. 3, 11, and 13 (*CCSL*
148A).

24. *Stat. Eccl. Antiq.* 93–98 (*CCSL* 148), accords each order its paraphernalia; but cf.
Const. Apost. 8.21; and Munier, *Les Statuta,* 170–85.

assisting the deacons.[25] The distinction between those vowed to the service of the Church at an early age, like Epifanius, and those entering it as men of worldly experience was taken into consideration. The correspondence of numerous popes indicates that men leaving public life for the Church had to prove they had truly been converted by living a life of exemplary piety and uprightness, especially in regard to the practice of chastity; minimum ages and years of service in each grade are often set down as well, though in real life minimum ages and periods of service might be overlooked.[26] Not only were sexual relations forbidden altogether after joining the clergy, but candidates were permitted to have been married only once prior to entering the religious life, and only to virgins.[27]

The material just brought together demonstrates that, while the minor orders were vital to the functioning of a thriving Church, their titulature and functions were far from uniform, differing from one metropolitan area to another. For Ennodius' particular situation we have no explicit information. What he does say in #438 about the piety and integrity of his intended bride, however, establishes her virginity beyond reasonable doubt. Joined to the couple's mutual decision to embark upon the religious life, that affirmation makes the question of whether Ennodius was married or merely betrothed irrelevant from a doctrinal viewpoint for, even if he had been married, the marriage was canonically acceptable and carnal relations ceased when religious obligations began.[28]

As a consequence of the diversity and ambiguity of the evidence, we cannot establish the precise trajectory of Ennodius' ascent toward the diaconate. His ecclesiastical career obviously began somewhere after the middle of 490, when his betrothal would have taken place, and 494, when he accompanied Epifanius on an embassy to Lyon to ransom captives held

---

25. Fifth-century evidence against remarriage: Orange (441), can. 24 (45); Arles 2 (442–506), can. 45; Angers (453), can. 11 (*CCSL* 148). Vence (461/491), can. 11 may be the first Gallic prohibition on married subdeacons, but the *Ep. Sancti Lupi et S. Eufronii Episcoporum* (453/461?) (*CCSL* 148, 140–41) is stricter; cf. Munier, *Les Statuta,* 198–213. Rome: Leo *Ep.* 10.3, 14.4 and 18, 167 (*PL* 54.631, 672–73, 707, 1204); Gelas. *Ep.* 9 (*PL* 59.46–57).

26. Siric. *Ep.* 1.8–10 (*PL* 13.1141–43); Innoc. *Ep.* 2. 6 (*PL* 20.474); Zos. *Ep.* 8.3 (*PL* 20.672–73). Leo *Ep.* 12 (*PL* 54.647–51). Siricius required deacons to be at least thirty; Zosimus had nine to thirteen years for mature men between ordination to the lectorate and diaconate. Cf. Gaudemet, *L'église,* 124–26.

27. The phrase most often found in Siricius, Zosimus, and their heirs is *unius uxoris virum* (1 Tim. 3.2; cf. Eph. 5.23; 1 Cor. 11.3), complementing Lev. 21.13–14; and Ezek. 44.22.

28. As Sirmond observed. Magani, *Ennodio* 1, 244–51, assumed that Ennodius rose through the hierarchy swiftly enough to become a deacon by 494; cf. Altaner-Stuiber, *Patrologie,* 478. Several popes were sons of clerics: *Liber Pontificalis* 44, 50, 59, 60.

by the Burgundians.[29] Since the most plausible reason for bishop Epifanius to have guided him into the clergy of Ticinum in the first place was his
technical literary attainments, Ennodius may have started out as a lector,
but his service among the *exceptores* certainly began soon after. His elevation to the subdiaconate is harder to pin down, but it probably occurred
after 494, or even after Epifanius' death in 497, when Ennodius seems to
have been transferred from Ticinum to the service of Laurentius, the metropolitan bishop of Milan.[30] By early 502 phrases like "in the infancy of
order and merit" (*in ordinis et meriti . . . infantia*) and "glorious duty"
(*famosum officium*) allude to his new status as a deacon, which resulted
from the publicistic work he performed for Laurentius of Milan on behalf
of the embattled Pope Symmachus.[31] The only preserved fifth-century formula for the installation of deacons states that they were ordained "not for
the priesthood, but for service."[32] Such a definition performs equally well
in principle, for the lesser orders that have otherwise escaped the record.
The important thing is that Ennodius assisted the bishops of Ticinum and
Milan as circumstances warranted; what we can see is that he served God
with prayer and pen.[33] During his Milanese period, however, Ennodius
was more forthcoming about his responsibilities as a subdeacon and deacon. That he was presumably a subdeacon during the composition of his
earliest preserved works is corroborated by his statements concerning
Epifanius, since Ticinum's general usage cannot have differed substantially from that of Milan in the fifth century: the *Life of Epifanius* explicitly
recognizes the latter's authority over Ticinum in respect to episcopal succession.[34] The fact remains that two characteristics of Ennodius' writing—
the deliberate avoidance of specific ecclesiastical terminology in his correspondence and the absence of any striking contrasts in address or purpose

---

29. Cf. Vogel, vi–vii; *produxisti ultionis tempora* (#438.23) invites conjecture. Lumpe,
"Ennodiana," 201, regarded Ennodius' entering religion in 493 as "bekanntlich." Mission,
ordination: #80.171 and 198.

30. The translation from suffragan to metropolitan see poses no problem: Gaudemet,
L'église, 113.

31. Dubois, *La latinité,* 10–11. See the discussion of the *Libellus* (#49) in chapter 5; he was
newly a deacon in 502: #2.3; #11.2. Ruggini, "Ticinum," 297, 304, is inconsistent.

32. *Stat. eccl. antiq.* 92 (*CCSL* 148); cf. Hope, *Leonine Sacramentary,* 92–95.

33. Gregory the Great gave great responsibilities to subdeacons and monks: *Ep.* 1.1, 1.9,
1.53, 1.54; 2.37, 2.46; 3.30, 3.34; 5.57; 6.4; 9.69; 11.14 (a *notarius* as deputy) (*CCSL* 140,
140A); *Dial.* 3.17. Cf. Gessel, "Reform am Haupt."

34. #80.36–39, on Epifanius' nomination and consecration; cf. Cesa, *Ennodio,* 141–44.
The usage behind this testimony may go back to the late fourth century, but Ennodius on
Epifanius was not utilized in reconstructing the clerical cursus in Ambrose's Milan: Mag-
istretti, *La liturgia,* 33–41; Monachino, *S. Ambrogio,* 24–25.

between the earliest works and the rest of the corpus—continue to obscure the fact that he most likely became a deacon in 501 or early 502.[35]

In the current state of the evidence, therefore, establishing a firm chronology of Ennodius' early ecclesiatical career with all details of titulature and duties tidily spelled out is impossible. What remains to us is of greater substance, namely that Ennodius was called to the service of the Church because his mentors realized he could make himself useful, not just because they perceived a certain nascent holiness. Epifanius of Ticinum would hardly have taken an incompetent with him to Lyon—Ennodius' first recorded activity as a cleric—or sanctioned the *dictio* in celebration of the thirtieth anniversary of his consecration as bishop, nor later would Laurentius have brought Ennodius into the service of the Milanese Church.

Ennodius' writings for the bishops he served, because they refer to externally datable historical events, do make it possible for us to extract definite dates—494, for instance, or 502—to attach to moments in his own life. Contact with the two excerpts from #438 should, however, caution us against attempting to extract chronological data from allusions in every single one of Ennodius' *opuscula*. A just interpretation of the writings and the man who wrote them depends on a fundamental awareness of the basic temporal contours of Ennodius' literary production. This can be divined only from the sparse, reflexive clues the author and the accidents of time have left behind. To grasp them, let us now consider how the physical constitution of the works has influenced and been influenced by their reception.

For hundreds of years the benevolence of editors has obscured the character of Ennodius' writings. Not satisfied with improving the lexical accuracy of a little-known and sometimes corrupt text, they refashioned its overall appearance to make it correspond more closely to contemporary ideas of literary protocol. Ennodius' works first appeared in print in 1569, sloppily transcribed from a single fifteenth-century manuscript sporadically supplemented by another, as part of a bulky omnibus of "doctrinally correct" patristic writers produced by a Swiss Protestant named Grynaeus.[36] In 1610, however, the Flemish Jesuit Andreas Schott detached the *carmina* for separate publication, fearing to inflict any more of "an author so bristling and murky" on his unsuspecting public at one time. The next

---

35. Lumpe, "Ennodiana," 201–3; Wermelinger, "Ennodius," 654.

36. Grynaeus, *Monumenta S. Patrum Orthodoxographa, pars altera,* 269–480; analyzed by Hartel, viii–x.

year Schott issued the complete works, apportioning the letters into twelve books in emulation of Cassiodorus' *Variae,* followed by the other works, personal, hagiographical, oratorical, apologetic, and poetic.[37]

Meanwhile, in that same year of 1611 another Jesuit, the gifted and indefatigable Jacques Sirmond, a native of the Auvergne, presented the entire text of Ennodius in a form "emended as much as possible" and reassembled all the works "out of the original disorder into definite orders and, as it were, classes."[38] His endeavors resulted in nine books of epistles in the manner of Symmachus, one book of miscellaneous prose works, another comprising three types of oratory, and two books of poetry. Sirmond based this arrangement on his own historically conditioned aesthetic perception of formal genres. It still continues to shape, and deform, the way in which Ennodius' works and their author are perceived. The first scholar since 1611 to undertake a new edition of Ennodius, Wilhelm Hartel, though critical of his predecessor's criteria for classification, nevertheless retained Sirmond's now-traditional scheme for the otherwise exemplary text he published in 1883, lest he discommode readers by "indulging in new conjectures."[39] From 1855 until now modern researchers have gladly acquiesced in Sirmond's comfortable re-creation of an order that never existed.[40]

The physical constitution of Ennodius' works as they survive in the manuscripts, however, offers scholars tangible help in comprehending their author. Instead of Sirmond's tidy parcels of letters, *opuscula, dictiones,* and poetry, a bewildering jumble of orations, letters, poems, and other works confronts the unwary investigator, with the manuscripts betraying no trace of division according to genre or book. As Hermann Usener was the first to recognize, that jumble represents the archetype as it was constructed by the posthumous copying of Ennodius' works from a series of smaller, approximately chronological journals or registers; by their very

---

37. Schottus (Schott), *Beati Ennodii Ticinensis Episcopi Opera;* each book of letters contains approximately twenty-five items.

38. *Ep. ad Nicolaum Fabrum,* Sirmond's preface to *Magni Felicis Ennodii Episcopi Ticinensis Opera.*

39. Hartel, *Magni Felicis Ennodii Opera,* xv.

40. Neither Fertig (*Magnus Felix Ennodius,* 5) nor Birt (*Das antike Buchwesen,* 378) realized the nine-book letter format was Sirmond's doing. Dubois, *La latinité,* 14–42; Benjamin, "Ennodius," 2632; Wermelinger, "Ennodius," 654; Näf, *Senatorisches Standesbewusstsein,* 197; Rohr, *Theoderich-Panegyricus,* 5–11.

form, those journals in fact constituted a sort of archive.[41] Though internal evidence makes it clear that some larger pieces and clusters of items were entered out of compositional sequence, these can be assigned their proper place.

Of the three editions that appeared between 1569 and 1611, only Grynaeus' *editio princeps* followed the manuscripts' archival order, ironically because of haste and inattention rather than conscious editorial method. Friedrich Vogel thus became the first and only scholar who, when producing his edition for Monumenta Germaniae Historica, intentionally sought both accuracy and fidelity to the order shown by the manuscripts. He followed the sequence of works as given by the oldest manuscript (a quarto at Brussels, thus B), save when items were distorted or missing altogether, in which case he introduced supplements and emendations from a family of manuscripts whose principal representative is kept in the Vatican Library; the result, while not without certain flaws, can on the whole be trusted.[42] Without his accomplishment this study would not have developed as it has. Vogel accompanied his breakthrough in textual and semantic clarity with an essay in establishing when and under what circumstances each *opusculum* had been composed; Tanzi took this line of inquiry further, making strikingly subjective, atomizing assertions about composition and redaction and championing a rearrangement whose connection with the content of the works I am at a loss to discern.[43]

My discussion of the text proceeds from Johannes Sundwall's "Die zeitliche Folge der Schriften des Ennodius" because it combines sense with simplicity. Founded on a lively confidence in the manuscript order as a whole, it refines Vogel's effort by seeking to coordinate statements inside the works with chronological information from elsewhere in the form of people, objects, and events existing independently of Ennodius' testimony.[44] Letters and other documents alluding to particular subjects do

---

41. Usener, *Anecdoton Holderi,* 13; cf. Hasenstab, *Studien,* 4–5. Manuscripts described: Vogel, xxix–xlviii (Usener's verdict revised); Hartel, i–viii, xv–xxvii. Posner, *Archives,* 4–11, 27.

42. Bruxellensis 9845–48, copied before 850 for the abbey of Lorsch, and Vaticanus Latinus 3803, another quarto, probably written at Corbie between 850 and 900: Bischoff, *Die Abtei Lorsch,* 48, 75. Kennell, "Ennodius and His Editors."

43. Vogel, i–xxviii, liii–lv (rationale in ordering the works). Tanzi, "La cronologia"; cf. Rohr, *Theoderich-Panegyricus,* 16.

44. Sundwall, *Abhandlungen,* 1–71, 84–170, is based on Fertig, *Magnus Felix Ennodius,* and Hasenstab, *Studien.* Vogel and Tanzi were excessively generous in identifying *opuscula* copied out of sequence.

appear in a recognizably consecutive order in the manuscripts: the letter congratulating Faustus on his son Avienus' consulate, the epigram to Messala on his own consulate, and the epitaph of Rustica are the clearest examples of this disposition.[45] Though gaps often occur and incoming letters were unfortunately not copied into the collection, matters proceed logically enough to be comprehensible, supporting the premise that the items at the beginning were composed earlier and that those toward the end of the manuscripts originated correspondingly later. Once we accept the principle that a combination of internal cohesion and exterior coordinates indicates the general contours of the compositional sequence, we can read the works in ways that sometimes differ from conventional wisdom.

The notion of a completely ecclesiastical context for the composition of all Ennodius' works—large and small, sacred and secular, poetry and prose—will shock those accustomed to the Sirmondian segregation of sinner from saint.[46] The realization that the author, true to prevailing human nature, possessed his own assortment of vices, virtues, passions, and aversions and tried to maintain friendships and personal interests while performing the duties incumbent on him as a member of the Catholic clergy should offset some of that shock. Ennodius' Catholicism is indubitable. For nearly the entire period of the works' composition, he was a deacon of the Church of Milan; all interpretation of them must coexist with that central fact.

As Ennodius' pre-episcopal writings constitute the unique firsthand source of information for the earlier part of his life, their witness will inevitably be subjective and selective. Circumspection is, to be sure, advisable in using them to approach larger topics such as Ostrogothic rule in Italy or the bishops of Rome, but the critical feature for a study of Ennodius himself is that each and every item in the corpus was composed after he had entered the service of the Catholic Church. Even the earliest, the prosimetric *dictio* celebrating the thirtieth year of Epifanius' episcopate, indisputably dated to 496, is the product of a man who has already spent several years in the lower ranks of the clergy of Ticinum.[47] The subjects

---

45. #9, #140, #462. All have externally verifiable dates: *PLRE* 2. Rustica's epitaph also appears as *CIL* 5.2, 6266. Cf. Bagnall et al., *Consuls,* a. 502 (Avienus), 506 (Messala), and 513 (Probus).

46. Magani, *Ennodio;* Fontaine, "Ennodius," 401–2; Chadwick, *Boethius,* 15; Rohr, *Theoderich-Panegyricus,* 14–15. Helm, "Heidnisches und Christliches," 25–26, was not deceived.

47. #43, prosimetric *dictio.* In #80.171 (*Vita Epifani*), Ennodius calls himself an eyewitness of the events of Epifanius' mission to Gundobad; cf. Vogel, vii; and Sundwall, 13–14.

and recipients of the other four hundred and sixty-odd *opuscula* firmly situate them after the death of Epifanius in 497, when Ennodius was transferred from Ticinum to the service of the metropolitan bishop of Milan.[48] More precisely, the writings belong to the years between 501 and 513, ceasing when he returned to Ticinum as that city's bishop. There, in addition to the liturgical and teaching duties of his office, he also led two delegations sent by Pope Hormisdas, Symmachus' successor, to the emperor Anastasius in Constantinople in 515 and 517 in a bid to end the Acacian schism that had sundered the eastern and western Churches for over thirty years. Though not immediately successful, these missions may have contributed to the speedy reconciliation effected by Anastasius' successor Justin in 518, three years before Ennodius' death.[49]

As I said in the introduction, Ennodius is not a great man for all time, intellectually and ethically speaking, but a man of his time; thus, we should consider him both a clergyman and an above-average rhetorician. His habit of expressing everything in rhetorical terms has consistently run afoul of post-Romantic moral sensibilities, so that de Labriolle could proclaim, apropos of the early sixth century, that "the truly manly intellects of this somewhat dispossessed time—the question here is only of those who benefited from the gift of writing—were Boethius and Cassiodorus."[50] That is not how Ennodius and his contemporaries saw it, though: rhetoric was just as much a fact of life for them as televisual idioms are for us; we are not bound to adore the Classical canon as the embodiment of intellectual virility and to regard originality and consistency as the highest goods.

What image of Ennodius are we trying to replace? Up to now people examining Ennodius adopted one of three courses. The first is founded upon the tradition of Ennodius the career clergyman and nascent saint, with Magani, whose three-volume study is now over a century old, still its most eminent representative. His overall characterization has the merit of being sympathetic: "he felt strongly, deeply; he was a man all of a piece and all of a color. He was not a hero, nor yet a saint or, to say it better, like the saints he had merely his weaknesses, his little faults, but ones that served to give prominence, like the shadows in a painting, to his comely

---

48. The letters to various parties in Rome and Ravenna on behalf of Bishop Laurentius indicate residence in Milan.

49. So his epitaph suggests (Vogel, lviii, vv. 11–12 = *ILS* 2952); these activities are discussed in the postscript.

50. de Labriolle, *Histoire de l'église* 4, 565; cf. Wermelinger, "Ennodius," 654–57. Pietri was shocked that Ennodius praised Boethius by invoking Demosthenes and Cicero ("Aristocratie et société cléricale," 438); cf. Kushner, "Articulation historique," 111–18.

individuality; he was, I hasten to declare and with pleasure, the sort of man who is accustomed to be called a man of character."[51] Magani's efforts to assimilate all available evidence, however, relied on moral preconceptions—that everything secular preceded the author's conversion, everything Catholic came after—rather than chronological indications in the transmitted form and content of the literary corpus. Manifest errors of interpretation resulted. So fervent was Magani's reverence for the bygone bishop of Pavia that he could not accept a Gallic birthplace for Ennodius, maintaining that he must have been born in Milan because no one in Arles venerated him.[52]

The second way of approaching Ennodius is animated by the spirit of academic thoroughness. It analyzes specific elements of the corpus with exemplary historical and literary-critical rigor, yielding a crop of sources and influences for certain details but making the works as a whole into a lexical no-man's-land.[53] The Greek culture quotient of later Latin authors has traditionally been an issue, but asking whether Ennodius "knew" Greek, read and emulated Greek authors, or perhaps entertained Greek philosophical and theological speculations elicits a dismal response.[54]

From the weaknesses of the first two approaches a third way has arisen that allows Ennodius to be both writer and clergyman by rending him in three to produce pedagogical, ecclesiastical, and political Ennodii, each with his own selection of works.[55] Such a technique has been found helpful in describing the essence of divinity, though heresies can arise; applied to human beings, the result is graceless.

Like Humpty Dumpty, Ennodius needs putting back together again, but without excesses of zeal, whether nationalistic or philological. By looking at the totality of Ennodius' works, we can say some things about them and their author as representative of their age. The diverse forms of

---

51. Magani, *Ennodio* 1, 54, 167, 183. Cf. Galbiati-Poma-Alfonsi, *Magno Felice Ennodio;* Cattaneo, *Terra di Sant'Ambrogio,* 85–91; Léglise, *Oeuvres* 1.

52. Magani, *Ennodio* 1, 8–17. Arelate origin is inferred from letters to relatives and friends resident in southern Gaul (#5, #313, #461) and poems (#148, #191; cf. #423, with Vogel, iii) referring to his origins and the explicit denial of Ligurian birth in #311; see Ruggini, "Ticinum." The formulaic opening of #2 no more proves biological nationality than "O Canada, our home and native land."

53. Morabito, *Paganesimo e cristianesimo;* Fontaine, "Ennodius"; Pietri, "Le Sénat, le peuple chrétien," and "Aristocratie"; Navarra, "Le componenti"; Carini, "*L'itinerarium*"; Lebek, "Deklamation und Dichtung."

54. Courcelle, *Les lettres grecques,* 134–35, 241–46; Riché, *Education and Culture,* 45–50. Cf. Kirkby, "Scholar and His Public," 54; Ruggini, "Ticinum," 306; *SEG* 43.672.

55. Navarra, *Ennodio.*

individual pieces designed to function as instruments of communication reveal the attitudes both of Ennodius and of his various audiences. If the range of his contacts and interests is any indication, a fair number of his contemporaries seemed to have thought well of him, which begins to explain how a flawed human being could be transformed into a saint.

Certain dichotomies have been thought to animate Late Antiquity: the civilian-soldier opposition; laymen versus clergy (the *plebs*/*clerus* divide); tensions between Romans and barbarians; the traditional elite literacy (which fostered an outlook we may call cultural Hellenism) versus the miracle-ridden, parochial Christianity of the masses; the contested relationship of the plastic and verbal arts. Traces of all are present in Ennodius' writings; their textual cohabitation should not shock us any more than depictions of saints in philosophical garb or the river Jordan as a horned divinity attending the baptism of Jesus. As recent studies of the period's cultural and political circumstances have demonstrated, a positive portrayal of the age's anxieties and affinities is possible and desirable.[56]

The creeds of early Christianity stress the mysterious and incorporeal in their formulations, but their central fact—the Incarnation of the Word of God—constitutes a validation of language and the material world that bears directly on Ennodius and his work. As a Christian, he perceived things wonderful in the present world as signs of realities yet unseen and as creatures admirable in themselves; many of his compositions, especially the poems, communicate this view. The ekphrastic style beloved of Late Antique poetic conventions required poets to cultivate every subject's visual allure, emphasizing its brilliance, color, and texture. Ennodius applies these conventions; the brilliant things he represents, however—jewels, marble, metalwork—are both favorite metaphors and the genuine article.[57]

Ennodius' work in resolving the Symmachan schism, which helped him reach the diaconate, illustrates his ability to manipulate opinion by inducing laymen to restore and enhance clerical prestige in the belief they were receiving benefit. His devotional and disciplinary writings fulfill the demands of their respective individual situations, but the fact that the edi-

---

56. Pietri, *Roma Christiana,* and "Aristocratie"; Maguire, *Art and Eloquence in Byzantium;* Brown, *Cult of the Saints,* and *Power and Persuasion;* Roberts, *Jewelled Style;* Bowersock, *Hellenism in Late Antiquity;* Wharton, *Refiguring the Post Classical City.*

57. Ennodius' texts about things often represent one end of the material culture spectrum, with Kingery, *Learning from Things,* and Tilley, *Reading Material Culture* at the other end; see chapter 3.

fying examples and precepts of the writings destined for an ecclesiastical audience coexist with more whimsical choices of theme and expression in works intended for lay correspondents suggests that the Church allowed members of its administrative elite some latitude in their views and behavior so long as their performance in the office and their physical chastity met accepted standards. Regardless of stylistic medium, Ennodius intermingles pagan heroes, traditional gods, and their mythic landscape with monuments of "popular" Christianity, the latter represented in his appeals for prayer. Faith in the communion of the saints in heaven with the still-earthbound faithful moves his requests; St. Victor's life-saving patronage elicits his special gratitude.

Two principles ultimately governed the way Ennodius composed his works and conducted his life. The first is the preeminence of friendship. The words of affection and concern contained in his letters are no less heartfelt or devoid of consequence because they accord with epistolary convention; the courteous elegance of their phrasing attests to the value Ennodius placed on nurturing amicable, civilized relationships. The other principle, a cornerstone of liberal education honored by pagans and Christians alike, is that appropriateness is paramount, governing both diction and behavior. St. Ambrose, impeccable in rectitude and rhetoric, had already divided the field when he appropriated the best elements of civilized discourse: speech should be "full of sweetness and grace, not improper," but a person in the religious life must scorn "wealth and the tales of worldly old women . . . permitting nothing that does not train for piety."[58] As deacon and bishop-to-be, Ennodius would find himself constrained by both precepts, particularly the second.

Both the corpus of Magnus Felix Ennodius' works and the character of its author have been thought seriously deficient in interest. Outbursts such as "for the training of his mind, for the direction of his thought, Ennodius is assuredly not responsible . . . but what is terrible is that he has no awareness of his maladjustment to the time in which he lives," imply an individual so ill-adapted to his surroundings as to require psychiatric treatment.[59] Though his language does pose challenges, the real reason for such disfavor is that, except when the blatantly historical cannot be overlooked, the works' generic and rhetorical attributes have received all the attention.

---

58. Amb. *De off.* 1.23 (*PL* 16.59); cf. 1.19–20, 1.36, 2.20; McLynn, *Ambrose,* 255–56, 277.

59. Bardy, "Saint Ennode de Pavie," 263. Cf. Piétri, "Aristocratie," 438: "une consternante nullité de pensée."

The technically belletristic aspects of Ennodius' writings, admittedly worthy of comment, do not exist in vacuous isolation. The practical circumstances of composition indicate anything but delusion: every manifestation of genre is indivisible from occasion, recipient, and time. Not simply the larger encomiastic and controversial pieces composed at the request of others, like the *Panegyric* of Theoderic and the little work against Eastern heresies, but every single composition—letters, epigrams, *dictiones*—was intended for a specific situation and audience at a specific moment in time.[60] He wrote on particular themes for particular people who would appreciate it (and him), not on philosophical abstractions for an intangible, unimaginable posterity. This fact, rather than any agglomeration of stylistic vagaries, is what renders Ennodius so opaque to a casual synchronic approach but also makes him a mirror of the tendencies of his age, more clearly reflecting what literary life in Italy was like around 500 A.D. than do the monuments of Boethius and Cassiodorus.[61]

Magnus Felix Ennodius, the deacon, is thus the single, enigmatic firsthand source of chronological information concerning his earlier life and literary activities simply because only his own works from the period prior to his episcopate survive; we have no contemporary corroboration. Ennodius the bishop of Ticinum, on the other hand, becomes the object of second- and third-person discourse of inferior quantity and questionable quality through the loss of all subsequent writing; we will consider this silent Ennodius in the postscript.

The age at which Ennodius entered the Church and the lower orders through which he may have passed, as well as their concomitant duties, we have gathered from the few mentions he lets drop along with what little is known of northern Italian ecclesiastical organization and some tenuous parallels from elsewhere in the West.[62] The years of his diaconate and the months just preceding it present an altogether different situation. Much of his correspondence is devoted to matters of Church business; many other letters are at least partially concerned with similar issues. To be sure, whether Ennodius is operating in an official capacity or simply as a well-connected friend or relative is frequently unclear and must be sorted out on a case-by-case basis. Taken in their entirety, however, the writings of this period are an invaluable and necessarily tendentious record of the

---

60. Panegyric, #263; the anti-Acacian piece, #464.

61. Differentiating between past and present taste: Głowinski, "Les genres littéraires"; cf. Fantham, *Roman Literary Culture*, 2–11.

62. Allusions: #80, #438.

activities and opinions of a real live deacon whose behavior did not always conform to the canonical prescriptions for his state of life.

With all his imperfections, Ennodius' shortcomings demonstrably did not extend to the hypocrisy of destroying potential sources of embarrassment.[63] We should appreciate the illumination Ennodius' candor affords, for what he reveals of his personal experiences and the aspirations peculiar to his class, however unintentionally, helps to explain behavior that seems initially at odds with his modern reception as a degenerate poet and defective Christian. His internal struggles stem not from the opposition of paganism and Christianity but from the sharpening conflict of lay, secular values with the more arduous ideal of monastic perfection.[64] In particular, the correspondence with wealthy laymen tells as much of his slow, straggling journey toward the elusive state of "conversion" as his formal allegiance to ecclesiastical authority. Read in company with associated works of poetry and prose, those letters bear witness to his personal experiences and opinions as well as to his mastery of literary discourse that was the distinguishing mark of civilized persons in the ancient world.[65] In contrast, sermons, tractates, and canons of the age reproachfully proclaim that the majority of people usually failed to conform to official standards of virtue. Ennodius' writings survive to remind us that the past does not have to be construed as an elemental conflict between incorruptible nobility and abject sinfulness. Their true value lies in the care with which the author rendered his imperfections and those of his contemporaries.

The works are unquestionably a historical source. But Ennodius himself had no intention of writing history, nor should he be forced to do so. Aside from compositions of explicitly public significance, by which I mean the *Libellus* championing Pope Symmachus, the *Panegyric* of King Theoderic, and the *Lives* of Saints Epifanius and Antonius, most of Ennodius' works are concerned with a variety of situations and affects. In short, they are about states, not dates. Accordingly, this reading will represent an attempt to discover the condition and evolution of his mind, not to rewrite the chronicle of Church and State in Ostrogothic Italy. The world of Ennodius will enter into the investigation to the extent that, having impinged on his consciousness, it emerges in his utterances.

---

63. Vogel, xxix–xxx.

64. Ambrose was far more circumspect: McLynn, *Ambrose,* xvi–xvii, 368–77. The conflict: Markus, *End of Ancient Christianity,* 181–202.

65. Epistolographical topoi: #40, #76, #110, #392, with Thraede, *Grundzüge,* 109–79. Social dimensions: Riché, *Education and Culture,* 48–51; Kaster, *Guardians,* 12–14; Heather, "Literacy and Power," 177–97.

To outline Ennodius' life and clerical career, we have already had to consider certain passages from #438 (the so-called *Eucharisticon*) and the problems that beset them; now, however, I would like to revisit that curious document in its entirety. Thanks to Sirmond, the work has widely been known as the *Eucharisticon de vita sua;* in the manuscripts, it bears no title, just an invocation to the Trinity.[66] If we list the features modern biographers consider crucial to factual narration—birth, family, education, fortune, career, important dates—then compare them to what Ennodius writes about, we encounter large divergences. Sundwall's chronological analysis shows that such "facts" do not appear where we might expect them or in the quantity and during the intervals of time we would demand from an accurate record of Ennodius' life. Whereas information relative to his status and function in the Church appears throughout the time frame of the works, this confessional work contains the only extant references to his birth and early years, and his activities as bishop fall completely outside the first-person account, although adumbrated in two compositions.[67]

For the most part Ennodius avoided reminiscing about his pre-ecclesiastical life, but what little he let slip is embedded in #438. Since Augustine's *Confessiones* are the origin and paradigm of spiritual autobiography as a genre, it is no accident that Ennodius' own personal narrative sometimes recollects the style and themes of that seminal work. Exhaustive comparison of the twenty-nine paragraphs in Vogel's edition with the thirteen books of Augustine's opus has unfortunately brought disappointment to those seeking a timeless work of searing self-examination in the tradition of the bishop of Hippo, although the *Confessiones'* own structure and authorial intentions are themselves more enigmatic than often supposed.[68] As far as he can, Ennodius candidly recounts his faults and vanities without endeavoring to write history; ancient formal constraints thwart modern expectations of factual reporting.

What literary form was it that constrained Ennodius when he decided to unburden himself before God? Context supplies a clue. This work is sit-

---

66. #438: *In nomine patris . . . gloria patri et filio et spiritui sancto.* One Augustinian phrase (#438.17) led some to call it *Confessiones* or *Confessio:* Benjamin, "Ennodius," 2632; Misch, *Das Altertum,* 443–44.

67. Status, functions: #3, #6–12, #14, #235, #438. Though #336 meditates on the episcopal office, only #464 foreshadows his later deeds.

68. Courcelle, *Les Confessions,* 214–17, calls it "un pastiche assez médiocre des Confessions"; Fontaine ("Ennodius," 401) questioned its fundamental Christianity. Cf. Steinhauser, "Literary Unity"; Scott, "From Literal Self-Sacrifice"; O'Meara, "Augustine's Confessions."

uated in the corpus toward the end of a sizeable group of correspondence that Sundwall assigned to the period between summer 510 and the end of 511.[69] Written for the sake of keeping in touch, they requested prayers for Ennodius' deliverance from an undisclosed and persistent illness. If we subtract its invocation to the Trinity and compare its text to the letters nearby, #438 looks rather epistolary itself in fact, like a letter to the Almighty conveyed by a highly trusted bearer (St. Victor), not a self-contained, chronologically arranged spiritual autobiography.

Let us therefore examine the characteristics of this letter to God, as several of them are common throughout the correspondence; we will meet them again. After a proem on the theme of human infirmity and divine power, Ennodius gives thanks to God, his real addressee, for the subtle dispensations of his mercy, then embarks on the narration of his major subject.[70] Desire for poetic fame and worldly fortune made him neglect his responsibilities to his Creator: time and again, humbled by loss and sickness, then raised up to honor and prosperity, he kept forgetting to whom he should be grateful. At last, reminded of his essential frailty and indebtedness, Ennodius beseeches God's presence, praising the piety of his former spouse (her steadfastness rendered all the greater in popular paradox by the presumed weakness of her sex) and glorifying the Trinity.[71]

In addition to its introductory thematic elaboration, which is a recurring feature in both Ennodius' letters and those of Cassiodorus, this piece contains two other details that betray its fundamentally epistolary nature.[72] Just after his narrative ends, Ennodius writes, "These and many other things, as I have said before, I have suggested be made known through a most approved witness, blessed Victor . . . he acknowledged, responded to, and obtained my petition."[73] This type of statement has direct parallels in his correspondence with mortal men and women, particularly in the use of *suggerere* and its cognates and the reference to the

---

69. #390–#446; Sundwall (*Abhandlungen,* 59–67) assigned the group #424–#438 to summer 511, since #439–#440 (to addressees at Rome) imply the magistrates changed at the end of August.

70. #438.1–3 (introduction), 4 (thanksgiving), 5–26 (narration).

71. #438.27–29; cf. the hymn to St. Euphemia (#348, vv. 3–5). Christian paradox: Cameron, *Christianity,* 155–88.

72. Thematic openings: #10.1–2; #63.1; #77.1; #254.1; #322.1. E.g., Cass. *Var.* 1.3, 5, 6, 8, 15, 45; 2.14; 3.3; 4.2, 25.

73. #438.27: *Haec et alia plura, sicut praefatus sum, per testem probatissimum beatum Victorem intimanda suggessi . . . petitionem meam suscepit replicavit optinuit.* The final trio of verbs indicates he conceived the relationship as one of traditional patronage. Cf. Dubois, *La latinité,* 200, 204; Jungmann, *Missarum Solemnia* 1, 489; Brown, *Cult of the Saints,* 54–64.

bearer as witness of the truth of the missive.[74] As in letters to mortals, Ennodius has left the communication of the inelegant and the distressing to the discretion of the messenger; information deliberately omitted because it was already known thus becomes inaccessible to subsequent readers.

The other letterlike feature occurs in the next to last sentence of the piece. There Ennodius says, "Behold, Lord, I have gone over the very things that you had known, and in that respect I was so faithful as not to snatch away what you were holding."[75] Although both Vogel and Hartel regarded it as synonymous with "read" (*legere*), the use of "go over, review" (*recensere*) is hardly an accident, given the author's religious and literary inclinations. Both Aulus Gellius and Statius, an author known to Ennodius, employed it to mean "review" or "revise," and participants in synods used *recensere* in the same way Ennodius does here.[76] In composing and revising this communication for his collected works, Ennodius suggests a relationship with God similar to those he maintains with his literary correspondents. With the latter he shares compositions on various subjects for comment and commendation; all parties are aware of drafts and revisions. With the former, the subject he seeks to communicate is his entire life. God knows its rough drafts and emendations too well for the author to snatch them away, as "the very things that you had known" admits, but when it comes to the final version Ennodius still finds some matters inappropriate for the written page.

Once we recognize that this composition possesses more formal similarities to the letters that adjoin it than to the tremendous volumes of Augustine's *Confessiones,* we are in a better position to assess the general accuracy and intentions of Ennodius' expressions in epistolary form. Unless he was more foolish and depraved than the most hostile critics could imagine, he should be at his most candid in addressing God, the omniscient Supreme Being. In his heart, Ennodius already said far more than he has committed to paper, consonant with what he considered appropriate under the circumstances. Here, as in other works, the particulars given are those he judged both relevant and suitable, not what a tabloid taste for graphic circumstantial detail might crave.

---

74. E.g., #122.3; cf. #22, #36, #92, #115, #138, #283, #301, #445. Dubois, *La latinité,* 201, 205.

75. #438.29: *Ecce, domine, recensui ipsa quae noveras, et in ea tantum fui fidelis parte, ut non raperem quod tenebas;* cf. #398.1. Zetzel, *Latin Textual Criticism,* 209–39.

76. Stat. *Silv.* 4.1.29, 5.3.20; Gell. 17.10.6; cf. Plin. *Ep.* 1.8.15. Augustine uses a different verb to allude to God's prior knowledge (*Conf.* 11.1.1.3), but the Ennodian sense occurs in the examination of a *procès*-verbal transcript: *Gesta Conl. Carth.* 2.23 and 25 (*CCSL* 149A).

By complying with the principle of appropriateness as the early sixth century of our era understood it, Ennodius has arranged illustrations like his aunt's death or his former wife's religious devotion according to their subjective importance, not to an absolute external chronology. They express what he in retrospect found most significant in his spiritual experience, namely the protracted and painful process of a conversion made more difficult by the tenacity of vain ambitions and the distractions of material and emotional prosperity. We can therefore examine the particular circumstances that he does trouble to mention in terms of his reaction to them, looking for what they tell of his affections and states of mind rather than for points on a time line.

Recurring within this work is the theme of Ennodius' own innate weakness, aggravated greatly by illnesses that, he now realizes, were part of the divine plan. The message of the introduction is that human infirmity (*infirmitas*), frailty (*inbecillitas*), and sickness (*aegritudo*) have been met and overcome by the power of God, the source of all recuperation and health. Ennodius seems initially to be referring to his own physical convalescence, since most of the letters immediately preceding #438 are concerned with that subject. Interest in his own well-being and that of his addressees, however, far exceeds this particular series of letters and is one of the principal topics throughout the correspondence. Literally dozens of letters courteously inquire after the correspondent's health or report on Ennodius' current bodily condition; some go into greater detail.[77]

In #438, which was evidently composed and revised several months after the worst of his illness, Ennodius views his sufferings in teleological rather than social terms, confessing that the health of the earthly body often thwarts the salvation of the immortal soul.[78] Physical well-being, accepted thoughtlessly, can itself become an inducement to worldly self-gratification. Only with the onset of illness did Ennodius' arrogance yield to repentance; although this most recent illness appears to have been the most serious, presumably because of advancing age, it was not the first time that bodily infirmity had providentially pulled him up short. In this work he wants to show that he has at last learned his lesson: so that the soul may turn to God and be strengthened, the body in which it too

---

77. Well over seventy letters deal to some extent with the health of the author and/or his addressee (for which see chap. 3).

78. The same word (*salus*) represents both "health" and "salvation" throughout the works. Ennodius can sketch his symptoms in suitably appalling terms (#438.9) but prefers to dwell on the emotional responses they evoked in himself and his confidantes.

blithely resides must be chastened by occasional sickness and distress. Physical and emotional suffering can teach what edifying books do not. "If the teachings of venerable books are lacking to you, you can be instructed for progress with torments and, unless you immerse yourself in the muck of perdition, have learning from punishment."[79] In this respect Ennodius' sensibility anticipates that of Gregory the Great.[80]

The narrative of his literary vanity takes up most of the work's development; the fact that Ennodius devotes so much space to eloquence signifies its importance in his life.[81] His love of beautiful language and confidence in its capacity to ennoble and immortalize is fundamental to his personality. Ennodius knew that the literary conventions of his time had the power to stamp him as an individual and to validate him as a member of the social elite. When describing his insanely prideful efforts to achieve literary renown after entering the religious life—"how often did my head, bared on account of religion, swell from the breaths of those applauding me"—he first admits he expected to gain the world through mastery of verse composition, then mocks that delusion with a pun in token of his repentance.[82] Having imagined that the world would be at his feet because he commanded an array of metrical feet, deployed in poems of dubious morality, Ennodius was salutarily disappointed.[83]

Notwithstanding the stress here on poetry's technical aspects, we should not take Ennodius' words as evidence that his hopes of fame were based exclusively on his verses. The poetic gift is emblematic of literary creativity in general, whether expressed in *carmina,* prosimetric works, *dictiones,* or even letters, which he clearly regarded as worthy of equal praise. The character of this declaration may also have been dictated by Ennodius' concern that the publicistic and administrative duties required by his superiors made him seem little more than a hack; his subsequent

79. #438.26: *si desunt tibi venerabilium magisteria librorum, ad profectum informare suppliciis et, nisi te caeno perditionis inmergis, habere potes de poena doctrinam;* the exemplary function of physical pleasure and suffering recurs, especially in his more vehemently devout utterances.

80. Straw, *Gregory the Great,* 219–21.

81. See Markus, *End of Ancient Christianity,* 220. With correspondents like the deacon Helpidius (#312), Ennodius was well aware of refinement's dangers.

82. #438. 6: *quotiens adclamantium flatibus propter religionem vertex nudatus intumuit.*

83. #438.5–6: *delectabant carmina quadratis fabricata particulis et ordinata pedum varietate solidata. angelorum choris me fluxum aut tenerum poema miscebat, et si evenisset, ut essem clarorum versuum servata lege formator, sub pedibus meis subiectum quicquid caeli tegitur axe cernebam.* Magani (*Ennodio* 1, 256) imagined only the briefest interval separated ordination from full conversion.

admission that ordination to the diaconate failed to rectify his wayward tendencies bolsters this inference.[84]

Ennodius meditates for the most part on "the deceptive happiness of eloquence" (*falsa dicendi felicitas*). While God laughed at his misguided effusions, "the allure of excessive accord" (*concinnationis superfluae . . . lepos*) impelled him through the meadows of rhetoric and poetry; "following a spurious wisdom," as he terms his belletristic urges, he distanced himself from the truth.[85] Illness reminded him of his spiritual misfortune and St. Victor's suffrages availed to save him, body and soul; basking in the Scriptural irony of his own name, he exclaims "unlucky person am I" (*infelix ego homo*).[86] Ennodius conveys his gratitude rhetorically because, as a well-schooled late-antique writer, he can conceive of no other mode. Within the context of St. Victor's patronage, expressed in legal, even contractual, terms, he had promised the saint he would pay recompense for the gifts of his trifling talent, "so that my writing style would never be debilitated by the puffed-up elaboration of worldly matters."[87] There is no question of giving up composition altogether, only of forsaking secular blandishments, as Ambrose would have wanted.

Desire for recognition of his literary accomplishments to confirm his worldly status was one recurring temptation for Ennodius. Anxiety about his material circumstances was another; he had been orphaned at an early age. It was with his anonymous aunt in Ticinum that Ennodius grew to adolescence; he says nothing of his parents.[88] He was not completely alone

84. #438.25–26: *ordinasti, ut per officium levitarum coactus sanarer . . . sed postquam venerandae me pressura dignitatis absolvit, habui de titulo genium, non de actionis nitore conscientiam.* Norden, *Die antike Kunstprosa,* 955–59; Ernout, "*Dictare,* dicter, allemand *dichten*"; Herescu, "Le mode de composition."

85. #438.7: *a vera sapientia mentitam secutus abscesseram;* though *inridere* appears several times in the *Confessiones* (Courcelle, *Les Confessions,* 215), Augustine was not alone in feeling the ironies of fate.

86. #438.7, invoking Rom. 7.24. Cf. #436.18: *felix et eruditus peccator.* St. Victor: #438.18, playing on the name he shared with Felix, another of Milan's holy patrons, and the expertise devoted to his transgressions; cf. Leclercq, "Milan," 1064, 1093.

87. #438.17: *promisi etiam . . . de manu linguae meae confessio ista procederet, de muneribus ipsius ingenioli mei eidem adipem litarem, ut numquam stili cura de saecularium rerum ventosa executione lassaretur.* On *de,* see Dubois, *La latinité,* 417.

88. Sirmond inferred a father named Camillus from Sid. Apoll. *Epist.* 1.11, *CIL* 8.1358, and Ennodius' #158; Vogel, however, noting the appearance of Firminus as a grandfather in #69 (a *dictio* for Ennodius' nephew Lupicinus; cf. #52), stated Firminus was the father (iv). See Stroheker, *Der senatorische Adel,* 174 (Firminus 155); Wermelinger, "Ennodius," 654; Cesa, "Integrazioni prosopografiche," 236–40; Reydellet, "Ennodio," 689. His mother's identity eludes even conjecture.

in the world: his epistolary confession omits to mention that he had two or three older sisters, married and with children, though he alludes to that fact in the correspondence, and the members of his more extended family are numerous and often notable.[89] All in all, Ennodius preferred not to call upon relatives for anything beyond fulfilling the duties of friendship and giving assistance to the Catholic Church. In a letter early in the collection, concerned for the health of his bishop and ecclesiastical superior, Laurentius of Milan, Ennodius refers to him as "a second parent," implying a transfer of affection and dependence from blood kin to voluntary relationships (*Wahlverwandtschaften*) based on religious affiliation.[90]

Perhaps because of its later date, however, #438 assumes a more frankly confessional stance in communicating doubts about the prospect of relying on relatives to supply the necessities of life. His betrothal to the unnamed *filiola* happened, Ennodius states, when he was "alone, lacking means and in need of counsel, to whom only adversity could grant relief," so God saved him from having to ask his relatives to support him, "which is a thing more bitter than captivity's lot," and to experience the evils inflicted on those obliged to wander.[91] He then concedes that he was blinded by his new affluence, which he all too easily took for granted, and so fell prey to chronic and heedless sin. The implicit message is that privation, or at least the threat of it, tended to draw him closer to God while the availability of material comforts, whether wealth or health, more than once seduced him away from the source of all good things. Ten years before his death, with a long way through the woods still to go, Ennodius nonetheless managed to analyze and articulate the desires and fears underlying his besetting sins.

We can find news of Ennodius' activities away from the office and the altar beyond #438. In the *Life* of Epifanius, Ennodius mentions that he

---

89. Euprepia, mother of Lupicinus (#52, #84, #109, #219, #268, #293, #313), Parthenius' unnamed mother (already dead; in #369 Ennodius learned of his nephew's derelictions from the father), and a third *germana anonyma* (#423, vv. 22–26). Fertig (*Magnus Felix Ennodius,* 13) allowed only the first two; of the third's existence, he said, "Ich möchte es beinahe glauben." Three sisters: Ruggini, "Ticinum," 305; two: Reydellet, "Ennodio," 689.

90. #19.4 (*alterius parentis*), from 503. Ruggini ("Ticinum," 304) and Reydellet ("Ennodio," 689) call Laurentius Ennodius' *parente.*

91. #438.21: *remansi solus, inops re et consilio destitutus, cui sola remedium tribuere posset adversitas, ne inter parentes, quod est captivitatis sorte amarius, subsidia vivendi liber poscerem et cognitus peregrinantium mala tolerarem;* cf. 22–24. Momigliano characterized him as "poor relative of the Anicii" ("Gli Anicii e la storiografia," 233); so also Ruggini, "Ticinum," 304.

accompanied the bishop to Gaul on a mission to ransom Ligurian prisoners.[92] Church business obliged him to travel on other occasions, most notably to and from Rome during the period of the Symmachan schism and to Ravenna to promote Milanese interests at the Ostrogothic court.[93] Three of his poems indicate that Ennodius turned these rigors of the highway to poetic profit: two of them concern trips to identifiable locations, while a shorter one describes a horseback ride on a moonlit summer's night.[94]

As the following chapters will show, we need to make several passes through the whole collection, each time reading with an eye for different things, to appreciate the full range of Ennodius' official activities. Though not the earliest piece in terms of absolute chronology, a *dictio* celebrating the anniversary of Laurentius' consecration as bishop of Milan is the first work in the manuscripts and gives an idea of the loftier assignments Ennodius had to handle.[95] Additional epideictic pieces for other bishops and their works of spiritual and literal edification are scattered about the corpus. A number of epigrams perform a similar function by displaying and glorifying the material accomplishments of living leaders of the Catholic community, among them new basilicas, baptisteries, and strongholds, renovations, and even vehicles.[96] The holy dead, still present in the community as vessels of God's grace, also receive their due. Epifanius of Ticinum and Antonius of Lérins receive the full hagiographical treatment by special request, with other saints and feasts of the Church commemorated in epigrams and hymns.[97] Moreover, the leaders of the Church used Ennodius' words to praise King Theoderic, notwithstanding his religion and ethnicity. Both the *Panegyric* and a later communiqué showcase the harmony of policy and purpose, largely facilitated by Ennodius himself, that prevailed

---

92. #80.171.

93. E.g., #2, #260, #286, #288, #361.

94. #245, *itinerarium Brigantionis castelli;* #423 (another *itinerarium,* describing the River Po); #330.

95. #1 (for Laurentius). Cf. #43 (Epifanius' thirtieth anniversary; out of sequence), #98 (Honoratus of Novara replaces a pagan temple with a basilica), #277 (Maximus of Ticinum dedicates a church).

96. #96, #97, #183 (basilicas repaired by Laurentius); #128, #181 (baptisteries); #260 (Honoratus' *castellum*); #469 (wagon).

97. #80 (Epifanius), #240 (Antonius); #179 (St. Lawrence), #195–#206 (bishops of Milan from Ambrose to Theodorus, Laurentius' predecessor), #341–#352 (various saints, feasts), #366 (Ambrose's victory over Symmachus).

between the Catholic Church and the Ostrogothic authorities until after
the schism between Rome and Constantinople was resolved.[98]

When writing as subdeacon and deacon, Ennodius keeps more down-
to-earth pastoral issues largely in the background; despite the elegant allusiveness he shares with his contemporary and fellow functionary
Cassiodorus, however, his responsibilities are clear enough. Model
descriptions of the duties of deacons tell us that they acted first and foremost as assistants to their bishops; certain documents remind deacons that
they were also subordinate to priests, since associating with bishops might
make them forgetful of the fact.[99] In particular, deacons had to look after
the material and spiritual well-being of the Christian community, of which
administering and replenishing the diocese's assets formed a vital part, and
to assist in the sacraments of the Eucharist and of Baptism, from which
their role in the liturgy of Holy Saturday naturally proceeded.

Already well-off even in Ambrose's time, the Milanese Church, like
those of Rome and Ravenna, possessed extensive assets by the sixth century as a result of gifts and bequests.[100] Not surprisingly, therefore, financial matters occupied a conspicuous place among Ennodius' diaconal
duties as did the Church's obligation to defend the rights of the oppressed.
Some letters request that powerful laymen give aid to individuals, who are
more often vexed by seizures of property, missing slaves, or pecuniary disagreements than by the afflictions of utter poverty (excepting certain persons in religion).[101] Many receive appeals for assistance, but a larger share
of Ennodius' correspondence is directed to the Roman senatorial family of
Faustus and his sons Avienus and Messala than to any other group of
addressees. When the correspondence begins, Faustus had already been
consul, his sons would receive the honor with the passage of time (also

98. #263 (from 506) and #458; Sundwall, *Abhandlungen,* 42–43, 69. Ennodius and Cas-
siodorus underscore Italy's good order and prosperity under Theoderic's reign of *civilitas:*
Reydellet, *La royauté,* 180, 222–24; Näf, "Das Zeitbewußtsein des Ennodius," 108–14; and
Senatorisches Standesbewusstsein, 196–215.

99. *Stat. Eccl. Antiq.* 57 (*CCSL* 148.1), Gelas. *Ep.* 14.7. Standard accounts: Gaudemet,
L'église, 103; Klauser, "Diakon," 899–902.

100. Cassiod. *Var.* 2.29; Lanzoni, *Le diocesi,* 1023; Mochi Onory, *Vescovi e città,* 135–74;
Jones, *Later Rom. Emp.,* 904–10; Wickham, *Early Medieval Italy,* 18–19; McLynn, *Ambrose,*
55–56, 67–71; Markus, *Gregory,* 134–37, 141–42.

101. To Faustus: #60 (property), #89 (slaves), #115 (a *mulier religiosa*); cf. #90, #424. To
Alico: #118 (*presbyter*). To Iulianus: #306 (dispute over a pound of silver). To Edasius: #392
(slaves). To Meribaudus: #425 (for Ambrosius, son of Faustinus). To Liberius: #457 (tax
relief for Camella, an impoverished Gallic relative).

occupying posts in Theoderic's government), and, most important, the family supported Pope Symmachus.[102] Wealth, high office, and religious sympathies rendered them useful; moreover, genuine rapport developed and so, scattered all through the corpus, Ennodius' letters to them show great variety of tone and subject matter. Other studies will shape this material in other ways, but because I decided to approach Ennodius through what he writes about rather than through the people to whom he writes, every chapter of this book contains some reference to his relations with the family of Faustus.

Whatever his subject or choice of words, however, Ennodius communicates with everyone either as a friend (its spectrum of meanings contains many wavelengths) or as a relative (chap. 4), or sometimes both. Potentially disorienting for us, such familiarities were essential to the complex, complementary interaction between the domains of traditional secular personal patronage and the good works emblematic of the institutional Church. Ordained members of the Church could call upon its lay supporters to exert political and legal influence in matters that by themselves they might not obtain directly; for their part, powerful laymen could also appeal to their ecclesiastical friends for special assistance as circumstances warranted. The following sample of letters, in which medium and message intertwine, will serve as our introduction to the varieties of interaction between laymen and ecclesiastics that consume so much of Ennodius' writing.

One way of orienting patronage comes through in a letter from the end of 506, to Laconius, a Gallic relative and advisor to the Burgundian king Gundobad, who had written to ask Ennodius a question about canon law. The reply begins most encouragingly: "heavenly dispensation has given an outcome to things well desired and . . . has made what was thought necessary to be yearned for."[103] Even with the introductory play on words, however, the nature of Laconius' question becomes clear only in the second sentence: "celestial care has bidden a suitor not altogether foreign to

---

102. Consuls of 490, 502, and 506, respectively: *PLRE* 2, 454–56 (Fl. Anicius Probus Faustus iunior Niger 9), 192–93 (Rufius Magnus Faustus Avienus iunior + Fl. Avienus iunior 3), 759–60 (Fl. Ennodius Messala 2); Bagnall et al., *Consuls,* 40–46; Moorhead, *Theoderic,* 157. For their relationship, see chapter 4.

103. #252.1: *bene cupitis superna dispensatio dedit effectum et . . . quod putabatur necessarium fecit optabile.* #38 (early summer 503) and #86 (mid–late 504) call Laconius "friend" and complain of sporadic replies; "brotherly attention," "your brotherliness," and "from our blood" declare he was family, pace Stroheker, *Der senatorische Adel,* Laconius 211.

our blood to approach my niece, so that, while the moment to take counsel presses, sustenance is afforded to holy love."[104] Happy that the proposed intra-family match caused Laconius to contact him, Ennodius approves the idea. Laconius should of course know the union is permissible for the degree of consanguinity described, but Ennodius will send his people to Rome immediately "to obtain an answer on this opinion from the venerable Pope, so that the authority of a more powerful ruling will strengthen your disposition."[105] Most private persons planning a dynastic marriage could not expect the Successor of Peter to decide their case; Ennodius' intervention on Laconius' behalf signifies both his own privileged ecclesiastical position and the level of pastoral care to which Laconius thought himself entitled.

Ennodius' dealings with two individuals located in southern Gaul, an abbot named Stefanus and a certain Aurelianus, successively layman, priest, and bishop, are more complex, revealing some of the pitfalls of conducting ecclesiastical business.[106]

The first letter to Stefanus is difficult to surpass in its application of allusive obliqueness to practical considerations: "How sweet is the trouble of your letter, because it has bestowed spiritual reward on me! How desired the need for couriers, which the yearnings of others minister to in its eagerness for relief!"[107] Calling himself a sinner, Ennodius celebrates Stefanus' missive as a happy event to which he would otherwise not have been party; adversities, however, have prompted this conversation. The abbot may have lost touch with him for some years, if the references to "the burden of bad company" (*malae conversationis fasce*) and "the world's filthy laxity" (*saecularis licentia inmunda*) explain his former isolation, but given Ennodius' voracious appetite for correspondence and the reiterated self-abasement that reaches fullest expression in #438, the

---

104. #252.1–2: *caelestis cura nepti meae procum non omnino a sanguine nostro peregrinantem iussit accedere, ut dum consulendi instat oportunitas, sancto amori pabula praestarentur;* she must be a nameless daughter of one of Ennodius' sisters.

105. #252.2: *homines meos . . . exacturos a venerabili papa super hac parte responsum, ut animum vestrum potioris praecepti firmet auctoritas.* Laconius' son/kinsman wanted to marry Ennodius' niece. Canon law was inconsistent in this area (Magani, *Ennodio* 1, 162; 3, 68–70) and might be set aside (McLynn, *Ambrose,* 259). Cf. Agde (506), *Sententiae insertae,* can. 14 (61) (*CCSL* 148); Cassiod. *Var.* 7.46; Gaudemet, *L'église,* 527–28.

106. To Bishop Senator: #66 (slaves). To Avitus of Vienne: #248 (Boniface's captive cousin), #253 (Sabinus' son). To the priest Adeodatus: #303 (unspecified patronage).

107. #71.1: *Litterarum vestrarum quam dulce negotium est, quod mihi spiritale munus exhibuit! quam votiva perlatorum necessitas, quae remedii sui studio desideriis medetur alienis* (Jan.–Apr. 504).

absence that made his courteous heart grow fonder need not have been ter-
ribly long.[108] He then thanks God for making him worthy and acceptable
to his holy friends, for long-cultivated submission has raised him up so
Stefanus now addresses him as "almost an equal."[109]

Staking out his position on the high ground of humility by requesting
Stefanus' sturdy spiritual patronage, Ennodius gets down to business in
the last quarter of the letter: "that blasted cleric was very much afraid to
state his case in front of the bishop after he saw the men to whom you have
delegated my allegiance being defended by me."[110] He then suggests that
one of Stefanus' people, armed with appropriate letters of recommendation, be sent to Faustus at Ravenna so as to forestall an adverse judgment,
obtainable for a price (*venalis . . . sententia*), being handed down by the
magistrates at Milan. The men Stefanus sent to Ennodius are clearly
enmeshed in a suit, most likely concerning property, with an unnamed
member of the secular clergy who, temporarily daunted by an impressive
counter-attack (so Ennodius would have his correspondent believe), must
still be thwarted in his ambition by a change of venue from Milan to
Ravenna.[111]

This appraisal of the venality of the Milanese legal community is
remarkably candid, if not tactless, given Ennodius' own place in the local
ecclesiastical bureaucracy. By informing his correspondent that money
influenced the outcome of cases heard at Milan and intimating that Faustus' personal patronage was a better guarantee of judicial impartiality, he
voices his disapproval of suits decided more by money than by the merits
of the contending parties. In addition, Ennodius reaffirms the values of a
class that preferred its influence subtler than the crude exchanging of
money for service. Perhaps his forthrightness in warning Stefanus of the
pitfalls of conducting legal business in Milan eventually benefited his cor-

---

108. #71.1–2; cf. #438. Sundwall (*Abhandlungen,* 19–20) believed there had been no contact since Ennodius' move to Milan c. 499.

109. #71.3: *ecce iam quasi aequalis appellor.* Other letters on prayer and piety: #218, #251,
#431.

110. #71.4: *perditus ille clericus expavit causam dicere apud episcopum, postquam defendi a
me vidit eos, quibus meum deputastis obsequium.*

111. The use of *clericus* (instead of *monachus*) suggests Stefanus' people were monks
either defending their title to property that secular clergy in their area also sought to claim,
thus appealing beyond the local bishop's jurisdiction (cf. Angers [453], can. 1 and 8; Vence
[461/491], can. 9), or asserting their monastery's right to dispose of property without the local
bishop's permission (Agde [506], can. 9 of the later *Sententiae insertae* [*CCSL* 148]). Cf.
Mochi Onory, *Vescovi e città,* 292.

respondent and his colleagues; in any case, it lends no support to the view that Ennodius invariably emitted politic frivolities.

Our only indication of how the case concluded is Ennodius' second (and last) surviving letter to Stefanus, written soon after.[112] It opens encouragingly—"the gifts of God are doubled for those who hope, and heavenly grace abounds with twofold favor" (*geminantur dei dona sperantibus et duplici exuberat gratia superna beneficio*)—then waxes metaphorical, joining the living water of Christ with Stefanus' letters, whose power to refresh shows that "in them, flames and cups are kindred, and that a contradiction of nature has united in a strange concord" (*in quibus cognatas video flammas et pocula et diversitatem naturae in peregrinam coisse concordiam*). Such elaboration was designed to convey the most elegant of compliments while indicating that word had meanwhile arrived from Stefanus; we can consequently infer he assented to Ennodius' suggestion. Only the last sentence offers a clue to affairs beyond the borders of spiritual friendship: "my lord, afford the earth a sustained example of the most blessed life, God providing, and show through the philosophy of holy religion that one must hope not in this life alone, by despising the present age."[113] In view of the extreme deference Ennodius previously showed his correspondent, his shift from imploring advice to dispensing it excites curiosity. We can, at the least, take his exhortation to cultivate saintly detachment as a warning not to assume good things of mortal men; more probably, it implies Ennodius thought the judgment would not go in favor of Stefanus and was trying to adjust his correspondent's expectations.

The correspondence with Aurelianus, in contrast, presents a longer, subtler series of exchanges.[114] In the first letter he is simply a layman addressed as a dear relative, who needs commiseration for difficulties not unrelated to Stefanus'. After declaring the strength of his confidence and affection, Ennodius gives thanks to "the heavenly dispensation, you who bestow the fruit of prosperity on human affairs out of a moment of adversity and do not allow sadness to keep its place," in terms similar to the first letter to Stefanus.[115] He then addresses the matter at hand: someone's mal-

---

112. #79.1–3 (Jan.–Apr. 504); for the fire/water image, cf. #224.6.

113. #79.3: *domine mi, longum terris deo nostro tribuente vitae beatissimae exemplum praesta et per religionis sanctae philosophiam non in hac tantum vita sperandum esse contemptu saeculi praesentis ostende.*

114. Aurelianus: #270, #390, #412, #455; Sundwall, *Abhandlungen,* 41, 59, 63, 68–69.

115. #270.1: *superna dispensatio, quae humanis rebus prosperorum fructum de adversitatis occasione largiris nec pateris in ordine suo tristia permanere* (autumn 507).

ice has robbed Aurelianus of his patrimony, but the costs of regaining it have won Theoderic's great favor: "expending one's substance is good if the attention of our renowned prince is found through disbursements."[116] Ennodius calls this temporary loss "the mother of profit and the way of honors," exalting Aurelianus all the more as he writes to celebrate this heaven-sent manifestation of greatness.[117]

Aurelianus disappears from the corpus for almost three years, until mid-510, when Ennodius sends affectionate salutations and news about his health to an Aurelianus *presbyter;* as the same person receives two further letters distinguished by their confidential tone, his identity is tolerably certain.[118] The letter to Aurelianus written at the end of 510, however, opens with singular sharpness, for even in circumstances painful to the other party he has normally welcomed opportunities for contact. Here, the unpleasant burden of Aurelianus' message made what was ordinarily a happy occasion loathsome, "for the disaster that was reported overshadowed the letter's sweet beginning and the honey of tranquil conversation with, as it were, a shroud of night."[119]

What horrified Ennodius was the virtuous man's nightmare: a woman who betrayed family and decency by leaving her husband and living with another man. Still, dismay does not keep Ennodius from exploiting the irony of the woman's name by punning, "I was forced to have seen that Aetheria all too earthly, banished from the loftiness of her name to Tartarus, with sin as her leader."[120] He would write a formal letter, he avers, were he not so eager to have the business forgotten, but his correspondent's desire to expel the offenders from Gaul moves Ennodius melodramatically to suggest they settle in the Libyan desert (so as not to befoul Italy). He finally indicates that he communicated Aurelianus' injunctions regarding legal remedies for Aetheria's transgressions to the Prefect, "who soon obtained the royal precepts through which we believe good and ami-

---

116. #270.1–2: *bona est iactura substantiae, si incliti notitia principis dispendiis invenitur.* Stroheker, following Vogel, put the troubles in 507 (*Der senatorische Adel,* Aurelianus 49), but *hostilis* need not imply military action: *inimicus* occurs as a synonym five lines later.

117. #270.2–3: *lucri mater et honorum via.*

118. #390 (summer 510); #412, #455.

119. #412.1–2: *nam dulce principium et sereni mella conloquii relata calamitas quasi veste noctis obnubit.*

120. #412.2: *coactus sum illam Aetheriam nimis vidisse terrenam et a sublimitate vocabuli in tartarum duce culpa depositam.* Cf. Stroheker, *Der senatorische Adel,* 142 (Aetheria 5); Verg. *Aen.* 1.546. Puns on personal names: Auson. *Epig.* 21, 41, 42, 74 (Green).

cable men have found opportunity of giving assistance."[121] In the meantime he urges Aurelianus to calm down and trust in God's judgment.

Ennodius does not mention Aetheria again, but two letters in the fourth book of Cassiodorus' *Variae* give witness that Aetheria's second husband was a man named Liberius and that he actively defended her against charges of squandering her children's inheritance made by their grandmother Arcotamia.[122] Arcotamia was another correspondent of Ennodius, and her son was a priest-monk on the island of Lérins.[123] If Aetheria had been married and borne children to this same son, who then renounced matrimony for the religious life (as Ennodius himself had done), her unwillingness to emulate her ex-husband's marital (sexual) renunciation would have been crime enough. Alternatively, she may have been the widow of another of Arcotamia's sons who decided to remarry despite her mother-in-law's views of what God and the family fortune required.[124]

The last letter to Aurelianus, very near the end of the collection, is unlike its predecessors in that it contains no allusion to pressing matters requiring the aid of secular authorities. Ennodius simply offers up his unhappiness at discovering through "precarious rumor" (*instabili . . . rumore*) that Aurelianus has been promoted to bishop; his friend had definitely not been a good correspondent.[125] Conceding his own desire for contact and dejectedly proffering a valediction, Ennodius accuses Aurelianus of using his episcopal office as an excuse to neglect their relationship: "one noble by his life and his ancestry has ascended the peak of ecclesiastical distinction, and he disdains to address me."[126] Even at this point in his career, a year or more after the confessional #438 reached its final form, Ennodius found himself enmeshed in relationships whose divergent origins and aims could not avoid generating friction.

Performing good works and cultivating friendships constitutes only part of what Ennodius had to attend to, publicly and privately; furthering

---

121. #412.3–4: *qui praecepta regia mox exegit, per quae credimus viros bonos et amicos occasionem invenisse praestandi.* The prefect was probably Ennodius' friend Faustus: Moorhead, *Theoderic,* 229. Divorce and remarriage: Watson, "Religious and Gender Discrimination," 318–23.

122. Cassiod. *Var.* 4. 12 (ordering the case against Aetheria be heard), 46 (response to Liberius' appeal in her defense). Cf. Arjava, *Women and Law,* 172–92.

123. #319 (Arcotamia as pious kinswoman and mother of a monk).

124. #319.6 implies Arcotamia lost this second son, plus her husband.

125. #455.3 (around mid-512).

126. #455.4: *nobilis vita vel genere apicem ecclesiastici honoris ascendit, et me dedignatur adloquio.*

the advancement of orthodoxy also demanded effort. Sometimes he wrote
communiques for the chanceries of Milan and Rome, as for instance the
episcopal letter of consolation and encouragement he prepared for a group
of Catholic clergymen who had fled from the Vandal persecution in North
Africa.[127] This communication's official nature is apparent from the
absence of Ennodius' own name from the title (rare among his personal
letters) and from the use of the first person plural.[128] Although the standard collection of papal letters includes it among the documents of Symmachus, certain manuscripts of Ennodius give the phrase Vogel represents
as "letters sent to our son the deacon" (*directis ad filium nostrum diaconum
litteris*) with an empty space and an adjoining initial letter; in chapter 5, I
will argue that, even if Symmachus was involved, internal evidence indicates that the deacon was Ennodius.[129]

Most important in the long run was Ennodius' personal engagement in
the problems and policies of Pope Symmachus and the Church of Rome.
Though its city had become politically marginal, the see of Rome stood
firm amid the theological controversies of the fifth century, utterly convinced of its own correctness. Leo the Great's definition of Christ's dual
nature (God and man), ratified by the Council of Chalcedon, was one
proof; another was its inalienable primacy in preserving and validating
orthodoxy in opposition to the heretical self-assertiveness of Constantinople, "the New Rome."[130] From the Roman point of view, any diver-
gence from the teachings of Chalcedon equaled heresy and every attempt
by the Imperial government in Constantinople to reconcile doctrinally
antagonistic groups to Orthodoxy without Rome's guidance and approval
was an incitement to schism.

Latin-speaking Rome was immune to the subtleties of all alternative
Christologies that arose in the East—from the convictions of Nestorius,

---

127. #51 (summer 503); cf. Jaffé, *Regesta* 1, 99, assigned to Symmachus' pontificate but
written by Ennodius (507–12).

128. Hasenstab, *Studien,* 27–38.

129. Thiel, *Epistulae Pontificum Romanorum,* 708–9: *Symmachi papae (vel saltem ipsius
nomine scripto).* Sirmond and Thiel: *H* signified Hormisdas, Symmachus' successor (so *C* and
P; V left space on both sides of *diaconum,* Baronius read *Ennodium*); cf. Hartel, 55. Dekkers
Clavis, 546 (no. 1678; cf. no. 1487) put it with Symmachus' genuine letters, perhaps written
by Ennodius; Sundwall, *Abhandlungen,* 15, concurs.

130. Leo *Ep.* 28 (the *tomus, PL* 54.755–82), 93 (exhortation to the Council); Wojtowytsch,
Papsttum und Konzile, 304–50. Constantinople's assumption of apostolic status galled
Roman *amour propre:* Leo *Ep.* 104–7, 111, 114, 117, 119, 128, 134–36; Schwartz, "Der
sechste nicaenische Kanon."

which many speakers of Syriac found congenial, to the teachings of Eutyches, favored by Greeks, Syrians, and Egyptians alike—and firmly
believed its condemnation of them settled the matter permanently. In 482,
however, the Emperor Zeno and Acacius, the Patriarch of Constantinople,
determined that unity within the Empire was of paramount importance
and so promulgated their own document of union. It aimed to satisfy as
many people as possible theologically, but the Orthodoxy of its tradition-
alizing formulae condemned both those who denied Mary was the Mother
of God (Nestorians) and those who denied the humanity of Christ (Euty-
chians) without giving any weight to the formulations of Chalcedon.[131] As
soon as the new, energetic Pope Felix III found out about it, he excommu-
nicated both Zeno and Acacius (whom Western churchmen considered the
chief villain), so summoning the Acacian Schism into existence; it continued for thirty-seven years, until the accession of Justin in 519.[132]

Ennodius thus spent his entire working life as a Catholic clergyman in a
consciously post-Chalcedonian environment, with the Acacian Schism
functioning as both emotive background and intellectual focus. Dissenters
roamed the East, easy prey for the heresiological slanging of Western
Catholics, while the doctrinal sovereignty of the bishops of Rome had substantially come to depend on the fact of Italian self-rule (under Arian
Ostrogothic control, to be sure), notwithstanding papal affirmations of
righteous independence. As the events of the Byzantine reconquest would
make painfully clear, East-West doctrinal rapprochement was as great a
danger to Italian autonomy as political reabsorption.[133]

From these tensions arose the Symmachan schism, which ensued when
two men were elected bishop of Rome almost simultaneously in 498: Symmachus, a popular deacon uncompromisingly solicitous of Rome's prerogatives, and Laurentius, an ascetic priest disposed to conciliation.[134]
While the two prelates and their supporters struggled for supremacy, Ennodius composed a pamphlet on Symmachus' behalf now known as the

---

131. *Henotikon:* Evagrius *HE* 3.14; Liberatus *Brev.* 17; de Labriolle, *Histoire de l'église* 4,
289–92; Caspar, *Geschichte* 2, 14–32.

132. Schwartz, *Publizistische Sammlungen,* 193–262; de Labriolle, *Histoire de l'église* 4,
295–96.

133. Ensslin, *Theoderich,* 109–10, 117–32; Noble, "Theoderic and the Papacy," 411–17.
Pope Vigilius' tribulations (the Three Chapters controversy): de Labriolle, *Histoire de l'église*
4, 457–79; Caspar, *Geschichte* 2, 238–86.

134. Caspar, *Geschichte* 2, 87–88; Wirbelauer, *Zwei Päpste,* 9–17. Ennodius' superior
Laurentius of Milan was Symmachus' foremost ecclesiastical supporter.

Libellus and was in fact the first writer to reserve the title "pope" (*papa*) exclusively for the bishop of Rome.[135] In the *Libellus* he constructed a strong, articulate statement of papal ideology that asserted the occupant of the See of Peter possessed an unimpeachable authority independent of emperors and councils. By itself Ennodius' exalted justification of the rights of the pontiff, both as successor of the Apostles and as head of the Church of Rome, "parent of the world," might have secured him lasting fame, but his pro-Chalcedonian convictions also left traces in the corpus; with the jumbled memory of his diplomatic activities in the East, both helped ensure his survival.[136]

One final aspect of Ennodius' working relationship with Symmachus and his successor Hormisdas remains to be examined here. Ministering to the bishop of Rome's material needs was a less uplifting task than drafting declarations on issues of faith and morals, but on the earthly plane no less vital. At times, however, its demands clashed with those of Milan and of Ennodius himself. Notwithstanding his resolve to keep his discourse as euphoniously civilized as possible, Ennodius left us four letters that unambiguously request repayment of certain monies lent to Symmachus in connection with the Laurentian problems, plus a fifth, dealing with a delivery of horses to agents of the Roman Church.[137]

In maintaining his claim to the See of Rome against Laurentius and his partisans, Symmachus endured two phases of attack. The Laurentians initially challenged the canonical validity of his election, forcing Symmachus to seek Theoderic's endorsement; subsequently, they attempted by means of a synod to depose him on grounds of adultery.[138] Ennodius' first letter dealing with money is addressed to Luminosus, a layman with close ties to Symmachus, and outlines his own bishop's request "that the expenditure which was made at Ravenna for the necessities of the lord Pope be reimbursed, for to certain powerful individuals whose names it is not safe to indicate in writing, the lord knows that he paid out more than four hun-

---

135. #49; cf. Dubois, *La latinité,* 20–23, 223.

136. #49.128; Lumpe, "Die konziliengeschichtliche Bedeutung." Chalcedon: #348, a hymn to St. Euphemia, its patroness (cf. Hope, *Leonine Sacramentary,* 32); #464, a brief anti-Monophysite discourse. For #49 and #464, see chapter 5.

137. Vogel deplored them (xxix: *de sordido negotio Ravennae contracto*): #77, #139 (Caspar, *Geschichte* 2, 88), #283, #300; #235. Bribery, or not: Noble, "Theoderic and the Papacy," 405; Amory, *People and Identity,* 133–34.

138. The disciplinary directive #8 (late 501) may have been written for Symmachus' scandal-plagued Rome (Moorhead, *Theoderic,* 115) or perhaps Milan (Magani, *Ennodio* 2, 206–9; Barnish, *Variae,* xxvii).

dred solidi of gold."[139] As Ennodius himself had stood as guarantor, Luminosus' assistance in repaying the loan would relieve him of both contractual obligation and personal liability; Ennodius then asks, "still, if you believe my petition to be immodest, indicate it, and I will pay any restitution stipulated out of my own resources."[140]

Was the appeal frank enough to procure prompt repayment? No, Ennodius had to write to Luminosus again a year or so later, informing him that Laurentius of Milan had asserted that "the reimbursements owed to him were denied by the lord Pope under some sort of disagreement" and imploring "the favor of your defense in this situation."[141] That overture was no more effective than its now-missing successors in the years that followed, for one more missive to Luminosus in connection with the loan survives. Its preamble still elegantly metaphorical, Ennodius' letter rephrases his anxiety about the funds expended on Symmachus' behalf at Ravenna. Stressing the bishop of Milan's resolve not to grant Rome a deferral of the repayment, Ennodius reminds Luminosus that "you had promised a swift outcome of the sums to be restored," which would end Ennodius' vexation and financial loss from the ongoing failure to fulfill contractual obligations.[142]

This last letter to Luminosus was evidently just as unsuccessful, because shortly afterward Ennodius wrote straight to the deacons Hormisdas and Dioscorus of the Church of Rome using similar language. They received the particulars in writing, he points out, and should recollect the pope's promise to repay the Milanese Church for useful disbursements at Ravenna; meanwhile, Ennodius had to remedy the shortage with his own resources. The tone, however, is generally more deferential than in the Luminosus letters, and Ennodius leaves it to his esteemed correspondents to inform him of how they intend to settle the matter: "now, because what is being requested is not a great sum, and it is a supreme benefit for me to

---

139. #77.3: *ut expensa, quae pro necessitatibus domni papae Ravennae facta est, redhibitione pensaretur, certis enim potentibus quorum nomina tutum non est scripto signari, novit dominus quia plus quam quadringentos auri solidos erogavit* (Jan.–Apr. 504). Dubois, *La latinité*, 189, 218, 320–21; de Labriolle, *Histoire de l'église* 4, 347; Sundwall, *Abhandlungen*, 203.

140. #77.4–5: *tamen si verecundum esse non creditis, indicate, et de propria facultate restituo.*

141. #139.2: *reditus sibi debitos, quos ecclesia Romana facta cum auctore eius est pactione pollicita, a domno papa adserit sub nescio qua oppositione denegari; in quo negotio favorem per me vestrae defensionis inplorat* (Jan.–Sept. 505).

142. #283.2: *de qua restituenda celerem promiseratis effectum* (Jan.–Apr. 508).

subtract what seems just from its fruitlessness, ordain whatever heavenly compensation repays you."[143]

Apart from this, Ennodius already enjoyed an amicable correspondence with Hormisdas by early 506, though in the late summer of that year he had cause to write concerning some horses. Those animals had been given to the pope on condition that a just price be paid if the Roman Church did not need them for its own use; the understanding behind such beneficence was that, as Milanese churchmen had assisted their Roman brethren when asked, Romans should be prepared to reciprocate.[144]

We cannot know how successful Ennodius the deacon was in preserving the fortunes of the Milanese Church in the face of such fraternal acquisitiveness, but his persistence kindled no lasting enmities. Once he became bishop of Ticinum, a city whose prestige under Theoderic he himself helped to augment, his handling of another notably discouraging endeavor—representing Roman doctrinal interests in Constantinople—definitely enhanced his subsequent reputation. In fact, I suggest that his unfailing courtesy in circumstances ordinarily conducive to wordless frustration upheld him as well in the long run as more conspicuously ascetic religious practices did others. Matters of phrasing might sometimes obsess him, but nicety of expression is essential to his character, both as an individual and in his relations with others.

---

143. #300.2–3: *nunc, quia grandis summa non est quae reposcitur, et summum est beneficium me ab ingratitudine eius quae videtur iusta subtrahere, ordinate quod vobis retributio superna compenset.*

144. #235; also to Hormisdas: #172, #317, #410, #417, #427. Ambrose arranged his letters more artfully: Zelzer, "Die Briefbücher."

CHAPTER 2

The Divinity of Letters

For Ennodius communication was the essential activity; since we cannot hear him speak, his writing must speak for him. The letters, which bulk largest in the corpus, as well as the declamatory pieces (*dictiones*), manifest this concern with writing and speaking well.[1] Ennodius hoped that those around him would be of like mind, sharing in a comprehensive social enterprise that began with the mastery of simple school exercises. I have already made the point that Ennodius was first, last, and always a member of the Catholic clergy, though not yet a bishop, during the entire period in which we see him as a writer. Now we need to affirm his wholeheartedly literary nature. Although this chapter mainly considers Ennodius' cultural discourse with well-born laymen, it will soon become clear that literary considerations permeated his relations with ecclesiastical correspondents as well; his treatment of individuals is nuanced, not compartmentalized.

Despite the influence of ascetic Christianity, very few people in the late Roman world questioned, let alone challenged, the desirability of observing those earthly distinctions in which their identity and worth resided, among which was a fastidious mastery of language.[2] This basic assumption has seldom been more evident than in the elegant letters, *dictiones,* and poems Ennodius destined for his circle of acquaintances. With careful attention to each addressee, particularly the promising young men among his associates, he presents his interpretation of contemporary literary culture, furnishing copious examples of the theory and practice of belles-

1. Letters and *dictiones* roundly condemned by, inter alia, Schanz-Hosius 4.2, 143; Fontaine, "Ennodius," 400–403; Riché, *Education and Culture,* 48–51. After Sirmond, only Léglise, *Les lettres,* claimed merit, but cf. Constable, "Forged Letters," 13–18; Bruggisser, *Symmaque,* 3–30.

2. Scheibelreiter, *Bischof in merowingischer Zeit,* 9–50; Klingshirn, *Caesarius,* 157–58; Hopkins, "Conquest by Book"; Heather, "Literacy."

lettres. We can observe Ennodius' thinking on what the Greeks called *paideia:* how education ought ideally to work and what he believed the well-educated man should be capable of (words and deeds conformable to both moral and aesthetic criteria).

Our appraisal accordingly begins with these letters and *dictiones* precisely because they testify to Ennodius' conviction that an intelligent command of rhetoric was still a necessary constituent of full participation in civilized Roman society. At no time is he content with an unadorned enunciation of principles and ideals; throughout his correspondence, he takes the trouble to demonstrate the utility and pleasure to be had from expressing oneself appropriately on a variety of subjects. In doing so, he displays characteristic tendencies of thought and metaphor. Technical details of the business of communication also emerge from these writings about writing, illustrating internal considerations as well as external constraints. As often as not, the physical difficulties attendant upon composition and transmission affect Ennodius' ability to vary his linguistic usage with harmonious synonyms, paraphrases, and the like. Struggling to write in a moving vehicle or while oppressed by eye trouble cramped his style; so did finding dependable people to carry letters.

We begin with a set of four letters whose techniques and aims encapsulate Ennodius' views on the practice of belles-lettres and their broader cultural significance. The missive to Pope Symmachus is the most intriguing, with a nice blend of verbal refinement and sensitivity to social considerations; the addressee's spiritual eminence contrasts with the letter's pragmatic purpose, which is to introduce and recommend Ennodius' nephew Parthenius, who was traveling to Rome to further his literary studies.[3] Three adjacent messages to the eminent laymen Faustus Albus (consul of 483), Luminosus (whom we met in chap. 1 in a financial connection), and the Faustus (Niger) to whom Ennodius dedicated so many of his surviving letters, complete the set.[4]

The letter to Symmachus begins by acknowledging the addressee's cares and responsibilities, giving just a hint of what is on Ennodius' mind: "As long as the concern of your crown guides the Apostolic See and you rule the peak of the heavenly empire, there obtains a situation favorable

---

3. #226 (early Aug.–Sept. 506).

4. #225 (Anicius Acilius Aginantius Faustus), #227 (Luminosus: *PLRE* 2, 692–93), #228 (Anicius Probus Faustus, differentiated as F. *iunior* or *niger*). Bagnall et al., *Consuls,* 36–46 and *ad a.* 483, 490; Moorhead, *Theoderic,* 156–66.

for the advancement of my relatives which holds promise for my efforts."[5] Then he talks about the hope that proceeds from fidelity, for the merits of a single individual may redound to the benefit of many: he cites the case of David's virtues and the sparing of the Israelites, wherein "the faith of one man either rescued a people from error or assisted it in grace."[6] Only after creating an ambience favorable to the request he means to make does Ennodius introduce Parthenius, the bearer of the missive and his sister's son. He asserts that an interest in liberal education has compelled this young man, imbued with the confidence just depicted, to seek Rome: "Holy is the study of literature, in which vices are unlearned before experience accumulates; by this way venerable counsels are accustomed to come to boyish years, as long as precepts know how to furnish what youth shuns."[7] When Ennodius finally appeals to Symmachus' benevolence, he expresses it as a virtual prayer: "Cherish him, therefore, whose reasons for coming you have learned by the revelation of his relationship."[8] Ennodius suggests that the *papa,* as he consistently and exclusively signifies the occupant of the See of Peter, should regard Parthenius as a sort of hostage for his uncle's good behavior; having discharged his social duties as a correspondent and a subordinate, he prays that his nephew, as Symmachus' letter bearer and servant, "may acquire a good name among you by a stranger's happy lot, because what will have been bestowed by my prayers, your office embellishes above its own endowments."[9]

This item is an obvious example of that subgenre, the letter of recommendation (*epistula commendaticia*); we can say more about its details. The brilliance of the introduction, which constitutes about forty percent of the letter's total length, artfully prepares the ground for the request while paying obeisance to the addressee's eminence. That Ennodius, a deacon of Milan, can write to a bishop of Rome in the year 506 to affirm the sanctity of literary studies without apology is noteworthy, considering Gregory the

---

5. #226.1: *Dum sedem apostolicam coronae vestrae cura moderatur et caelestis imperii apicem regitis, blanditur profectibus parentum quod meis promissum tenet officiis.*

6. #226.2: *fides hominis aut eripuit de errore populum aut iuvit in gratia.*

7. #226.3: *sancta sunt studia litterarum, in quibus ante incrementa peritiae vitia dediscuntur; hoc itinere cana ad annos pueriles solent venire consilia, dum quod aetas refugit, norunt instituta praestare.*

8. #226.4: *fovete ergo cuius veniendi causas patefacta consanguinitate didicistis.*

9. #226.4: *perlator praesentium famulus vester felici sorte peregrini apud vos nomen excipiat, quia quod adtributum fuerit precibus meis, vestrum supra dotes suas ornat officium.* #416 (also to Symmachus) similarly recommends Beatus but less sentimentally; cf. Näf, *Senatorisches Standesbewusstsein,* 47–48, 143–45.

Great's treatment of Desiderius, the grammarian-bishop of Vienne.[10] Invoking the virtues of cultural pedagogy, however, is a line of argument common from Isocrates to Allan Bloom; Ennodius' appeal is on behalf of traditional general education as preparation for life in a civilized society, not the minimal literacy simple monks needed to read the Bible and its expounders.[11]

Every step in the formal process of pleasing, informing, and moving the correspondent in order to preserve social relationships and at the same time obtain a specific practical result, just as an orator would his audience, is implicit in the letter's intentional indirection. Ennodius' handling of Symmachus shows him to be yet another great man, a dispenser of patronage mindful of considerations of consanguinity.

This letter to Symmachus also reveals an attention to matching metaphors with addressees especially conspicuous when the latter share in the religious life. To represent the idea that faithful followers of steadfast men can expect to be rewarded and, still more, that the integrity of one individual can be the salvation of an entire community, Ennodius selected the figure of King David from the Old Testament. Although this choice may seem a remarkable display of impudence on his part, the Scriptural identity of David as narrative character and as the author of the Psalms permitted Ennodius to represent him both as a figure of sacred history, shepherd of God's chosen people and ancestor of Jesus Christ, and as a divinely inspired poet. By virtue of their poetic qualities and liturgical applications, the Psalms of David are among the most quoted books of the Bible; several episodes from the story of David were also applicable to various contexts, as Ennodius found. In an early letter to Faustus, written in the time of Symmachus' greatest troubles, Ennodius claimed he was imitating the patriarchs, among them David who consumed the consecrated loaves to assuage his hunger while a fugitive.[12] Elsewhere in the works David appears as a graciously victorious figure, merciful in his treatment of Saul, or as Absalom's sorrowing father.[13]

---

10. Markus, *Gregory,* 37 (on *Ep.* 11.34).

11. The precepts of #452 (early 512) to Ambrosius and Beatus reinforce this idea; Brown, *Power and Persuasion,* 35–70. Contrast #431 and Markus, *Gregory,* 34–40.

12. #7.3–4 (from 501). Ennodius used both Vetus Latina and Vulgate texts, often paraphrasing: Dubois, *La latinité,* 67–75; Petitmengin, "Les plus anciens manuscrits"; Gribomont, "Cassiodore et la transmission."

13. Epifanius' words to Anthemius and to Theoderic (#80.63 and 144); last words (#80.194). Absalom: #34.6. Cf. Reydellet, *La royauté,* 161–63, and "La Bible miroir des princes."

On the other hand, Ennodius found the David of the fiercer Psalms quite useful when invective was needed, as in the *Libellus* that expansively defended Pope Symmachus.[14] The composition of the *Libellus* must in fact be the main reason why, three years later, Ennodius confidently approached Symmachus about receiving Parthenius in Rome. In purely hierarchical terms the deacon of Milan was subordinate to the bishop of Rome, but as long as social relationships were based on reciprocal services and obligations he could benefit from his way with words, applying it to situations where others would recognize its utility.

Because there are three letters about Parthenius to other addressees, we should not overestimate the distinctiveness of Ennodius' overture to Symmachus. At the same time, comparing the ways in which he varies the subject of Parthenius from one letter to the next does give an excellent impression of his ability to translate the general principles of rhetorical education into individualized practice.

He addressed the first piece in the dossier to a Faustus (also called Albus) who was Prefect of Rome in 502–3 and supported Symmachus' rival, the former priest Laurentius, during the Roman schism.[15] We may suppose that either this Faustus had been won over by the arguments of the *Libellus,* or Ennodius was relying on the forces of polite acquaintance and the political reality of Symmachus' triumph to sustain his overtures, for the easy familiarity that we will see in the letter to Ennodius' frequent and cherished pro-Symmachan correspondent Faustus Niger is largely absent here. Ennodius uses the introduction to evoke the common social values to which he will presently request his addressee's practical assent. "Let the divinity be favorable to worthy desires, let happy omen not be denied to good studies, let free-born ventures grow strong with the fruits of success!" he urges, exalting the liberal arts and claiming that "only those who have received a moral education are predisposed to the ornaments of eloquence."[16] He then brings on Parthenius, already given the promise of Faustus' "paternal backing" (*suffragia paterna*); Ennodius' entreaties on his behalf comprise the main part of the letter. Using the lexical unity of "prayer" and "oration," he implies the great man's consistent conduct

---

14. #49.16 (Ps. 49); cf. #49.8, 21, 26, 54, 96, 98, 106, 118.

15. #225. Distinguishing the Fausti: Bagnall et al., *Consuls,* 40–46; Moorhead, *Theodoric,* 139, 150, cf. 163–66.

16. #225.1: *Secundet desideria honesta divinitas, felix auspicium bonis non negetur studiis, ingenuae intentiones prosperorum fructibus convalescant! . . . ad eloquentiae ornamenta non tendunt nisi moribus instituti.*

counts for more than his own persuasive skills, "as long as what habit demands we implore with pleas, as if anyone believed that by his speech he deserved the sun to rise or a river to flow."[17] He does expect that, "beyond the rounds from which you in no way depart," something will result, as he sends this heartfelt commendation through an authentic representative, and concludes by acknowledging esteem for Faustus and the kinship (*proximitas*) that ties him to the messenger.[18]

Immediately after the letter to Symmachus comes one to Luminosus, with whom Ennodius has already corresponded on the subject of the pope's unpaid debt.[19] That distressing business, however, has no place in this graceful exercise in social intercourse. Its first quarter simply compliments Luminosus on his hospitable patronage of those commencing rhetorical training, with requisite allusion to "liberal concern" (*liberalis cura*) and "the palm of eloquence" (*eloquentiae palmam*). The central part presents Parthenius, "seeking Rome for the venerable disciplines" (*ad venerabiles disciplinas Romam petenti*) and Ennodius' hopes for what Luminosus will do for him—"if it is not at variance with humanity" (*si ab humanitate non discrepat*) and "if I am dear to your heart" (*si vobis cordi sum*)—so that the correspondents can delight each other by a display of mutual affection.[20] The last quarter attends to valediction's cheerful niceties as Ennodius avers that if Luminosus had already known the bearer's identity, it might have been recommendation enough; his confidence the request will be fulfilled ensures the letter's brevity.[21]

The last letter in the group is the shortest of all, to Ennodius' relative and constant correspondent Faustus. Unlike the other missives in the group, it opens without an elaborate attempt to disarm the addressee by extolling his virtues or those of traditional literary education. Instead, Ennodius devotes the first third of the letter to thanksgiving for recovery from a painful eye ailment that had plagued him for "numberless days" (*innumeros dies*) made more trying by Faustus' absence.[22] After this prologue he arrives at the business that compels him to write: "Parthenius, the son of my sister, wants to appear a gentleman through the disciplines of

---

17. #225.2: *datur culmini vestro per supplicantem genius, dum quod usus exigit precibus inploramus, ceu si quis credat se ortum solis, cursum fluminis oratione promereri.*

18. #225.3: *ego tamen supra cursum a quo nequaquam disceditis aliquid accepturus occurro.*

19. #227; cf. #77, #139, #283.

20. #227.1–2.

21. #227.3–4.

22. #228.1–2; Ennodius' friendship with Faustus Niger, entitled here "the Younger" in quasi-consular fashion, goes back to #6 (501).

liberal study; he wishes, if I am not mistaken, to have evidence of your liberality."[23] Because Ennodius is confident of Faustus' past, present, and future trustworthiness, he simply requests the latter's protection of his nephew; the last couple of lines simply bid farewell and hope the letter brought by Parthenius will stimulate further conversation.[24]

Taken together, these four letters share some features of diction. The Faustus Albus and Symmachus letters depict Parthenius as a sort of hostage (*obses*) and also, along with the one to Luminosus, denote "sister" by *germana* rather than *soror,* which occurs only in the letter to Faustus Niger. As for the principal subject of all four letters, the importance of higher education, we can make a distinction between the treatment for Pope Symmachus and that for the lay correspondents. In the former, Ennodius portrays education exclusively as a means to virtue, while in the latter he also recognizes that literary training results in the practical eloquence that glues civil society together. The difference is one of emphasis, since these functions coexist in Ennodius' mind; in an epigram celebrating a dining room belonging to an erudite man, perhaps his friend Faustus, he matter-of-factly calls literature the "leader of righteousness" (*dux littera recti*).[25]

Common to these four letters is the sedulous practice of opening and closing the communication by affirming the addressee's responsibilities, interests, and social status, complete with forms of address like "Your Magnitude," the altitudinous "Summit," "Sublimity," and "Crown," as well as the all-purpose "Lord."[26] Compared with the worldly wealth and power with which he mingled on this plane of consummate civility, Ennodius' own position was rather marginal. Thus, he took correspondingly greater care in calibrating his subtle overtures than, for example, did Q. Aurelius Symmachus, fourth-century senator and prefect of Rome, or Sidonius Apollinaris, literary landowner, Imperial son-in-law, and bishop of Clermont-Ferrand in the later fifth century. Ennodius' approach to the pope is founded less on official status (their respective positions in the Catholic hierarchy) than on the awareness that past services have required eloquence and virtue in equal measure. The way he handles all his corre-

---

23. #228.2: *Partenius, sororis meae filius, per liberalis studii disciplinas ingenuus vult videri; optat, ni fallor, peculii vestri habere testimonium.*

24. #228.3, with elegantly modulated emphasis and parting words.

25. #112, v. 7; cf. Corbier, "L'écriture," 105–11.

26. *magnitudo:* #225, #227, #228. *culmen:* #225, #228. *sublimitas:* #227. *corona:* #226. *dominus:* esp. #225–28, to express respect or subordination. Cf. Chastagnol, "Le formulaire."

spondents stands for the efforts of an entire, lost group of cultured individuals to maintain the fabric of social intercourse.

Parthenius' aspirations to further schooling at Rome imply a wider context for the correspondence just examined: the fullness of education as
expressed in what Ennodius habitually calls "the commerce of letters"
(*commercia litterarum*). Whereas this brief dossier introduced Parthenius
to a Roman public, Ennodius had already presented his nephew to posterity two years earlier, through a *dictio* thanking the Milanese grammarian
Deuterius for a successful recitation Parthenius had lately given.[27] Turning
back to that first appearance of Parthenius shifts our investigation from
individual, personalized epistolary requests to the more imposing memorials of Ennodius' involvement in the propagation of traditional Latin literary culture, the letters and *dictiones* for and about youths whose responsibility it would eventually be to perform the rituals of civilized discourse. In
a society in which speech still marked the true Roman, the phrases characteristic of this task underline its seriousness: *obsequia salutationis, episto-
lare commercium, salutationis servitia / officia,* and *munus servitutis.*
An indispensable component of such *Romanitas* was the command of
rhetoric's arsenal, whose use was governed by the principles of linguistic
propriety and conceptual paradox. Ennodius' oratorical pieces remind us
that this armament was acquired and maintained only though the assiduous practice of public speaking.

The thanksgiving *dictio* for Parthenius is one among a group of twenty-
two speeches that relate directly to literary-rhetorical education. Some of
them were composed for particular moments in the academic careers of
the individuals named in them.[28] One piece celebrated the transfer of the
school's lecture hall (*auditorium*) to the forum of Milan.[29] Furthermore,
three of the compositions on quasi-legal conundrums (*controversiae*) bear
the names of their recipients, while a fourth is accompanied by a brief preface that refers to "an outstanding young man" (*egregius adulescens*) soon
revealed as Arator, the future poet and subdeacon of Rome.[30] The remain-

---

27. #94 (between Easter and the end of 504); the *dictio*'s title, likely devised by Ennodius,
is properly informative. See Schröder, *Titel und Text,* 208–9.

28. For Ennodius' other nephew, Lupicinus (#69); for Arator's entry into the *auditorium*
(#85) and attainment of fame (#320); for the inaugural lessons of Eusebius' son (#124) and
of Paterius and Severus (#451).

29. #3 (early 503); *auditorium:* Pompeius 235.16–24; *CTh* 14.9.3.

30. #239 and #243, to Arator; #261, to Ambrosius, corecipient with Beatus of #452;
#380, its *egregius adulescens* none other than Arator, the future author of *De Actibus Apos-
tolorum* (*PL* 68.45–252; *CSEL* 72).

ing seven *controversiae* (Sirmond's classicizing label) and the five pieces on situations from epic literature (Sirmond's *ethicae*), however, hold no explicit clues to their recipients or occasions. Ennodius perhaps intended them for recitation by some unnamed youth or to serve as models for that youth's own efforts in a forensic or epideictic vein; some may have been composed simply for his own entertainment and that of his friends. The rhetorical form and thematic range of the *dictiones* long condemned them to the history of education's nether regions.[31] Let us, who now tend to forget that social communication depends on learned, traditional structures of discourse, judge them less harshly. Without first acquiring the tools to communicate with others, we embrace solipsism, not self-expression; for Ennodius, those tools were grammar and rhetoric.

The *dictio* for Parthenius, among the earliest and certainly the most specific, is a good place to start because it combines standard and personalized items. As I said, its primary aim was to thank the grammarian and rhetor Deuterius for turning Parthenius into a polished speaker. The work is divided into three main sections. The preface talks about thanksgivings: genuine ones are inspired by something truly praiseworthy (here, a talented member of Ennodius' family) rather than hijacked by arrogant self-aggrandizement. The person of Parthenius, whose hitherto hidden natural gifts have been developed and refined by Deuterius' expert methods, prompts this outpouring of gratitude, and the section culminates in a question-spouting *aporia* applauding the teacher's immense learning and care.[32] The explicit *gratiarum actio* completes the piece, as Ennodius addresses Deuterius directly, saluting his laudable achievement. The latter has not only weeded and cultivated the fields of Parthenius' intellect, but also trained him up in virtue, so that Parthenius knows which family's hereditary tendencies he should cooperate with and which he needs to resist; now, after a winter of lethargy, Parthenius' tongue has poured forth the resplendent spring flowers of educated and humane discourse.[33]

This particular *dictio* contains metaphorical traits typical of Ennodius' educational thought, which we can now pursue more fully. The ambiguous nature of rhetorical skill is the introduction's central concern: "by a single mouth, indeed, are celebrated the praises of a tyrant and of good rulers, nor is there any difference between the eulogies of him who deserves them

---

31. Roger, *L'enseignement des lettres classiques,* 191–92; Fontaine, "Ennodius," 419; Riché, *Education and Culture,* 48; Navarra, "Ennodius," 272–73.
32. #94.1–3, 4–9.
33. #94.9–13.

and the one who arrogates them."[34] Ennodius' statement shows that he understands rhetoric, the technique of using language to please and persuade, is morally neutral; the technique gains moral worth only from the occasions and subjects to which it is applied. This conception of the craft is consistent throughout the corpus. Two early *dictiones* rejoice in their task because of the excellence of the persons to be celebrated: Bishop Laurentius of Milan, on the anniversary of his consecration, and Ennodius' other nephew Lupicinus, as he enters into the lecture hall of Deuterius. In the former, Ennodius states that "often the things to be said are attributed for the sake of the merits of those for whom speech has been empowered, especially if the person about to speak discharges his service by praising with pure affection."[35] Apropos of his nephew, Ennodius likewise says, "if a speech gives allegiance to a theme, it obtains worth from that very theme; be not therefore filled with consternation at the slenderness of your own talent, when the baseness of your utterance is exalted by the value of the speech you have undertaken."[36] Whether it is practiced by St. Cyprian or the figure of Rhetoric herself, the way in which the art of speech operates remains the same. Ennodius represents the saint's activity in these verses— "the speaker speaks, pleads, and obtains, / severity subtly restrains; / makes the guilty become blest, / by breaking bonds of sin with song."[37] The art's personification asserts "both sinner and saint is born from our mouth: / while we speak, the will is led captive."[38] Ennodius never disguises the basic amorality of the *technē* that serves him and his superiors so well. His religious profession may require him to insist rhetoric be used only for good ends; his refusal to condemn it outright shows a soundly teleological pragmatism.[39]

This thanksgiving *dictio* also contains a distinctive complex of

---

34. #94.2: *uno quidem tyranni laudationes et bonorum principum ore celebrantur, nec est aliqua inter eius qui meretur praeconia diversitas et illius qui usurpat.*

35. #1.4: *saepe pro eorum meritis quibus se mancipaverit oratio dicenda tribuuntur, maxime si mera affectione laudando militet narraturus* (for Laurentius, Feb.–Mar. 503); cf. #240.1.

36. #69.3: *si themati obsequium praestat oratio, ab ipso suscipit dignitatem; proprii ergo macies non turberis ingenii, quando eloquii vilitas pretio susceptae dictionis elevatur* (for Lupicinus, first third of 504).

37. Cyprian: #343, vv. 14–18: *orator orat optinet / et dura causis temperat, / facit beatos ex reis, / peccata rumpens carmine* (winter 508/9).

38. Rhetoric: #452.17: *et reus et sanctus de nostro nascitur ore: / dum loquimur, captum ducitur arbitrium.* Though from early 512, it hardly presumes that rhetoric "is fundamentally flawed," pace Relihan, *Ancient Menippean Satire,* 174.

39. Cf. the stance taken in the opening sentences of his *Libellus* for Pope Symmachus (#49); see chapter 5.

metaphors, illustrating the person of Parthenius and Deuterius' pedagogical role, which interlace and flow uninterrupted into the concluding section. All depend on the opposition of nature and culture, no surprise given the educational environment of the piece, but the particular circumstantial details Ennodius uses to bring life to this crucial topos are diagnostic for his thought throughout the works.

As already mentioned, kinship is what imparts real value to this rhetorical occasion, "for the swelling of arrogance is veiled by no garment of probity, since words are not in the service of glory, but of blood."[40] The word *blood* (*sanguis*) occurs three more times in the speech; additional locutions indicating Ennodius' interest in heredity reinforce the context.[41] Family serves as the initial incitement to speech, though the inherited gifts it presupposes here are just a part of the story. Only as a result of the training Deuterius has provided through Ennodius' intercession is Parthenius' natural talent (*ingenium*) manifested, "for he whose ancestry training does not reveal capitalizes on no proof of noble birth," and without proper instruction, "the light of good breeding is imprisoned in the night of boorishness."[42] That notion leads Ennodius' thoughts into the silent world of vegetables and minerals to seek parallels for expertise's effects upon inar-ticulate matter when ancestry is "hidden away by the disguises of ignorance" (*imperitia fuscante*).[43] That training should exist to develop an individual's inherited strengths is the traditional view all the way back to Pindar. With Parthenius, however, we will see that Ennodius sees an additional function: besides revealing and refining talents, education must offset whatever deficiencies it encounters.

Gold leads the analogical array of improvable things in nature. Most precious of metals and most tangible of metaphors, it epitomizes what is intrinsically valuable yet requires the addition of further value by skilled artisans. In its natural state, gold's purity is sufficient to proclaim its identity, but without knowledgeable men to find, extract it, refine it, and make beautiful objects of it, gold remains hidden and deficient in value. "When industry leaves off, the brilliance that would have come from nature is

---

40. #94.1: *nullo enim adrogantiae tumor honestatis velatur indumento, cum non gloriae militant verba, sed sanguini.*

41. #94.1 and 4, 5, 10. E.g., "stock" (*prosapies*), "bloodlines" (*stemmata*), "family" (*familia*), "propinquity" (*propinquitas*), "blood relation" (*consanguineus*).

42. #94.4: *nullo enim teste nobilitatis utitur cuius sanguinem non prodit instructio . . . bonorum semper meritorum labes est habere lucem sanguinis et nocte rusticitatis includi.*

43. #94.4–5.

slight."[44] The skill of the artificer enables him to transform "the progeny of hidden veins" (*latentium fetibus venarum*) into a solid to be mastered by his tools, which in its turn "takes the savage hearts of men captive with dominating passion."[45] The correspondences between the goldsmith's art and the grammarian-rhetor's are many and plain: the basic material's obscurity of origin and character, technical processes involving heat, pressure, and torsion, a finished product whose powers of attraction control men. The *objet d'art* and the polished speaker, fashioned in much the same manner, affect those beholding them in analogous ways.[46]

We can appreciate the ambiguous nature of verbal persuasion, but gold's splendid allure remains, glinting here and there among Ennodius' works, a token of intrinsic value enriched by artistry. The earliest *dictio* that obviously belongs in an educational setting deploys much of the same vocabulary for a briefer, more general treatment of cultural erudition. In this speech the nobility of the vein of unrefined gold, namely the promising youth's undertaking grammatical studies, "is faded almost to nothing by maternal shadows" (*maternis paene hebetatur tenebris*) unless the teacher's skilled touch polishes it.[47] Such an image is tactfully absent from the *dictio* for Parthenius, the son of Ennodius' sister. Among the friends, Ennodius finds Avienus, the elder son of Faustus, remarkable for his "vein of rich talent" (*ingenii divitis vena*), and so remarks that he knows where all eloquence's mines and quarries are, yielding not only gold but the precious stones to adorn it further.[48] A related image recurs in a late work, the Menippean pedagogical letter (*pagina*) for the promising young men Ambrosius and Beatus.[49] In his desire to showcase the multiplicity of virtues to which his addressees should aspire, Ennodius symbolizes the transition from modesty and chastity to faith with a single diadem constructed from a variety of jewels and the alloy of "ever-admirable electrum" (*semper admirabilis electri*), the offspring of multiple metals.[50]

The equation of gold and eloquence in all phases of production so attracts Ennodius that he devotes half an epigram to it. "Speech is held to

---

44. #94.6: *cessante industria exigua est claritas quae venerit a natura.*

45. #94.6–7: *quod . . . effera hominum corda domitrice adfectione captivat;* cf. Beagon, "Nature and Views," 292.

46. E.g., the verses about jewelry (#165, #229) and clever *defensores* (#186, #194).

47. #3.6 (early 503), on the dedication of the new *auditorium* in the forum.

48. #23.1–2.

49. *PLRE* 2, 69, 222; Moorhead, *Theoderic,* 161, 166.

50. #452.8 (early 512). The piece's virtuosity has been thought parody: Relihan, *Ancient Menippean Satire,* 164–75.

be a sure sign of character" (*Eloquium certus naturae constitit index*), he begins, calling it the source of perfection, but in remarking that "raw nobility is hidden by shadows" (*infabricata latet nobilitas tenebris*), he returns to a place where gold is held captive in the earth's veins, awaiting its discoverer and refiner: "he who polishes talent thus makes it his own" (*qui polit ingenium, sic facit esse suum*).[51] Complementing this dynamic image of grammarians and rhetoricians as the goldsmiths and jewelers of language are poetic star turns for literal works of craftsmanship. The lady Firmina's cunningly wrought golden chain and ring receive special ekphrastic treatment; so do the silver and gold whip of "baby Arator" and a set of shield-shaped silver dishes.[52] We will return to them in chapter 3, together with other pleasures and pains of material existence.

While the goldsmith's art is certainly among the showier examples of technical know-how, other skills of a more immediately practical nature join it in the Parthenius *dictio:* seafaring and agriculture. Although only a single sentence of the thanksgiving to Deuterius is given over to sailors, its expressive force suffices: "it is a thing of skill, that a man confidently enters the sea's watery element and, with scant danger, surmounts a journey of death through the exercise of his talents."[53] Although the proportion of artifice in this passage admittedly equals if not surpasses the art it sets out to describe, a tendency wholly in keeping with late antique taste, Ennodius firmly acknowledges the importance of navigational expertise.[54] Sailors are integral to his canon of men adept in handling particular situations, as their presence in works both early and late indicates.[55] In the later poetic settings sailors acquire a more redolently literary aura, as with one poem's classically poor boatman and a letter that boasts an array of nautical equipment, or are merged with fishermen to stand in contrast to hunters; the latest instance (the verses about Ennodius' Po River journey) contains a perfectly real boatman, however, vital to the poet's tale of literal travels.[56]

The skills of the farming population now come to the fore in the Parthe-

---

51. #105, vv. 1–8, meshing literal and metaphorical topoi; cf. Luc. 4.298.

52. #165 and #229; #267, #267a–b (*de flagello infantis Aratoris*); #232, #233 (*de scutellis*).

53. #94.7: *artis est, quod liquidum maris elementum homo securus ingreditur, et parvo discrimine per ingenia iter mortis exuperat.*

54. Kennell, "Hercules' Invisible Basilica," 164–65.

55. #1.8; #2, v. 2; #3.1; #26, v. 34 (all early 503); implicit in #208.8 (early 506); #451.1 (early 512).

56. #26 (boatman), #42 (sea, sails, oars, etc.), #112 (fisherman), #423 (river boatman).

nius *dictio*. They initially form the theme of a longer statement immediately preceding the rhetorical questions that express Ennodius' admiration, then become the metaphorical heart of the section in praise of Deuterius' intellectual husbandry, whose profound and pervasive debt to Vergil's *Georgics* is readily apparent. Portraying the work of the viticulturist who "sculpts the face of the earth . . . sets out the vineyard and from the progeny of trees extracts that liquid whereby health may be sustained," he concludes with this observation: "by many signs, it becomes evident that the workers' dedication either instills what the stock has not contributed or safeguards the good it has contributed."[57] Since Ennodius then asks whether everything works this way, obviously expecting a reply in the affirmative, the correlation was as clear to his audience as to him. The cultivator's fundamental task is the same for plants as for humans: to reinforce innate goodness and make good the deficiencies of nature.

The result, in the first image, is wine. Its associations embrace both inspired eloquence and the saving draft of the Eucharist, to say nothing of the traditional Greco-Roman way of life embodied by the figure of Dionysus-Bacchus. On occasions given over more to the spirit of convivial pleasantry than to high-minded professions of cultural continuity, Ennodius can indeed be quite expansive, as in the epigrams intended to adorn the wine cellar and vine-shaded garden of a comfortable establishment, or the series on the bibulous *princeps*.[58] He even devotes a ten-line poem to the season of the vintage that ends by declaring the fittingness of "dry rhythms" (*ieiunos . . . rhythmus*), since "none of the Muses is joined to Bromius" (*nulla Camenarum iungitur ad Bromium*).[59] In the *dictio* for Epifanius' thirtieth anniversary as bishop of Ticinum, however, a special situation that demands loftier sentiments, Ennodius draws on the imagery of cultivation and vintage as well. He likens the saint to the overseer of a farm who, while awaiting the return of his master, ceaselessly works the soil and improves the plantings: "so does he comb the face of the soil with plows that, as he runs along, the vintage foams from brimming jars."[60] Epifanius

---

57. #94.7: *magistra agricolarum simplicitas telluris faciem dum brachiis distinguit, vineta conponit et de prole arborum liquorem quo salus nutriatur extorquet . multis manifestatur indiciis operantum diligentia aut infundi quod origo non tribuit aut quod bona tribuit custodiri.* Cf. Verg. *G.* 1; Quint. *Inst.* 2.4.4–8.

58. #162f, #164; #364, #365, #374.

59. #188, vv. 9–10.

60. #43, vv. 135–38: *sic dominum expectat domitatis vilicus arvis, / cum bene molitus incurvi dente ligonis / scribit agros faciemque soli sic pectit aratris, / ut spumet plenis currens vindemia labris;* cf. Verg. *G.* 2.177–94, 259–72, 346–419.

is emphatically a "cultivator of souls" (*animarum cultor*) whose learned devotion in the field of spiritual horticulture prompts an allusion to the parable of the barren fig tree, which the proprietor wanted cut down but the field laborer sought to save by cultivating and manuring the soil; in their way, the bishop's counsels and intercessions were as effective as a knowledgeable gardener's toil.[61] Though saving immortal souls is a higher task than transforming the uncouth into the civilized, they share a common metaphor.

Viticulture and the tending of trees constitute only one area of Ennodius' agricultural construction of his intellectual environment, which he completes in the Parthenius *dictio* by bringing in cereal crops, distinguished by their nutritive qualities, and spring flowers. He praises Deuterius for removing the "brambles and darnel" from Parthenius' bosom with "the hoe of knowledge," enabling "the wheaten harvest by which he may nourish his kinsmen."[62] The youthful object of these attentions metamorphoses from hidden ore and ground ready to receive the vine into a field for growing wheat, bidding fair to produce a generous crop provided that weeds of every sort are uprooted. A variety of harvests appears all around the corpus, from the "harvest of experience" (*messem peritiae*) Ennodius refers to in his first letter to Avienus, Faustus' elder son, to "the harvest of joys" (*messe gaudiorum*) in one of the last; he also combines love, conversation, human beings, and ancestral excellence with this notion.[63] Let us note one further vegetable motif that came up when the Parthenius *dictio* was first mentioned. Though it has more to do with the change of seasons from winter to spring, organic nature's exuberance counterbalances the deployment elsewhere of intellectual technique: "behold, already from wintry breast and chilly heart little flowers of *dictiones* blossom forth and the smiling sprouts of words adorn the calyxes as they unfold."[64]

Compared with other works concerned with the literary education of young men, the amount of space Ennodius gives agricultural metaphor in

---

61. #43, vv. 154–61; cf. Luke 13.6–9.

62. #94.9: *tu de eius pectore scientiae sarculo paliuros et lolium submovisti, tu triticeam messem qua propinquos pascat elevasti.* This motif, already used for Lupicinus in #69.5, is also applied to Arator in #320.6. Cf. #119.2, to Bishop Eulalius.

63. To Faustus' son Avienus: #17.6 and #459.3. Cf. #240.42 and #290.4, to Parthenius himself.

64. #94.12: *ecce iam ex hiemali pectore et corde algido dictionum flosculi vernant et ridentia verborum germina depingunt calathos exhibentes.*

this *dictio* is actually not that large. When he celebrates the induction of his other nephew, Lupicinus, into the arena of public speaking with Deuterius' guidance, expressions whose vividness relates to the cultivation of plants and trees occur with formidable frequency. Beginning with exotic spices, "noble scion" (*nobile germen*), and "the merit of the sod" (*meritum cespitis*), the introductory paragraph lingers briefly on the occasion and ancestral attainments, but the majority of the text constitutes a brief treatise *de pueri cultura*, spoken prosopopoeically by the youth's grandfathers. The tasks of metaphorical husbandry Deuterius is to undertake are so manifold that it is difficult to render them effectively in English. His uncle represents Lupicinus as "the shoot and seed-head of both families" (*utriusque plantam familiae et culmum*), ready to sprout ears of grain, and as "fertile land" (*uberem terram*).[65] As the metaphorical scenario for the youth's education unfolds, farming vocabulary evoking *Georgics* 1 proliferates, for the terrain of Lupicinus' mind requires hoeing, grafting, weeding, plowing, and pruning to produce a fair yield.[66] Such bounteous specificity makes the word usually applied to such activities ("cultivation") seem banal and insipid, while the notion of applied effort (*industria*) assumes the same central location that it occupies in the metallurgical section of Parthenius' *dictio*. Although more agricultural images are yet to come, Ennodius stops to underline the moral of his metaphors. "Such is the nature of mortals: to that of shrubs is rightly likened the education of the young—after the solicitude of kinsmen has plucked them from the mother's root, it should entrust them to a man who is to care for them only in accordance with its wishes."[67] Domesticating plants and bringing up youths in a civilized way are basically the same; to make even good stock bear good fruit, informed effort is necessary. As Ennodius says in an early letter to Iohannes, another younger friend seeking to improve his writing, blossoms, however beautiful, still do not guarantee fruit that meets the highest standards without corrective guidance: "granted, what you promise in the snowy flower of eloquence may be magnificent; nevertheless, I myself do not give thanks except for the harvest, as the grasping farmer who only measures the bounty of the year in his granaries is

---

65. #69 (prosopopoeia: 5–12); cf. Verg. *G.* 2.458–74.
66. Cf. Verg. *G.* 1.145–226.
67. #69.8: *talis est natura mortalium: rite conparantur arbutis rudimenta parvulorum, quos postquam parentum sollicitudo a matris radice decerpserit, providendum est cui solo iuxta vota conmendet.*

wont."[68] Iohannes was apparently the father of Vigilius, a future bishop of Rome; more relevant, as we will see in chapter 4, is that his father-in-law was Olybrius, one of Ennodius' older correspondents and a kinsman by marriage.[69]

Ennodius accords the agricultural treatment not just to nephews and friends like Iohannes. One of his closest literary associates was the young Arator, a future Christian poet in whose work interest has burgeoned in recent years.[70] Arator's very name elicits an exceedingly pun-filled exhortation on the occasion of his entry into the halls of rhetorical performance, though matters of general education (*paideia,* that is) form the theme of the *dictio* for his first day at Deuterius' school in Milan. When Ennodius first turns to address the "slip of a youth" (*adulescentulum*) to whom the entire discourse pertains, he remarks that "we are put to the yoke, constrained by the urgency of affection."[71] Such phrases give just a taste of things to come; the rest of the address elaborates on the implications of "plowman" (*arator*) as an appropriate name for a young man of great promise.[72] "Happy in learned circles is that omen of your name," Ennodius proclaims, urging Arator to "cleave the backs of rich soils" and dig down with his new-forged plowshare to "practice in the ground of studies whatever suits the best plowman."[73] Not only must Arator learn to plow but also to cut back what is overgrown or fails to thrive at all; only after he has brought forth the diverse fruits of knowledge may he truly be called "the Great Plowman," in a stellar pun on the significance of his name.[74]

The last of Ennodius' *dictiones* for Arator can stand alone as an encomium of literary studies, as its subtitle, "a praise of literature" (*laus*

---

68. #15.4: *sint licet grandia quae in cano eloquentiae flore polliceris; ego tamen nisi de messe non gratulor, ut solet avarus agricola qui ubertatem anni nisi in horreis non metitur* (mid-502); cf. Verg. *G.* 1.47–8. See also #4.5–6 (from 501) and #175.4, to Marcianus, son of Asterius.

69. Other letters to Johannes: #55, #141, #304. In the last (from 508), he is another *magnitudo* who fails to answer letters; cf. *PLRE* 2, Iohannes 67. Olybrius: #13, #27, #32, #37, #42, #48.

70. Roman subdeacon to-be, author of *De Actibus Apostolorum:* Roberts, *Biblical Epic;* Schwind, *Arator-Studien;* Hillier, *Arator.*

71. #85.9: *sub iugum mittimur dilectionis necessitate constricti.*

72. #85.9–10.

73. #85.10: *felix istud nominis apud doctos auspicium!* . . . *finde, adulescens egregie, pinguium dorsa terrarum, inprime dentem vomeris novella adhuc incude formatum, exerce in studiorum solo quicquid optimum convenit aratorem.*

74. #85.11–12; cf. Verg. *G.* 1.19 and, ecclesiastically, #336.4.

litterarum) indicates.[75] More synthetic and comprehensive in scope, it includes a greater range of sub-themes and illustrations, among them agricultural metaphors. Arator's verbal attainments inspire a proem of verdant fields that delight and captivate, green shoots pleasant in themselves that grow to "harvests of talents" (*messes ingeniorum*). He is praised especially for affording "a way to pursue justice" by cleansing "the weed-choked path that leads to higher things," for producing a crop of wheat where tares had been, and for bearing "swelling ears to the granary of knowledge lest the famine of ignorance prevail."[76] Over the centuries the skills of the agriculturalist, essential to Mediterranean civilization, had gradually become the dominant metaphor for language acquisition and use within that civilization. Now the metaphor epitomizes civilization itself, for language—the knowledge and right use of words rather than literal scythes, plowshares, and pruning hooks—is what creates Ennodius' civilized society.

After absorbing all these allusions to the subjugation of the vegetable kingdom prompted by Lupicinus and Arator's education, we can now return to the Parthenius *dictio* that invoked them, looking at its final section and at what eventually becomes of Parthenius. Ennodius now gives the original theme of heredity and environment an uncomfortably personal twist with the portrayal of Deuterius' particular service to Parthenius: "in one and the same person, with what skill you have shown what he should learn and what he should unlearn, because each originated in his ancestry."[77] The trouble with Parthenius, it seems, is that one side of his family is happy to acknowledge him while the other side is not; Ennodius feared that his nephew would take after the wrong side and so turn out badly. The words he uses—*dissonantia, permixtio, diversitas*—emanate as much from the vocabulary of the grammarian as of the moralist, proclaiming the inseparability of academic training and social initiation within the upper classes of late antiquity. Deuterius has skillfully modulated the "dissonance of families" (*familiarum dissonantiam*) to produce a

---

75. #320 (Aug. 508), *dictio data Aratori quando ad laudem provectus est;* he also received two *controversiae* (#239, #243).

76. #320.6: *ad investigandam iter iustitiam vos praebetis, dum oppressum dumetis callem quo expetuntur superna purgastis. vos triticeam de loliis segetem . . . efficitis et gravidas aristas ad scientiae horrea ne fames infantiae possit praevalere portatis.* Cf. Beagon, "Nature and Views," 299–300; August. *Conf.* 2.

77. #94.10: *in una eademque persona qua arte, quod utrumque descendebat a sanguine, quid disceret et quid dedisceret, indicasti;* cf. 4–5.

happy, harmonious outcome in which Parthenius has learned what to emulate and what to avoid, in other words, how to make the distinctions in regard to his life that Deuterius, grammarian and rhetor, makes in relation to language.

Parthenius subsequently managed to forget the moral lessons he received and to shirk his responsibilities as a student once he came to Rome, requiring additional correction. His delinquency, however, in no way invalidates his uncle's pedagogical conceptions, for Ennodius describes and castigates Parthenius' dereliction in terms very close to that of the *dictio*. The need for constant attention and application occurs in both the letter to Faustus requesting the latter's personal intervention with Parthenius and the letter to Parthenius himself, as do images of wheat infested by tares and brambles, idle plows, and harvests of progress.[78] As in his original letter recommending Parthenius to Faustus, Ennodius forthrightly broaches the issue. After stating his general theme—cultivation versus weeds—he explains that, according to Parthenius' father, fear of Faustus had kept the young man on the scholarly straight and narrow, but that he was now "undertaking indecent things" (*molitur obscena*). Candidly admitting that "that age, rather too friendly to sins, finds many guides to error" (*aetas illa peccatis amicior multos repperit ad errata ductores*), which Faustus as a man of the world and father of two grown sons should understand, Ennodius exhorts him to apply correction's "healing hand" (*medicam manum*) to the youth lest his vices progressively undercut any prospect for good.[79] In view of how *obscenitas* is used elsewhere in the works and Ennodius' comment on the foibles of youth, Parthenius' misdeeds were at least partly sexual; not long ago, they might have been concealed under the euphemism of "partying."[80]

In writing directly to his nephew, however, Ennodius says nothing of "indecencies," instead addressing Parthenius' failings as a son and as a student. If he is indeed identical with the Parthenius to whom Arator dedicated his poetic paraphrase of the Acts of the Apostles and who later murdered his wife and her lover, dying finally at the hands of a Frankish mob, his uncle's fears were indeed justified; for now, he receives only a good scolding for his general ingratitude, failure to write, bad behavior, and

---

78. #368, to Faustus, and #369, to Parthenius (Aug.–Sept. 509).

79. #368.3: *ne vitiorum profectus universa in eo quae boni aliquid potuerunt ferre succidat.*

80. Tellingly in #278.7 (Minerva in a brothel). Cf. #13.4 (certain famous male friendships); #208.5 (Diomedes, on his wife's infidelity).

neglect of his studies, with emphasis on the last item.[81] We may suppose
that Ennodius tailored content to correspondent when he omitted mention
of sex as inappropriate for one of tender years; enough examples of his
candor exist elsewhere, mainly among the epigrams intended for a mature
secular readership, to indicate he could cope with sexual subjects.[82]

The pedagogical challenges Parthenius presented inspired some of Ennodius' most cogent statements on literary erudition and the power of language, but nephews did not monopolize his concern. There is a large ration
of literary example and moral exhortation in many other *dictiones* and letters that also emphasize the pleasure of "getting it right" verbally. When
conversing *per litteras* with his friends, many of whom happened to be
bound by business interests as well, the simple yet indispensable discharge
of social obligations is what moves him to write. An early letter addressed
to Firminus exemplifies Ennodius' delight at keeping in touch with individuals of taste and ability. By telling his correspondent, "pleasant are literary exchanges conceived by a learned writer, those in which the splendor
of language polished to perfection shines forth, where lavish eloquence is
controlled by the reins of experience," he intimates how much more entertaining it is to write to people whose linguistic accomplishments are comparable to his own and with whom he can trade self-deprecating Ciceronian quips about rhetorical technique.[83]

Ennodius enjoys communing with all his associates, a good many of
whom seem able and willing to share his fondness for the well-turned
phrase and the erudite allusion. Some, like the *vir illustris* and quaestor
Eugenes, receive letters that epitomize conciseness while still performing
the tasks—graceful tributes to the addressee and his relatives, cordial yet
discreet interest in his health and affairs, decorous condolence when
needed, affirmations of mutuality—that keep the fields of friendship luxu-
riantly green.[84] Writer and reader alike understood that the aim of literate
communication was simultaneously to discharge responsibilities and to

---

81. #369 *passim* (esp. 4–6). Mathisen, "Epistolography," 101–3, and *Roman Aristocrats,*
139–40 (one Parthenius); Riché, *Education and Culture,* 26, 49 (two).

82. #132, #133, #136, #136a–b, #180, #180a–c, #217, #233, #238, #329, #329a–c. #339:
Shanzer, "Ennodius, Boethius, and the Date," 183–86. #388 (the epithalamium for Maximus).

83. #12.1: *iucunda sunt commercia litterarum docto auctore concepta, illa in quibus ad
unguem politi sermonis splendor effulgorat, ubi oratio dives frenis peritiae continetur.* In #40.4
he deplores his imagined stylistic wants, declaring himself better at praise than imitation.

84. Eugenes: *PLRE* 2, 414–16; Moorhead, *Theoderic,* 157–58. Co-addressee (with Olybrius) of #32, sole addressee in #67, #159, #167, #170, #255, #279, #289; cf. #419, to
Agapius.

occasion delight. Ennodius' words to the *vir illustris* Eugenes encapsulate its essence: "be there for your side, and just as the privilege of a duty prescribed exalts me, so may the blessing of conversation conferred lift you up."[85]

Other equally estimable correspondents early in the collection provoke more peculiar reactions. A friend named Florianus received two letters in early 503, one thanking him for a letter "rich in Roman endowment," the other extolling his command of the Latin language, which Ennodius claims rivals that of Cicero, Sallust, and Vergil.[86] This future abbot and co-dedicatee (with Parthenius) of Arator's *De Actibus Apostolorum* appears to have put Ennodius on his guard with a complaint of "rhetorical cunning," since the latter affirms his inability to be "engrossed in the flowers of words" when his religious vocation calls him to lamentation and prayer.[87]

The single letter to Pomerius, dated to the spring or summer of 503, exhibits a similar deliberation in tone and content.[88] This correspondent has been identified as the African rhetor named Julianus Pomerius who lived in Arles and became a priest, best known as the author of a treatise on the contemplative life widely circulated in the medieval period.[89] Ennodius reproaches Pomerius for a lengthy epistolary absence with mock-Ciceronian magniloquence, then acclaims him ebulliently as master of both Greek and Latin: "clasp of both literatures, you have digested the greatest parts of the perfection coming from each branch by taking care that your talent fattens on such satiety."[90] Hinting at an ecclesiastical honor Pomerius has recently received by virtue of his spiritual endowments and complimenting his Latinity, Ennodius asks for advice on himself and his writing. Though such allusions have already contributed to a

85. #106.2: *adesto partibus tuis et sicut me imperati muneris praerogativa sublimat, ita vos exhibiti gratia sermonis attollat,* echoed in #107.1 to Avienus.

86. #20.2: *epistulam . . . Romana dote locupletem;* #21.3.

87. #21.4: *rhetoricam in me dixisti esse versutiam . . . nequeam occupari verborum floribus quem ad gemitus et preces evocat clamor officii.* Identified with the abbot Florianus, who recollected Ennodius (Vogel, lix–lx = *MGH Epp.* 3.116–17 Gundlach); Ruggini, "Ticinum," 305.

88. #39.3: "fosterling of the Rhône" (*alumnus Rhodani*) implies adoptive Gallic citizenship; cf. *PLRE* 2, 896. Other *alumni:* #80.19 and 80.

89. *Vita Caesarii Arelatensis* (*MGH SRM* 3) 1.3; Gennadius of Marseille, *de vir. inl.* 98; Solignac, "Julien Pomère"; Markus, *End of Ancient Christianity,* 189–91. *De vita contemplativa* (*PL* 59.415–520): Laistner, "Influence."

90. #39.2: *utriusque bybliothecae fibula, perfectionis ex gemino latere venientis partes maximas momordisti procurando ut tali ingenium tuum saturitate pinguisceret;* cf. #370.4 (Boethius' mastery of both languages).

career for the rhetor-priest of Arles, Sundwall's dating of this letter is particularly relevant to his ordination.[91] While declaring that he ought not and does not presume to run the risk of rhetorical ostentation, "because zeal for plain doctrine should satisfy my vocation," Ennodius trusts he will have an appropriate response ready if someone should ever impugn him, "as yet rejoicing in the novelty of liberal studies."[92] He signs off with an appeal for support and a list of Old Testament trivia questions for Pomerius: Melchisedech's parents, what the Ark means, circumcision's significance, and what the prophecies contain to confirm his rejection of "plans for worldly things, engrossed in transitory certainties like Penelope's web."[93] The peaceable cohabitation of Homer and the Bible inside Ennodius' head are evidence that he was not about to send ancestral treasures, including metaphorical ones, to the dump. The plastic arts of the period provide a nice parallel, as decorative imagery incorporates motifs from the Christian scriptures and traditional Mediterranean literature.[94]

Ennodius enjoyed a more confidential relationship with the patrician Agnellus, who receives both well-turned, erudite verses and pretension-rejecting reports on the state of his correspondent's health.[95] So eager is he to maintain contact with Agnellus that he claims one letter was rapidly dashed off so as to catch a departing bearer and another letter is sent with a slave "who is not to ask for missives in return, but to demand them."[96] Displaying personal devotion and confessing hasty composition in one brief, elegant missive, Ennodius keeps in touch while he deftly alludes to the innumerable matters, mundane but ever-nameless, that rob him and his correspondents of time they would otherwise spend in sociable literary pursuits. The fact that he wrote at all, let alone so gracefully, also serves as

---

91. Riché, *Education and Culture,* 32; *Césaire d'Arles: Sermons* (Deléage), 53. Ordained priest before 502: Klingshirn, *Caesarius,* 73–82.

92. #39.4–5: *cum professionem meam simplici sufficiat studere doctrinae . si me tamen quondam studiorum liberalium adhuc novitate gaudentem aliquis tali dente tetigisset, parassem vel quod ad excusationem esset idoneum vel quod non puderet obiectum.* Cf. Léglise, *Lettres,* 19: "le triomphe de l'esprit chrétien sur le paganisme littéraire."

93. #39.6: *saecularium schemata . . . caducis intenta persuasionibus, telae similia Penelopeae.* Parallels for the omnibus query: Jer. *Ep.* 64, 120, 121 (*PL* 22.607–22, 979–1038).

94. Ivories: St. Paul (Louvre); Poet and Muse (Monza, Tesoro del Duomo inv. 12), plaque with mythological scene (Trieste, Civici Musei di Storia e Arte, inv. 1335) = 5b.1d–e in *Milano capitale;* Cutler, "Five Lessons." For silverware, see chapter 3.

95. Agnellus: *PLRE* 2, 35–36; Moorhead, *Theodoric,* 124, 167. #257 (prose preface plus two epigrams on love and poetic inspiration), #309 (eye trouble), #397 (general health), #316. Similar disclosures in #271, #408 (to Boethius), #361 (to Adeodatus the priest).

96. #322.3: *qui non reposcat scripta, sed exigat* (Aug.–Sept. 508); cf. #321, #359, #448.

a tacit reminder that the accomplished writer needs but little time to perform basic acts of courtesy.

Correspondents who have suffered bereavement offer Ennodius a different sort of opportunity for demonstrating the value of literary accomplishment. Their loss prompts him to compose epitaphs—whose material aspect we will revisit in chapter 3—commemorating the various virtues of the blessed dead. Two men are remembered by name. The former, a *vir illustris* named Habundantius, has his merits enumerated by a string of nouns characteristic of Late Antique poetry: "ancestry, charisma, acumen, integrity, constancy, fortune."[97] The Fates here receive their Roman name (*Parcae*), and the only allusion to Christianity comes in the last two lines: "venerable customs used to renew the hoary ages, and brought pure hearts instead of a temple."[98] The latter honorand is St. Victor of Novara, whose name contains expressive possibilities; his life elicits another serial characterization, with Mount Olympus the archetype of celestial loftiness.[99]

Ennodius takes a different approach to the subject of individual mortality in the prose consolation for a kinsman named Armenius, whose son died while still of tender years. The work, by its author's own admission, owes much of its inspiration to St. Ambrose. Citing the examples of Abraham and David, Ennodius dwells positively on the youthfulness of the deceased, capitalizing on the fact that Armenius' son died before he was old enough to commit grave sins: "he sinned less, because he was snatched away untimely; what he preserved in that former life he has united to perpetual life of a better age."[100] In representing the dead son as a youth of good character and tender years, this letter to Armenius is substantially similar to the "epitaph of a good man" (*epitafium hominis boni*) whose unnamed subject's youth is more notable than his hereditary and personal excellence, although the poem's first lines do mark the latter. Posing the questions, "what honor is there in boyhood, what advantage are the thresholds of life? . . . What help is it for this one, that he preferred old age

---

97. #50, v.3: *sanguis honor genius probitas constantia census. PLRE* 2, 3 (Abundantius 2); Roberts, *Jeweled Style,* 59–61; Lausberg, *Das Einzeldistichon,* 145–50.

98. #50, vv. 9–10: *cana venerandi renovabant saecula mores, / inque vicem templi pectora munda tulit.*

99. #215; Lanzoni, *Le diocesi,* 1035. In the Milanese bishop epigrams (#195–#206), the names Venerius, Lazarus, Benignus, and Senator have a similar effect on Ennodius' imagination.

100. #34 (summer 503): "Our Ambrose" and his *libellus* on the death of his brother Satyrus (2–3); blameless youth (4–8: *minus peccavit quod inmaturus abruptus est; iunxit ad vitam perpetuam melioris saeculi quod in ista servavit*).

to tender years," the epigram addresses the deceased as "youth" (*iuvenis*).[101] Age, we are told, failed to detain a "conquering boy"; the poet finally states that the youth had passed "twice ten winters" when a hostile fate snatched him from sight.[102] Though not necessarily about Armenius' son, this epitaph is in the same chronological block as the letter; the same bereavement may have moved Ennodius' Muse to poetry as well as prose.

These three commemorations are not the only epitaphs Ennodius composed. A majority of the individuals he honored were women; their passing discreetly removed all suspicions of moral frailty imputed to their sex in life. The earliest of this group of sepulchral epigrams is for one Cynegia, transmitted in a letter for Ennodius' sister Euprepia. There is another epitaph for a woman of the same name, however, sent to the priest Adeodatus and to young Beatus three years later. Are these two epitaphs for the same person, or not?[103] Ennodius proudly states that he composed the first poem very quickly (in scarcely an hour) because he wanted to praise Cynegia's eminent virtues; his cover letter mentions neither death nor grief.[104] These five pairs of elegiac couplets call her a woman now united with God, who after death lives through her actions, "bearing masculine deeds with feminine comportment"; Ennodius catalogues her qualities in a list identical to that of Habundantius except for the last item, for which he substitutes *countenance*.[105] The verses, "she brought up her children to maintain a tranquil life, / while she instructs them by her example always to love God" record her admirable motherhood.[106] Save for twice mentioning

---

101. #46 (summer 503), vv. 5–7: *quid decus in pueris, quid praestant limina vitae? / non expectatis mors venit ordinibus. / quid iuvat hunc, teneris senium quod praetulit annis?* See also v.9.

102. #46, vv. 12, 15–16: *aetas vincentem non tenuit puerum. / . . . / bis denas hiemes, totidem transcendit aristas, / quem subito ex oculis sors inimica tulit.* Some think these sixteen lines a two-epigram cycle for a man named Homobonus: Schetter, "Zu Ennodius *Carm.* 2,1"; Polara, "I distici," 232.

103. #219 (early to mid-506). #361, to Adeodatus; #362, to Beatus, with poem (July–Sept. 509). Sundwall allotted #219 (Jan.–Aug. 506) to a Gallic aunt or other relative, denying she was Faustus' wife, Cynegia, who received #362 (*Abhandlungen*, 36, 56). See Polara, "I distici," 223, 232–33. Inscriptions: Pietri, "*Pagina in pariete reserata*," 145; Petron. *Sat.* 71.

104. #219.2: *vide necessitatem, ut illam tantorum meritorum feminam verborum saltibus explicarem.* Cf. #177.2 (early 506) to Helisaea: *postquam mihi domna Cynegia meritum vestrae conversationis exposuit, visionem vestram . . . requisivi.*

105. #219.2 and vv. 3–6: *mixta deo mulier vivit post funera factis, / mascula femineo tramite gesta ferens. / sanguis honor genius probitas constantia vultus / vicerunt tantis exitium pretiis.*

106. #219, vv. 9–10: *instituit natos vitam servare serenam, / dum docet exemplis semper amare deum.*

God, however, such a treatment would have worked well for a Stoic matron of the first or second centuries, which is not true of the second epitaph, professedly written after the dead woman had appeared to Ennodius at dawn and reproached him for not hallowing her grave with verses.[107] In it Cynegia herself speaks of having "obtained the reward for my prayers by Christ's gift," the power of the Cross, the flesh's dissolution with the soul remaining unscathed, and felicitously predeceasing her husband; an exhortation in hendecasyllables concludes the poem: since grief has ceased, "let the matron who keeps her bed faithful by her merits choose a similar lot."[108]

What distinguishes the first epigram from the second is not necessarily its subject but its diction. Lacking an externally corroborated Gallic Cynegia who died in 506, I believe Ennodius composed the earlier epitaph while its subject still lived, without being asked and simply because he wanted his sister to applaud his talent, whereas the *titulus* for the tomb of Cynegia was commissioned after her death; her apparition prompted Ennodius to compose something more appropriately religious, as the earlier epigram's lack of Christian imagery may have made it unsuitable.

Five other epitaphs for women occur in the corpus, three of them for matrons. The wife of a certain Severus—his name naturally elicits a punning allusion to her agreeable interventions—Mellesa was the mother of several children, among them another Severus, who subsequently became an object of Ennodius' pedagogical concern.[109] Eufemia, a widow distinguished in the final lines of her epigram by an exemplary power to inspire her daughter to the love of God, is also praised for her womanly virtues but, like the epitaph for Rustica, another chaste, heaven-bound widow who left a son, the effort lacks vividness.[110] Two virgins, Dalmatia and Melissa, receive the remaining epitaphs that emphasize their chastity. The eminence of the former's ancestors offers opportunities for spirited paronomasia while the latter's epigram barely mentions its personal subject, instead exalting the notion that the whole tradition of funeral rites should be rejected now that the soul is liberated from sin and flesh.[111]

---

107. Cynegia's reproach: #361.2, to Adeodatus; #362.2, to Beatus.

108. #362.5: *optinui pretium votorum munere Christi / . . . / quae servat meritis torum fidelem, / exoptet similem matrona sortem.* For the closing sentiment, cf. #412, #414; Prop. 4.7 and Luc. 9.201.

109. #325 (Aug.–Sept. 508), in the first person like #362; cf. #451.

110. #333; #462 (= *CIL* 5.2, 6266).

111. #375 (early 510), likely kin to the Milanese *vir sublimis* Dalmatius on whose behalf Ennodius sent #121 to Faustus (early 505); #465 (513).

When the same dear people whose lives he has sought to share from a distance fail to take the necessary pains with their letter writing, Ennodius lets them know he is shocked and disappointed. Particularly vexing was the behavior of one senator named Asturius.[112] Having first demanded a profusion of entertaining letters to enliven his retirement, Asturius failed to return the favor, then definitively violated social decorum by fulfilling his obligations with a form letter. Ennodius' reply begins with courteous magniloquence that turns to outraged exclamation: "for the Lord knows that, if the letter had not been marked with our name, I would not have known to whom it had been directed; keep your witticisms or save them for those with whom you share . . . the outcry of actions."[113] While still basically respectful, the final sentence of the letter reads as a lesson in epistolographic technique: "Behold, as I do you the honor of a salutation, I pray that in writing letters you pay attention to place, times, individuals, lest what I do not count as written to me should perhaps wound another, since I judge that you wrote the text of this letter to a great many people and, by just changing the names, are sending it to them individually without regard to their merits."[114] We can compare this early letter with Ennodius' own missives to plural addressees, which faithfully observe the conditions spelled out for Asturius' benefit; he clearly intends them to be read concurrently by two or more men of like interests living in the same city.[115]

Missing from these precepts of letter writing, though frequently reiterated throughout the corpus, is the requirement that a proper letter not be too long.[116] Ennodius strives to adhere to this principle even when, in a cover letter for a seven-line epitaph, he claims to reject it in the name of speed and sincerity: "I am not confining my letter within terse bounds,

---

112. (Or Astyrius) #31 and #47 (mid-503), seemingly another distant relative, perhaps a cousin: Léglise, *Oeuvres* 1, 153; *PLRE* 2, 174.

113. #47.4: *scit enim dominus quia si non nostro* [Sirmond; MSS *vestro*] *nomine notata fuisset epistula, ad quem fuisset directa nescirem; tibi habe facetias tuas aut illis reserva cum quibus vobis . . . clamor est actuum.*

114. #47.5: *ecce salutationis honorificentiam solvens deprecor, ut in dirigendis epistulis loca tempora personas adtendas, ne quod ego ad me scriptum non conputo alterum forsitan laedat, quia aestimo te huius epistulae formulam ad plurimos destinasse et sola nominum conmutatione eam per singulos sine meritorum consideratione transmittere.*

115. #279, to Liberius, Eugenes, Agapitus, Senarius, Albinus in Ravenna, "a communal letter" introducing a deacon to "powerful friends": Sundwall, *Abhandlungen*, 45; Moorhead, *Theoderic,* 157. #300, to Roman deacons Hormisdas and Dioscorus. #311, #315, to Florus and Decoratus at Ravenna, allies of Faustus: Moorhead, *Theoderic,* 230–31. #452, to Ambrosius and Beatus at Rome on education.

116. #9, to Faustus, one of his longest efforts; #29, to Opilio; #152, to Julianus; #298, to the Pope; #319, to Arcotamia; #443, to Agnellus.

mindful of Spartan euphony, nor am I laughing at your reply with enthusiasm for constrained diction. Far from me to say little with trifling words: it is characteristic of sophisticated men to remove lengthy material from slight things and without any constraint to fashion pages such as the measure of men demands. What in me you might have supposed plain about these things which I have said beforehand, haste, not always a friend of art, and accident has produced."[117] That the addressee is Beatus makes the rationalizations understandable, since he was one of the young men with whose literary development Ennodius was especially involved.

From writing inappropriately to failing to take the trouble to write at all was no great distance when it came to distressing Ennodius. The same Eugenes mentioned earlier, whose obligations as a civil servant Ennodius concedes as a reason for the paucity of communication on both sides, receives a dejected appeal to break his silence: "I confess that I am distressed because, when Montanarius was returning, although I had given him dispatches, I did not receive what I ask, which ought on principle to be returned, in decency to be doubled."[118] Ennodius recapitulates such affliction again and again; though perhaps an accident of transmission, letters to persons who have been failing to reply occupy much of the correspondence regardless of whether their subject is practical or personal.[119]

Up to now, our attention has lingered on Ennodius' relationships with laymen of culture, but we should note one *dictio,* while celebrating the educational progress of Paterius and Severus, does hint at his religious profession. Ennodius both praises the eminence of the boys' families and, in closing, proclaims a special concern for Paterius, "whose father I am also called as regards heavenly things."[120] Within the Church conditions for the verbally gifted could be rather grim; Ennodius' letters to and commissions for several ecclesiastics, however, suggest that good style and good faith did mix, at least for the lower clergy.[121] His letter to a Bishop

---

117. #362.1: *non ego epistolam meam intra breves terminos Spartanae memor concinnationis includo nec formam tuam studio coacti sermonis inrideo. abest a me loqui pauca cum modicis; urbanorum est exiguis producta subtrahere et sine aliqua necessitate paginas, quales poscit hominum mensura formare. quod in me de his quae praefatus sum subtile putaveris, festinatio non semper amica artis et casus exhibuit.*

118. #170.3: *confiteor quod remeante Montanario, cum dedissem paginas, non recepi quod debitum posco lege restitui, pudore geminari;* cf. #159, #289. Montanarius: Cass. *Var.* 2.8.

119. Cf. #247, #251, #304, #322, #377, #428, and the Aurelianus and Euprepia dossiers.

120. #450.11: *cuius pater et inter caelestia sum vocatus.* Paterius was his godson; deacons participated in the baptismal liturgy. Cf. Lynch, "Spiritale Vinculum," 183–89. The youths: *PLRE* 2, 886, 1004.

121. As we will see at the end of this chapter, the Italian papyri offer a bleaker vista.

Constantius appeals to the *caritas* existing between them by asking Constantius to promote Vigilius, one of his subdeacons, to the diaconate; Ennodius ventures to hope this favor will entitle him to further requests.[122] As noted earlier, the overture to Pope Symmachus on Parthenius' behalf was not unique, and Ennodius' relations with the deacons Hormisdas at Rome and Helpidius at Ravenna contain a mixture of the practical and the pleasant.[123] The sharpest contrast to Ennodius' correspondence with younger laymen like Iohannes and Beatus occurs in a letter to Hormisdas, the Roman deacon and future pope, indicating a more complex interrelationship of the sacred/secular and literary/devotional domains.[124]

In the preceding chapter we noted Hormisdas' role in Ennodius' financial vexations, also that he occupied the see of Rome when Ennodius' missions to Constantinople took place. Now we will observe that, on at least one occasion, Hormisdas was simultaneously capable of importuning Ennodius to exercise his talents by composing a letter and making him feel uncomfortable about them. Ennodius' reply begins by affirming his wish to avoid saying too much, for a long, rambling letter betrays the provincial, but eventually the accusation comes out. "You have demanded this, brother, with Roman and excessively ingenious subtlety, but candor tinged by no subterfuges defends us against contrivances."[125] On one hand, Ennodius means to compliment Hormisdas for his command of Latin style; on the other, he betrays unease that so flagrant a demonstration of rhetorical skill has been allowed in a context that normally required plainer, more modest diction, namely amicable correspondence between ecclesiastical colleagues.[126] Ennodius goes on to say, "I know how to limit a page, whose value I as its publisher understand; you nevertheless know that I do not fail my side, though a man both cosmopolitan and a cleric may call me before the tribunal, but how am I to produce a letter whose brevity I was promising above?"[127] He ends with best wishes for Hormis-

---

122. #153.2 (late 505 or early 506). Ennodius' acquaintance with Vigilius and initiative in requesting his preferment implies Constantius (diocese unknown) was a suffragan of Milan.

123. Helpidius, recipient of #312, #384, #437, and #445, was also Theoderic's personal physician: Moorhead, *Theoderic*, 167–68, 231.

124. Cf. #452. Hormisdas: #317 (July–Aug. 508).

125. #317.1: *Romana hoc, frater, et nimium artifici subtilitate flagitasti, sed nos contra fabricatos munit simplicitas nullis colorata praestigiis.*

126. #317; cf. #172.3.

127. #317.2: *scio artare paginam, cuius pretium promulgator intellego; noveris me tamen meis partibus non deesse, quamvis vocet in medium et urbanus et clericus, sed quid produco paginam, cuius superius angustiam pollicebar?*

das' health after yielding "such a crop of literature"; the whole letter is unusually prickly in tone compared with a letter to Helpidius written slightly earlier marked by Christian humility of spirit and speech, and with later, more routine letters to Hormisdas.[128]

The ironies of Ennodius' life in letters emerge most clearly from the twists and turns of his relationships with Arator and another young man named Maximus. Arator, the future subdeacon-poet, for whose character and abilities Ennodius always entertained the highest regard, is the named recipient of five *dictiones,* including the praise of letters inspired by his civilizing accomplishments that contains the phrase, "let us pour libation to the divinity of *belles-lettres,* which has flowed from their very altars."[129] Soon after that *dictio* appear Ennodius' first three letters to Maximus. They combine polished traditional allusions to the vintage and the hunt with a desire to converse about the life of chaste Christian virtue, particularly by spurning the blandishments of the world and of marriage; a poem on virginity and friendship is appended to the second.[130] About a year later another letter indicates Maximus was being compelled to marry, but Ennodius complains only that he has received no letters with diverting details; the last communication a few months later offers the simple wish, embellished with several Scriptural references, that God bless the union.[131] The manuscripts separate the polymetric epithalamium Ennodius enclosed with that final letter by a single item, a missive rebuking Arator for taking the delight out of Maximus' happy occasion (of which Arator was well aware) with his "disgraceful silence" (*turpi silentio*).[132] Arator's own dedication to a life of chastity is commendable, Ennodius concedes, but, "even if you do not like these things" (marriage, i.e.), "you ought nonetheless to praise them for the sake of showing your talent."[133]

This parting of the ways had been developing for some time. In a letter from the beginning of the same year Ennodius enjoins Arator to write

---

128. #317.2: *talis fructus est litterarum;* cf. #312 to Helpidius (mid-508). Also to Hormisdas, #410 and #417 recommend people, #427 reports on Ennodius' health; Caspar, *Geschichte* 2, 129 n. 6.

129. #320.1: *libemus litterarum numini quod de ipsarum fluxit altaribus,* discussed earlier.

130. All from fall 508: #334.2; #335.3; #337 also refers to wine, plus duck hunting.

131. #356 (Aug.–Sept. 509). #386 went with #388, the epithalamium (spring 510), discussed in chapter 3.

132. #387.1.

133. #387.3: *haec etsi non diligis, debes tamen pro ingenii tui ostentatione laudare,* sounding parental.

more often now that he has gone off to the country, lest his "taciturnity strengthen day by day and vile unconcern grow into a habit of silence."[134] Considering Arator's attitude toward Maximus' change of lifestyle, that tendency intensified, for Ennodius tried to placate him one last time, professing affection, reaffirming the legitimacy of marriage, and claiming to be sick of belles-lettres.[135] When he regrets that literary culture has estranged Arator from him, Ennodius does mean what he says, though his professed tedium seems to have had no immediate consequences. Two years passed before his elevation to the episcopate; meanwhile, he could not reject those who made claims on his still-useful expertise.

Arator is exemplary among the dedicatees of Ennodius' declamations in receiving five *dictiones* and having his own distinguished future as a Christian poet, but he was not alone in his experience of declamation, in which the ideals and skills imparted by education are put into practice. Having already seen that twenty-two out of the twenty-eight *dictiones* were meant to operate in an educational environment, we will now consider the actual thematic range of those declamations that seem so closely akin to the *controversiae* and *suasoriae* of the elder Seneca and his successors. As Ennodius left so little—only ten declamations of a quasi-legal sort and five utterances inspired by situations in epic—any findings based on a rigidly statistical approach would be specious. I therefore decided to look at the nearly three hundred speeches and excerpts contained in the corpora of the elder Seneca, Calpurnius Flaccus, and the Quintilianic major and minor declamations, which are susceptible to reasonable analysis vis-à-vis their thematic content. I summarize my main conclusions here.[136]

Setting aside waspish anecdotes from ancient media critics like Petronius, Tacitus, and Quintilian and specialized questions of rhetorical technique, let us examine these corpora of actual declamations. The themes that animate Roman declamation of the early and high Empire separate easily into two sets, one according to characters, the other by dramatic situation. The *dramatis personae,* so to speak, are dominated by freeborn fathers and husbands, who define the status of almost all of the other characters, most frequently represented in turn by sons and wives (mothers). As befits the stereotypical Roman family, daughters are less in evidence.

---

134. #378.2: *timeo, ne ista taciturnitas diuturnitate convalescat et in usum silentii turpis crescat incuria* (early 510). Recently, Ennodius had taken the other side of a declamatory theme (#363, against Arator), likely increasing the budding ascetic's aggravation.

135. #422 (early 511).

136. A more detailed version of this inquiry will appear as "Sex, Money, Death."

Beyond this basic social unit, the only other characters to appear in at least ten percent of the 291 declamations surveyed are tyrants, military men, and those described as rich or poor men.

As for the dramatic situations in which these characters move, those involving deaths resulting from violent or malicious acts are the most frequent, occupying thirty-one percent of the total. Sex crimes in the aggregate (rape, adultery, incest), crimes against official authority, disinheritance, and conflicts centered on money, property, or personal damages appear less frequently, but still more than fifteen percent of the time. Characters and scenarios notorious in the anecdotal literature are considerably less common than their reputation might suggest. Within these same 291 declamations lurk only 20 stepmothers, 10 bands of pirates, and 14 alleged parricides, while human sacrifice occurs in just two topics; among the most infamous offenses, only rape and suicide approach the ten percent mark.

Such, in outline form, are the most common thematic constituents of Roman declamation of the early Empire. This outline is, however, based on a synchronic approach that disregards the passage of time and assumes that the content of Seneca's *Controversiae* (early Principate) is completely indistinguishable from that of the *Minor Declamations* (2d c. A.D.). In some respects this assumption is accurate. Sons (brothers) and wives (mothers) appear more frequently in both than do any other characters, unnatural death is consistently the leading scenario, and the two corpora have five themes in common; Calpurnius Flaccus conforms to this pattern as well.[137] The *Major Declamations* can fit into this synchronic picture too, but I excluded them as an indicator of temporal change because, among the second-century collections, their number is too small and subjects too singular to be statistically useful.

Insofar as the imprecision of "second century A.D." for dating Calpurnius Flaccus and the *Minor Declamations* permits, the thematic picture does change when we view the corpora chronologically. Seneca contains nearly ten percent fewer sons than Calpurnius Flaccus, the *Minor Declamations* even fewer. From a one-in-twenty appearance rate in Seneca, pirates diminish almost to nothing in the two later collections

---

137. [Quint.] *Decl. Min.* 291 = Calp. Flacc. 48; [Quint.] *Decl. Min.* 354 = Sen. *Cont.* 6.6 = Calp. Flacc. 40; [Quint.] *Decl. Min.* 356 = Calp. Flacc. 37; [Quint.] *Decl. Min.* 369 = Sen. *Cont.* 4.4; [Quint.] *Decl. Min.* 380 = Sen. *Cont.* 3.9; [Quint.] *Decl. Min.* 381 = Sen. *Cont.* 9.6; [Quint.] *Decl. Min.* 386 = Sen. *Cont.* 6.5. When the Republic failed, fictional "unreality" supposedly supplanted "real" topics: Bonner, *Roman Declamation,* 22–25, 32–41; Clarke, *Rhetoric at Rome,* 85–98.

while the number of tyrants increases modestly. A more substantial change occurs in the categories of soldiers and rich vs. poor men. In the *Controversiae* the former are featured once every twelve and a half themes, the latter once every ten or eleven, but Calpurnius Flaccus has a military man in nearly every third topic, the *Minor Declamations* one in every seven, and the rich/poor antagonism turns up in every fifth or sixth synopsis. The second-century collections introduce several characters completely absent in Seneca: attractive youths, physicians, blind people, and parasites. Dramatic situations show comparable shifts. Disinheritance, or the threat of it, and crimes against the state, prominent in Seneca, become less so in Calpurnius Flaccus and the *Minor Declamations*. The later collections, on the other hand, have their peculiarities; both are more interested in violent death, a slightly higher number of sex crimes appear in Calpurnius Flaccus, and the *Minor Declamations* have a greater proportion of stories motivated by money and property.

From this vantage, the topics of declamations from Seneca to the Quintilianic corpora can be said to betray at least a passing awareness of daily life's realities in the first two centuries of the Roman Empire. Without dispensing with favorite characters grappling with the usual consequences of immoderate appetites and anxieties—heartless fathers, rapist sons, grief-stricken mothers—the later declaimers also suggest, by their increased use of military men, parasites, and variations on the rich man / poor man topos, newer tensions caused by the growth in size and influence of the Empire's army and the dangers inherent in rigid social and economic stratification. As Mary Beard has perspicaciously argued, what unites all declamation is the use of the rhetorical medium to construct a mythic world in which Romans could articulate and resolve social conflicts through an infinitely repeatable process of negotiation.[138] So what can we say about Ennodius' *dictiones?*

Over fifty years ago appeared a magisterial statement about the corpora considered here, along with the declamations of Ennodius: "these collections are spread over six centuries . . . always the same kind of subjects that keep reappearing, and they are the very subjects we have already come across in Hellenistic schools, with the same vein of phantasy, the same taste for paradoxes and improbabilities."[139] I trust we can admit that this

---

138. Beard, "Looking (Harder)," 53–62.
139. Marrou, *History of Education,* 286; Haarhoff, *Schools of Gaul,* 69–70, 162–64; Roberts, *Biblical Epic,* 65. But cf. Kennell, "Herodes Atticus."

pronouncement lacks foundation even in the case of declamations from the early centuries of the Empire, for it confuses the essential substance of basic themes with circumstantial details of style and interpretation supplied by the inventive technique of individual rhetors. We can more accurately state that, while some characters and scenarios remain popular from the first century B.C. through to the second century A.D., others go out of fashion and still others arise relatively late. Between the high Empire and the early sixth century lie approximately three hundred years; during their passage noticeably far-reaching changes of a political and religious nature took place. Did Ennodius' *dictiones,* the last progeny of epideictic oratory, that most rhetorical of genres, march obtusely along in their predecessors' footsteps, or do they bear some trace of these changes in Roman society? If declamation as a genre allows old themes to be argued with ever-new twists and more recent ones to assume traditional shapes in the ongoing process of (re-)negotiating social issues, it certainly left room for growth in the sixth century. Equipped with the basis for a proper thematic comparison, let us see how Ennodius' declamations fit into the tradition.

The ten rather brief quasi-legal *controversiae* left by Ennodius do contain certain characters in situations typical of the declamatory canon known to classical scholarship: an envoy who has betrayed his country, a hate-filled stepmother who resorts to poison, a parricide-honoring tyrant, and a disinherited son with homicidal tendencies.[140] Another *dictio,* the longest of the group, is more than typical, for its theme—children should either feed their parents or be imprisoned—coincides with one in the Quintilianic *Major Declamations,* a correlation that has been duly noted. Ennodius, however, takes the part of the son who had been left to the pirates' tender mercies against the earlier declaimer's advocacy of the now-indigent father and requests that his audience not think him arrogant.[141]

Attracted to some degree by their very familiarity, Ennodius was also moved to select these themes by their continuing relevance. Betrayal of the state by persons in positions of trust, whether alleged or proven, was no novelty in the Roman Empire's last years; neither were enslavements and usurpations. Alaric's maneuverings, the charges that led to Stilicho's

---

140. #221, #222, #243, #467.

141. #363 (no manuscript title) covers the same ground as [Quint.] *Decl. Maj.* 5, but its synopses differ. Ennodius stresses the moral disparity of the sons, while [Quint.] highlighted the father's liquidation of his estate to redeem the ailing son; a fuller discussion appears in chapter 4.

death, rumors that the general Boniface helped the Vandals capture Africa, and the strange tale linking Justa Grata Honoria and Attila the Hun time and again raised the specter of treason. Maximus, the early fifth-century bishop of Turin, even likened the threat of abduction by marauding barbarians to a pirate invasion sent to try the souls of the faithful, while the phenomenon of would-be rulers in both East and West showed no sign of diminishing between the age of St. Ambrose and Ennodius' day.[142] Christianity had, if anything, intensified the shock value of threats to the integrity of the family and the virtue of its members by its theological dependence on traditional family relationships, inspiring Ennodius to devise several variations on the subject of intra-family wickedness. He exploits two situations not seen elsewhere, prosecuting one son who starved his elderly father and another who gambled away the family burial plot; moreover, the disowned son mentioned above murdered not only his father, but also mother and younger brother.[143]

Such are the more conventional subjects among Ennodius' declamations, familiar enough to have persuaded some that he added nothing new to the repertory of standard themes yet possessing definite topical interest even on a superficial level when viewed in the light of their predecessors. Certain themes do seem truly odd. Into the victor's reward topos found in a fair number of the older declamations, Ennodius introduces the figure of a Vestal Virgin whose hand the city's successful defender has demanded in marriage.[144] Bent on combating this demand, the *dictio* portrays it as tantamount to rape and pillage. In the belief that "vowed virginity, given over to sacred worship, should not be ravaged by the raider's torch," the speaker asks the "great-souled hero" (*heroa magnanime*) why he saved the city only to inflict what a conquering enemy would have and concludes, "I fear lest favorable fate, with temples consumed by no flame, lead a Vestal Virgin captive."[145] The memory of Ambrose's promotion of virginity and opposition to traditional Roman religious custom still lived in Milan; were this Vestal merely a figure of pagan antiquity, defending her virginity

---

142. Treason: Jones, *Later Rom. Emp.*, 183–86 (Alaric); 177, 197–200 (Stilicho); 176–90 (Boniface); usurpers: 112–13 (Magnentius); 158–63 (Magnus Maximus); 159, 168 (Eugenius); 225–29 (Illus and Basiliscus); 234–35 (Vitalian). Justa Grata Honoria: Stein, *Histoire du Bas-Empire* 1, 333–35. Pirate invasion: Max. Taur. *Serm.* 72 (*CCSL* 23, 301–3), on Job 7.1 (*Piraterium est vita hominum*, from the Vetus Latina).

143. #239, #261; #467 has a tabloid / "Court TV" flavor.

144. #223. For the *praemii nomine* of a *vir fortis,* see Sen. *Cont.* 8.5; Calp. Flacc. 21, 25, 29, 32; [Quint.] *Decl. Maj.* 4; [Quint.] *Decl. Min.* 249, 258, 287, 294, 303, 304, 315, 371, 375, 387.

145. #223.6–8: *ne votiva virginitas sacris mancipata culturis praedonis igne raperetur . . . vereor ne templis nulla face consumptis ducat vestalem virginem sors secunda captivam.*

would have been pointless, or impious.[146] If, however, the Vestal Virgin of this scenario represented a consecrated virgin forced to repudiate her vows and marry a man of war whose real power Ennodius masked by the archaizing *in praemii nomine* for the sake of declamatory form, his audience would have caught the allusion.[147]

Another *dictio* on a related theme, that of letting the priests and Vestal Virgins of a captured enemy city go free, takes the opposite tack, but Ennodius intended it to complement a *dictio* Arator composed on the same subject.[148] Ennodius capitalizes exuberantly on the coloristic possibilities presented by the notion "enemy city" (*urbem inimicam*), a desolate place where plundered temples have been forsaken by priests and priestesses who wander hopelessly among the crowds cowed by captivity, their faces and deportment a poor testimony to religious faith; he rejects their advocate's supposed loquacity, since the undeserving should be handed over so that good priests might be had.[149] Described less in terms of its edifices and institutions than through the moral debility and disbelief of its inhabitants, the city arguably deserves the fate the *dictio* wishes particularly upon its religious professionals. Though their characteristics sooner recall the enervated pagans of Christian apologetics than the villains of Catholic heresiology, unworthy priests are far more evident than virgins, suggesting the Roman schism inspired Ennodius.

A third declamation focuses more directly on virginity. This time, Ennodius illustrates the idea not by involving Vestals, but with the desecration of a statue of the virgin goddess Minerva, by placing it in a brothel.[150] His oration utterly condemns the deed, dispensing with Minerva's traditional array of attributes in order to present her simply as a symbol of virginal purity, a manifestation of virtue requiring no apology. To immure her image in a den of carnal gratification is thus to commit a type of ethical catachresis (*abusio*), for Ennodius couches his castigation in terms appropriate to both grammatical and moral correctness.[151]

Ennodius' quasi-legal *dictiones,* then, differ explicitly from their prede-

---

146. #366 (June–Dec. 509) epigrammatically recalls Ambrose's victory over Symmachus; McLynn, *Ambrose,* 60–68.

147. Pope Symmachus to Caesarius of Arles, on excommunicating *raptores viduarum vel virginum* (*PL* 62.53–55); Justinian's Pragmatic Sanction (554) *Nov.,* appendix 7.17. Cf. Arjava, *Women and Law,* 157–66.

148. #380 (early 510) is suggestively bloody minded, since neither the Roman Church nor Constantinople was entirely tranquil.

149. #380.7–12; cf. Maguire, *Art and Eloquence,* 24–34.

150. #278; Kennell, "Ennodius and the Pagan Gods," 237–42.

151. Kaster, *Guardians,* 12–14; Relihan, *Ancient Menippean Satire, 175.*

cessors in insisting upon the good of virginity and the heinousness of violating it; implicit divergences exist as well. As I have said, Ennodius tailors both subject matter and treatment to the needs of his audience. Given the common educational milieu and the dedications to specific individuals borne by several of these declamations, Ennodius' refusal to enter certain traditional thematic areas is not surprising. Most notable is the absence of sex crimes among the *controversiae*. They contain no instances of adultery, rape, or incest, only the threatened nuptials of the aforementioned Vestal Virgin, in which the argument rests upon the sacrosanctity of those vowed to the service of higher things, not upon issues of consent or dowry. Aside from that speech, military men are missing from the cast of the *dictiones,* while slaves, daughters, comely young men, and members of the rich man/poor man contingent are altogether absent. We can explain this circumstance partly by the small number of preserved declamations and partly by authorial predilection. Personal preference is also evident in the choice of story lines, which exhibit no qualms about violent death but exclude circumstances like mental illness, which impairs moral judgment, and suicide, which a Catholic audience would find unacceptable.

Turning briefly to the "ethical" declamations inspired by famous moments in literature, we at last glimpse the word *adulterium,* safely embedded in epic contexts. The first instance occurs in an address that Deuterius the grammarian had asked Ennodius to compose, expressing Diomedes' sentiments upon discovering his wife's infidelity at the end of his wanderings. The thrust of the discourse, however, tends more to invocation of the gods and disillusioned soliloquy than to passionate indignation as the returning hero mourns the loss of his hopes and of his once-admirable spouse; he denotes her merits and sins with arid abstractions, not vivid portraiture.[152] Ennodius' heart may not have been in this task. A later speech imagining the thoughts of Menelaus (another wronged husband) as he beheld Troy in ashes achieves a more convincing effect. Saying very little about the fallen city and a great deal about the punishment meted out to those who seduce other men's blameless wives, the king of Sparta states his purpose: "we have dictated the laws of married women, not with speech but with swords, laying waste a crop of effronteries with avenging scythe."[153] His closing words expose the speech's true moral: all

---

152. #208.6–7 (early 506); virtue turned instantly to vice by "a Circean cup" (*Circeo, ut aiunt, poculo*).

153. #414.4: *dictavimus matrimoniorum iura non sermone sed gladiis, praesumptionum segetem ultrici falce vastantes* (early 511).

women must observe the same discipline of chastity, either willingly or by compulsion. A sentiment that Romans of old and Christian men alike would heartily endorse, its utterance gains in emotional weight from the *dictio*'s temporal proximity to a letter we looked at in chapter 1, concerned with a sex scandal in Ennodius' own family (the Aetheria problem).[154] The personal connection here calls all presumptions of an academic context for the work into question, since any well-schooled, reasonably tactful author would find it more appropriate to mediate strong opinions through a dramatic surrogate rather than to utter them in his own voice.[155] The other *dictiones* on epic themes all express griefs, disappointments, or losses through feminine *personae,* but even Dido's meditation on her abandonment by Aeneas emphasizes the need for rationality and sympathy over the senselessness of sexual passion.[156]

The substance of Ennodius' writings about learning and literature—from short letters of advice to the declamations that forcefully illustrate Late Antique rhetorical prose's appropriation of poetic style and content—thus emerges as less frivolous, more intent on presenting images of chastely virtuous rationality compatible with Catholic morality. As we might expect, the quality of his writing in every genre owes a great deal to immersion in poetry, especially that of Vergil, whose all-pervading influence deserves fuller documentation. Among the standard prose writers, Ennodius repeatedly acknowledges Cicero and Sallust by name (as Tullius and Crispus, as often as not); the Symmachus who once opposed Ambrose also had undeniable effects on his theory and practice of the Latin language.[157] Recent work on late antique education and the literature it produced corroborates how thoroughly Ennodius' writing reflects the characteristics beloved of literary stylists in the centuries between Constantine and Gregory the Great.[158] Other men, rebelling against the niceties of traditional erudition, might discover moral virtue in the utterly unliterary, but Ennodius shows a full and complete devotion to

---

154. #412; cf. Possidius, *Vita Augustini* 7.2. The theme recalls the heresy-infidelity equation: Mark 8.38; 2 Cor. 11.2–3. Cf. #240.25–29 (the *Life* of Antonius); Goodman, *Mission and Conversion,* 100–101.

155. Ahl, "The Art of Safe Criticism," 185–96, 200–205.

156. #220, Thetis, anticipating Achilles' death; #436, Juno on Antaeus' defeat (cf. Luc. 4.589–660); #466, Dido on Aeneas' flight.

157. Vogel, 332–33 (*auctores profani*) and 348–63 (*index nominum*), provides merely a place to begin.

158. Kaster, *Guardians;* Roberts, *Jeweled Style;* Cameron, *Christianity;* Brown, *Power and Persuasion.*

the kind of cultural literacy that only grammar and rhetoric had the power to transmit.

After all, Ennodius could never forget what the alternatives were, nor should we: his practiced verbal elegance stands in conscious counterpoint to his daily work as an ecclesiastic. Many of the diaconate's responsibilities were of a solidly practical nature, so his compulsion to produce and talk about producing what was regarded as good literary Latin is not so very strange. Milan's archdiocesan archives from Ennodius' day do not survive, as I mentioned earlier, while the Roman Church's *Liber Pontificalis* presents evidence of a somewhat different kind. From the archives of the diocese of Ravenna, however, scattered papyrus documents from the mid-fifth to the mid-seventh centuries have survived to testify to some of the responsibilities of deacons and to the condition of the Latin language outside the literary salons of late antique Italy. The most recent collection of these fragments, whose editor prefers to call them "Italian" papyri because they represent only a fraction of the documents produced throughout Italy, affords us an invaluable opportunity to evaluate the quality of Ennodius' Latin in the light of its broader milieu.[159] The orthographical phenomena of these papyri, when compared with Vogel's "index of words barbarously written in the manuscripts," suggests Ennodius' orthography may have been less "classical" than his editors have assumed.[160]

The second-oldest papyrus in the collection is a text contemporary with Ennodius, created in the last years of Odoacer's rule in Italy and dealing with a royal grant of property in the vicinity of Syracuse to a *vir illustris* named Pierius.[161] Teeming with clumsy efforts to clarify words whose original significance had slipped from use and confusions of letters and sounds, its details bring the late fifth-century linguistic environment to life.[162] The ponderously prosaic nature of conveyancing comes through as

---

159. Tjäder, *Die nichtliterarischen Papyri* 1, 23. Cf. Culler, "La littérarité"; Horsfall, "Statistics or States of Mind."

160. Tjäder, *Die nichtliterarischen Papyri* 1, 150–65 and 2, P. 29–59; Dubois, *La latinité,* 46–48. Vogel lists (334–48) anomalies segregated from the text, e.g., confusions of *ae* and *e, b* and *p, b* and *v, i* and *e, i* and *y, o* and *u;* evanescent *h; ph* changing to *f.* Cf. Hartel, xl–lxxxvi; Rohr, *Theoderich-Panegyricus,* 179–93.

161. P.1 (prescriptions for a patrimony in Sicily belonging to Lauricius, a former *praepositus sacri cubiculi* of Honorius); P.10–11 A–B, after 18 March 489 (copies entered in the *gesta municipalia* of Ravenna and Syracuse to complete Pierius' property transfer).

162. Spellings in P. 10–11 (I. 6–7): *ad Marcianum . . . qui ipsam donationem scribsit . . . adque praesentes principales viros et exceptorem, ut, dum eius nobilitati ipsa pagina donationis hostensa fuerit adque relectam;* (II. 3–4): *quos utendi, possidendi, alienandi vel ad posteros transmittendi livero potiaris arvitrio. Quam donationem Marciano v[iro] c[larissimo], notario nostro, scribendam dictavimus;* (I. 8): *recitate necessae mae [= necesse me] est.*

well, signaled by quantities of affirmations and subscriptions at several points during the process, the obligation to record that the estate was extensively inspected and approved, and that the change of ownership was entered in the public records.[163]

From January 491 comes a very fragmentary donation by Maria, a *femina spectabilis,* to the church of Ravenna; also to the apparent benefit of the church of Ravenna is a group of six wills together with the formalities for the official opening and reading of each, copied after the early 550s but going back at least to 474.[164] All the documents in this latter group contain virtually identical wording regardless of the date and the status of the person making the disposition, to be expected in the circumstances. We may consider them representative of general practice in making donations to the Church throughout Italy in the time of Ennodius; with a simple change of recipient, the document transferring land to Pierius in the preceding paragraph also offers procedural analogies for Ennodius' work. As explained in the first chapter, his duties as a deacon would have included looking after the diocese of Milan's material resources; some functional aspects of these responsibilities corresponded to those preserved in the papyri. Whether Ennodius was occasionally obliged to draw up conveyances himself or simply to act as the Church's official representative and witness in such transactions is unknown, but the sheer repetitiveness and banality of the language required for orderly transfers of property to the Church and other beneficiaries would have afflicted his verbal sensitivities.

Furthermore, even the simple ability to sign one's own name had not been required for making a will in favor of the Church since the time of Constantine. Among the literate persons in the papyri were a bishop of Ravenna who, as befitted his office, left everything to the Church in 552, and a deacon of the same church who actually composed and copied out his own will in 480, but many individuals throughout the collection were obliged to make their mark underneath what the scribe had written; few in

---

163. Legalisms in P.10–11 (III. 4): *pro Aurelio Virino magistrato gesta aput eum habita recognovi. Mel-(minius) re-(cognovi);* (IV. 1–3): *Et cum alio die ambulassent et pervenissent ad singula praedia adque introissent vel [c]omvocassent tam [. . .]m et inquilinos vel servos, et circuissent omnes fines, terminos, agros, arbos, cultos vel incultos, seu vineas, et traditio corporalis celebrata fuisset [a]ctoribus Pieri v[iri] i[nlustris] nullo contradicente;* (IV. 10–11): *Unde rogamus, uti iubeatis a polypthicis publicis nomen prioris dominii suspendi et nostri dominii adscribi.*

164. P.12, a fragment of the original protocol. P.4–5 A–B, more *gesta municipalia* before the praetorian prefect in Ravenna: the earliest dated unsealing protocol is from 5 Nov. 474 (the will's date is missing), the latest from 13 Jan. 552.

Ostrogothic and Byzantine Ravenna seem to have possessed writing skills, and the situation at Milan must have been little different.[165] As his letters indicate, Ennodius was regularly involved with matters of real estate, money, and movables, so he did have to deal with people like those in the Italian papyri.

Still within the papyri but further afield chronologically, in the 560s, we find more information about the church and clergy of Ravenna. In the famous *chartula plenariae securitatis* dictated by a certain Gratianus, a subdeacon of Ravenna and tutor of Stefanus *honestus puer,* is presented a detailed accounting of a one-third portion of an estate that had been left to the boy.[166] Gratianus lists everything in the household, item by item, often adding the cash value of each, as in this part of the inventory:

according to the apportionment, two pounds of silver: this is spoons, seven in number, one dish, a pin for braces and for garters, twelve molds, two damask bedspreads worth one *solidus,* one *tremis . . .* a box fastened with a key worth two *siliquae,* a silk-blend garment with short sleeves worth two gold *siliquae,* linen trousers worth one gold *siliqua . . .* one bronze pitcher, a bronze lamp with a little chain attached, twelve pounds of scrap iron, a barrel of vinegar worth one *tremis,* a smaller barrel worth two and a half gold *siliquae,* forty *nummi.*[167]

---

165. Constantine's law on bequests to the Church: *CTh* 16.2.4 (321 Jul. 3). Caelius Aurelianus, in 552 (P.4–5. B, V. 7–8): *cogitans casus fragilitatis humanae, sana mente sanoque consilio hoc testamentum meum Agnello . . . scribendum dictavi.* Colonicus *diaconus* in 480 (P.4–5. B, III. 5): *graviter tedians, cogitans humanae condiciones casus, ne, ut adsolit, repentina morte praeveniar, conrogatis mihi testibus . . . manu mea olografa subscribsi, et valere iussi.* Domitius Iohannes, *tinctor publicus:* his will of 474 is an early example (P.4–5. B, IV. 4): *cuique ipse litteras ignorans subter manu propria signum feci.* Rampant illiteracy: Tjäder, *Die nichtliterarischen Papyri* 1, 271 n. 2; but cf. Horsfall, "Statistics or States of Mind," 69–72. Of fifty-one preserved subscriptions in these papyri, only eighteen are actual Latin signatures; most of the rest are done with a *signum* (twenty-six) or betray some incapacity (two with bad eyes, one with gout, four in Gothic); cf. Gratianus the subdeacon.

166. P.8, dated 17 July 564; see esp. II. 1–16, III. 1–3, 8–14.

167. P.8 (II. 5–8): *secundum divisionem argenti libras duas, hoc est cocliares numero septem, scotella una, fibula de bracile et de usubandilos, formulas duodecim, stragula polimita duo valentes solido uno tremisse uno . . . arca clave clausa valente siliquas duas, sareca misticia cum manicas curtas valente siliquas aureas duas, bracas lineas valentes siliqua aurea una . . . orciolo aereo uno, lucerna cum catenula unixa aerea una, ferro fracto libras duodecim, butte de cito valente tremisse uno, butte minore valente siliquas duas semis aureas, nummos quadraginta.* Real estate: II. 14–III. 2.

Like the legal representatives in Odoacer's donation to Pierius, Gratianus affirms that he has inspected and personally witnessed the handing over of everything; instead of signing his name, he puts his mark on the document, for he is illiterate.[168] This *chartula* contains a great many unusual words with odd spellings to intrigue philologists, and economic historians find much of interest here; by ancient standards of style, however, a more artless, unliterary piece of writing could scarcely be imagined, aggravated by the fact of Gratianus' "ignorance of letters." The ravages of the Byzantine reconquest may excuse some lowering of educational standards for the clergy; they do not alter the legal nature of the document or what it tells of the responsibilities of one subdeacon. Reflecting the practice of Rome, Milan, and every other reasonably prosperous diocese in the Latin-speaking world, further papyri record various bequests of money, houses, farms, and assorted movables to the church of Ravenna.[169] Matters such as these were customarily handled by deacons like Ennodius and subdeacons like Gratianus; if basic literacy could be waived as a qualification for the subdiaconate, literary cultivation was altogether expendable.

In view of the monotony, indifference, and verbal ineptitude he encountered in the course of his work as a deacon, Ennodius' tenacity in insisting on a certain standard of linguistic proficiency among his intimates shows how essential good verbal form was to his life. At the same time, he was receptive to current usage in orthographical matters (as comparison of the readings of his manuscripts with the Italian papyri indicates) and vocabulary, when it furnished a piquant answer to questions of sound and sense. The series of five couplets, "about a certain fool who was called Vergil," vividly illustrates the latter, playing upon the contradiction in terms posed by the existence of a literary imbecile who professed to have the same name as the supreme Latin poet.[170] This defective Vergil, who by his insolent ineptitude committed a species of *laesa maiestas* against the nature of poetic greatness, apparently aggravated the offense by his claim of kinship

---

168. P.8 (III. 8–10): *signum fecit, et ei relictum est, testis suscribsi, et omnia mobilia, quae superius leguntur, ei traditos vidi. Immobilia vero . . . sicut superius legitur, de percepta omnem tertiam portionem . . . quae superius leguntur, ei traditos vidi.* The document was dictated, but not signed; Gratianus put his mark (*signum*) because he was illiterate (III.2: *pro ignorantia litterarum subter signum feci;* cf. III.3 and 6). See Grundmann, "Litteratus-Illiteratus," 24–32.

169. P.13–28: the earliest (P.13) is from 553, the latest (P.23) around 700.

170. *de quodam stulto qui Virgilius dicebatur:* #326, #326a–d. Cesa, "Integrazioni prosopographiche," 239–40, identified him as a would-be littérateur distinct from the homonymous *sublimis vir* mentioned in #93.

with the poet; calling him "insane" (*demens*), Ennodius orders him to stay away if he has any sense.[171] The last epigram, especially Martial-flavored, demands, "Why, o atrocious man, do you pervert our Vergil? / You cannot be Maro, but you can be a moron."[172] Although doubt has been cast on the last word of the second line, my translation represents the unambiguous reading of the manuscripts, which show Ennodius using a "vulgar" word borrowed from Greek with a form common for the period.[173] Considering the defects of his target, Ennodius' preference for slang here is apposite for both meter and meaning.

Another epigram, directed against an anonymous Roman would-be teacher of literature, demonstrates a similar feeling for the later Latin vocabulary, stating, "A sign of your nature, no schooling comes to you. / No alphabet patronizes the transactions of a brute tongue. / Never a student, tell me whence you qualify to be a teacher?"[174] Only in Late Antiquity does *bruta* acquire the bestial associations that place it among the adjectives denoting irrationality and by extension, deficient humanity; these lines, by pointing out the ignorant Roman's want of proper instruction and beastly inarticulateness, stand as the antithesis of the Parthenius *dictio*'s exaltation of the virtues of pedagogy, from the mouth of whose happy beneficiary "pour forth the words that betoken humanity."[175]

Against the linguistically and politically changing background of post-imperial Italy, Ennodius' involvement with belles-lettres is a clear manifestation of late antique cultural Hellenism. The concept of *civilitas* as rule of law and way of life encapsulates its implications for Ostrogothic Italy. Had Ennodius lived and worked in the Greek East, his verbal propensities would never have seemed so shockingly problematic.[176] Even in the West his literary passions were far from unique; the extent of his correspondence and speeches suggests how much we have lost.

---

171. #326a, #326b, #326c.

172. #326d: *cur te Vergilium mentiris, pessime, nostrum? / non potes esse Maro, sed potes esse moro;* cf. Mart. 3.43.1, 5.39.6; Sall. *Cat.* 48.6.

173. Vogel prints Barth's *baro* and (Gk.) *matēn,* adding *mero,* but the word is just the classical Greek *mōros* with final sigma omitted: Gignac, *Grammar of the Greek Papyri* 1, 124–25; cf. Dubois, *La latinité,* 105–6.

174. #216: *index naturae studium tibi non venit ullum. / littera nulla colit brutae commercia linguae. / numquam discipulus, valeas dic unde magister?;* cf. Kaster, *Guardians,* 45, 440 (Anonymous 17).

175. #94.12: *ecce post gentile murmur de ore eius quae humanitatem significent verba funduntur.* Cf. Greg. Mag. *Mor. in Job* 10.13.23, 17.30.46.

176. E.g., Firmus of Caesarea; Maguire, *Art and Eloquence,* 9–21; Bowersock, *Hellenism,* chaps. 3, 5, 6; Moorhead, *Theoderic,* 77–80.

CHAPTER 3

Living in a Material World

Upon beholding the luxuriance of Ennodius' style, people have tended to suppose his compositions were made up of empty nothings about nothing in particular. Nothing is further from the truth. His allusions cloak no void but matters so evanescently topical that they elude our distant comprehension: whether concrete items or current metaphors, they carry no explanations because everyone he wrote for was already familiar with them. We can test the validity of this proposition by looking at the evidence for his relations with the world around him, since he takes considerable pains to transpose objects of sensory perception into verbal form. As always, considerations of medium, occasion, and audience temper how he describes and weighs the animate and inanimate creatures with whom he interacts. His writings about selected facets of his environment provide a textual complement, at once objective and subjective, to the tangible, nonverbal record of artifacts, architecture, and human remains. In his day Ennodius articulated what his contemporaries saw, and to some extent how they saw it. Fifteen centuries later his words can sharpen our vision of the material world of Late Antiquity by bringing objects long-vanished into view and altering how we perceive those that yet survive.

Makers of poetry have found inexhaustible inspiration in the natural world and its seasonal changes. As an inheritor of millennia of Greco-Roman literary tradition, Ennodius shares his predecessors' interest. Let us therefore consider the implications of his premodern, preindustrialized environment. Fertile countryside lay just beyond the comparative safety of the city walls and, by Ennodius' time, also within it, as the example of Rome indicates; past the zone of cultivation stood inhospitable wilderness, where bears roamed and bandits lurked.[1] Hence, he has less affection for the great outdoors than do the post-Romantic nature enthusiasts of today. Conversely, he reserves his most fervent admiration for the fruits of civilization, from gardens to baptisteries, well-trained horses and adept orators to silver plate and golden rings.

Although Ennodius spends as little time and affection on it as he can, the world of untamed nature makes its first appearance early in the corpus. Even then, Ennodius' relationship with Faustus was already close, enabling him to compose a letter that glorifies God for bestowing a variety of agricultural gifts upon the provinces, then asks the addressee why he honors the cold, craggy barrenness of Comum with his presence. Ennodius finds this landscape, "which, with rugged, shut-in valleys and sweeping expanses of clustering mountains, is good at showing a harmony woebegone with summer snows" so unpleasant to contemplate that he enlarges on the subject for several paragraphs, decrying its deceptive lushness, the inhabitants who exist only to pay taxes, the eternally rainy and sinister sky, and Faustus' reputedly habitable island, approached only at the risk of death since the lake's swollen waters contain frightful fish that devour the shipwrecked.[2] At the end he recants his contrary eloquence: "I have not written these things as it were with feelings different from you, but so that from them a reader may admit it is better to behold Comum through your pen than to see it."[3] Embroiled in affairs political and ecclesiastical, Faustus found Comum an agreeable refuge from the turbulence of Rome and Ravenna. Defusing potential bad feeling with flattery of his correspondent's powers of description, Ennodius' representations elaborately decline what must have been an invitation to visit Faustus' island retreat. Though we cannot estimate the extent to which dislike of the outdoors motivated this refusal, Ennodius' other encounters with wild nature suggest he considered it an excellent pretext.

When he writes to Asturius, the man who subsequently afflicted him with a form letter, Ennodius candidly shows his allegiance to urban man-

---

1. Krautheimer, *Rome,* 56–57; Smith, "Where Was the 'Wilderness'"; Christie, "Barren Fields?"

2. #10.4: *quae per praerupta convallia et patulos cohaerentium hiatus montium aestivis nivibus miseram scit exhibere concordiam* (early 502); Beagon, "Nature and Views," 286, 306–7.

3. #10.7: *haec ego non quasi a vobis diversa sentiens scripsi, sed ut ex istis lector agnoscat Comum per stilum vestrum melius esse legere quam videre;* cf. Plin. *Ep.* 9. 7, on the lake's piscatorial amenities.

ners, asserting that his addressee's lengthy residence in the vicinity of the Alps reflects and influences his literary behavior. While Asturius gazes at the frosty peaks, rustically nourished "by the acorn of writing," the surly charms of his letters confirm the truth of the matter: "this food's significance has become apparent in the belching of a swollen breast and of an Alpine mode of speech."[4] Men are supposed to cool down in their old age, not become hotter and more choleric, but Asturius' wintry dwelling and rustic diet seem to have had the opposite effect, stirring up his natural fire with "nourishments of cold"; Ennodius warns that "after this, if you choose to receive my letters frequently, it is your business to appreciate the caveat."[5] Ennodius' threat to stop corresponding with a "senator and man of learning" (*senator et doctus*) may seem facetiously overstated to us, but the nature-culture opposition still remains, whereas Asturius' social skills did not.[6]

The example of Asturius highlights the risk of retreat: any withdrawal into the wilderness has the potential to make people as rude as their surroundings. Ennodius amplifies this view analogically in King Theoderic's speech in the *Life of Epifanius,* stating that land bereft of cultivators is barren ground, overrun by thorns and weeds, that elicits grief in a civilized beholder.[7] Journeying from one place to another sometimes requires crossing the wilderness, but Epifanius' eminent holiness moves him to water his transitory surroundings with prayerful contrition, while the ardor of his Catholic faith overcomes the Alps in winter, inspiring the playful aphorism, "he whose foundation a rock has made firm never slips on the ice."[8]

Sanctity is the only condition that makes retreat into the wilderness morally defensible, as the *Life* of Antonius of Lérins shows. Even then, the saint's predicaments bolster Ennodius' view that life in human society is preferable to inhuman isolation. The blessed monk escaped from a Pannonia depopulated "by the incursions of various foreigners," going first to the fertile Valtellina in northern Italy, where he fell in with Marius, "a

---

4. #31.1: *glande te vesci scriptione signasti . . . cibi huius significantia in ructu turgidi pectoris et Alpini sermonis adparuit.*

5. #31.2–3: *quasi ignis tuus algoris pabulis inritetur . . . vestrum est post haec, si eligitis litteras meas frequenter accipere, de admonitione gratulari,* implying Asturius' remoteness owed nothing to asceticism.

6. #31.1; only one other letter to him (#47).

7. #80.138; cf. Christie, "Barren Fields?" 259–68.

8. #80.147: *numquam in gelu labitur, cuius fundamentum petra solidavit;* cf. 84.

priest lorded over by unclean spirits," who was soon won over by his virtuous conduct.[9] To Antonius' distress Marius wanted "to make him an
associate of the corporation of clergymen," an association in which he
wanted no part, so he fled again.[10] Attempting to avoid the enticements of
human society, equipped with only a few vegetables and a hoe, Antonius
penetrated hitherto untrodden Alpine tracts populated by wild beasts: "in
this place the servant of God chose his abode, in which the only reason for
gratification was that it in no way beguiled with its looks."[11] Even there he
encountered two elderly recluses of exemplary life and morals, one of
whom soon departed the earthly life. The edifying spectacle of a fiery column reaching up to heaven marked this event, "so that the venerable
man's faith and ardor, that evaporator of vices, might be manifested by a
symbolic conflagration."[12] The burning love of God shown by this individual who rejected society's evils contrasts markedly with Asturius' isola-
tion-inflamed self-indulgence.

Thereafter, Ennodius judiciously lauds Antonius' rectitude in striving
unremittingly toward perfection: "You would have seen him wild-eyed,
opposing the world's iniquities, the soldier of Christ carrying on a tireless
campaign against the blandishments of the age; when did that figure relax
its attitude into a smile and shatter the severity of its proper condition with
the infirmity of delight?"[13] An anecdote illustrates Antonius' eremitic condition. The veritable solitary, to whom "the mountain loneliness used to
give wild beasts for comrades, the bear's bellow and the sinister growling
of other brutes taken as an exchange of suave conversation," confronted a
thieving bear who had devastated his cabbage patch.[14] After soundly
thumping the offender with his staff, the saint instructed him to go and testify to the other beasts, "so that the unfailing promise of the Lord would
be fulfilled, which promised His followers the obedience of every poi-

---

9. #240.12–16: *per incursus enim variarum gentium cotidiana gladiorum seges messem
nobilitatis absciderat . . . illic Mario presbytero qui spiritibus inmundis dominabatur adiunctus
est.* Antonius in Noricum: Lotter, "Antonius von Lérins."

10. #240.17: *beatus Marius . . . voluit eum clericorum sociare collegio.*

11. #240.18–19: *in hoc dei famulus sedem delegit, in quo sola fuit placendi causa, quia
nequaquam lenocinabatur aspectibus.*

12. #240.22: *ut venerabilis viri fides et ardor ille vitiorum decoctor typico monstraretur
incendio.*

13. #240.24: *videres adversus flagitia mundana torvos oculos et indefessa contra saeculi
blanditias Christi militem bella tractare; quando illa imago statum suum resolvit in risum et ab
ordinis proprii rigore laetitiae debilitate confracta est?;* cf. Barnish, "Ennodius' Lives," 16–19.

14. #240.32: *dabat feras pro sodalibus montana solitudo, mugitus ursi aliarumque beluarum
minax inmurmuratio pro blandae confabulationis communione ponebatur.*

sonous creature and of all wild things."[15] The bear faithfully carried out these orders. The rumor of Antonius' holiness, however, attracted a growing number of people who persecuted him with what he regarded as diabolical temptations of praise. Seemingly all alone, Antonius decided that life in an established religious community would be better because it offered safety in numbers against Satan's assaults, then dismissed the hitherto unmentioned "brothers" who had gathered for love of him and reappeared at Lérins, "that island, nursemaid of saints" (*illa nutrice sanctorum insula*), where he died two years later.[16] A distinctly anti-eremitic note sounds throughout the *Life,* asserting communal life's aesthetic and moral virtues.

Outside the realm of hagiography, Ennodius conveys his perceptions of the great outdoors through travel sketches, many of them inspired by seasonal phenomena. Not far distant in the corpus from the *Life* of Antonius, the first of these pieces gives impressions of a summer journey the poet made on church business between Briançon in Gaul and Torino in northern Italy.[17] Its elegiac couplets forego the detailed description of Horace's journey to Brundisium or Rutilius Namatianus' return to Gaul while maintaining thematic coherence. Emphasizing the paradoxes of Alpine travel in the hot season, represented by the sun's height and the dominance of Cancer, the sign of midsummer, Ennodius calls frozen roads a greater danger than burning fields, recalling "a war of nature which a contradictory year had made: one day brought summer and winter."[18] Light clothing exposed him to the elements as the summer sun turned to unforeseen ice; he endured the pathless crags of the *Matronae,* traditionally associated with a triad of Celtic goddesses.[19] He says these goddess-mountains at first enticed wretched travelers with their aspect then, trodden underfoot, menaced life and limb with jagged, nearly invisible tracks. After labyrinthine wanderings ornamented with images of Daedalus and Noah's dove, Enn-

---

15. #240.33: *quem ille baculo mulcatum districtius abire praecipiens . . . nuntium passionis ad alias ire bestias mox coegit, ut impleretur domini fidelis pollicitatio, quae sectatoribus suis totius veneni et omnium ferarum promisit obsequium;* cf. Zelzer, "Das Mönchtum," 435.

16. #240.35: *universa tamen secum ipse pertractans brevi animum suum adlocutione firmavit;* cf. 38: *his dictis, dimissam fratribus cellulam quos ibidem praedicti amor congregaverat, apud Lirinum inprovisus adparuit.* Cf. Markus, *End of Ancient Christianity,* 160–67, 213.

17. #245, vv. 5–6 (Oct.–Dec. 506). Carini, "*L'itinerarium,*" repeats old arguments (cf. #246, #305) without digesting Sundwall.

18. #245, vv. 13–14: *bellum naturae, quod discors fecerat annus, / aestatem atque hiemem detulit una dies.*

19. Mont Géneve, if Carini, "*L'itinerarium,*" 159, is correct. Pascal, *Cults of Cisalpine Gaul,* 116–22; Chevallier, *La romanisation,* 434, 478.

odius descended into the "riverine sea" (*pelagus fluviale*) of the Po watershed, where he names the Piedmont's major rivers only to recoil from their dangers by paraleiptically requesting the Muses' silence, "for the Dora, the boiling Sesia, and the Stura and the Orco surpass the glassy Ionian's fury."[20] But he has had enough of untamed nature. Spurning poetry's mnemonic function, he wants only to forget his terrors and recover from fear and fatigue now that he has once more reached civilization, most of all the dwellings of Torino's saints whose intercession he prays will keep his life unspotted by sin.[21] Opening with general considerations of the season and the unnamed task that had taken him over the Alps, the poet then endures savage extremes of temperature and terrain, assailed by perils of body and mind, finally reaching the security of Christian urbanism; his "itinerary" is an unambiguous narrative of return from the wider, wilder world to the edifying sanctuary of edifices.[22]

Horseback riding in the summertime inspired another, briefer poem that contemplates different, more pleasant things up in the pre-dawn sky, where beauty and order prevail and learned traditional associations abide. "The multitude of stars had not yet lost light / from the sun's brightness, but from the bosom of mature night / kept pouring gleaming radiance in a drenched shower; / Cynthia was shining milky through her golden chariot," the poet begins, evoking the visual delights to be found outside Milan during the hot months.[23] The subsequent image—"silent grandeur was being renewed by the night's largesse, / shattering Cancer's blazing season with chills"—implies a visit to the country could also soothe other senses, for Ennodius then slips into the first person, declaring that the beauties of the countryside called him as he yearned to cast his cares aside.[24] Away from the city, astride a mount no match for Cyllarus the wonder horse, the poet conjures up the persistent vehicular illusion of motionless movement,

---

20. #245, vv. 17–40, at 39–40: *Duria nam Sessis torrens vel Stura vel Orgus / marmoris Ionii saevitiam superant.*

21. #245, vv. 47–50. Solutor, the last-named saint, suggests a spiritual laundry product; cf. Max. Taur. *Serm.* 61, 61a *extr.* (*CCSL* 23).

22. Carini ("*L'itinerarium,*" 162) saw only disordered, flashback-style emotional impressions.

23. #330, *versus de vectatione sua nocte in aestate* (late August or early September 508), vv. 1–4: *astrorum populus necdum de lumine solis / perdiderat lucem, gremio sed noctis adultae / fundebat rutilos madefacto aspargine crines; / Cynthia per croceas fulgebat lactea bigas.*

24. #330, vv. 6–9: *vernabat tacitus splendor de munere noctis, / torrida frigoribus confringens tempora Cancri: / cum me curarum cupientem spernere fasces / ruris amoenati facies depicta vocavit.*

of standing still while the world whirls by: "his rider races immobile through the byways, flying in place while hooves are constantly driven home."[25]

Autumn at its least tractable overshadows the latest poem in which Ennodius purports to describe a journey. This time, he takes the pretext of visiting a bereaved sister whose name and plight he forbears to relate and transforms it into a series of ekphrases of a route that obliged him again to confront the wildness of rivers.[26] Calling upon the Muses' Castalian spring, whose inspirational liquor will sustain his celebration of the Po's waters, Ennodius sets the scene with the bounty of an autumn that "springs" (*vernat*) with the vintage's grapes, their skins swollen by the season's rains. By those same downpours "the law of the banks was overturned" (*uberibus pluviis riparum lege subacta*) as the foam-whitened Po waxed threatening and took fields captive with its floodwaters.[27] Not just farms, but human homes were swept away as well: "villas were running through the wave's crest as they stood; / the flood then saved a plundered shelter on the shore, / and changing their ground, the luck of small houses held."[28] After taking a moment to justify so hazardous an excursion, namely to succor the grief-stricken sister, the poet returns to his elaboration of the great flood. It includes a few lines of Ovid-inspired description: the soggy, cloud-covered air drew up moisture only to pour it down upon an earth unable to catch sight of the sky, while "fish, but not caught ones, wandered in the houses, / and the citizenry of the river licked up their food from tables."[29] The human element of this natural disaster occupies center stage, though. The flood displaced everyone as it resurfaced people's fields with water. Ennodius himself was also appalled when he finally foundered trying to ford a rather deep section. One of the locals caught sight of him and cheerfully hauled him onto his vessel, bringing him safe to shore. The

---

25. #330, vv. 12–13: *inmobilis currit cuius per devia sessor, / in statione volans pedibus constanter adactis.* Cf. Verg. *G.* 3.90; Mart. 4.25; Stat. *Theb.* 6.327; Döpp, "Cyllarus und andere Rosse." Today car would replace horse.

26. #423 (early 511, with several months between journey and final version); less than a quarter (vv. 22–32) of the fifty-two-line poem concerns the sister.

27. #423, vv. 5–13, 14–16.

28. #423, vv. 17–21: *currebant stantes per fluctus culmina villae, / servavit raptum pelagus tunc litore tectum, / et mutans terras mansit fortuna casarum. / respiceres silvas stationem perdere iussas / ad flammas properare Pado ducente voraces.* For the trees, cf. Ov. *Met.* 1.285–92.

29. #423, vv. 37–38: *erravit piscis sed non captivus in aedes / et populus fluvii per mensas lambuit escam;* cf. Ov. *Met.* 1.295–300.

poet ends this slightly Vergilian episode by sensibly honoring his rustic benefactor, who knew how to handle a boat with Christ's guidance.[30]

Judging from the brief and generally uncomplimentary references we have seen in the works examined here, the less said about winter the better. Spring is an altogether different matter. As chapter 2 explained, this season appears frequently in various metaphorical contexts throughout Ennodius' works, but one composition is distinguished by its brilliant display of spring's essential qualities: the epithalamium for Maximus. I situate this piece in the context of Ennodius' interactions with the material world because only through metaphors of vernal fecundity and mythological situations could he articulate the physical nature of marriage positively and with apposite candor.[31] Of necessity, his poem minimizes the Christian background to the impending nuptials. With the Muses' endorsement, Ennodius praises the virtues customary for Maximus' familial and personal endowments, then states, "our ages have presented you as a monument of faith, / equal in virginity of body and soul."[32] Despite the pious statement that Maximus' triumphantly chaste spouse will win him the palm of purity, flames and blushes also have their place. This juxtaposition of traditional Roman virtues with the physical detachment required of Christian virginity sums up the central problem of the poetic and communal occasion: how to represent the solemnization of marriage? Although the event was necessary and desirable for the maintenance of human society, Catholic teaching sanctioned it without enthusiasm. For Ennodius as a poet, and still more as a Catholic clergyman, exalting the social status and attainments of Maximus' family was far simpler than expatiating on the delights of marriage with a virginal female whom he might never have met.[33] Even at the risk of apparent irreligiosity, envisioning the latter theme required a more inclusive perspective, one that embraced the mate-

---

30. #423, vv. 43–52; cf. Verg. *Ecl.* 1.62–63 with *G.* 4.372–73 and *Aen.* 6.295–416 (esp. the inversion at 315–16).

31. #388 (spring 510), though the epithalamic vernal landscape may be too generic to date the event (Roberts, "Use of Myth," 346); the cover letter (#386) is fully Christian.

32. #388, vv. 19–22: *saecula te fidei monumentum nostra dederunt, / corporis et cordis virginitate parem. / vincentem meritis sponsam dat candida vita, / quae cum te superat sic tibi palma venit.* Esteeming Maximus' chastity, Ennodius hoped it foretold a future in the Church; Ambrose perceived the conflict between baptism and sexual renunciation: McLynn, *Ambrose,* 222–23.

33. Acquainted with all parties and not yet ordained, Sidonius Apollinaris fared more easily with his two epithalamia (*Carm.* 11 and 15). Gallic churchmen would censure Ennodius' attendance at Maximus' festivities: Vence (461–91), can. 11; Agde (506), can. 39 (*CCSL* 148).

rial universe of the traditional wedding-song. With its masterful deities and chaste lovers, Ennodius' procreative world of Spring does just this.

The poem opens in elegiac couplets, with the year's new sun fashioning delicate ears of grain and Nature sitting in bed while the earth warms and flowers paint the world, and ends in hexameters promising plentiful offspring to those struck by the darts of passion; attached hendecasyllables seek the goodwill of noble listeners.[34] In between, description and debate carry the audience from the season when the earth and all its creatures burgeon with generative energy to the point where the force of natural love impels a well-bred, virginal couple to fruitful union.[35]

The depiction of Venus and Cupid that follows the elegiacs and trochees was designed to help Maximus come to grips with the significance of marriage on a personal level by mirroring and magnifying the initial description of the Earth and her vivid offspring.[36] Growth, warmth, color in the world of nature are first brought together in "one face of the soil: charm, cultivation, love," vital juices begin to coalesce, nourishing fiery energies, and the female body of Earth "raises herself up, swollen by the Genius of fertility."[37] The metaphor of nature's female fecundity progresses into parched woods now vigorous with wanton growth, milky grass, and the arms of vines giving forth fingers jeweled with buds.[38] In another distinctly Roman turn the law acts as matron of honor; air and water also join in, uniting all the elements.[39] Immediately after these lines, which stress the naturalness and necessity of Spring's livelier characteristics, Ennodius embeds a direct address to Maximus, briskly informing him of his special connection with the business of Spring. An invocation to the appropriate poetic divinities follows, then Venus appears in all her glory and is present for the balance of the narrative. We already know about

34. #388, vv. 1–24 (elegiacs); vv. 25–28 (trochees); vv. 29–52 (sapphics); vv. 52–122 (hexameters); vv. 123–28 (hendecasyllables).

35. #388, vv. 1–10 (cereals, flowers, trees, grasses, grapevines); vv. 11–14 (beasts of air, water, land).

36. Coinciding with the Late Antique tendency of epithalamia to become love poetry (Spring, Love, Venus parallel motifs in the medieval amatory landscape): Roberts, "Use of Myth," 346.

37. #388, vv. 4–8: *una soli facies: gratia cultus amor. / arbuta vitali coalescunt uda vapore, / ignea* [MSS; Vogel *lignea*] *concretus semina sucus alit. / erigitur genio tellus tumefacta marito, / torrida lascivis silva viret spoliis,* in a traditional Roman vein. Ennodius mentions trees (vv. 5–6), but echoes of *De rerum natura* (cf. Lucr. 5.783–854 and 6.200–227) fill the poem.

38. #399, vv. 8–10; *gemmare* simultaneously expresses both bud and jewel, appropriate to season and literary style.

39. #388, vv. 11–14; cf. Verg. *Aen.* 4.160–67. Roberts ("Use of Myth," 347) detected a "distinct subtext . . . a protest against excessive devotion to Christian celibacy."

Maximus' devout chastity, which Ennodius has surrounded with the exuberance of Spring, but the dynamic relationship of the traditional nuptial figures of Venus and the well-armed Cupid to the Christian virtues of Maximus and his intended is this poem's most interesting aspect.

After retaining the Muses and Apollo to assist in hymning the stateliness of Maximus' family, Ennodius launches into sapphics for his description of Venus, naked upon the pebbles of the cold salt sea; the mention of coldness is not, as we will see, haphazard.[40] Like Nature at the poem's beginning, the goddess plays among the flowers of Spring; spurning golden dresses and the hairdresser's art renders her nudity all the richer and more brilliant: "beneath an ethereal open weave, her bosom's buds had gleamed on rosy breasts; as long as she denies her limbs the odious mantle, she is a second day."[41] Then, irked by his moldering quiver and unbloodied arrows, her winged son arrives to inform her of the sorry state of things: "we have lost, mother, the prerogatives of our excellence: / already 'Cythera' resounds nowhere, the legend of the Loves / is laughed at, and progeny does not suffice for the nascent age."[42] "Frigid virginity" now rules, he continues, and "high-minded vows subdue the flesh"; surveying the ages, he finds a sparse crop of marriages since, in this universal recess from the business of sex, a modest man may not even speak of the marriage bed by name.[43] Ennodius himself could obviously not have uttered the sentiment Cupid voices here. The report rouses Venus, for she rises to gird herself, binding up her hair and breasts and abandoning her glorious *déshabillé* to defend her divine rights against ill-advised laws of demureness.[44]

Not only does Venus respond actively to the words of a son Ennodius consistently avoids naming, but the world starts to change as well; even the sea's entrails burn. The goddess asks her son where they are bound, declar-

---

40. #388, vv. 25–28 (Muses and Apollo). Venus appears (in apt Sapphics) at vv. 39–40.

41. #388, vv. 41–44: *fulserant raro sub hiante filo / pectoris gemmae in roseis papillis; / invidum membris dum negat amictum / altera lux est,* in pointed contrast to Claudian's Venus (*Epith. Hon. et Mar.* 99–100). For the euphemism, cf. vv. 9–10.

42. #388, vv. 54–56: *perdidimus genetrix virtutis praemia nostrae: / iam nusquam Cythere sonat, ridetur Amorum / fabula, nec proles nascenti sufficit aevo.* See Lucr. 1.1, 2.599 and Verg. *Aen.* 1.590, 689, on *genetrix* as parent of Aeneas, the Romans, Amor, and synonym of *tellus.*

43. #388, vv. 57–67: *frigida consumens multorum possidet artus / virginitas fervore novo, sublimia carnem / vota domant . . . / et si quid teneros potuit transducere mores, / praeceptis calcare malis, servatur ubique / iustitium: culpa est thalamos nominasse pudico.*

44. #388, vv. 70–72 (summons); 74–81 (girding).

ing "after idleness, a greater flame is fitting; then let the peoples learn that
a goddess grows stronger when she lies neglected."[45] When Venus sees that
Maximus, "lone hope of an eminent family," is following the lead of his
mother, "a woman / who is purer than the very heaven," she resolves to
change his ways; there will be more fires.[46] Reprising the description of
nature with a twist, the goddess commands, "let my torch reach this boy's
hidden entrails: / let him sigh, yearn, fret, burn, entreat," then embraces
Cupid before he flies off, "uniting all the elements with voluptuous passion."[47]

Possessing the elemental power to promote reproductive urges, Cupid
derides Maximus' arrogance and warns that passion too long delayed
burns hotter and replenishes itself. Piercing Maximus with the same dart
that he used on all the gods, Cupid calls him "runaway" (fugitive), asks
what he is afraid of, and proclaims him a sacrificial offering to Mother
Venus, whom he has long failed to honor. Ennodius treats the bride-to-be
incidentally—the only telling detail is the use of an appropriately lighter
arrow—but depicts Maximus' inevitable fate in ambiguous, almost tragic
terms.[48] Cupid's parting words of comfort are for Maximus alone: "our
wounds, youth, will reinforce your strength, / for whoever is struck by my
point grows; / these fine blows make, if you believe, many descendants. /
May you be fortunate and always bring my presents with you!"[49] The
action ends here, rounded off by a captatio benevolentiae addressed to the
wedding guests.

Other epithalamia, Claudian's and Sidonius Apollinaris' for example,
prefer dramatic narratives thronged with divine and human personages or
lingering descriptions of some symbol-laden venue. What distinguishes
this work is its opening evocation of burgeoning Spring and the figures of

---

45. #388, vv. 83–85: *post otia maior / flamma decet: discant populi tunc crescere divam /
cum neglecta iacet;* cf. v. 73. Ancient thinkers recognized rising temperature as a necessary
concomitant of the generative process: Brown, *Body and Society,* 17–18.

46. #388, vv. 87–90: *Maximus ecce, vides, generis spes unica summi, / dulcibus inludit per
longa oblivia taedis. / sectatur matrem quae caelo purior ipso est / femina quam scimus mulierem
vincere mente.*

47. #388, vv. 93–94: *huius ad abstrusas veniat mea lampada fibras: / suspiret cupiat discur-
rat ferveat oret;* 97–98: *ille volat celeri tranans per nubila vento, / omnia lascivo socians ele-
menta furore;* cf. v. 11.

48. #388, vv. 100–107 (warning, deed); 112–17 (bride dispatched).

49. #388, vv. 119–22: *nostra tuas, iuvenis, confortent vulnera vires, / nam quicumque mea
est percussus cuspide crescit; / haec faciunt multos si credis bella nepotes. / sis felix semperque
feras mea munera tecum!*

Venus and Cupid, who unabashedly personify Nature's reproductive
forces claiming their place in Maximus' chastely ordered universe. In a
Christian world where permanent virginity was the loftiest goal, Ennodius
and his audience were well aware that marriage and family life were not
really about birds and flowers, let alone benevolent deities who induced
the madness even traditional polytheists called love, but about sex and
procreation. Sexual desire was indispensable for the physical consumma-
tion of marriage and the begetting of legitimate heirs, which was precisely
that tract of human experience Maximus had shunned. When Ennodius,
who had held Maximus' spirituality in high regard, came to compose
something suitable for Maximus' wedding, he had to employ his rhetorical
skill to promote a way of life diametrically opposed to what the Church
officially approved; likewise, Maximus may have needed considerable
rationalization and special pleading to shift from continence to marriage.[50]
These considerations help explain why Ennodius' epithalamium proceeds
as it does—from the natural universe to the sphere of human nature by
way of Venus and Cupid in poetic images as explicit as decorum allowed—
and why it is aimed so narrowly at Maximus himself. The gospel of Jesus
Christ altered the cosmic relationship of man to God, but earthly arrangements still had to admit human beings were in and of the created universe.
Ennodius could affirm this fact, at least while still a deacon. His rhetorical
outlook enabled him to imagine a situation quite different from his own;
his affection for the created world let him portray it with spirit and sympathy.

Ennodius discovered a less problematic meeting-place for nature and
culture in the hot springs of Aponus. The place had been honored by devotees since prehistoric times and, in the Roman period, by writers as well; as
a spa under the name of Abano Terme, it is still frequented today.[51] The
springs' proximity to Padua, whose foundation was traditionally ascribed
to Antenor the Trojan, linked them to the heroic age, while their contradictory physical features and beneficial effect on the human body lent
themselves to portrayal by paradox. Thus, Ennodius composed six elegiac
couplets plus a pair of hexameters on the "Antenorean whirlpool"
(*Antenorei gurgitis*), which he offered as "poetry to stir a smile" (*risum*

---

50. Cf. Brown, *Body and Society,* 396–427; Gregory of Nazianzen had already made
Spring respectable for Greek Christians: Maguire, *Art and Eloquence,* 42–52.

51. #224 (Aug.–Sept. 506). Ex-votos: Pascal, *Cults,* 95; Lazzaro, *Fons Aponi,* 28–43.
Noted by, among others, Plin. *HN* 2.103, 106 [227]; Suet. *Tib.* 14.3; Luc. 7.193; Mart. 6.42.4.

motura poemata) at the end of a letter for one Petrus, a negligent literary friend off to take the waters.[52]

Introduced with the suggestion to "read, therefore, the hot waters which you will visit," Ennodius' verses appeal to Petrus through topographic anthropomorphism: the Earth herself is brought on, raised up and supported lightly by the swelling of a ridge's brow, neither raising her proud head to the peaks nor seeking the valley bottoms.[53] Through this dignified, reposeful landscape, "steaming Aponus flows," placidly mingling fire and water, where "wave tends hearths, flame does not swallow up liquid, / the sacred fountain roars from a soaked pyre."[54] In the last descriptive segment Ennodius acknowledges the spring's traditional cultic associations, but the irreverent beginning of the next line betrays his humorous tendency: "a drunken heat affords a remedy for all here, drying out bodies with vaporous dew."[55] The final verses revert to cosmic paradox. "Here, fire undulates in whirlpools, moisture in sparkles: / life comes by the friendship of alternate death. / Lest he perish, Vulcan merges with those nymphs; / a combative concord breaks nature's treaties."[56] Such are the abstractions that decorate the gastric gist of the poem. Beyond performing prodigies of nature, the true value of Aponus' waters is to rectify the excesses of banqueting, drying up the flesh of those bloated with too much fish and other things.[57] Two other Late Antique literary men, Claudian and Cassiodorus, also alluded to Aponus' sovereign digestive properties, which were evidently the practical reason for the spring's continuing popularity; now, it is patronized more for the treatment of arthritic disorders.[58] Though not the

52. #224.5; cf. *PLRE* 2, 871 (Fl. Petrus 28, consul of 516). It gives no positive indication of Petrus' current location; Sundwall, *Abhandlungen,* 77; Ensslin, *Theoderich,* 269.

53. #224.6: *lege ergo aquas calidas quas invises* [MSS; Vogel *invisis*]; the tense suggests Petrus intended a trip to Aponus, far closer to Ravenna than to Rome; Lazzaro (*Fons Aponi,* 75) inexplicably suppose Ennodius had been taking the waters for his own eye ailment.

54. #224.6: *fumifer hic patulis Aponus fluit undique venis, / pacificus mixtis ignis anhelat aquis. / unda focos servat, non sorbit flamma liquorem, / infuso crepitat fons sacer inde rogo.*

55. #224.6: *ebrius hic cunctis medicinam suggerit ardor, / corpora dessicans rore vaporifero;* for the epithet, cf. Luc. 7.193.

56. The image (*hic pyra gurgitibus, scintillis fluctuat umor: / vivitur alternae mortis amicitia. / ne pereat Nymphis Vulcanus mergitur illis, / foedera naturae rupit concordia pugnax*) recalls the fate of Castor and Pollux: Verg. *Aen.* 6.121.

57. Representing food by "offspring of waters" (#224.5: *aquarum fetibus*) and Earth as a reclining diner, Ennodius dispenses poetic justice to bloated stomachs.

58. Claud. *CM* 26.95–100 and Cassiod. *Var.* 2.39; Kennell, "Aponus and his Admirers." Lazzaro, *Fons Aponi,* 74–75, rates Ennodius' work a mere imitation of Claudian's. Cf. Anth. Lat. 1.1, 101 (*Carm. Cod. Salmas.* 36, Avitus' *de balneis*). Macadam, *Blue Guide: Northern Italy,* 398.

only work in which Ennodius develops the implications of conspicuous consumption, his ironic awareness of human excess here adds zest to an ekphrasis of a dramatic and useful wonder of nature.

As I said earlier by way of introduction, Ennodius' preferred theme was not nature's wonders, but the world of culture. We now turn to consider his real interests: buildings, artifacts, living beings. Closest to hand were the edifices of the Church, a subject apt to please much of his potential audience; in fact, the dedication of churches did engage his literary energies for several years. The earliest piece in this category concerns a "basilica" in honor of St. Syxtus, or Xystus, restored at the command of Ennodius' own superior Laurentius, Bishop of Milan.[59] Art historians equate this structure with one of the chapels attached to the church that has been called San Lorenzo since at least 590.[60] Since Ennodius features Laurentius' merits in the opening lines, making the epigram as much a praise of the bishop as of the building, that prelate was assuredly behind the poem's composition. The significance of the church's dedication to Xystus, however, deserves a second look: with three different popes bearing the name Xystus, identifying the honorand may not be so straightforward as we might suppose.

Little is known about the first Xystus save that he was a martyr of the second century; Xystus II, the superior and fellow-martyr of the third-century Roman deacon who was Bishop Laurentius' namesake, is more celebrated by far.[61] Xystus III was Leo the Great's immediate predecessor as bishop of Rome, ruling from 432 to 440, and a great builder of churches, among them the basilica of S. Maria Maggiore; he is also a featured character in two documents roughly contemporary with Ennodius' epigram that were part of a publicistic campaign promoting the much-assailed Pope Symmachus' claims to be exempt from judgment by his episcopal colleagues.[62] Ennodius' personal advocacy of the Symmachan cause in the

59. #96, *versus in basilica sancti syxti* [B; other MSS *sixti/xysti*] *facti et scripti quam laurentius episcopus fecit* (mid-504), probably inscribed somewhere in the building; cf. Pietri, "*Pagina in pariete reserata,*" 141–43. *Basilica* effectively means *ecclesia* at this period: Lazard, "Les byzantinismes lexicaux," 367.

60. Kinney, "Evidence for the Dating of S. Lorenzo in Milan," 92–107 (her translation based on Hartel's text at 93–94); Krautheimer, *Three Christian Capitals,* 82 and n. 26. Xystus I: *Liber Pontificalis* (= *LP*), 8 (with obvious anachronisms). Xystus II: *LP* 25; Combet-Farnoux, "Sixte II."

61. Hope, *Leonine Sacramentary,* 31, 44–45.

62. Xystus III the builder: Krautheimer, *Rome,* 46–54, Pietri; *Roma Christiana,* 503–14. The literary creation: the *Documentum* of Xystus III of Rome (*gesta de Xysti purgatione*) and the *Documentum* of Polychronius of Jerusalem. See *LP* 46; Caspar, *Geschichte* 2, 108–9; Wirbelauer, *Zwei Päpste,* 262–83; 66–72, 84–89; Hope, *Leonine Sacramentary,* 44–45, 63–68.

Libellus is a matter of record; the poetic commemoration of his bishop's "temple" (*templum*) suggests Laurentius' partisanship, displayed at the Roman synods of 501 and 502, assumed material form in Milan.[63]

The manner in which Ennodius sketches Laurentius' undertaking leaves open the question of how much reconstruction was involved and tantalizingly hints that the structure might originally have been associated with Xystus: "joining the light of life / to the worth of the work, he established this temple, / decayed through indefinite abandonment (no tidings circulate); / but the ordinance for the old establishment, / which fortunate Syxtus may gain by the liberality of Laurentius, / lives increased through time. / Thus endures the charge which once fell to the saints: / this man offered the temple which that one, coming, consecrates."[64] As his deacon relates it, Laurentius' pious work was both another diocesan construction project and an element of the pro-Symmachan publicistic effort; by conflating and confounding Xystus III with his homonymous martyred predecessor, the dedication of this structure helped to establish his character as a precedent-setting pontiff supported by his faithful deacon.[65]

Immediately following this epigram is a slightly longer one that praises another of Laurentius' churches. Its title indicates the hexameter verses were meant to be inscribed in a new and splendid *Basilica Sanctorum,* built where previous structures had been destroyed by fire.[66] The body of the text certainly gives no cause to doubt the church was new rather than renovated since, as Ennodius tells it, "First did ignoble abodes yield to the blessed flames. / If splendor comes through losses, if rooftops destined / to house God rise from the flames, if ruins grow / from benign brands, if the expenses do reverence, / what sort of man will restore what was consumed

---

63. Wirbelauer, *Zwei Päpste,* 29 and n. 87.

64. #96, vv. 2–8: *et lumina vitae / ad pretium iungens operis haec templa locavit / lapsa per incertos—non spargit fama—recessus. / sed veteris facti vivit lex aucta per aevum, / quam dexter capiat Laurenti munere Syxtus. / sic manet officium quod sanctis contigit olim: / obtulit hic templum, veniens quod consecrat ille.* Cf. Thomas and Witschel, "Constructing Reconstruction."

65. Medieval tradition is obscure about St. Xystus and the Milanese bishops interred at S. Lorenzo, but multiple identifications can coexist (Xystus II and Laurentius; Xystus III and Leo): Wirbelauer, *Zwei Päpste,* 264, 276–80; Pietri, *Roma Christiana,* 1542; Picard, *Le souvenir,* 59–66. #179 celebrates the martyr Laurentius' steadfastness. Cf. the veneration of Stephen the protomartyr as "Pope Stephen": Hope, *Leonine Sacramentary,* 42–43.

66. #97. Picard, *Le souvenir,* 32–33 discerns a new construction, identified with a church once adjacent to S. Babila dedicated to S. Romanus but anciently called *Concilia Sanctorum.*

in crackling ruins?"[67] Apostrophizing Laurentius as the conqueror of the conflagration, he credits his bishop with seizing the opportunity to build offered by the felicitous flames whose cleansing action has enabled him to instruct through construction: "with facts train those to be taught, lest a mind ignorant of right falter at words."[68]

However predictable we may find the preceding opposition of words and deeds, it accords with Ennodius' disposition to regard exemplary acts as more effective instruments of edification than the ambiguities of speech. He further develops the idea of teaching through buildings in an adjacent piece, a *dictio* composed for delivery by Honoratus, Bishop of Novara, at the dedication of a basilica to the Apostles "where a temple of idols had been."[69] The keynote is renovation within tradition. Instead of demolishing and rebuilding from the ground up, Christians have allowed both the edifice and its very name (*templum*) to remain; old beliefs and rites have perished while the surviving structure is made new. Honoratus' predecessor Victor, whose name is exploited for the sake of an edifying pun, receives some credit for this excellent work, as his spiritual triumphs over the world's vices made it possible for the building to be rededicated to Christ's service; a bygone age had rebelled, squandering its substance on a multiplicity of offerings.[70] The address glides over the nature of the renovations, stating merely that they were accomplished with little exertion, and glories instead in a variety of contrasts, between old and new, darkness and light, filthy vileness and exalted purity. Signified by deceitful illusions and sacrifices (alternately gory and air polluting) and the ex-votos and cult images whose only value lay in their materials and craftsmanship, the evils of ancient times have been put to flight by Christ, assisted by the apostles Peter and Paul.[71] With the appearance of these

---

67. #97, vv. 1–5: *vilia tecta prius facibus cessere beatis, / si splendor per damna venit, si culmina flammis / consurgunt habitura deum, si perdita crescunt / ignibus innocuis, si dant dispendia cultum, / qualis erit reparans crepitantibus usta ruinis?* #183, vv. 7–8, calls Laurentius "repairer of the old . . . founder of the new" (*vetustorum reparator . . . novorum / conditor*); Picard, *Le souvenir*, 25–26, 614–16.

68. #97, vv. 9–13: *sed postquam superi flammas misere secundas, / ad lumen cineres traxerunt ista colendum. / huc oculos converte pios qui cuncta vapore / praedicis mundanda, pater, rebusque docendos / instrue, ne verbis titubet mens nescia recti.*

69. #98 (Easter/end 504), *dictio . . . in dedicatione basilicae apostolorum ubi templum fuit idolorum.*

70. #98.1–5; 2–3 (Victor's victory: *cum vocabulum didiceris, gesta cognoscis*).

71. #98.2; 4–7 (pollution, images). We may infer that, after minimal defacement and re-labelling, an altar and some crosses (painted and/or incised) were installed: Vaes, "*nova construere,*" 303–4.

two luminous figures, the temple's new patrons, the idea of construction hitherto suppressed on the literal plane blossoms on the metaphorical one: "for what would be required for the restoration of a sanctuary save the master builder and the rock, save the stone and the one who builds upon it, save the foundation and the workman?"[72] An invocation follows, entreating God to come and enter fully into the consecration of his work by cleansing this place of worship from its former corruption and being present in the sacrifice of the Mass. The last few lines of the *dictio* diplomatically shift from extolling the excellence of the basilica to praising of an eminent guest, the metropolitan bishop. As in the epigram on the *Basilica Sanctorum,* Laurentius of Milan's greatest virtue is that he "has bestowed his lessons for life not with talk, but with examples."[73] In Ennodius' eyes the most effective teaching is the visible witness of a blessed life or a building hallowed by divine worship.

This "basilica of the Apostles" at Novara received additional attention from Ennodius around the same time in the form of elegiac couplets whose phrasing recalls much of the official speech, omitting the praise of Laurentius.[74] This poem gives Honoratus and Victor joint honors for making this once-dirty old temple shine forth with new light: as befits his name, Victor has indeed been victorious in expelling the former possessors, the old gods, while Honoratus follows in his predecessor's footsteps by increasing devotion by converting the premises to Christian cult use.[75] Beautifying this temple's rooftops in God's sight proves Honoratus' purity of heart, for the act manifests his merits; a six-line poem Ennodius composed several years later on the bishop's stronghold illustrates them anew.[76] This poem develops the theme of Honoratus' mighty fortress to express his earthly defense of his people. Like the rampart it represents, the poem is annular. Ennodius opens by affirming the fort "is the most trustworthy hope for life," continues with praise of Honoratus as holy guardian and shield—before his virtues, warfare withdraws—

---

72. #98.8: *qui enim in restaurationem aedis essent necessarii nisi architectus et petra, nisi lapis et superaedificans, nisi fundamentum et opifex?* Cf. Verg. *Aen.* 3.89; Pietri, *Roma Christiana,* 1537–92.

73. #98.10: *non sermone vitae instituta tribuit sed exemplis;* cf. #1 for Laurentius (early 503).

74. #100 (esp. vv. 6–8) clearly refers to Honoratus, as Sirmond and the scribe of V realized.

75. #100, vv. 1–2, 5–10.

76. #260 (early 507), *versus de castello Honorati episcopi.*

and closes the circle where he began, immuring the threat of war by repudiating fear, hope's antithesis.[77]

This scatter of occasional pieces was not the only fruit of Ennodius' poetic strivings, for other Christian edifices, especially those associated with Milan's bishops, also inspired him. Let us look first at the baptisteries he credits to Laurentius and his successor Eustorgius. The former's baptistery receives five pairs of elegiac couplets that dazzle, not enumerate decorative and devotional features. Throughout, Ennodius accentuates effects of light and color, from the metal of Laurentius' holy life, smelted in the furnaces of tribulation, to the edifice whose material aspects— "marbles, mosaics, paintings, lofty coffered ceiling"—fade before its founder's integrity.[78] As in the epigram for the basilica of Xystus, Laurentius' own worth enriches the work, which reappears in a white and purple blaze of similes: "as the fleeces of China are dyed with purple, you say, / so the sojourning light adorns inlaid gems / whenever the snow of stone blushes more beautifully with craftsmanship."[79] Paradox comes powerfully to the fore when Ennodius hails Bishop Eustorgius' hydraulic improvements to the baptistery of St. Stefanus. "Lo, under the roof it rains without a cloud in placid shower, / the pure face of heaven provides waters," he marvels.[80] The baptismal context raises the elemental contrast of liquid and solid, of water flowing from a shelter that normally kept people dry, to become an earthly manifestation of God's miraculous power. Through Eustorgius' good offices, those baptized into Christ participate analogically in the parting of the Red Sea, an image that Ennodius' friend Arator later elaborates: "the heavenly wave comes back to its children, / holy liquid flows out through celestial recesses."[81]

---

77. #260: *pontificis castrum spes est fidissima vitae. / cui tutor sanctus, quae nocitura petant? / hic clipeus votum est: procul hinc, Bellona, recede. / quod meritis constat, proelia nulla gravant. / conditor hic muros solidat, munimina factor; / nil metuat quisquis huc properat metuens;* Settia, "Le fortificazioni dei Goti," 117.

78. #181 (early 506), alluding to the ordeals of war and schism; vv. 5–6 (*marmora picturas tabulas sublime lacunar / ipse dedit templo qui probitate nitet*) refer to figural mosaics (*pictura:* Verg. *Cul.* 64), not carved figures (3 Reg. 6:32 [Vulg.], of Solomon's temple).

79. #181, vv. 8–10: *vellera ceu Serum murice tincta feras, / qualiter inclusas comit lux hospita gemmas, / nix lapidis quotiens pulcrior arte rubet;* cf. Verg. *G.* 2.121.

80. #379 (early 510), vv. 1–2: *en sine nube pluit sub tectis imbre sereno / et caeli facies pura ministrat aquas.* Utilizing stored rainwater, it was apparently part of the cathedral complex attached to S. Maria, Ambrose's *basilica minor:* Amb. *Ep.* 20.24 (*PL* 16.1001); Picard, *Le souvenir,* 100–104, 370.

81. #379, vv. 5–7: *arida nam liquidos effundit pergula fontes, / et rursus natis unda superna venit. / sancta per aetherios emanat limpha recessus;* cf. Hillier, *Arator,* 151–79. How the system actually functioned is unclear: Picard, "Ce que les textes nous apprennent," 1460.

Beyond providing for churches and baptisteries, the metropolitan bishops of Milan also required accommodations suitable to their worldly eminence and number of clergy. Ennodius' verses "written in a house in Milan" seem to contribute to the sixth-century evidence for the city's episcopal palace, which existed since at least the time of St. Ambrose; the information they offer, however, is more allusive than conclusive.[82] A few mention Laurentius by name, others do not; all develop the subject of a beauty at once visibly material and invisibly spiritual, since the house ought properly to represent the luminous excellence of its inhabitants, especially if they are the bishop and his clergy. The first poem proceeds from the proposition that a house may be brilliant in two ways, either from its proprietor's personal merit or by virtue of its luxurious decoration. The ostentatious house thus requires highly literal description: "grass-green rocks simulating lush pasture / may entice the eyes, a work may strike them / by a nobler trick, nature may yet control figures with art / while she molds stones' flesh in shapes, / she may learnedly suffuse their whiteness with rosy vigor / and paint sections harmonious with sprinkled flecks."[83] The use of the subjunctive indicates moral reservations, for this vision of gleaming colors, indeed the whole array of "gold, roofing, ivory, paintings, coffered ceilings," simply points a moral: nothing "is granted to shine more than good people do."[84] Though Ennodius concludes that building a human life of lasting virtue is what requires true effort, the glories of his ideal house are more eye-catching.

The subsequent poems about the Milanese house are tantalizingly allusive. In the next piece in the group, Ennodius credits Laurentius with giving the building a fresh day in the sun after a spell of dilapidation clearly due to fifth-century political and military developments: "splendid roofs rise through the ruin of assets; / what comes from the Lord knows no sunset."[85] Though mentioning only courtyards and modest colonnades, he declares the bishop has done so well that legend will bear his time-

---

82. #99, *versus in domo mediolani scripti.* Early sixth-century evidence: Ward-Perkins, *From Classical Antiquity,* 177 (#101 and #453 also adduced, but not #103, #127). Cf. McLynn, *Ambrose,* 252–56, 284–85.

83. #99, vv. 3–8: *herbida pasturam simulantia saxa virentem / inliciant oculos, nobiliore dolo / pellat opus, tamen arte regat natura figuras, / viscera dum lapidum fingit imaginibus, / candorem roseo perfundat docta robore* [B; Vogel *rubore*], */ depingat sparsis congrua membra notis.*

84. #99, vv. 9–10: *aurum culmen ebur tabulas laquearia gemmas / non datur humanis plus rutilare bonis.*

85. #101, vv. 5–6: *splendida per census consurgunt tecta ruinam, / occasum nescit quod venit a domino; 9–10.*

vanquishing name to the stars. Another ten-line epigram characterizes the house as a "happy little home" flourishing under its present stewardship; he omits mention of Laurentius' name, but the final couplet, "learn what sharing in common offers for a holy life, / if consecrated edifices render men pure," returns to the motif of metaphorical edification afforded by the bishop's house.[86] A third epigram has little to indicate a connection with the episcopal residence beyond its introductory prayer "that sure hope come to pious guests."[87] Further along, however, are some "verses on the marble lion which spouts water in the house."[88] The dwelling's identity is implied by the thematic juxtaposition of dreadful beast and salubrious water: "losing its nature, the beast quenches us; / while savage throats pour out glassy fountains, / terrible hearts are washed in healing waters."[89] Any source of liquid refreshment is welcome in summer's heat, but a lion-shaped fountain in the bishop's own house inspired special moralizing.

The last epigram that may pertain to houses owned by the diocese of Milan occurs late in Ennodius' works. Riddle-like, its opening lines say "a single house is joined in twofold divided structure / and splits the fabric that binds it well"; the succeeding statement, "in twin roofs reverent glory shines plainly and honor is combined from things divided," implies ecclesiastical ownership.[90] The final couplet's allusion to the ample room allotted for sacred functions to prevent confusion may refer to a double cathedral (Ticinum, for instance, had one for summer, another for winter), though a palace-chapel complex that sequestered liturgical observances from day-to-day administrative matters is conceivable.[91]

Not every religious edifice that Ennodius commemorated was founded by prominent clergymen. His friend and kinsman Armenius was respon-

---

86. #103, vv. 1: *qui possessa diu felix habitacula liquit?* 9–10: *quid praestet consors ad vitam discite sanctam, / si reddunt mundos tecta dicata viros.*

87. #104, vv. 1–2: *da, pater omnipotens, per saecula longa precamur, / spes ut certa piis hospitibus veniat;* cf. Picard, *Le souvenir*, 506–7.

88. #127 (from 505), *versus de leone marmoreo qui aquam mittit in domo*. See Schröder, *Titel und Text*, 206.

89. #127, vv. 4–6: *naturam perdens belua nos satiat; / effera dum vitreos effundunt guttura fontes, / dira salutiferis corda lavantur aquis.*

90. #453 (mid-512), vv. 1–4: *una domus duplici discreta iungitur aede / partiturque suum quod bene nectit opus. / in geminis simplex radiat pia gloria tectis / et de divisis consociatur honos.*

91. #453, vv. 5–6: *ne procul aut ibidem sacros confunderet usus, / constanti numerum sors dedit ampla loco.* Double cathedral: Mirabella Roberti, *Milano Romana*, 106–8; Ward-Perkins, *From Classical Antiquity*, 177; *Milano capitale*, 106–8.

sible for a third baptistery, "where the martyrs whose relics are kept there are depicted," according to the epigram's title.[92] Unfortunately for us, Ennodius has not identified the martyrs by name and instead celebrates the saving wave of baptism and the artist's achievement: "the painter brought bodies snatched from tombs to life; / seeing corpses live, let Death go to the grave."[93] From the same year comes a related four-line epigram intended to accompany a depiction of Armenius' dead son being presented to Christ by angels.[94] Neither title nor text of this testament to youthful virtue makes mention of the baptistery, but the epigram and picture evidently formed part of the building's interior appointments; as founder and as father, Armenius wished his construction to signal the heavenly destiny of the son he had recently lost.[95]

Ennodius' attentions also fell upon real estate whose potential to edify was less immediate, for several properties he describes possess no discernible ecclesiastical connections. The earliest among these is a ten-line epigram that would have been inscribed above the colonnade of a dining room.[96] Bracketed by two friendly letters to Avienus, the poem praises a house at whose paneled doors "art, virtue, name, and ancestry is learned," proclaiming its master's talents and cultivated Latinity.[97] Considering this homage's literary detailing and elevated tone, the urbane proprietor of the house in question was probably Faustus, since Ennodius had already devoted a twenty-line poem to Faustus' book cabinets.[98]

The destination of a set of nine epigrams designed to introduce various areas of an unidentified house is more difficult to ascertain. Each of these little pieces is labelled to indicate its placement—"in the house, before the oratory," "in front of the oil storage room," "in front of the granary," "in front of the stairs," "in front of the pantry," "in front of the kitchen," "in

---

92. #128 (505), *versus in baptisterio ugello factos ubi picti sunt martyres quorum reliquiae conditae sunt ibi;* Armenius is not in *PLRE* 2.

93. #128, vv. 5–6: *rapta sepulturis animavit corpora pictor; / funera viva videns, mors eat in tumulos.*

94. #147 (end 505 or early 506), *versus scriptos ugello ubi filium Armeni angeli Christo offerunt qui paenitentiam egit.* Only B reads the unparalleled, perplexing *ugello* here and in #128 (other MSS: *agello*, dim. of *ager*, "field"); *agello* is easier, but *ocello* (dim. of *oculus*, "eye") might work as "apple of one's eye, gem."

95. #147: *suscepit oblatum, veniam cui contulit Iesus; / post culpas animae sunt holocausta dei. / perge, puer, teneros superans bene conscius annos; / vectores meruit candida vita pios;* Pietri, *"Pagina in pariete reserata,"* 142–44.

96. #112 (Easter–end 504); Ellis, "Late-Antique Dining," 42–44.

97. #112, vv. 5: *discitur in valvis ars virtus nomen origo;* 7–10. Pecere, "La cultura greco-romana," 368; Scott, "Power of Images," 60–65.

98. #70, *de epigrammatis per armaria domni Fausti factis.*

front of the wine cellar," "at the entrance of the garden," "inside the garden above the doorway"—while the content of each oscillates between common description and symbolic exposition.[99] Thus, the first five are modest couplets that represent their object either as a metaphysical message, as in the case of the oratory's paradoxical exchange of earthly weeping for heavenly joys and the staircase's symbolic function, or as concrete essentials of human life, as with the oil storage room, the granary, and the larder, whose meaning is self-evident.[100] Concerned with rooms of a more expressively sociable nature, the next two epigrams devote four lines each to the kitchen and the wine cellar: quality, not quantity, distinguishes the former's dishes, while the latter, a "temperate chamber," contains a pure beverage that, unlike the ordinary cup, soothes truculent hearts.[101] Indispensable to every well-furnished house, the rooms acquire a concomitant moral function in the course of this poetic directory, whose seeming commonplaces of domestic life convey higher truths.

The last two poems, the longest of the set, lead the visitor outdoors into the garden. At its entrance, the blossoms of literature that arise at poets' behest temporarily supplant real vegetation: "who begets flowers with song has spring in winter; / through the ice, words breathe forth warming zephyrs."[102] In contrast to the sober storeroom of the preceding epigram, inspired erudition inebriates the utterances that create this pleasant place, bringing the cultivated natural world glowingly alive for its own sake years before Maximus' epithalamium. The final poem celebrates the garden's exquisite completeness, made all the more charming by the narrow confines of its urban setting. "It is true nobility which shines in small things," the speaker declares, affirming that "grace has come to an enclosed space, preferring it to the open fields; / what zeal may accomplish in tight spots, she has shown."[103] Notwithstanding the smallness of the

---

99. #162, *epigramma in domo ante oratorium;* #162a, *ante olearium;* #162b *ante horreum;* #162c, *ante scalas;* #162d, *ante cellarium;* #162e, *ante coquinam;* #162f, *ante canavam* (cf. Lazard, "Les byzantinismes lexicaux," 388); #163, *in ingressu horti;* #164, *intra hortum supra limen* (early 506).

100. Metaphysical: #162, #162c. Essential: #162a, #162b, #162d; cf. Lausberg, *Das Einzeldistichon,* 186.

101. #162e, vv. 3–4 (cuisine); #162f, vv. 1 (*sobria cella*), 3–4. Both allude to Ambrose's hymn *Splendor paternae gloriae,* vv. 17–24 (Raby, *Oxford Book of Medieval Latin Verse,* 10). *Nostro* may be quite specific; cf. Nevett, "Perceptions of Domestic Space."

102. #163, vv. 4–5: *ver habet in bruma qui flores carmine gignit; / per glaciem zephyros exhalant verba tepentes.* This is the only epigram of the group in dactylic hexameters.

103. #164, vv. 3–6: *ditior extentos superat dos larga minorum; / nobilitas vera est quae nitet in modicis. / venit ad inclusum postponens gratia campos; / prodidit angustis quid faciat studium.*

place, every essential feature is present in its season: a columned walk shaded by God's own verdant grapevines; lilies, rosebushes; bay and olive trees that the earth bestowed on her offspring as tokens of victory and amity.[104] The closing couplet concedes that more affluent individuals may demand grander surroundings, but "what pleases without deceit is enough for us."[105] In its satisfaction with what can be done in a modest setting, the poem resembles the boast of a proud apartment gardener. Since the house and garden are clearly too unpretentious to belong to one of Ennodius' illustrious acquaintances, who might the "us" represent? This *hortus conclusus* appears real enough, as do the domestic appointments that precede it, though also alluding to the timeless and perfect garden of Paradise.[106] Perhaps the discriminating unpretentiousness of this group of epigrams camouflages Ennodius' own dwelling and garden, for he is manifestly appreciative of other people's houses and, at times, interested in acquiring property for his own use.

Regardless of whether or not some of these verses about domestic arrangements refer to pleasant aspects of Ennodius' own household, let us examine what can be discovered about his material resources (*facultates*) and the demands made on them, mindful of the material world's profound influence on his well-being and general outlook. In chapter 1 we observed the evidence for his financial involvement with the partisans of Pope Symmachus, which indicates that he owned enough real property to provide him with a respectable income (for a clergyman) and thus to act as guarantor of a loan, but not so much that he could afford to overlook protracted failure to repay it.[107] Was he eventually obliged to reimburse the lender with his own funds? In the present state of the evidence, the question is unanswerable. Of some relevance, however, is that Ennodius' final missive on the subject of the Symmachus loan comes approximately two years after the suite of house and garden epigrams, and about another year

---

104. #164, vv. 7–14, 15–16; cf.#188, on the vintage. Triumphant laurel: #346, vv. 14–15; #351, v. 10.

105. #164, vv. 15–16: *largus opum poscat maioris praemia voti, / hoc satis est nobis, quod sine fraude libet.*

106. Curtius, *European Literature and the Latin Middle Ages,* 200 and n. 32. Sharing some vocabulary with #163 and #164, #264 uses Theoderic's horticultural preserve to address themes of hereditary merit (propagated by grafting) and Hesperidean plenty.

107. Clergymen were expected to be financially independent without engaging in sordid occupations, which means income from real estate. Arles 2 (442–506), can. 14; *Stat. Eccl. Antiq.* 28–29 (47, 52); Agde (506), can. 22 (*CCSL* 148). *Brev. Hippon.* 15; Carthage (345–48), can. 6, 9, 13; *Canones in causa Apiarii* 16, 32 (*CCSL* 149); *CJ, Nov.* 6.1,5,9.

and a half later, indications of interest in other real estate begin to appear in the corpus.[108] The first sign is a letter to Boethius regarding a house; four more will follow. Ennodius apparently sought either another refuge from his cares or a property to replace the one he lost to creditors; in any event, the Church would benefit.

When he wrote to Boethius on the occasion of the latter's appointment as Western consul for 510, Ennodius had already sent him at least two letters, trying to cultivate a friendship with someone whose family background, wealth, and erudition overshadowed any difficulties his political and religious views might have occasioned.[109] All recognized consulships as a time for exceptional generosity, so Ennodius took the opportunity to seek a more substantial sign of Boethius' favor through the exercise of great subtlety and decorum. Performing his epistolary duties "full of the best hope," he elaborates on his correspondent's merits, most notably his present office and incomparable mastery of Greek and Latin style, and declares himself happy at seeing a kinsman so exalted.[110] Then, five-sixths of the way through his missive, Ennodius comes to the point. He beseeches the honor of a reply and "that, in whatever style you wish, you grant me the house in the city of Milan which both your affluence and neglect have practically abandoned already."[111] Ennodius supports his request by stating, in traditional Roman fashion, that it was only right that Boethius benefit members of his own family with his patrimony. By showing his generosity in this way, moreover, Boethius can expect something from Ennodius in return. "Believe me, as God is my witness, that if I should deserve to obtain my request without harming your assets, I will reciprocate, bound as it were by the gift, with more vigorous devotion"; the unusually businesslike final sentence asks that the donation be confirmed in writing.[112]

The remaining letters in the series show that Ennodius received some form of confirmation, but not the house itself. The next communication,

---

108. #300 (Easter–June 508); the Boethius dossier (#370, #408, #413, #415, #418) begins in late 509 or early 510.

109. #271 (autumn 507) and #318 (high summer 508). He had favored Laurentius for pope; his fortune: *Cons.* 3.3.5.

110. #370.1–7, beginning *optimae spei plenus.*

111. #370.7: *ut domum quam in Mediolanensi civitate et abundantia vestra et neglectus propemodum iam reliquit mihi quo vultis genere concedatis;* cf. #9, to Faustus on Avienus' consulship.

112. #370.8: *credite mihi deo teste quia si inpetrare sine detrimento census vestri meruero, quasi dono obligatus obsequiis potioribus respondebo . . . si securus esse debeo, plenarii mihi documenti dirigite firmitatem.*

hurriedly composed almost a year later (end 510), claims Ennodius sent "masses of letters about the house" he had requested, exhorting Boethius to hand over the property if possible, "because all of its structures are decaying from neglect."[113] Shortly after this, three more letters appear in close succession. In the first one, Ennodius compliments Boethius on his epistolary gifts, then fears his addressee is being equivocal and even cold towards him, but makes no mention of the house.[114] The second and third focus directly on the house, appealing to a written promise Boethius made not to refuse Ennodius the property and asking him, yet again, to get on with it, but this dossier is something other than "a series of shameless begging letters."[115] For whatever reason—personal antipathy, carelessness, unspecified legal encumbrances—Boethius appears to have reneged altogether on his commitment to transfer title to a house. Ennodius had cited this dwelling's dilapidated condition as proof that its proprietor had no use for it. Like many extremely wealthy people in antiquity, Boethius owned a variety of far-flung properties, most of which he probably never saw; we may wonder if he even wanted to, given his interests. On the other hand, Ennodius the deacon of Milan was ever alert to opportunities that would benefit his church's patrimony, especially when it came to neglected pieces of urban real estate. Although nothing in the legal sources suggests he was bound to leave property acquired during his diaconate or at any time before his episcopal consecration to the Church, that institution would have been the moral inheritor of a man with few definite relatives and no evident biological heirs.[116]

During the same period of frustration with Boethius, a second set of communications shows Ennodius pursuing inquiries among his friends with an eye to purchasing a property outside Milan (*suburbanum*) with other money.[117] He begins in summer 510 with a letter to Florus, a younger associate of Faustus, asking him to urge Faustus to order that a villa already discussed be purchased, "if the price given by me is deemed worthy"; Ennodius is to enjoy the property while he is in Liguria, while

---

113. #408: *crebras super domo quam poposci litteras destinavi . . . iam referte, quia omnia aedificia eius sub neglegentia consenescunt.*

114. #413 (early 511).

115. #415.2–5, #418 (early 511). So Moorhead, *Theoderic,* 167, though his "8.12 to Florus" (#389), is not even about Boethius' house.

116. Carthage (435) III.49 (*CCSL* 149); Agde (506), can. 6 (*CCSL* 148); *CJ* 1.3.41, 5–7, (a. 528); Just. *Nov.* 131.13; Greg. Mag. *Ep.* 4.36, 12.14.

117. Moorhead (*Theoderic,* 168) thought this villa "took the place of the *domus* sought in vain from Boethius."

Faustus and his people shall have it after his decease.[118] Faustus himself then receives two letters on the same subject, the second by way of Florus, while Ennodius was still gravely ill.[119] A year later, he has recovered but the transaction has still not gone through when he writes Avienus, requesting that Avienus conclude the negotiations for the property with Liberius' help; Ennodius tells him that if the agreement should change, the price be paid to prevent further doubt.[120] A few months afterward (autumn 511), the deal finally closed. Ennodius sent a slave back to his master, the doctor-deacon Helpidius in Ravenna, to inform him and Faustus that "the legal documents concerning that villa" had arrived so that then Helpidius and Triggua the Goth could see to the necessary arrangements.[121] The number and sort of people involved in obtaining this out-of-town property invite comment. Ennodius' ill health disposed him to buy a place in the country, but the delay suggests his choice was hampered by legal and/or financial difficulties, perhaps related to the settlement of Theoderic's Goths in northern Italy.[122] Such a factor would account for the participation of Liberius the patrician, the Goth Triggua, and Helpidius, as well as explain why Ennodius wrote Liberius around the same time to praise him for having accommodated the Goths without financial detriment.[123]

The letter to Helpidius just mentioned reminds us that Ennodius, both as a private individual and as part of his ecclesiastical responsibilities, was concerned not only with real estate but with people who were property. Some, like Helpidius' slave, belong to his correspondents and act as messengers.[124] Others fled acts of cruelty to seek refuge with the Church: his duty was to protect them even if, as once happened, someone accused him of seizing his domestics. In that case, Ennodius stated violence had been done to "the two boys" (*pueri duo*), who publicly appealed to the Church

---

118. #389.1: *insiste domno, ut suburbanum illud, dato si dignatur a me pretio, comparari iubeat: quod dum in Liguria fuero, feliciter habeam et post obitum meum ipse suique possideant;* cf. #16.2. *PLRE* 2, 482 (Florus 4). Moorhead, *Theoderic,* 230–31.

119. #395, #396, both contemporaneous with Florus' letter.

120. #429.2 (summer 511); cf. #447 to Liberius. Moorhead, *Theoderic,* 168, locates the affair within Faustus' term as praetorian prefect; Avienus and Liberius presumably saw to the details.

121. #445.2: *me de suburbano illo documenta legitima suscepisse.*

122. The settlement: Moorhead, *Theoderic,* 33–35.

123. #447 to Liberius, contemporary with #445; O'Donnell, "Liberius the Patrician," 44. Triggua (aka Triwila, Triwa): *PLRE* 2, 1126–27; Moorhead, *Theoderic,* 73–75, 228; Amory, *People and Identity,* 423–24.

124. E.g., #446.2 to Faustus: *servos vestros de Venetiis iam regressos.*

for aid.[125] He also assisted a blind woman to recover her slave from the clutches of an unscrupulous tenant farmer.[126] Still other slaves are fugitives rightfully sought by their masters. The unidentified bearer of a letter to Laconius in Gaul is "a well-born person coming on account of his runaways," and Ennodius tells Faustus, "I suspect that I have found your runaway boy, Germanus by name, who slipped off three years ago."[127] Fugitives figure in one late letter (summer 510), when Ennodius copiously thanks someone for an unspecified favor, then asks that he have "the rest of those slaves" held forthwith; whose they were is unknown.[128]

In addition to interacting with masters and slaves as part of his ecclesiastical responsibilities, Ennodius also possesses slaves of his own, several of whom apparently spend a good deal of time conveying their master's dispatches and retrieving replies. An early letter to Faustus states that "boys" have been sent to find out how the correspondent and his family are; the same is done for Avienus, with references elsewhere to "my own bearer," "my own people," and a "boy" sent to bring back a horse.[129] This is typical of how he refers to his servants. When he wishes to emphasize humility and subordination in his friends and himself, he resorts to "domestic" (*famulus*) or, implicitly conveying his own status, the continual use of "lord" (*domine*).[130]

Slaves could be emancipated by means of a testamentary disposition or a proclamation in church; Italian papyri and Gallic ecclesiastical documents amply attest to the procedure.[131] For Agapitus, a future urban prefect and consul, Ennodius composed something special: a formal declaration of manumission in a Roman ecclesiastical setting. For us this text

---

125. #11.3–4, to Faustus; the unnamed man was relying on Theoderic's support. Cf. Saller, *Patriarchy, Property and Death*, 147.

126. #275, also to Faustus. The tenant's attitude (*rustica temeritas*): Brown, *Cult of the Saints*, 119.

127. #86.2: *bene natum hominem propter fugaces suos venientem;* #89: *fugacem puerum vestrum Germanum vocabulo, qui ante triennium lapsus est* (both Easter–end 504).

128. #392.2 (*residua illa mancipia*), to the otherwise unknown Edasius: *PLRE* 2, 385.

129. #19.4 (*pueros destinavi*); #75.1 (*puerum turbatus direxi*). Cf. #83.2; #288.1 (*domesticus perlator*); #152.1 (*familiaris perlator*); #252.2 (*homines meos*); #301.3 (*proprius perlator / homo meus*); #397 (*puerum . . . ad suscipiendum caballum*).

130. Cf. #396 to Faustus, referring to a friend (*Florum confamulum meum*). Religious vocation did not impede slave owning: Jones, *Later Rom. Emp.,* 851 and n. 66; McLynn, *Ambrose,* 67–68; Garnsey, *Ideas of Slavery,* 31–34, 84–85, 233–35.

131. Tjäder, *Die nichtliterarischen Papyri,* P.9 and P.20; Nîmes (394/396), can. 7; Orange (441), can. 6; Arles 2 (442–506), can. 33–34; Agde (506), can. 7 (*CCSL* 148). Cf. Dubois, *La latinité,* 30; Vismara, "Le *Causae Liberales*"; Garnsey, *Ideas of Slavery,* 98–100.

marks the event; at the time it was presented the document may have encouraged Agapitus to do something besides freeing the "boy" Gerontius whose virtues it praises, for the letter that precedes it asks him to act upon a "hint" (*suggestionem*) made by the bearer.[132] After introducing his subject, the speaker pleads that Roman citizenship be given to an individual he knows well, Gerontius, "whose faith, modesty and probity both demand freedom and gain renown by their gifts"; speaking before Pope Symmachus, he claims to appear "not so much the bestower as the witness" of Gerontius' release.[133] The equation of emancipation with "citizenship" transcends actual legal distinctions of slave/free and *humiliores/honestiores* to invoke a more venerable image of Roman political identity.[134] His next observations serve to justify the proceedings: "The just servitude of the aforementioned has shown me his character is not servile. I therefore desire not so much to grant freeborn status to the person named as to restore it. I know that he, who deserved to be thought a free man before he was called it, has rightly rejected a contemptible name."[135] Rationalizing the act and making public the exemplary nature of Gerontius' life, the address' performative utterance is "I restore freedom to the same individual, supplicating Your Crown that by the acts of the Church he may be released from all subjection, so that he can delight in the perpetual association of the City of Rome, granted all of his property without any diminution."[136]

After attending to the practical legal details, the speaker promises a future of "gifts still more mighty" for Gerontius; whether they were spiritual or material in nature, as would befit the freedman of a future consul, remains unclear.[137] The highly pragmatic context of undiminished prop-

---

132. #123 (Jan.–Aug. 505), freeing the *Gerontius puer* of Agapitus, addressee of #122, PVR 508/9, cos. 517: *PLRE* 2, 30–32 (Fl. Agapitus 3). The next letter to Agapitus (#146) is late 505 or early 506. Gerontius does not reappear; Moorhead, *Theoderic,* 151–52, 156.

133. #123.3: *cuius a me conperta fides pudor integritas et exigit libertatem et suis dotibus innotescit . . . cuius ego absolutionis non tam largitor quam testis existo.* Symmachus was present (5: *supplicans coronae vestrae*); cf. #226.1 and #409.1.

134. Garnsey, *Ideas of Slavery,* 201–2.

135. #123.4: *ostendit mihi iusta praedicti servitus personam non esse servilem. ergo nominato non tam cupio ingenuitatem tribui quam refundi. scio quod recte vile nomen expulerit, qui ante ingenuus credi meruit quam vocari.*

136. #123.5: *eidem restituo libertatem, supplicans coronae vestrae ut gestis ecclesiasticis ex omni obnoxietate solvatur, ut perpetuo Romanae urbis possit exultare collegio, omni peculio suo sine aliqua inminutione concesso.* Implications of "Roman citizenship": Amory, *People and Identity,* 21.

137. #123.5: *nec fas est ei de adquisitis quidquam minui, quem polliceor donis etiam potioribus subsequendum.*

erty and more gifts to come favors an interpretation that embraces both possibilities. The most plausible scenario is germane to Ennodius' diaconal responsibilities and personal preoccupations: Gerontius received his freedom so he could join the Roman clergy, taking his money with him, and perhaps bringing an additional benefaction from his former master. While Ennodius remained a deacon, he had no need to worry about the canonical legality of any gifts that came his way; if he had to assist the Church's work with his own resources, he could do so freely. Bishops, however, had to beware of inciting scandal when handling money and property; recall the allegations that Pope Symmachus unlawfully alienated Church property.[138]

Nonetheless, Ennodius managed to keep the minutiae of conveyancing and property management under control, leaving time to admire smaller things whose attraction lay in their beauty and utility. In chapter 2 we saw that the goldsmith's skills were a dominant metaphor throughout Ennodius' works, but he also treasured the tangible products of similar work in silver, featuring them in at least ten epigrams. Several of them describe dishes embellished with personages from traditional mythology or, in one case, a live human being, that stand as verbal analogies to the "picture plates" that survive from Late Antiquity.[139]

The earliest item in Ennodius' works, "on a plate which has a cuirassed youth on a horse holding Victory in his hand," depicts a large round silver dish meant for display (*missorium*) ornamented with the figure of a "youth" on horseback holding an image of Victory.[140] The iconography of victorious rulership it represents had developed since the Hellenistic period, circulating in a variety of media from coins to sculpture to gameboards.[141] If we look at this epigram in full, certain details of the object Ennodius describes suggest a singularly topical variation on the theme:

Behold, his victorious right hand holds the winged divinity.
He has come, and has no gear for the return journey.

---

138. Noethlichs, "Materialien zum Bischofsbild," 50–51; McLynn, *Ambrose,* 55–56; Pietri, "Le Sénat," 133–38; Wirbelauer, *Zwei Päpste,* 18.

139. Toynbee and Painter, "Picture Plates."

140. #126, *in missorio quod habet loricatum iuvenem super equum tenentem victoriam in manu* (early 505). *Missoria:* Leclercq, "Disque"; Delbrueck, *Die Consulardiptychen,* 70; Strong, *Greek and Roman Silver Plate,* 199–201; Kent and Painter, *Wealth of the Roman World,* 20–25.

141. Grabar, *L'empereur dans l'art byzantin,* 31–84; MacCormack, *Art and Ceremony,* 222–59; McCormick, *Eternal Victory,* 11–68.

Bearing the fighting man, the thunderfoot rears up,
A good stranger at whom terror smiles in a work of art.
Let the scion renowned in Hyperborean fields learn
His nature's gift when he sees its likeness.

Ecce tenet victrix pinnatum dextera numen.
Venit et ad reditum non habet arma viae.
Pugnacem gestans sonipes per terga minatur,
Advena cui terror ridet in arte bonus.
Discat Hyperboreis famosum germen in arvis
Naturae genium, cum simulacra videt.

The fusion of hand-held statue and youthful rider, the latter alien yet abiding, is unusual but not unparalleled: standing or seated figures holding small Victories are known; so are equestrian generals, but not ones gripping *imagines.* Two ivory panels suggest what this *missorium* may have looked like. One commemorates the consulship of Probus, in which the emperor Honorius stands holding a Victory atop a globe; the other, the so-called Barberini diptych, shows an emperor astride a rearing horse, accompanied on his left by a palm-bearing winged Victory.[142] Ennodius' verses tell us both about the intended viewer and about the object itself, since the entire poem operates as a kind of gift tag or greeting card.[143] This rider is a fierce yet friendly young Goth possessed of the sign of victory, a traditional representation of the Roman emperor-general converted to the commemoration of Theoderic's military successes in Illyricum.[144] For its Gothic beholders the plate's substance and special embellishment conferred self-evident worth; Roman observers must have found still more in its implication that archetypal military vigor dwelt among them in barbarian guise. Ennodius' epigram celebrates the paradox of a thoroughly Roman medium of artistic production transforming a scene of mortal ter-

---

142. Kitzinger, *Byzantine Art in the Making,* figs. 70, 176; Delbrueck, *Die Consulardiptychen,* 188–96. Cf. Schramm, *Herrschaftszeichen und Staatssymbolik* 1, 227–29 (the Senigallia medallion).

143. #126, vv. 3–6. Horse as *advena:* #212 (Ennodius' Hunnish horse). Gift tags: Lausberg, *Das Einzeldistichon,* 343–58; Leary, *Martial Book XIV,* 5–9, 21–23. Format and audience: Heather, *Goths,* 235.

144. #263.28–30 and 83 (his early years; the Gothic *pubes indomita*). No survey of Theoderic's portraiture includes #126 (Vollenweider, *Deliciae Leonis,* 197–98; Wolfram, *History,* 289, 307; Johnson, "Toward a History," 74), which links to events in Illyricum (#263.60–69): Croke, "Mundo the Gepid," 129; Moorhead, *Theoderic,* 174–75. *Iuvenis* as Gothic military might: Cass. *Var.* esp. 1.24, 38; Amory, *People and Identity,* 93–96.

ror into a brilliant exaltation of alien military might. In so doing, he has conserved a hitherto unrecognized panel of the mosaic of Theoderic's self-presentation, for a king who desired to appear a Goth to Goths and a lover of Rome to Romans found the tradition of Roman imperial art too impressive to reject.

Decidedly less political in nature is Ennodius' virtuosic thumbnail sketch (a single elegiac couplet) of a set of seven rectangular dishes. Since each dish bears a figural decoration taken from the ever-popular pursuit of hunting, he has fitted the name of each figure, beginning with that of the goddess of the hunt, into the compass of a single line: "Delia, stag, boar, tiger, lion, wild cow, leopard."[145] Representing the vessels on which they stand, this parade of game animals conveys a variety of dishes to the learned owner's table in the second half of the poem, which reminds us they had a practical function alongside the decorative one.

Next to this vision of beasts serving at table Ennodius celebrates a serving dish divided into seven sections.[146] What victuals this piece of table silver actually held interests him less than the fact that the same vessel can contain different sorts of food without mixing them together: "how well does one belly hold in silver what a conjoint order divides by fixed bounds!"[147] Ennodius manifests a similar preoccupation with divisions and separations elsewhere in his epigrams, most strikingly in a series inspired by tableware decorated with the figures of Pasiphae and the bull. One cluster concerns the drinking vessel "of a certain person" whom Ennodius leaves nameless, obviously because of the man's fascination with sexual perversity, and contemplates the artifice both of the article and of Pasiphae's mythic situation.[148] The longest poem of a later group about a set of rectangular dishes embellished with Jove's sexual intrigues also dwells on Pasiphae's story.[149] Given Ennodius' passion for correct linguistic usage, we can readily appreciate his interest in this myth, since the union of Pasiphae and the divinely-sent bull gave rise to the monstrous

145. #129: *Delia cervus aper tigris leo bucula pardus / adportant mensis fercula, docte, tuis.* Cf. Toynbee and Painter, "Picture Plates," 19–20, pl. XVIb, XXa, XXIa–b; Schröder, *Titel und Text,* 206–7.

146. #130, *epigramma de conpostile habente septem gavatas.* The vessel's name: Lazard, "Les byzantinismes lexicaux," 377; cf. Mart. 11.31.

147. #130, vv. 3–4: *limitibus certis quod iunctus dividit ordo, / unus in argento quam bene venter habet!*

148. #133, #136, #136a, #136b (all 505), *versus de cauco cuiusdam habente pasiphae et taurum.* The vessel's name is a Greek loan-word (*kauka*): Jer. *Adv. Jovinian.* 2.14.

149. #232 (the silversmith's work; Jove's crimes teach by negative example), #232a (the divine adulterer's falsehoods moralized), #233 (Daedalus' *vacca biformis* for Pasiphae).

Minotaur, a graphic illustration of the awful consequences of combining things better left apart. The issue of improper combinations surfaces in other instances of juxtaposition in both verse and prose. One epigram concerns a person "who was said to be the son of a whore and a donkey"; the Latin makes the mother a she-wolf, alluding to the myth of Rome's foundation.[150] The union of material contraries provokes two moral *dictiones:* one censures a man for placing a statue of Minerva in a brothel, another denounces a tyrant who proposed to honor a parricide with a statue among the heroes.[151]

An epigrammatic tribute to a true wonder of the ancient world, the craft of marble-cutting, belongs among the writings on smaller works because Ennodius focuses on the application of a specialized decorative technique rather than the construction of an entire house or church. He portrays marble masons' zeal to "create nature, with the flesh of stones constrained by the law of fusion . . . he who can assemble a single look from diverse pieces leads rock to obey him."[152] Using the beauties of ordered matter to embody the concept of obedience (*obsequium*), Ennodius salutes the universal principle that, for him, orchestrates both civilization and civilized nature.[153]

Some items that Ennodius thought interesting enough to transpose into verse belonged to noble ladies of his acquaintance. Two pieces of gold jewelry owned by Firmina, a Gallic *inlustris femina* known for her good works, are so featured: a necklace of workmanship "so delicate that it is kept in a little holder" and a ring engraved with a hunting scene.[154] Wrought of incredibly fine interwoven golden filaments that seem to float and glow like a cloud, the necklace deceives the eye even as the hand grasps it. The ring's appeal is akin to that of the *missorium* of Theoderic discussed earlier, a static work of art that has the capacity to contain an

---

150. #132, *versus de eo qui dicebatur meretricis filius et asellionis esse;* v. 2: *quem lupa sordenti conceptum fudit asello.*

151. #243 (tyrant/parricide); #278 (Minerva/brothel).

152. #209, vv. 1–2: *visceribus lapidum permixta lege coactis / naturam faciunt artificum studia;* 5–6: *unam de variis speciem conponere frustis / qui potuit, saxum duxit in obsequium;* Kennell, "Hercules' Invisible Basilica."

153. *Obsequium* is ubiquitous in Ennodius' writings. Cf. #240 (the bear); #43; #163; #266 (a tractable horse).

154. #165, #165a–c: *de murena inl. f. Firminae quae in septacia* [B; *septicio* other MSS; *pistacio* Vogel] *clauditur, ita tenuis est;* #229. Cf. #305 (from 508) and Pope Gelasius, to a "Firmina," *Epistolae Romanorum Pontificum,* 501; Hill, "Constantinopolis," 146; Killick, "Optical and Electron Microscopy."

affective subject and so alter its significance: fleeing rabbits, raging bears, and roaring lions become charmingly docile when captured in metal.[155] Gold also appears in complimentary connection with another Gallic lady, Bassus' wife Viola, metaphorically embellishing her sedan-chair (*basterna*). That "roving shelter" gleams gold from the light of its mistress, whose radiance spreads everywhere; Ennodius praises Viola's merit, mediating her spiritual splendor through the matter of her conveyance.[156] In contrast, a poet of the *Anthologia Latina* saw only sedan-chairs' generic function: portative preservers of matronly purity that permitted women to travel without seeing or being seen by men.[157]

Besides silverware and jewelry, Ennodius also accorded epigrammatic treatment to a whip and a sword-stick. According to his words—"whoever gets a beating with metals of silver and gold mingles greedy joys with his weeping" and "no one scorns to suffer beautiful blows"—the whip's precious materials confer delight or honor on those it flogs.[158] Alluding to the owner, who is distinguished by his "learned mind," the title refers to the Arator we met in chapter 2 as "baby Arator."[159] The purpose of the whip, too grand to waste on unappreciative dumb animals, remains enigmatic, although the first epigram implies that Arator is using it on himself. The meaning of the "sword in a cudgel," on the other hand, is clear enough: "we use a blade enclosed by deception in a stick; / how well death hides, covered in husks of wood!"[160] Ennodius himself owns this discreet instrument of self-defense. He timelessly explains that "you carry protection because you are considered a terror by all: / what prohibits submission is our peacemaker."[161] While brigandage of all sorts made travel dangerous,

---

155. #229, vv. 2–6. Cf. #340, v. 6.

156. #332, v. 1: *quam vaga constantem retinent haec tecta decorem!* She was the wife of Bassus (*PLRE* 2, 219); cf. #25.6, #158.

157. *Anth. Lat.* 1.1, 125 (*Carm. Cod. Salmas.* 101).

158. #267; #267a: *argenti atque auri vapulat quicumque metallis, / gaudia cum fletu miscet avara suo;* #267b: *dentibus argenti fulvum concluditur aurum: / contempnat nullus verbera pulcra pati.* See Saller, *Patriarchy, Property and Death,* 145–46; Garnsey, "Sons, Slaves—and Christians," 116–20. *Infans* conveys familiarity, not age or status: #398.3 (*infantem Rufinum*); #448.2 (*infante Valentino*); Mart. 8.46.

159. #267, *versus de flagello infantis Aratoris.* Text: *quae capiant mundum, iunxit mens docta flagello / exornans censu nobilitante plagas.*

160. #338, *de spata in fuste* (winter 508/9) vv. 1–2: *utimur incluso per fraudes ense bacillo; / mors ligni tunicis quam bene tecta latet;* cf. Amory, *People and Identity,* 96.

161. #338, vv. 3–4: *subsidium portas, quod cunctis terror haberis: / pacificum est nobis quod negat obsequium.*

brandishing swords was not recommended for Romans and clergymen, either; Ennodius evidently found a covert form of defense desirable.[162]

In addition to this ingenious concealed weapon, Ennodius also apparently owned a *missorium* and dazzling drinking bowl, whose existence he signaled in a pair of one-line epigrams. He moralizes on the bowl's thirst-quenching utility in a manner recalling the house epigrams we examined earlier.[163] The plate's design is rather curious, for the likeness it bears is the poet's own: "Ennodius' reward is his form in rich metals."[164] Characteristically, one of the gifts Ennodius treasured most was a small-scale portrait in silver, fitting counterpart to the miniature verse ekphrases he composed for his friends and himself; once he became a bishop and founded a church, a larger likeness would be possible.

The vignettes involving animals reveal with particular clarity how Ennodius associated with the better sort of people and participated in their pastimes. Horses interest him most. In one epigram, he characterizes a tractable old horse as yet another participant in the universal ritual of obedience; without the cooperation of this creature whose smooth gait he commends, he might not have enjoyed the night ride he later turned into poetry.[165] Ennodius described another horse he received as a gift as "Hunnish," and his verses leave no doubt that the animal came from a Gothic acquaintance: "after conquering the nations, after rivers of gore so great, / a second master owns you, but the same work remains; / leave the war-trumpet, you about to suffer blessed chants."[166] This animal reappears in a later epigram, "on the bay horse and the dappled one," its looks and merits distinctly inferior in comparison to what must be the old reliable Po Valley horse.[167] Ennodius may have had others, but only these two horses rated poetic immortality. The more trustworthy animal was rather elderly;

---

162. Were hidden weapons less apt to provoke aggression? *CTh* 15.15.1, forbidding civilians to bear arms, was suspended in 440: *Nov. Val.* 9; cf. *Nov. Maj.* 8. The post-519 situation: *An. Val.* 83.

163. #211 (early 506): *parturit unda sitim quam splendens conca ministrat.*

164. #210 (early 506): *divitibus pretium est Ennodi forma metallis.*

165. #266, *de equo suo sene*, vv. 1–2: *fixior annoso sonipes moderamine noster / nunc iuvenem blando sustinet obsequio;* cf. #330. See Scheibelreiter, *Bischof in merowingischer Zeit*, 205–6 (Eligius of Noyon's favorite horse: *MGH SRM* 4, 726).

166. Perhaps a gift from Triggua: #212, *de equo quem accepit hunisco*, vv. 5–8: *post domitas gentes, post flumina tanta cruoris, / alter te dominus, sed manet ipse labor. / linque precor lituum, cantus passure beatos: / captivus pacis mitteris obsequiis.*

167. #355, *de equo badio et balane*, v. 5: *Padanus sonipes;* cf. #266. A Germanic word: Blaise, *Dictionnaire latin-français*, s.v. *balan*, "noir tacheté de blanc"; Amory, *People and Identity*, 103.

two letters to the patrician Agnellus show that Ennodius made inquiries about a possible replacement. According to the first letter, though Agnellus had not written lately he had extravagantly promised Ennodius a horse, so Ennodius asks him to amend the omission by seeing to the beast's arrival.[168] Ennodius fell very ill afterward and did not write to Agnellus again until the following summer to explain his situation. He informs his friend that he has delegated a slave to fetch the horse, so all Agnellus need do is send it along; the deed will redound to his credit and Ennodius' joy.[169] Since Ennodius sends someone after the horse, then makes no further reference to it, he presumably received it.[170]

After horses, creatures of the hunt claim a fair share of Ennodius' regard. The likeness of a hunting dog appeared on the lady Firmina's ring, and a nearby epigram presents a Cretan hound, anthropomorphically called "little man" (*homullus*) yet vividly endowed with doggy attributes—nose, lope, bark—which energetically affect the domain of wild things.[171] Another epigram describes waterfowl peaceably bobbing upon the swollen Po, but Ennodius is more interested in hunting them with hawks and sending them to his friends; in fact, a gift duck accompanies one letter that mentions a successful day of fowling.[172] This combination of clerical status and venery, though jovially medieval, is difficult to justify in ascetic terms; a sixth-century Gallic canon suggests the deacon of Milan may have been sailing rather close to the prevailing moral wind, even with borrowed hunting gear.[173]

Outside the world of hunting, it is mules that draw Ennodius' attention for empirical and aesthetic reasons. As a literary man with direct knowledge of Gaul, he found Claudian's encomium of Gallic mules deserving of rebuttal. His poetic predecessor perhaps witnessed the prodigiously silent docility of one group of these beasts, but Ennodius writes of another whose manners are quite different.[174] The origin of mules suggested an

---

168. #359.1: *de caballo promisso* (Aug.–Sept. 509).

169. #397 (summer–fall 510).

170. Cf. #443, the last letter to Agnellus (fall 511); contrast Moorhead, *Theoderic,* 167 (a fruitless venture).

171. #231, perhaps a jewelry ekphrasis as well; cf. Vollenweider, *Deliciae Leonis,* 81–82 (no. 127). The other side of *homullus:* #326a.

172. #353; #337.3: *de volucribus tamen munus singulare destinavi quod cepit accipiter . . . solam anatem direximus,* to the still-virginal Maximus (fall 508); cf. Verg. *Ecl.* 8.75.

173. Léglise, *Oeuvres,* 1, 403. Epaon (517), can. 4: *Episcopis, presbyteris aut diaconibus canes ad venandum aut accepitres habere non liceat* (inserted as Agde [506], can. 8 [55]) (*CCSL* 148).

174. #328, *epigramma adversus Claudianum de mulabus,* against Claud. *CM* 18 (51).

aesthetic theme to him as well; the observations he makes in four epigrams exploiting the idea of miscegenation between asses and mares intersect with the treatment of Pasiphae and the ass-wolf hybrid.[175]

From a menagerie of beasts often reminiscent of people, Ennodius takes a short step to epigrams that illustrate a variety of humans, generally wicked or at least peculiar, who sometimes turn into animals. Many of the individuals he presents are prey to the common social vices connected with food, drink, and sex, whereas others incur his disapproval for more diverse reasons. All reveal his talent for traditional invective.

Ennodius' animadversions on the way certain people deal with food and drink first take epigrammatic form in three little pieces about a man noted for synchronizing the funerals of his children with his dinner parties, an irresistible amalgam of grief and gluttony.[176] About fifty items further along stands a cluster of verses from early 506 inspired by greed. There are three epigrams "on a certain old enemy, a fool who eats well" because he devours the lifeblood of the poor, another about a man who gives dinners for the wrong reasons, and one that concerns an unnamed glutton who kept impugning the poet's "holy work."[177] After such harshness, Ennodius allows himself something more light-hearted: an elaborate, food-related ethnic pun with a historical basis. It remarks on the amusing coincidence that a man of Gallic parentage (*Gallus*) is fond of consuming the birds that once saved Rome (*anseres*), in other words, a rooster who likes to eat geese.[178] With direct address heightening the sense of familiarity, several later epigrams involving aristocratic Ligurian acquaintances dramatize the pleasures of the vine, referring even to the now-questionable Bacchus.[179]

Although Ennodius never admits to having had anything personally to do with sex, apart from the one allusion to his early, short-lived marriage discussed in chapter 1, he is undeniably intrigued by the structural implications of copulation and sexual difference. We have already encountered an epigram about a supposed son of a she-wolf and an ass in connection

---

175. #329, #329a–c, *de asino et equa;* cf. D'Angelo, "Tematiche omosessuali," 650–51.

176. #134, #134a–b (early 505). Cf. Caes. Arel. *Serm.* 54.5–6; Halsall, "Origins of the Rei-hengräberzivilisation," 205.

177. #184, *de quodam veteri inimico stulto et bene pascente,* and #184a–b catalogue the man's greedy excesses; see #184a, v. 1: *visceribus miserorum et sanguine pauperis aucte.* #189 may allude to the *Libellus* (v. 1: *nescio cur sancto non parcas, stulte, labori*); Symmachus awaited full vindication: Vogel, xxix; Wirbelauer, *Zwei Päpste,* 39–40.

178. #191, *de eo quod cum ipse Gallos parentes haberet anseres amabat comedere,* is a pair of elegiac couplets alluding to the Gauls' invasion of Rome (390 B.C.).

179. #364, #364a–c; cf. #365, #374. Honoratus (*PLRE* 2, 567–68), probably Decoratus' brother (*PLRE* 2, 350–51): #311; Cassiod. *Var.* 5.4; Moorhead, *Theoderic,* 230.

with the Pasiphae myth, but Ennodius knows of other individuals who
mingle attributes of both sexes in a single body. Four of his epigrams comment on a bisexual adulterer. Setting the tone for the rest, the first expos-
tulates, "A man by your face, a woman in your bearing, but in the leg,
what both are, / Settling the disputes of nature with no resolution, / You
are a hare, and you tread the neck of so great a lion underfoot!"[180]
Another poem, four lines "about a certain person of indefinite lifestyle and
sordid habits," decries a "she-man" who may or may not be the same individual as the human rabbit of the previous set, since the person here aggra-
vates his failure to commit to a single gender by compulsive chatter that
moves Ennodius to call him a "hermaphroditic magpie."[181] Lacking in
sexual ambiguity but revolting all the same remains Ennodius' graphic
portrayal of a degenerate blind man who refuses to let his suppurating eyes
deter him from the straight path of vice.[182]

Not everyone Ennodius lampoons lacks a name, though at least one
may come from the epigrams of Martial and Ausonius. Ennodius gives the
name Galla to an older woman who, he claims, feigns pregnancy's nausea
in order to preserve her shameless union with a younger man, thus contra-
vening the whole Roman (and Christian) notion of marriage as a means of
producing legitimate offspring.[183] The two males he troubles to name have
more definite identities. One is a eunuch called Tribunus with whom Ennodius must have become acquainted at the court in Ravenna. Despite passionate efforts to win riches and respect, Tribunus remains a twitchy bun-
dle of insecurities, compounded by his irreparable rootlessness; lacking
manhood and fatherland, he can never amount to anything in Ennodius'
eyes.[184] The other male object of Ennodius' satire is the estimable
Boethius, otherwise known as a paragon of virtue and erudition. With

---

180. #179; #180: *vir facie, mulier gestu, sed crure quod ambo, / iurgia naturae nullo discrimine solvens, / es lepus, et tanti conculcas colla leonis;* #180a–c. Cf. Ps. 90 (91).13; Sid.
Apoll. *Epist.* 5.7; D'Angelo, "Tematiche omosessuali," 650.

181. #238, *de quodam incerti propositi et vitae turpis.* Text: *tot rebus fallax quid garris, pica
biformis, / semivir et tremulo qui vexas turpia lumbo? / quod tibi propositum, qui sexus constitit
umquam? / quid non mentiris, vir femina, sancte profane?* Cf. #452.3; *Anth. Lat.* 1.1, 262 (Luxorius, *Carm. Cod. Salmas.* 317). Manliness under constant attack, eunuchs a counterex-
ample: Brown, *Body and Society,* 10–12.

182. #265, vv. 1–2, 10: *nil videt, et rectum servat iter scelerum.*

183. #217. Cf. *Anth. Lat.* 1.1, 254–55 (Luxorius, *Carm. Cod. Salmas.* 301). Mart. 2. 25, 34;
3. 51, 54, 90; 4. 38, 58; 7. 18, 58; 9. 4, 37; 10. 75, 95; Auson. *Epig.* 14. Her iniquity: Brown,
Body and Society, 20–25.

184. #190, vv. 5: *vis dici locuples sublimis pulcher amicus;* 8–10: *mendicus vetulus timidus
confusus anhelus, / his verum perdens utere nominibus;* #190b, v. 1: *instabilem faciunt naturae
damna Tribunum.* Cf. #190a, #190c; D'Angelo, "Tematiche omosessuali," 651.

other reasons to be unhappy with him, Ennodius alleges the great man was better suited to amorous exploits because he was so unwarlike that he could turn swords to flowing water or womanly distaffs.[185]

Because this chapter focuses on Ennodius' interactions with visible, material reality, it includes his criticisms of people who fail to behave appropriately. His work for the diocese of Milan enmeshed him in a multitude of legal matters, bringing him face to face with various odd personalities. Ennodius lampoons an inept advocate for summoning up an assortment of divergent affects while understanding nothing, and throws color-based puns at a man from the Veneto who presumed to mock his Gallic compatriots.[186] He castigates another well-born malefactor for his weakness for horses, alleging the man's posterior dishonored those noble creatures.[187] A Roman acquaintance who grows a Gothic-style beard and dons a barbarian traveling cloak rouses his indignation as well, since Ennodius' essentially grammatical views on the mingling of incompatible things require that Romans be distinguished from Goths.[188] The strictures of Ennodius' faith and vocation occasionally emerge as epigrams: one judiciously allusive poem comments on religious life's effect on human nature and another ponders on the fall and redemption of man.[189]

A few individuals command Ennodius' admiration regardless of their power to help or harm. Two poems celebrate a fellow litigant's winning technique and tactics: "you stir up wars and thrive on the plunder you have carried off."[190] His true sentiments cloaked in ambiguous oxymorons, Ennodius salutes the invincibility of his adversary, "who accuses with a smile, who slays serenely," perfection of style and substance forbidding all demur.[191] The eminent grammarian Deuterius, whose skills Enn-

---

185. #339, *de Boetio spata cincto* (winter 508/9), vv. 2–4: *solvitur atque chalybs more fluentis aquae. / emollit gladios inbellis dextera Boeti; / ensis erat dudum, credite, nunc colus est.* Shanzer, "Ennodius, Boethius"; Barnish, "Maximian, Cassiodorus," 17–21. It follows #338, the sword-stick item.

186. #143, vv. 5–6: *ira pavor rabies patientia tempore in uno; / tot facies gestas pectoribus vacuis;* #148.

187. #193, vv. 1–3: *gaudet equis recti dissuasor <et> prodigus aequi, / nomina qui digna studio superante caballis / subtrahit, opponens ad sancta vocabula clunem.* Unlike *Anth. Lat.* 1.1, 143 (*Carm. Cod. Salmas.* 148), it lacks sexual innuendo.

188. #182: *barbaricam faciem Romanos sumere cultus / miror et inmodico distinctas corpore gentes;* #182a–c; Murga, "Tres leyes de Honorio"; Moorhead, *Theoderic,* 83; Amory, *People and Identity,* 338–47.

189. #192, cf. *Anth. Lat.* 1.1, 255–56 (Luxorius, *Carm. Cod. Salmas.* 303); #169, cf. Gen. 3.3.

190. #186, *de defensore callido,* v. 9: *bella cies spoliis crescis, defensor, ademptis;* #194.

191. #194, vv. 5–6: *credite, non aliter Iustinus proelia tractat, / qui accusat ridens, qui perimit placidus.*

odius commended so profusely in the *dictio* for Parthenius, receives whole-hearted veneration. He praises the savant, who has been called to teach at Rome, literally to the skies in a verse *dictio* that fuses traditional and Christian imagery, mentioning both the Muses and their friends and Christ's triumph over death.[192] A separate epigram acclaims Deuterius for his "countless endowments," his equally exemplary words and actions: the silent Deuterius' "countenance and awesome baldness suffice for his students: they behold the Moon's full light."[193]

We have seen that Ennodius greatly admired those who put their book learning to practical use in teaching and litigation. Let us now look at the poems that are concerned with actual books. I mentioned earlier that Ennodius used Faustus' book cabinets to represent that gentleman's taste for literary learning.[194] He also left poems that refer to his own literary production and to an array of codices. About halfway through the corpus is preserved a ten-line "preface of the whole poetic work that he made," in which Ennodius claims to have received a kind of salvation from the Muses.[195] After having been awash in a sea of cares, the gifts of Delphi warmed, garlanded, and invigorated him so that he might welcome the bliss of song.[196] These verses capture the fleeting pleasures of literary inspiration. His religious vocation, however, would force him to be more circumspect about such idolatrous effusions, suggesting why he never produced a finished edition of his works. The trochees that gloss the virtues of a neatly arranged library show a comparable satisfaction in books as "that path which dispenses heavenly power."[197] Even if these books were not part of Ennodius' own holdings, his poem emphasizes the moral nourishment they supply rather than their precise content, like the suite of epigrams inspired by his own house.

In the context of Ennodius' interactions with the material world, the

---

192. #213 (early 506), vv. 7: *docta Camenarum coeat pia turba sororum;* 19–20: *te pene demessum ceu florem dextera fati / dum lacerat, Christus perculit exitium.* Call: vv. 13–14: *luminibus locuples solem te Roma vocavit / celsa, Quirinali suscipiens gremio;* cf. Kaster, *Guardians,* 267–69.

193. #234, vv. 1: *innumeris doctor dotibus ille cluit;* 9–10: *discipulis satis est vultus tacitique verenda / calvities: Phoebae lumina plena vident.* He resembles an exemplary bishop (but no sun of salvation). Cf. Synesius, *Encomium Calvitii.*

194. #70, *de epigrammatis per armaria domni Fausti factis.*

195. #187, *praefatio totius operis poetici quod fecit* (early 506).

196. #187, vv. 7–10: *tunc hederae viridis rubuerunt fronte corymbi, / Castalii mellis murmura blanda bibi. / continuo ponens marcentes pectore curas / conplector laudem carmina laetitiam.*

197. #327 (Aug.–Sept. 508), v. 1: *iste callis est supernam qui parat potentiam;* cf. #440 (books returned/borrowed).

Panegyric of Theoderic may seem out of place, but the king whose memory it preserves and the volumes of scholarship it has generated do outweigh the rest of Ennodius' *oeuvre* in concrete historical terms. By virtue of its subject, length, and rhetorical splendor, the *Panegyric* is the most fully realized monument of Ennodius' ekphrastic and narrative talents; its perceptiveness, tact, and brilliance of description commend the author as much as the king who inspired it. Recent studies have good reason to accept the standard dating of early 507, but other issues continue unresolved. Ennodius' personal allegiance to Theoderic is evident in his connections at the court of Ravenna and professional activities as spokesman and later bishop of Ticinum, a city of strategic importance to the Ostrogothic regime, but we do not even know which Church—Milan or Rome—called upon him to compose the *Panegyric*. Furthermore, there is no consensus regarding the *Panegyric*'s logical coherence and circumstances of delivery, or indeed whether it was delivered at all, and to what audience.[198] Unfortunately, constraints of length preclude trying to answer such questions here but, in pondering them, we all need to be conscious of how distant we are from the *Panegyric*. Great gulfs sunder the eloquent elite literacy of the Classical world from today's egalitarian inarticulateness, late antique aesthetic values from the twentieth century's, and Ennodius' sociopolitical circumstances from our own.

A reminder of those linguistic and aesthetic gulfs lies near to hand, in the suite of epigrams Ennodius composed to keep alive the memory of the bishops of Milan from Ambrose to Laurentius' predecessor Theodorus. These poems exist now only on paper, but they once possessed an eye-catchingly different form.[199] While demonstrably not the same as epitaphs, since that of Glycerius, fifth bishop after Ambrose, survives, they must have been inscribed somewhere in Milan with representations similar to the medallion-style *imagines clipeatae* of the popes formerly adorning the walls of S. Paolo fuori le mura in Rome.[200] Like much of Late Antique lit-

---

198. #263. No contributor to Whitby, *Propaganda of Power,* even cites it, but see Mac-Cormack, *Art and Ceremony,* 230–34 ("chaotic" performance/message); Rohr, *Theoderich-Panegyricus,* 16–26 (symmetrical structure; too "unverständlich" to deliver); Amory, *People and Identity,* 113–20 ("written for the government";"formally impressive"; "recited"). Cf. Grundmann, *"Litteratus-illitteratus,"* 14–34; Reydellet, "Ennodio," 692.

199. #195–206. Ambrose receives fourteen verses, Simplicianus twelve; the others have ten each. See Lausberg, *Das Einzeldistichon,* 149–50, 473–74; Pietri, *"Pagina in pariete reserata,"* 143–44.

200. Glycerius' epitaph: *CIL* 5.1, 620 no. 5; Picard, *Le souvenir,* 54–55, 505–7; Gusso, "Sull' imperatore Glycerio," 189–90.

erature, these epigrams contain a strong pictorial element, but if, as their general uniformity of length suggests, we consider them as part of a complete decorative scheme embracing images and text, they would either have provided artists with attributes useful in graphic representation or, more likely, have elaborated on selected visual details and aspects of the hagiographic tradition that lent themselves better to words than pictures.

Ennodius' epigrams for honorably deceased lay persons imply immortality of a different sort. Chapter 2 examined their social function as literary memorials, but present discussion requires that we return to consider the physical nature of inscribed epitaphs. An epigram for a man named Albinus illustrates the desired effect with a play on the word *titulus,* at once epitaph and renown: "You see that Albinus, who cuts death's throat with his lively merits, placed his fame beyond the grave."[201] Operative here is Ennodius' conviction that Albinus' posthumous renown, irrespective of his virtues and undoubted Christianity, requires the material instrument of an inscribed epitaph. Even the doomed emperor Majorian's curious tomb can serve as an ethical counter-example when labeled in this way.[202]

The business of Cynegia's epitaphs, whose poetic and prosopographical content we examined in chapter 2, reinforces this down-to-earth view.[203] Writing to the priest Adeodatus at Rome with the second epigram, Ennodius lays down what is to be done: "respect for the lady has been saved—the verses that I have sent, by the day of judgment I conjure you, to have them inscribed forthwith on the wall above her feet."[204] Born of negligence, his breathless amendment took place after three nights' travel, when a disgruntled Cynegia appeared to him at dawn: "I was much reproached by her about my hasty journey, wherefore her sepulcher was still honored by no verses; she complained strongly, not subject to mildness of words."[205] Ennodius affirms that the ensuing epitaph springs neither from true prophetic vision nor from random nocturnal delusions, but from a devoted affection that pays its debts; pragmatically rationalizing an

---

201. #230, vv. 1–2: *aspicis Albinum titulos post busta dedisse, / funera qui meritis vivacibus iugulat; PLRE* 2, 51–52.

202. #354 presents textual problems. See also Krautheimer, *Rome,* 187; Nichols, *Marvels of Rome,* 86.

203. #219, #362.

204. #361.3: *salva est dominae reverentia. versus quos direxi per diem iudicii te coniuro ut in pariete supra ad pedes scribi mox facias* (May–Aug. 509); see Pietri, "*Pagina in pariete reserata,*" 145–48.

205. #361.2: *multum ab ea me de itineris properatione culpatum, quare etiam nullis versibus sepulchrum eius esset honoratum, non sub verborum lenitate conquestam.*

apparent irruption of bad conscience, he refuses to let supernatural novelties eclipse his sense of social obligation.[206]

The resolutely unphantasmagorical attitude Ennodius adopted to deal with Cynegia's belated epitaph is consistent with his wonder-free treatments of Epifanius of Ticinum and Antonius of Lérins. By celebrating him in both poetry and hagiographic prose, Ennodius preserved the holy bishop of Ticinum so well that one later reader, a tenth-century bishop of Hildesheim, took Epifanius' remains home with him to Germany.[207] We cannot know whether Ennodius was responsible for Epifanius' epitaph as well, but the longer work apparently had greater effect.

Matter-of-factness and substantial form are not the only ways in which the second Cynegia epitaph brings Ennodius' relationship with the material world into sharper relief. Another piece of correspondence about the epitaph also demonstrates that literary criticism and bodily infirmity do not mix. Because of his ill health at the time, Ennodius inadvertently allowed a metrical irregularity in that second epitaph. He sent a copy to Beatus, a younger friend, who did not reply with the bad news until the next year; after that, Ennodius explained he was "nearly dead" (*pene mortuus*) when he composed it and asked that Beatus' father Probus emend the fault.[208] That could have been the end of it, but bad feeling erupts in two more letters as Ennodius, still oppressed by illness, reacts to new criticism of the prosody and content. Choosing "to believe the well-disposed rather than the clever," he seeks the great Symmachus' advice as he censures Beatus and his "gnawing comrades" for venturing to impugn a poem Faustus himself has welcomed.[209] Beside himself with irritation, Ennodius goes so far as to quote Scripture about not casting pearls before swine.

This literary row with Beatus, which ended without lasting rancor, shows us Ennodius in an uncharacteristically disagreeable mood that the conjunction of his extreme debility and Beatus' inopportunely relentless critique may explain, though not altogether excuse.[210] Precisely because his health was so often precarious, Ennodius was generally more aware of

---

206. #361.3; cf. the *admonitio* of #362.2. Miracles: Van Uytfanghe, "La controverse biblique et patristique," 212–17.

207. The "translation" occurred in 964: Picard, *Le souvenir*, 648–49.

208. #362 (May–Aug. 509); #398.1–2 (fall 510). See *PLRE* 2, 222 (Beatus), 913 (Fl. Probus 9); Moorhead, *Theoderic*, 151.

209. #405.1: *eligo benignis plus credere quam peritis;* #406.2–3: *te et participibus tuis rodentibus.*

210. Cf. #428, #452; his condition evident in #391–#411.

his body than most people; for him this physical weakness was both a means of attaining intimacy with others and a way to God.

Well over eighty of Ennodius' letters make some reference to his health along with that of his correspondent; the frequency and quality of these notices far surpasses anything in the letters of Symmachus, to whom Ennodius has often been compared, and is in fact more reminiscent of ancient valetudinarians such as Fronto, Aelius Aristides, and Synesius, or, in more recent times, the Duc de Choiseul.[211] In one letter to his friend Helpidius, who was both a fellow deacon and a physician, Ennodius even likens himself, with a certain homeliness, to a little frog (*ranula*) drawn out by its tormentors to unnatural length.[212] Ennodius' representation of his own condition contrasts strongly with the way he describes the physical aspect and regimen of bishop Epifanius and the victorious, vigorous king Theoderic.[213] When he anoints himself with the oil of St. Victor, after every physician had given up in despair at the extremity of his sickness, Ennodius illustrates in his own body how divine grace operates through material creation.[214]

Augustine of Hippo, as epitomized in the *Confessions'* "take and read" incident, came to his knowledge of God through the act of reading.[215] Ennodius, in contrast, shows a curiously Yeatsian insistence on feeling and singing for his tattered mortality.[216] It is through understanding and articulating personal suffering, whether physical in nature, as here, or spiritual, that he approaches his fellow human beings and his Creator.

---

211. #17, #19, #22, #24, #25, #28, #29, #30, #38, #40, #41, #44, #47, #62, #64, #68, #76, #82, #83, #89, #106, #117, #151, #157, #168, #170, #218, #224 (bad eyes), #228, #253, #258, #259, #268, #269, #272, #273, #276, #286–89, #292, #293, #299, #302, #305, #307, #319, #323, #356, #370, #382–84 (not #386 and #389, curiously), #390, #391, #393–407, #411, #418, #420, #421, #426, #427, #429, #434, #435, #437, #439, #440, #446–49, #454. Cf. Matthews, "Letters of Symmachus," 58, 81–83; Butler, *Choiseul* 1, 848–51, 906.

212. #384.2 (early 510), recalling schoolboy tortures?

213. Epifanius: #80.13–16, 47–50, 183–84; Theoderic: #263.19–21; all Goths: #263.26–28, 89–92.

214. #401.2 (to Faustus), #438.14. The oil came from the lamps at Victor's *martyrium:* see Cabrol, "Huile," 2990; Neunheuser, "Oil," 611.

215. Stock, *Augustine the Reader.*

216. Cf. "Sailing to Byzantium" (*The Tower*) and "Vacillation" (*The Winding Stair*).

CHAPTER 4

Family's Boons, Kinship's Bonds

The vocabulary of familial relationships features prominently in Ennodius' works. As we have already seen, most of his correspondence was addressed to or concerned persons with whom he was somehow related, though his utterances eschew the precision of Ausonius, Symmachus, and Sidonius Apollinaris. In consequence, we might presume that a greater degree of intimacy attends Ennodius' blood relationships, whatever their degree, and that letters to relatives sound a happier, more cordial note than those to business acquaintances, although the success of his dealings with others, both on his own behalf and on that of the Church, depended as much upon social proficiency as upon ecclesiastical rank or ancestral alliances.

But how close were the ties that bind, the "chain of blood" (*sanguinis catena*) that Ennodius professed to honor?[1] In chapter 1 we noted how evasive he was when talking about his family. Recall, for instance, the roundabout way in which he recorded the death of his nameless aunt. Ennodius transmits the name of his father, which seems to be Firminus, by a similarly circuitous procedure: only because he chose to introduce his nephew Lupicinus' grandfathers by name when he composed a *dictio* in honor of the youth's rhetorical debut can we deduce Firminus' place in his family tree. Ennodius never mentions his mother at all. In no other work does he leave any discernible clues, let alone definite statements, that might help us to establish who his parents were and what they did, though his frequent use of the word "parent" (*parens*) seduced even the great Sirmond into inferring the existence of a father named Camillus (or Camellus).[2] The

---

1. #177.1 (early 506), to Helisaea.
2. Sirmond, note to *Ep.* 4.25 (#158). Firminus' identity is obvious once the clue is recognized (Vogel, vi–vii). Ambrose's usage of *parens:* McLynn, *Ambrose,* 263–64; cf. Barnes, "Augustine, Symmachus, and Ambrose."

perceived implications of *parens*, which throughout the works means "relative" or "kinsman" more often than "mother/father," plus Ennodius' generally vague manner of referring to his kinfolk have thwarted scholarly efforts to supply him with a full complement of relatives. Thus, we will begin this chapter by looking at a few individuals who seem to be related to Ennodius but whose existence does not depend on being mentioned in his works, then turn to what the corpus can tell us about members of his family and how he interacted with them on various levels. Finally, we will consider Ennodius' other way of communicating views about family matters—through fictions in poetry and prose—with an eye to the attitudes shown by some of his Gallic compatriots.

A scan of *PLRE* 1 and 2 informs us that, in addition to our Magnus Felix Ennodius and his kinsman and friend Ennodius Messala, consul of 506 and son of Faustus, the Western consul of 490, other Ennodii did exist.[3] The tendency of late Roman onomastic practice to give multiple names that commemorated several ancestors while leaving the last name as the personal identifier makes some of our Ennodius' forebears more obvious than others.[4] An emendation of the *Codex Theodosianus,* which records a man called Ennoius as proconsul of Africa in 395/6, produces the earliest known Ennodius.[5] The first Felix Innodius [*sic*], even with the orthographical variation, is a better prospect for our man's family tree, a *vir clarissimus* who served as proconsul of Africa in the first quarter of the fifth century.[6] Closer in time, another possibility is a man whose name, in a novel of the emperor Majorian, is actually spelled Ennodius; he was *comes rerum privatarum* in the 450s.[7] The name Magnus points toward a further set of conjectural alliances, for two associates of Sidonius Apollinaris were called Magnus. Former praetorian prefect of Gaul then consul for 460, the elder Magnus was among the recipients of Sidonius' volume of poetry.[8] His son, called Magnus Felix, also served as prefect some years later and acquired patrician status, but turned to a life of religious devo-

---

3. Fl. Ennodius Messala 2: *PLRE* 2, 759–60, and Stemma 23. Magnus Felix Ennodius 3: *PLRE* 2, 393–94, and Stemma 19.

4. Late-antique polyonomy: Salway, "What's in a Name?" 141–44.

5. *CTh* 12.1.149 = *CJ* 6.30.16 (which shows "Ennodius"). *PLRE* 1, 278, with Barnes, "Late Roman Prosopography," 257.

6. Felix Ennodius 2: *CIL* 8.1358 + p. 938, *v.c. procons. Africae;* cf. *PLRE* 2, 393.

7. Felix Ennodius 1: *PLRE* 2, 392–93; *Nov. Maior.* 5a, *comes rerum privatarum* in the West in 458.

8. Magnus 2: *PLRE* 2, 700; Sid. Apoll. *Carm.* 24, vv. 90–91 (mentioned together with his son Felix).

tion after his exile in the 470s, presumably rendering him unavailable to assist the orphaned Magnus Felix Ennodius.[9]

Two, or perhaps three, additional Ennodii occur among the aristocracy of sixth-century Gaul after our Ennodius' death. Attested in inscriptions, royal letters, and Gregory of Tours's *History of the Franks,* we cannot avoid noting the coincidence of their name, though their connection to Ennodius, Bishop of Ticinum, remains obscure. One Ennodius was a governor of patrician rank in Provence; another (or perhaps the same man) became a bishop and ambassador to the Byzantine court in the mid-580s.[10] Around the same time, a third Ennodius commanded troops in Poitiers and Tours, later acting as a prosecutor at Metz in 590.[11]

Knowing that other individuals named Ennodius lived before and after Magnus Felix Ennodius is some help, but we still need to ask what the name Ennodius itself says about the family's origins. Over a century ago, Usener realized the name, like many in the later Roman West, must have originated in Greece or the Hellenized East.[12] After this promising start, however, he became entangled in efforts to explain why the letter *n* in Ennodius was doubled. Because he knew of only one dedication to a goddess named *Ennodia,* he believed *Enodia* was the original form and had acquired a second *n* on the same principle as *Euodos/Euuodius.*

With more inscriptions at his disposal, Robert was able to dispel Usener's orthographical doubts and, in the process, supply some clues to where Ennodius' family may have arisen.[13] One of the lesser-known Greek divinities was a goddess named Ennodia. Once assimilated with Hecate, she was depicted on horseback, holding torches in both hands; her cult flourished throughout Thessaly and Macedonia, lands famed for their horses.[14] These locales for Ennodia's cult coincide agreeably with Ennodius' known predilection for horses, but northern Greece was never a major source of emigrants to the West in the imperial period, whereas epi-

9. Magnus Felix 21: *PLRE* 2, 463–64. Sid. Apoll. *Carm.* 9; *Epist.* 2.3, 3.4, 3.7, 4.5, 4.10; Faustus of Riez, *Ep.* 6 (*PL* 58.850–52 [5]); Gennad. *de vir. ill.* 86 (*PL* 58.1109–10 [85]).

10. *PLRE* 3, 442–43. Felix Ennodius 1 (epitaph: *CIL* 12.388 = *Anth. Lat.* 1369) may be identical with Ennodius 3 (*Ep. Austras.* 25), sent to Constantinople in 587/88.

11. Ennodius 2 (Gregory of Tours *Hist.* 5.24, 8.26, 9.7, 10.19): *comes* (577), exiled by Chilperic, *dux* at Poitiers/Tours (580s), prosecutes a bishop at Metz (590); cf. Cesa, *Ennodio,* 8.

12. Usener, *Anecdoton Holderi,* 13.

13. Robert, *Hellenica* XI–XII, 588–95. Cf. *Bulletin Épigraphique* (1971) 345; (1961) 382; (1964) 225; (1939) 152; (1972) 252; (1973) 247; (1967) 332; (1972) 235.

14. *IG* 9.2 421, 575–77, 1286; *SEG* 3.485 (Artemis Ennodia).

graphical evidence shows that the majority of Greek-speakers in Gaul came from Asia Minor and the Middle East.[15] Within that broad expanse of territory, one other place had a cult of Ennodia: the city of Colophon in Asia Minor.[16] The connection with Gaul is admittedly tenuous; I nonetheless propose that a homonymous ancestor of Magnus Felix Ennodius moved from Asia Minor, hotbed of the Second Sophistic, to southern Gaul, replete with rhetors. Such an explanation supplies an invitingly plausible, if far-fetched, background for an individual profoundly concerned with verbal expression.

Even if Ennodius himself was unaware of its significance, we can see that his name is both Greek and theophoric. Moreover, many of the people he calls family (however close they actually were) have clearly Hellenizing names. Apodemia, Archotamia, and Euprepia are among the most striking and indicate that hereditary values operated as strongly as Christian belief in a region still subject to Eastern influences.[17] Apodemia's name suggests a further Gallic connection to the literary and religious circles of Bordeaux, for among the correspondents of St. Jerome a century earlier were two ladies from southwestern Gaul. They used a cleric named Apodemius to carry their questions about various points of Scripture to the great scholar in Bethlehem, who made much of their messenger's name and elucidated its meaning in Greek.[18] Ennodius' respect for Greek culture is owed to this still-vivid social and intellectual milieu, even if he did not consider himself competent to compose literary works in the Greek language.

What, then, does Ennodius make of his own family? Leafing through Vogel's index of words for things and ideas produces some entries for fathers, brothers, sisters, and children, as well as the irksome "parent," but they are neither exhaustive nor wholly accurate.[19] Furthermore, there is no

---

15. Jullian, *Histoire de la Gaule* 5, 15–24, with *CIL* 12 and 13.

16. Paus. 3.14.9: Colophonians sacrificed black puppies to the goddess.

17. I have found no exact Greek parallel for the awkwardly formed Archotamia: cf. *SEG* 12.360 (Cyprus), 14.699 (Caria), 19.633 (Antibes), 20.314 (Cyprus), 28.1539 (Egypt), 29.1614 (Palestine). The second century and later: *SEG* 37.825–834; Bréhier, "Les Colonies d'Orientaux."

18. Jerome, *Ep.* 121 and 122 call Apodemius a significantly named Holy Land pilgrim (*PL* 22.1007: *de Oceani littore atque ultimis Galliarum finibus*). Greek *Apodemioi:* Thessalonica, Rome (*CIG* 1977, 9572: Apodemes Deuteria); Klaudioupolis in Bithynia (*SEG* 36.1136).

19. Vogel, 363–418 (*Index Rerum et Vocabulorum*), s.v. *fraternitas, germanitas, germanus/germana, pater* (synonym of *bishop* or *godfather*), and *pignus,* equating to "son" or (pl.) "children." *Parens* is classified variously as *pater* (5x), *propinquus* (7x), *soror* (1x), or *original sin* (3x). *Parentela* and *parentivus* appear once each.

mention of mothers and families, although the word *mater* in fact appears over fifty times in a variety of literal and metaphorical contexts. His index of proper names is excessively sanguine in designating sundry persons *adfinis* or *propinquus:* if we search it for all persons somehow related to Ennodius, we find about forty individuals.[20] Though the status of a few is remarkably definite, most are highly questionable, including a number of gentlemen addressed variously as "brother" or "your fraternity," a term of elective intimacy.[21] Consulting *PLRE* 2 adds nothing.[22]

The only member of Ennodius' immediate family to whom any correspondence has survived, his sister Euprepia receives seven letters in all, making her the relative about whom we can be most certain.[23] Thus, the documents involving Euprepia offer an excellent point from which to observe the precision and intensity of the author's utterances about family matters. Euprepia is also the only sibling Ennodius names in letters to other people, for when he writes Faustus to request his assistance in protecting her possessions, he alludes to the latter's "paternal support" of Lupicinus, "our Euprepia's son."[24]

In the opening sentence of the first letter to her, from the summer of 503, Ennodius presents their relationship with studied precision: "By the dispensation of heaven's mystery, at the same time I was denied a sister's affection and Lupicinus a mother's fondness, and after a while our double family tie was entitled to receive your absent devotion."[25] From the lament and variations that follow, Euprepia appears to have been in Milan with her son, at which time Ennodius made her acquaintance properly, then returned to Gaul alone, leaving Lupicinus and his uncle to fret about her

---

20. Vogel, 348–63.

21. Euprepia and Lupicinus are discussed later. *Frater, fraternitas:* Agnellus (#155; cf. #256–57, #309, #316, #321–22, #359, #397, #443), Constantius (#68; #54, #56–57, #142, #153, #251), Epiphanius and Gaianus (#315, #381), Florianus (#20–21), Florus (#396; cf. #5, #16, #311, #315, #400), Helpidius (#312, #384, #445), Panfronius (#144; cf. #53, #146, #242, #435), Paulus (#430).

22. The footnote to Magnus Felix Ennodius' family tree (*PLRE* 2, 1320) contains more relatives (fifteen who could not be placed) than the stemma itself; both omit at least four others. Magnus 2, Gennadius Avienus 4, and Pope Vigilius' do not help, either (*PLRE* 2, 1318, 1322, 1323).

23. #52, #84, #109, #219, #268, #293, #313; she is called both *soror* and, with technical precision, *germana*.

24. #60.1: *paterna subsidia . . . Lupicinum Euprepiae nostrae filium.*

25. #52.1: *caelestis dispensatione mysterii uno tempore mihi sororis, Lupicino refusus est matris affectus, et geminae copula necessitudinis peregrinantem recipere meruit post intervalla pietatem.*

situation until news of her well-being arrived unexpectedly. Although they of course realized that she had suffered hardships, the negligence she showed by not keeping in touch was burdensome. Ennodius' interest in the relationship is evident in his protest—"Where in the world has maternal concern been hiding? Where has what used to be owed to a brother strayed?"—but he reserves his harshest words for Euprepia's disregard of her offspring: "the child who indicts a parent's silence has difficulty bearing her neglect of kindness."[26] He asserts that she could mend such mistakes, if not by her presence, then by profuse letters, then asks her to remember him, for his "prayers and wishes for our shared son" precede her own, and to pray for both him and Lupicinus.[27]

Before we examine the other six letters to Euprepia as evidence of Ennodius' attitudes toward familial attachments, let us notice a few things about the language of this earliest communication. The chiastic associative sequence of the first sentence (Ennodius : sister / mother : Lupicinus) is glossed by *double family tie*, expressed in an utterly unambiguous way by *necessitudo*, a word common in kinship contexts throughout Ennodius' works. The appearance of *parens* is equally straightforward: the word here has the same weight as "parent" in English, signifying "mother" and/or "father."[28] *Shared son* sounds slightly strange without reference to adoption, but additional passages pertaining to the orphanhood and guardianship of Lupicinus himself will clarify matters.

The other letters to Euprepia manifest Ennodius' continuing distress at the disregard she showed him and Lupicinus by not answering their letters. The second and third items in the series appeared at least a year later. The earlier of them (Easter–end 504) again stressed motherly feeling, comparing Euprepia's deficiency of sentiment unfavorably to that shown by barbarians and beasts of the field: "you, forgetful of your sole successor, have taken away both the commiseration due an orphan and the happiness of one whose mother survives."[29] Ennodius even wonders what more she

---

26. #52.2: *ubinam gentium materna hactenus cura delituit? ubi quod fratri debebatur erravit?;* 5–6: *graviter fert circa caritatem neglegentiam, qui parentis silentium liber accusat. Liber/parens:* [Ps.-Quint.] *Decl. Maj.* 2.8; *CJ* 3.38.33; 5.9.8. *Circa* instead of *pro:* Dubois, *La latinité,* 406.

27. #52.6: *qui preces tuas circa communem filium et vota praecessi.*

28. Dubois, *La latinité,* 213; Vogel, 400, incautiously equated it with *soror* within the set of *propinqui.* Cf. Saller, *Patriarchy, Property and Death,* 106–14.

29. #84.3: *tu unici oblita pignoris et miserationem orbati et felicitatem eius cui mater superest abstulisti* (Easter–end 504); cf. Dixon, "Continuity and Change," 80–83.

could desire or fear from her son, "since an inheritance is never well sought when the heir is despised."[30] Although Euprepia may think he reproaches her at Lupicinus' behest, Ennodius affirms that he is gloomy because he misses her and realizes from her silence that she is heedless of all affection. He tries to conclude more positively by mentioning Lupicinus' progress, but his parting wish for her return sounds rather wan: "if it can come to be, restore yourself to our sight with God's ordinance."[31]

The other letter from the same period is appreciably more brusque. Euprepia has at last conceded Ennodius a letter "compatible neither with affection nor with kinship," but silence would be childish, so he is obliged to reply.[32] Their relationship is not progressing as he had hoped. Although he tries to be understanding of "sister Euprepia" and the afflictions besetting Provence, he suspects she is trying to avoid his attentions, warning that "we do not flee our faults by a change of location."[33] "Was your intention concerning your relatives such that you would neither weigh their good deeds with impartial judgement nor merely criticize their excesses with deserved reproach?" he asks before conceding the futility of his efforts.[34] As the letter ends, Ennodius strikes a final blow for the cause of proper feeling: "You will have learned nevertheless that I will expend on Lupicinus not what I owe you, but what is appropriate to my soul, because affection that deserves a greater recompense from God is granted only when it has been summoned by no gifts of men."[35] The implication that Euprepia avoids wasting kindness on those from whom she receives no material benefit anticipates Ennodius' comment, seven years later in the confessional letter, that surviving on the charity of unspecified relatives is worse than captivity.

The only item to survive from the next two years is Ennodius' short cover letter to the first epitaph he wrote for Cynegia sometime before the end of summer 506. Grief was not his motive; he gives no indication that

---

30. #84.4: *quia nunquam bene hereditas quaesita est herede contempto.*

31. #84.6: *si fieri potest, nostris te cum dei ordinatione redde conspectibus.*

32. #109.1: *paginam . . . nec affectui nec necessitudini congruentem* (also from Easter–end 504).

33. #109.2: *soror Euprepia . . . vitia nostra regionum mutatione non fugimus.*

34. #109.2: *circa propinquos tibi fuit tale propositum, ut nec benefacta ipsorum iusta interpretatione pensares nec excessus debita tantum reprehensione corriperes.*

35. #109.3: *me tamen Lupicino noveris non quod tibi debeo, sed quid animae meae conveniat inpensurum, quia sola est quae maiorem a deo retributionem meretur affectio, cum nullis hominum dotibus provocata conceditur.*

Cynegia was in fact dead. Proudly bemoaning the atrophy of his talent and powers of invention, the speedily-written poem simply serves as his pretext to contact Euprepia. Of course, he does want her to praise his skillful handiwork and to pray that their kinswoman Cynegia's spirit—not her soul—take no affront at his "rough acts of duty."[36]

Additional letters likely passed between them in the meantime, but the next item in the corpus appears about a year later, around autumn 507, with Ennodius' grandiloquent response to a missive from Euprepia that has finally exceeded his pleas for amiable intimacy. After an expansive preface opposing the "heavenly affinity of the mind's dominion" to the body's "earthly ignominy" and playing on the empathetic proximity shared by kindred souls, he proceeds to the letter's heart, whose nature could come as no surprise to Euprepia.[37] "I could scarcely bear the sweet talk that you had sent me before: after my remonstrance, you poured forth doubled honey in your letter that buffeted all my inmost breast and transported my captive soul to longing for you, leaving my physical situation behind."[38]

Ennodius here draws on the standard epistolary topos of bodily separation and spiritual closeness in styling his self-presentation because that topos happened to work for him, not because he craved "rhetorical" flavor without meaningful substance. For him, rhetorical topoi were part of a verbal palette whose color range was far wider than those in general use today; furthermore, we should remember that, now as then, commonplaces exist because they are in some measure true, not because they are pungently unique. Granted more than he had dared to expect, Ennodius feared that Euprepia's display of affection would ultimately come to nothing if her attention wavered. Though admitting he might be deceived, he still desired a meeting of minds, "to achieve not the semblance but the very truth of spiritual union."[39] The paternal role he has effectively assumed towards Lupicinus, whose name he does not mention here, governs his choice of words. He maintains that the success of the projected relation-

---

36. #219.2: *ora, ut spiritus illius scabridis nequaquam laedatur officiis.* See Dubois, *La latinité,* 137; Ven. Fort. *Carm.* 2.9.7; 2.13.7.

37. #268.1–2: *rerum omnium cursus obsequiis corporis animarum constat imperio. aliud nobilitat caelestis adfinitas, aliud abiectio terrena summittit,* alluding to Sall. *Cat.* 1–3.

38. #268.3: *vix quae ante direxeras blandimenta sustinui: post admonitionem meam duplicia in litteris mella fudisti, quae tota pectoris secreta concuterent et ad desiderium tui captivam animam relicta corporis sede transferrent.*

39. #268.5: *spiritalis coniugii non simulacrum sed ipsam implere veritatem.*

ship depends on cooperation, stating "You, with God's intervention, just promise that you will maintain a solid and immutable constancy against every attack that is born of envy."[40] Now Euprepia must respond.

That letter's eager yearning for communion was unrequited, it seems. Many months pass before another letter to Euprepia appears, in the first half of 508. Ennodius' communication is brief—less than fifteen lines long—and to the point. Fear had kept him from writing, but affection won out in the end; he states that he and Lupicinus are in good health and wishes that Euprepia do likewise.[41] Five years after he first undertook the care of his nephew, Ennodius returned to the matter of "our" Lupicinus. Disclaiming any desire to cause distress, he reminds Euprepia that "I owe him more through dedication than you yourself were capable of showing through nature . . . Truly, I declare, with you going off too far away, the worries of both parents that we could energetically have shared in one location are incumbent on me."[42] Since he can expect nothing more, he desires only the charity and prayer she deems necessary to obtain her wishes.

Ennodius composed his last letter to Euprepia only a few months later, after receiving a more cordial message from his sister that broke the silence to which, he says, he had become accustomed: "cut open is the scar that had helped to heal devoted love."[43] If she wished, she could produce a letter of great taste, pleasing enough in its finesse for her brother to stress the artifice inherent in their teasing contest of inconstant words: "behold, see how artfully you contend with me, whom you allow neither the satisfaction of your presence nor the oblivion of silence to succor."[44] Though these sentiments coincide with many of the familiar topoi of late antique epistolography, their appearance here expresses a literal truth. Euprepia is the only individual with whom Ennodius can try to experience the immediacy of a real sibling relationship. She stymied his efforts, however, by remaining in Arles while her brother was "shut up in Milanese walls"; his

---

40. #268.6: *tu tantum deo medio adversus omnem quae ex invidia nascitur inpugnationem firmam promitte et indemutabilem servandam esse constantiam.*

41. #293.1–2 (Apr.–June 508). Frankish-Gothic tensions must have heightened anxiety: Klingshirn, *Caesarius,* 94–96, 106–11.

42. #293.2: *plus illi per studium debeo quam ipsa exhibere poteras per naturam . . . vere dico, vobis ad longiora digredientibus utriusque parentis sollicitudo me respicit quam potuimus in unum positi cum ambitione partiri.*

43. #313.1: *rescissa est cicatrix quae ad medicinam pii amoris accesserat.*

44. #313.1: *ecce vide qua mecum arte contendis, cui nec satietatem de praesentia tua nec oblivionem de silentio pateris subvenire.*

mind might run freely out to meet her, but his body's captivity shut him up within Italy.[45] Of all the letters to Euprepia, this last one contains the most explicit statement of their physical separation. In its valediction, whose phrases recall and reverse the happy consternation induced by the "double honey" of her letter from the previous year, Ennodius asks that she preserve herself "for the good of mutual well-being, to alleviate my grief, which you have doubled with your missive in all-too-clever fashion."[46]

Although we have no way to prove that Ennodius intended this to be his last published letter to Euprepia, he mentions her only once thereafter. In writing to Arcotamia, another relative living in Gaul, he lists Euprepia among his informants who have attested to the addressee's exemplary piety.[47] Ennodius says that Arcotamia is bound to him by "propinquity" (*propinquitas*) and calls her son, a monk of Lérins, "my lord and priest, the splendor of our family."[48] Family is good, but religious devotion is better. Quoting Scripture for Arcotamia's benefit, Ennodius loved and admired her moral excellence, especially because she continued to live in the world; reciprocal contact is just as important here as accidents of consanguinity.[49] Moreover, when he wishes he had an excuse to visit, he attaches no blame to the fact Arcotamia and her son live in Provence, in strong contrast to his views on Euprepia's place of residence.

Apart from his recurring role in Ennodius' letters to Euprepia, Lupicinus himself seldom appears in the writings, though the letter to Faustus requesting protection for Euprepia's "little holdings" (*facultatulas*) initially refers to them as Lupicinus' property, claimed by a group of Goths.[50] Because both Ennodius and Lupicinus were in Milan, the latter needed no letters from his uncle, but one other document shows something of Ennodius' attitude towards his nephew and matters of familial relationships: the *dictio* celebrating Lupicinus' entry into the arena of public speaking under the tutelage of the *grammaticus* Deuterius, from which we

---

45. #313.2: *habuit Arelatensis habitatio, cum Mediolanensibus muris includerer, et dum ad dulcem sedem libertas mentis excurreret, intra Italiam me corporis captivitas includebat.*

46. #313.3: *precor ut valeas et ad sublevandum maerorem meum, quem scriptione tua nimis daedala arte geminasti, bono prosperitatis mutuae reserveris.*

47. #319.3 (July–Aug. 508): *hoc nostrorum relatione propinquorum, praecipue tamen domina et sorore Euprepia referente, percrebuit.*

48. #319.5: *dominum meum et familiae nostrae iubar presbyterum.* #291 calls her *Archotamia*. She is identified with the *Arcutamia senatrix* of *Vita S. Apoll. Valent.* (Krusch, *MGH SRM* 3, 201); her devout son may be the scandalous Aetheria's ex-husband: #412 and chap. 1.

49. #319.7: *laudent te proximi tui,* quoting Prov. 27.2.

50. #60.1–2 (late-fall 503); Amory, *People and Identity,* 419, 422.

have already gleaned the name of Ennodius' father.[51] Though, as we saw in chapter 2, this piece has obvious bearing on belletristic issues, what matters here is how Ennodius dwells on his nephew's relationship within the family and his obligation to live up to ancestral achievements.

The emphasis on his nephew's hereditary nobility already implicit in the opening sentence's allusion to the "noble seed" (*nobile germen*) of aromatic spices from distant lands emerges fully in the statements, "lofty growth suffers not for itself to be hidden; the honor of famous blood is not kept in concealment."[52] The subsequent discourse expatiates on the duty Lupicinus and his instructors have to develop and perfect his innate gifts. Ennodius uses the figures of Lupicinus' grandfathers Firminus and Glycerius, speaking as prosopopoeiae, to promote the educational obligations of noble birth. They call the young man "the leaf and bud of both families," entrusted for cultivation to the most learned Deuterius, who imparts a tongue that "reveals the family's luster," for "nobility without learning forswears the reward of heaven."[53] After bidding Lupicinus "to undertake things worthy of your lineage," which will benefit his future senatorial career, the grandfathers leave the platform. Then Ennodius speaks at last in his own voice: "I have shown myself a kinsman toward you as a relative, a man of God toward one orphaned of his parents."[54] Confessing that his love for Lupicinus is inevitable because of propinquity, he affirms, "if devotion is gracious by intention, they who are deprived of the bulwark of their parents become our sons; one bond therefore comes from ancestry, by another does duty constrain us."[55] Uttered with particular reference to his nephew, this statement symbolizes Ennodius' general position on human relationships: undertaking spiritual responsibilities does not annul natural social ones, but raise them to a higher level.

Another sister whom Ennodius leaves nameless married a man, likewise nameless, and had a son named Parthenius. This nephew received a *dictio*

---

51. #69 (Jan.–Apr. 504).

52. #69.1: *amomi flosculus aut messis casiae . . . occultari se non patitur fetura sublimis; decus clari sanguinis non tenetur abscondito.*

53. #69.5–10: *suscipe, doctissime hominum, utriusque plantam familiae et culmum . . . splendorem familiae prodit lingua quam tribuitis . . . inerudita nobilitas caeleste munus abiurat.* Because Sirmond identified him as the subscriber of Caes. *B. Gall.* 2, *PLRE* 2, 694 calls him "Fl. Licerius Firminus Lupicinus 3"; cf. Zetzel, *Latin Textual Criticism,* 222. "Glicerius" is the other grandfather in only one MS (B); Gusso, "Sull' imperatore Glicerio," 169.

54. #69.13: *propinquum ad te consanguineus, orbum parentibus religiosus exhibui.*

55. #69.13: *si necessitudo respicitur, liber ab amore esse non possum; si pietas amica proposito, nostri fiunt fili qui parentum suorum praesidio denudantur. unum ergo vinculum venit a prosapie, alio nos astringit officium.*

whose dominant technological metaphors I discussed in chapter 2; we will now revisit that piece because of what it implies about Parthenius' parentage.[56] The "mixture" (*permixtio*) of ancestries Deuterius so skillfully moderates is still a mystery: though Ennodius obviously took great pride in his own side of the family, a subsequent letter shows that he remained in contact with his nameless brother-in-law, who informed him of Parthenius' bad behavior in the big city.[57] Beyond the problems this man had in controlling his son, what Ennodius thought was wrong with him is difficult to see. The only clue lies in the phrase *gentile murmur,* with which Ennodius describes the way Parthenius spoke before Deuterius transformed him into a proper Roman; allowing for exaggeration, these words could mean anything between a Gallic provincial accent and fluency in Gothic or Burgundian.[58] The former is far more likely, considering the kind of instruction Deuterius imparted, although one French scholar surmised Parthenius' father was actually a "German"; others have taken the evidence for Ennodius' nephew and a Parthenius son of Agricola (whose grandfather was the Ruricius of Limoges noted by Gregory of Tours) to create a single Parthenius.[59] I find neither proposition wholly convincing. For all that Ennodius seems to have had civilized dealings with Goths, it is easier to suppose that his sister married a Gallo-Roman whose wealth exceeded his breeding and academic achievements than to believe that Parthenius' father was either a barbarian or one of the Ruricii. A paternal deficiency of this sort would explain why Ennodius and Faustus had to supplement what guidance Parthenius' father provided.

We can summarize Ennodius' more definite relatives in the following manner. Euprepia, Lupicinus' mother, and the mother of Parthenius are securely attributable as sisters. Besides these women and their sons, Ennodius' nephews, the bereaved anonymous sibling (*germana*) for whom he braves the Po's floodwaters constitutes a probable third sister; to our tally, we can also add the niece whose matrimonial prospects Ennodius endorsed in his letter to Laconius.[60]

---

56. #94.

57. .#368.2; cf. #369.5.

58. #94.12.

59. Léglise, *Oeuvres* 1, 28 ("Parthenius . . . a pour père un Germain"); cf. 266. Stroheker (*Der senatorische Adel,* Parthenius no. 283–84) divided Ennodius' nephew from Ruricius' grandson; cf. *PLRE* 2, 832–34 (Parthenius 2 and 3). Wood ("Administration, Law and Culture," 67–69; *Merovingian Kingdoms,* 25) uses Mathisen's identification ("Epistolography," 101–3).

60. The third sister: #423, vv. 22–26. Laconius: #252; cf. Cesa, "Integrazioni prosopografiche," 240; and chapter 1.

Aside from these six individuals, Ennodius connects other persons presumed to be members of his family with vague expressions of affinity in which he may or may not mention the tie of blood explicitly.[61] He often expresses these relationships through abstract nouns like "affinity" (*adfinitas*), "rapport" (*necessitudo*), "consanguinity" (*consanguinitas*), "intimacy" (*proximitas*), and "closeness" (*propinquitas*).[62] At other times he refers to people variously as "near" or "intimate relatives" (*adfines, proximi*), "kinsmen" and "kinswomen" (*propinqui/-ae*), or simply "relations" (*parentes*).[63] The last of these terms, *parens*, has been a notable source of difficulties but, having examined the confessional letter in chapter 1 and the Euprepia dossier earlier in this chapter, we can see that the word's significance is either patently literal, like the English use of *parent*, equivalent to *father* and/or *mother*, or more broadly familial and even ancestral, as with *parent* in French.[64] The former and latter senses are applicable to real people and invented literary situations alike, to relatives both literal and metaphorical, distinguished only by the context in which they appear. If Ennodius' father was named Firminus, as the Lupicinus *dictio* affirms, then the "Camellus *parens*" of the letter to Bassus and "my *parens* Camella" in the last letter to Liberius are no more than uncles or cousins.[65]

Ennodius portrayed his own relationship to Lupicinus as that of "a second father" by virtue of love and duty. This must likewise be the sense of his characterization of Bishop Laurentius as *alter parens,* just as *parenti omnium,* referring to Pope Symmachus, is rendered in French as "au père

---

61. Astyrius, Camella, Domnica, Helisaea, Promotus, Senarius (#30.3), and Venantius are linked by *sanguis.*

62. *adfinitas:* #9.1 (of Avienus), #285.1 (to Domnica); cf. #90.1. *consanguinitas:* 34.1 (of Armenius), #291.1 (of Arcotamia). *necessitudo:* #12.3 (to Firminus), #17.2 (to Avienus), #82.1 (to Apollinaris), #83.1 (to Promotus), #285.1 (to Domnica), #455.3 (of Aurelianus). *propinquitas:* #285.1 (to Domnica), #319.1 (of Arcotamia), #441.1 (of Apodemia), #455.2 (to Aurelianus); it can also mean "kinsman"; see Amm. Marc. 14.11.7. *proximitas:* #177.1 (to Helisaea), #178.2 (to Avitus of Aquileia), #250.1 (to Venantius), #271.3 (to Boethius).

63. *adfines/proximi:* #48.7 (to Olybrius about Speciosa), #90.1 (of Iulianus). *propinqui/propinquae:* #40.2 (to Firminus), #318.3 (to Boethius), #426.2 (of Ambrosius). *parentes:* #31.3 (to Asturius), #59.1 (of Faustus to Albinus), #158.1 (of Camellus), #334.1 (to Maximus), #370.7 (to Boethius), #412.2 (of Aetheria), #457.4 (of Camella).

64. *Parens* (a selection of the over seventy-five occurrences). As actual father and/or mother: #4.4 and 6, #85.17, #386.1, #459.5. Metaphorical or fictional: #49.128, #81.5; cf. #438.15, #132, #363.6, #452.3. Generic relatives: #59.1, #150.1, #225.3, #263 *passim,* #370.8, #438.21, #449.3, #461.6 (actual); #261 (fictional).

65. #158.1–2 (to Bassus). #457.4 (to Liberius). Asturius (#31, #47) is no closer.

commun."[66] Following common practice, Ennodius calls bishops "father" (*pater*) but uses *papa* to denote the bishop of Rome; Bishop Laurentius of Milan was both Ennodius' actual superior and the man who took him under his wing after Epifanius of Ticinum died.[67] Ennodius did not intend to provide precise information about his connections save in instances when *parent* is unambiguously literal and specific. Looking beyond the obvious family members surveyed here, we find some of the same relational nuances present in his other compositions. The *dictiones* for Arator, for the son of the deceased Eusebius, and for Paterius and Severus imply that those entrusted with intellectual and spiritual education are the truest *parentes* of all, for in the last of these Ennodius identifies himself specifically as Paterius' godfather, his "father among heavenly things."[68]

While his more remote kin are virtually impossible to sort out genealogically, the fact that Ennodius preserved his letters to them indicates he willingly partook of their company, so we can regard them as relatives of choice (*Wahlverwandten*). Diagnostic for Ennodius' manner of relating to these select individuals is the case of Faustus and his sons Rufius Magnus Faustus Avienus and Ennodius Messala, who receive a multitude of letters throughout the corpus. Although they appear as family members of vague and tenuous degree in the early letters, a closer relationship evolves from the initial contact occasioned by the Symmachan schism. Son and father of consuls, and consul himself for 490, Faustus was Symmachus' only senatorial defender of note, according to the sources.[69] The first two letters addressed to him consequently emphasize the embattled state of the Church rather than family matters, although the first acknowledges the delights of Faustus' friendship and the second alludes to Avienus' imminent good fortune.[70] By the third letter, however, Ennodius felicitates Faustus at length on Avienus' consulship, adopting a more confident tone that continues to the end of the collection.[71]

Faustus' wife is more obscure. If Ennodius addressed any letters to her, none survives. Of those to Faustus or to Avienus and Messala inquiring

---

66. #19.2; #416.1, translated by Léglise, *Oeuvres* 1, 469; cf. Cassiod. *Var.* 11.3.

67. Bishops as *patres* and *parentes:* #1.6, #11.4, #19.3, #43 (vv. 124, 168), #80.27, #85.17, #409.1, #416.1, #455.2. *Papa:* Dubois, *La latinité,* 223.

68. Arator: #85, #320. Eusebius' son: #124. Paterius and Severus: #451.11 (*Paterium . . . cuius pater et inter caelestia sum vocatus*). See Lynch, "*Spiritale Vinculum,*" 182–87.

69. Wirbelauer, *Zwei Päpste,* 57–65; cf. Moorhead, *Theoderic,* 129–31, 166.

70. #6, #7 (both 501); the second alludes to Avienus' consulship.

71. #9.3 (beginning of 502); #446 (Sept.–Dec. 511) is the last.

about the lady of the house's health or, later on, lamenting her decease, none ever names her explicitly, calling her only "my lady" or "your mother."[72] Her identity turns on the suggestive names of her sons and the coincidence that Ennodius composed two epitaphs for a woman named Cynegia. Avienus was obviously called after his paternal grandfather Gennadius Avienus, but Magnus was one of his other names, whereas his younger brother was called Ennodius Messala. As we have already seen, the name Ennodius is found in no other Roman family of the time, and neither it nor Magnus appears in Faustus' family before Messala; since ancestors are prominent in later Roman names, we can conclude that both names entered the family of Faustus through Messala's mother.[73] The precise degree of her relationship to our Magnus Felix Ennodius is unrecoverable, but Ennodius' authorship of two different epitaphs at two separate times for someone named Cynegia helps us to uncover her name. As set out in chapter 2, the material fact of these two epigrams caused prosopographers to distinguish two different Cynegias.[74] I consider this distinction unnecessary. The Cynegia of the first epigram, mentioned in letters to Euprepia and to Helisaea, another kinswoman, has hitherto been counted among the Gallic members of Ennodius' family although her husband's name remained unknown.[75] However, the second epigram, usually thought to be for another Cynegia, contains the line, "a fortunate and happy thing, I die before my partner."[76] The choice of words plainly alludes to the name of Cynegia's husband (Faustus), since other metrical options exist for that part of the verse and one of the letters accompanying the epigram contains a greeting to Faustus' sister Stefania.[77] This latter Cynegia, whom Sundwall deduced was the wife of Faustus, must consequently be the mother of Avienus and Messala, whose failing health had caused concern in the year prior to the second epigram.[78] If, as my analy-

---

72. E.g. #272.2: *domnae matris;* #323.1: *inaequalitas domnae meae matris vestrae.*

73. *PLRE* 2, 1322 (Stemmata 23); Salway, "What's in a Name?" 141–42. Altogether untrustworthy: Mommaerts and Kelley, "Anicii of Gaul and Rome."

74. Sundwall, *Abhandlungen,* 36, 56; *PLRE* 2: "Cynegia 1" (relative of Ennodius, d. 506: #177, #209); and "Cynegia 2" (wife of "Faustus 9 Niger," d. 509: #323, #361–62, cf. #272, #434).

75. #177.2, to Helisaea, of whom Cynegia had spoken highly; #219.2, to Euprepia; the epitaph's cover letter. Neither implies Cynegia was dead.

76. #362.5: *quod faustum et felix, coniuge praemorior.*

77. #325, v. 8 gives one alternative: *quod votum est sanctis, coniuge praemorior;* #361.4 (greetings to Stefania via the priest Adeodatus).

78. #323 (late summer 508), to Avienus on his mother's ill health. See Sundwall, *Abhandlungen,* 117; Barnes, "Late Roman Prosopography," 249.

sis of both epigrams in chapter 2 indicates, and the ebullient tone of the letter to Euprepia prefacing the first epitaph intimates, the Cynegia of the second epigram is actually the same person as the Cynegia of the first epigram, the kinship Ennodius and his Gallic relatives claim with Faustus' Roman family becomes somewhat clearer.[79]

The sheer quantity of Ennodius' letters to Faustus on sundry matters of business shows how useful the latter's official posts and personal influence made him.[80] Through Faustus, Ennodius became acquainted with enterprising individuals like Florus, Castorius, and Decoratus, as well as the worthy Albinus.[81] We can easily say that he regarded Faustus as useful; more than that, however, he found him to be a genuinely congenial relative.[82] The outpouring of letters in the corpus confirms that Ennodius communicated with Faustus far more than the call of ecclesiastical duty required, amicably inquiring about the health of Faustus and his family, giving news of his own well-being, lending a sympathetic ear, and requesting prayers.

Other members of Faustus' immediate family received their own share of Ennodius' confidences and entreaties. His correspondence with Avienus and Messala begins by admiring the great man's sons as holders of consulships and devotees of literary studies. Later, they became friends and helpers in their own right, as we have seen in chapter 3, when Avienus assisted in obtaining a suburban property for Ennodius. Not only did he exchange letters with the brothers, but also poetry, *dictiones,* and critiques; furthermore, Messala apparently requested a versified grammar text.[83] The corpus of Ennodius' writings even preserves an epigram composed by Messala himself, which makes much of the name he shares with Ennodius.[84]

Avienus and Messala's paternal aunt, Faustus' sister Stefania, whose existence Ennodius first disclosed when writing to Adeodatus about Cyne-

---

79. #219 adduces inspiration and poetic skill, not grief; cf. Wirbelauer, *Zwei Päpste,* 59.

80. Besides having been consul, Faustus also did service as quaestor and praetorian prefect: *PLRE* 2, 454–56; Moorhead, *Theoderic,* 146.

81. Up-and-coming friends: #5, #16, #149, #311, #315, #389, #400. Albinus: subject of #59.1 (referring to Albinus as Faustus' *parens*), recipient of #58, #279, and #230; cf. Moorhead, *Theoderic,* 163.

82. Faustus' network of connections: Barnwell, *Emperor, Prefects and Kings;* Moorhead, *Theoderic,* 157–58, 229–30; Näf, *Senatorisches Standesbewusstsein,* 194–204.

83. Avienus' talents: #17, #23, #65, #107–8, #111, #113, #244, #376, #448; cf. #9.10. Messala: #377; #434; #373, vv. 1–2 (grammatical interests). Cf. Pecere, "La cultura greco-romana," 385–86.

84. #371. Two epigrams devised by Ennodius follow (#372, #373).

gia's epitaph, receives three conspicuously devout letters from Ennodius, the first prompted by his illness, the second and third by considerations of spiritual health.[85] The last, complaining that her diction is too sophisticated when telling of humble things, asks that she "never mix the uncouth compositions of academic exercise with holy dictations: for me, it is enough to admire what I ought to find in your sentiments, if I deserve to follow it."[86] Even when a woman possessed intellectual talent equal to her piety, like the rest of her family, she was not to compete with men on the field of traditional rhetoric; only the blessed martyrs could break the connection between virtue and virility, and only momentarily.[87]

Ennodius' regard for the affluence, culture, and religious devotion of Faustus' family is readily apparent in his letters. To be sure, age and sex did limit his ardor, but his dealings with Avienus and Messala, the closest to him in age, show how intensely involved he could become. Ennodius felt free to unburden himself to Avienus when his hopes of becoming the new bishop of Milan were dashed in July or August of 508 by the election of Eustorgius. Ennodius declares, "no consolation can come from my miseries, when the things I deserved are set before my eyes and the more the preferred man appears less worthy, the more the loser's faults end up in the open."[88] The choice of *locata* to signify what he thought of his rival's preferment is intentionally ambiguous, since the word can mean both position in space and hiring something out. Considering the awareness of money matters we have seen Ennodius display elsewhere, financial considerations doubtless carried some weight in his rival's promotion; still, Ennodius himself may have been excessively optimistic.[89]

Thwarted ambition, as we see, could induce Ennodius to speak candidly with a friend. The matrimonial plans of the brothers Avienus and

---

85. #394.3 (Aug. 510) desires only faithful letters, invoking her deceased husband's soul: *nullum alium dictare . . . per domni Asteri animam;* #439, #442. Cf. *PLRE* 2, 173–74.

86. #442.2–3 (Sept.–Dec. 511): *graviter tamen fero quod rusticas voces nimis urbana et subtili elocutione narratis . . . rogo vos . . . ut numquam scholasticorum indociles compositiones sanctis dictationibus misceatis; sufficit mihi quod admirer quod si mereor sequi debeam in vestris sensibus invenire.*

87. Cf. #348, to St. Euphemia: Jones, "Women, Death, and the Law," 23–34; Clark, *Women in Late Antiquity,* 134–38; Hope, *Leonine Sacramentary,* 32. Understood as public speaking, rhetoric was men's work; cf. Arjava, *Women and Law,* 244–47.

88. #314.1: *sed miseriis meis evenire nulla consolatio potest, quando ante oculos sunt locata quae merui, et quantum praelatus indignior extiterit, tantum in aperto fiunt peccata superati.*

89. Sundwall, *Abhandlungen,* 51–52. As Eustorgius had the baptistery of #379 built, he was evidently a man of ample means.

Messala in Rome drew him out even further. Having received "a report late, to be sure, but wished-for," he allusively felicitates Avienus on his wedding plans in a letter devoted to other business in the summer of 511, after the nuptials of their mutual friend Maximus and his nameless bride and Ennodius' own battle with grave illness.[90] What Avienus receives is visibly terser than the message Ennodius sends to his father Faustus about the family's future, or the letter that tells Messala of God's blessing on his brother's match; after several months, Ennodius resumes direct communication with Avienus, in a message meant only to elicit some reply that does not mention marriage at all.[91] In contrast, his last two letters to Avienus speak of little save marriage, praising it as a divine institution represented by the Old Testament patriarchs and complimenting the unnamed bride's breeding and merits, which make her worthy to succeed Avienus' departed mother as lady of the house.[92] Although the final message ends with an item of business, just like so many of the letters to Faustus, Ennodius prefaces it and its predecessor with expressions of ardent longing to see Avienus again, the neglected correspondent emulating the forsaken lover.[93]

The prospect of Messala's nuptials surfaced about a year after Ennodius began to discuss Avienus' wedding. In pugnacious tones, Ennodius mistrusts his ability to overcome Messala's negligence: "if, Christ our God granting, the hope of marriage breathes upon you, you'll not rout Ennodius' memory of you, since no greater affection yields like that and devoted love is shut out."[94] Asking "will I be removed as much from your heart as from your sight?" he hopes for the best and solicits Messala to pray for him at the shrines of Peter and Paul.[95] One further letter, the last in the corpus, indicates Ennodius' fears were not groundless, for it contrasts good fortune's usually agreeable effects on men's attitudes with the inflated self-esteem Messala suffers from now that he has obtained his desires. Ennodius asserts, "on account of your future wife's wealth alone, you disdain old friends, ignorant of the burden to come," vindicating his

---

90. #429.1: *de coniunctionis vestrae munere . . . venit ad me sera quidem relatio, sed votiva.*
91. #433, to Faustus; #434, to Messala (both summer 511); #448 (early 512).
92. #459 (Jul.–Dec. 512); #463 (early 513).
93. #463.3; see #459.1–3 and #463.1.
94. #454.2 (mid-512): *ergo si te Christo deo nostro tribuente spes nuptialis adflaverit, Ennodi memoriam non fugabis, quando nulla sic cessit maior diligentia et pius amor exclusus est.*
95. #454.3: *rogo . . . ut apud domnos apostolos pro me digneris preces offerre.*

own stance with a warning that Messala has no right to act thus.[96] After such reproof, he moderates the tone considerably with familiar phrases about Messala's abstention from correspondence; as in the Euprepia letters, he makes his correspondent responsible for making amends or justifying behavior.

We could rationalize the lack of a conciliatory sequel by reference to accidents of textual transmission, but the last letters to Messala do contrast markedly with those to Avienus; a certain degree of closure is implicit in their proximity to Ennodius' becoming bishop of Ticinum. In Avienus' case Ennodius effects a rapprochement of sorts in a missive that fades away on a pragmatic note while Ennodius' esteem for the bride remains constant. With Messala, on the other hand, Ennodius began to fear estrangement from the moment news of the engagement arrived, so he represents Messala's fiancée as a hindrance rather than a support on the journey toward sanctity.

Contacted less frequently than members of Faustus' family are other individuals with whom Ennodius seems to have had cordially profitable relations, loosely termed relatives. Their precise relationship to him is impossible to ascertain. Some lived in Italy. In Aquileia we find Helisaea, who had been warmly recommended to Ennodius by Cynegia herself, and her son Avitus, whom Ennodius called upon as a useful contact in arranging the election of a new bishop for that city, as well as for attending to other legal problems.[97] Ennodius regarded Senarius as unbreakably linked by "twin bonds of charity and blood" and "the greater portion of my soul," thus a kinsman; he was a friend of Faustus and worth knowing in his own right, involved in both secular administrative matters in Ravenna at Theoderic's court and religious debate in Rome.[98] In chapter 3 we noted the letters of praise and petition addressed to the philosophic senator Boethius, testimony that the latter's erudition and fortune rendered the degree of their relationship ultimately irrelevant to Ennodius.[99] The invo-

---

96. #468.2 (sometime in 513): *de sola amicos veteres futurae uxoris opulentia contemnis, nesciens sarcinam venire.*

97. Helisaea: #177. Avitus (*PLRE* 2, 195): #168, #178 (episcopal election); #248, #249 (for Bonifatius' brother, detained near Aquileia); #253, #280, #281 (legal problems of Sabinus' son).

98. Senarius: #30.3 (*gemina vincula . . . caritatis et sanguinis*), #241 (*animae meae maior portio*); cf. #78, #116, #160, #171, #273, #279, #294, #310, #383. *Comes patrimonii* and *patricius: PLRE* 2, 988–89; Moorhead, *Theoderic,* 157, 210; Amory, *People and Identity,* 413.

99. A real tie, if hard to define: #271.3 (*proximitatis*), #318.3 (*propinqui*), #370.5, 8 (*propinquum/parentes*); Moorhead, *Theoderic,* 166.

cation of "proximity of blood" (*proximitas sanguinis*) links Ennodius with Venantius, consul of 507, as well as with Venantius' father Liberius, the patrician and perennial civil servant to whom Ennodius wrote six letters of friendship and business.[100]

A man called Olybrius is the key to three of Ennodius' relationships, one very close. Although he disappears early in the works, after a correspondence of only six letters, from him spring Ennodius' connections to the littérateur-functionaries Iohannes and Eugenes and a religious woman named Speciosa. When Ennodius first writes to Iohannes claiming friendship of a literary sort, he forbears to name the young man's father, distinguishing him only by his "tranquillity of character," but proclaims his father-in-law to be Olybrius, exemplary in his eloquence.[101] The elevated diction of the correspondence addressed directly to Olybrius confirms this accolade by displaying a wealth of mythological allusion and poetic invention along with the declarations of concord and affection indispensable to gracious letter writing.[102] When Olybrius temporarily stops writing to him, however, Ennodius makes mention of the conduct obliged by blood in a missive addressed jointly to Olybrius and Eugenes.[103] The fact that Eugenes first appears as a co-addressee with Olybrius, then receives condolences on the death of a brother the next time Ennodius writes to him makes it fairly likely that the dead brother was Olybrius, who receives no letters after summer 503.[104]

Only two letters from Ennodius to the nun Speciosa exist, both early in the corpus. Ennodius expresses his profound respect, praising her as a shining adornment of the Church, "the cloudless splendor of a good conscience."[105] Some phrases deserve a closer look. In the first missive he apologizes for failing to write, then calls her "light of the Church," giving her the credit for leading the way in religious devotion as he recalls his promise to emulate her in all things, conforming his silences and speech to

---

100. #250 (Venantius' consulship: *PLRE* 2, 1153); #429.2: *cum parente vestro domno Liberio,* about the "suburban property." Petrus Marcellinus Felix Liberius (*PLRE* 2, 677–81): #63, #174, #279, #399, #447, #457; see O'Donnell, "Liberius the Patrician," 41–42.

101. #4.6: *te pater morum tranquillitate, socer eloquentia similem producat;* cf. #15, #55, #141, #304. Olybrius: *PLRE* 2, 795–96; Moorhead, *Theoderic,* 148–49.

102. Especially in #13 (early 502) and #27 (winter–spring 503; prose preface to elegiac couplets).

103. #32.1: *deberem quidem sanguini et proposito silentii venustatem.*

104. #32 is the first letter to Eugenes, #67 (Jan.–Apr. 504), mentions his brother's decease (so Sirmond). #37, #42, #48 (all late-spring–summer 503) are to Olybrius alone.

105. #35.3: *bonae splendor sine nube conscientiae;* #36 (May–July 503).

hers; at the end, he simply asks her to extend the example of her holy conversation and remember him.[106] The second, filled with regret, explains
why he could not visit her in Ticinum. Just as Ticinum's walls were coming
into view and he was planning what to say, the *vir inlustris* Erduic (whom
she had asked him to see) met him on the road and took him back home to
Milan in a state of extreme anguish. Who was Speciosa? Why was Ennodius so upset at failing to visit her when official business intervened?

In his final letter to Olybrius, after musing about the principles and
aims of epistolography, Ennodius says that he is distressed that he could
not perform the service for Speciosa and her sisters in religion that Olybrius had requested of him, "for now there is nothing left to me of intimacy or pledge with them, especially when they live in distant cities," but
affirms his commitment "in the instance of your relations" (*in adfinium
vestrarum causa*).[107] This statement confirms Speciosa's kinship with Olybrius, a man with whom Ennodius is demonstrably familiar, while the second letter Ennodius wrote to her establishes that she lives in Ticinum,
where Ennodius first entered the religious life under the guidance of
Bishop Epifanius. Now, he declares, the place is revered for her sake, and
offers the letter as evidence of his intellectual and spiritual integrity. In his
letter to Olybrius, on the other hand, he stresses Speciosa's remoteness and
lack of mutual obligation.

Ennodius' choice of words for each correspondent is illuminating.
From his reply it appears that Olybrius had based his request on the presumption of a relationship between Ennodius and Speciosa that Ennodius
no longer considered valid, whereas the humble veneration of the letters to
Speciosa herself implies a continuing relationship on a different level.
Pignus can signify both vow and child; although offspring would not have
impeded Ennodius' entry into the clergy, it seems better to take the word
as referring to vows. We already know, from chapter 1's discussion of the
confessional letter (#438), that Ennodius had become engaged and that his
former wife or fiancée entered the religious life when he did, but by itself
that document does not provide information sufficient to determine
whether the marriage took place, and with whom. On the basis of the cor

---

106. #35.2: *aequo ergo animo sustine quod deliqui: dum in ea re praecedis, lux ecclesiae, ipsa
voluisti. ego servo animum quem promisi, ut in universis si mereor aemulator existam; cuius rei
fidem dum tacentibus vobis taceo et quod loquentibus loquor ostendi.*

107. #48.6–7: *nihil enim nunc mihi cum illis residuum est familiaritatis aut pignoris, maxime
quia in disiunctis civitatibus degunt;* Moorhead, *Theoderic*, 149. *Pignus* signifies not only
"pledge, token" but also "child, progeny": #80.24, #84.3, #120.1, #293.2, #363.34, #452.13.
Cf. Dubois, *La latinité*, 218.

respondence just examined, however, it becomes attractive to identify Speciosa, the kinswoman of Olybrius, as Ennodius' ex-wife.[108] If so, the fact that the first letter in the entire collection of Ennodius' writings is addressed to Olybrius' son-in-law Iohannes makes more sense. Ennodius' words to Speciosa intimate that she had given herself over to repentance and prayer more promptly and completely than he; his intrusions may have been unwelcome to her and, moreover, disciplinary canons gave clergymen sound reasons to avoid associating with most women.[109] The use of a bearer to communicate more than the written word's conventions permitted suggests Ennodius may still have kept in touch, though no more letters survive.[110]

Though founded on a notion of clerical sociability his correspondent did not share, Olybrius' request for Ennodius' assistance reminds us that the propinquity Ennodius so often invokes involved two-way relationships. He might ask people to do him a favor for the sake of family ties but, as relatives, they could just as easily claim the same prerogative. This could occasionally be gratifying, as we saw in chapter 1, when Ennodius agreed to investigate the feasibility of Laconius' marriage plans for his niece; he undoubtedly preserved the letter as a sign of his familiarity with both the successor of St. Peter and the advisor to the king of the Burgundians.[111]

Laconius was not the only Gallic relative to appear in Ennodius' letters. As mentioned earlier in this chapter, he much admired Arcotamia and her holy son at Lérins; he accords the highest tribute to her virtue in the face of worldly temptation; her daughter-in-law Aetheria served as its inadvertent foil.[112] Aurelianus, another Gallic correspondent whom we met in chapter 1, in fact provided the news about Aetheria. When Aurelianus at last became a bishop, the responsibilities of his new office caused his letters to Ennodius to cease; Ennodius was greatly distressed by this failure of rapport, but he must have had a similar experience when his own episcopate began.[113]

---

108. Vogel, vi–vii. Cf. Ferrai, "Il matrimonio," 956–57; Ruggini, "Ticinum," 304; Sundwall, *Abhandlungen,* 12–13.

109. #8 (from 501) advises bishops what company they should keep. Orange (441), can. 21–22 (22–23); Arles 2 (442–506), can. 3; Anvers (453 Oct. 4), can. 4; *Stat. Eccl. Antiq.* 27 (46) (*CCSL* 148). Other clergymen with sons: *LP* 44.1, 50.1, 59.1, 60.1; Caspar, *Geschichte* 2, 25, 129, 181.

110. Both #35.3 and #36.4 refer to the *portitor* and his functions.

111. #252 (late 506 or early 507).

112. #319; Aetheria: #412.2; Cass. *Var.* 4.12, 46.

113. #270, #390, #412, #455 (now a bishop).

Not only as a kinsman, but also as a Catholic clergyman, Ennodius had a special obligation to succor widows and orphans. The Gallic Camella, clearly related to the *parens* Camellus mentioned earlier in this chapter, put him in a peculiarly difficult position, however, by insisting that her son be instructed in two intrinsically opposed disciplines. Ennodius' single letter to her reflects this dilemma. He dispenses with the usual thematic preface and comes straight to the point. Camella's plan, he states, has caught him completely off balance: when she sent her "little one" to Milan with a deacon called Patricius, who related her wish that the boy study the liberal arts, she had already had her son "marked with the titles of religion."[114] Ennodius naturally found this situation highly problematic; though he approved of the son's dedicating his life to the service of God and withdrawing from the world, he had misgivings about Camella's demand that he also receive the full panoply of secular education. But he could not refuse her: "Truly, you have driven my mind from the anchorage of calm to the open sea of ponderings; still, with God's favor, I have taken up the little native of my blood."[115] We may suppose that Ennodius saw that the boy was educated as Camella wanted, but a year later had to ask Liberius the patrician to give her, now both widow and captive, official assistance in obtaining provisions.[116]

What generalizations can we make about Ennodius' dealings with all these people who are in some measure connected by kinship? Considering how nebulous many of his connections are, at least from our vantage point, it is apparent that a particular individual's characteristics—rank, sex, age, interests, and personal situation—make more of a difference than whether he or she is a relative or not. With Olybrius and the family of Faustus, for instance, Ennodius can combine literary playfulness with practical business, whereas he tries to adopt a more austere verbal stance for pious ladies and men of the Church, always working within the expressive conventions of the epistolographic tradition. The pleasures of polite correspondence between living humans, however close they may be,

---

114. #431 (summer 511): *intercepisti nostrum nescio quem secuta consilium. nam parvulum tuum quem studiorum liberalium debuit cura suscepisse, ante iudicii convenientis tempora religionis titulis insignisti.* The plural likely indicates both lectorate and notariate: Riché, *Education and Culture,* 99.

115. #431.3: *vere animum meum de quietis statione ad cogitationum pelagus expulisti; suscepi tamen deo auspice sanguinis mei vernulam.* Camella's aspirations for her son were not outmoded: Wood, "Administration, Law and Culture."

116. #457 (mid-512). Conditions in Gaul: Wolfram, *History,* 309–13; Klingshirn, *Caesarius,* 111–24.

depend on putting comfort before candor, but many distress him by failing to keep up their end of the correspondence. His sister Euprepia remains a special case because, having defined her relationship to him more precisely than any other, Ennodius expects more from it. Otherwise, he shows unusual reticence about his own parentage, allowing negative family feelings to escape only once, in the confessional letter. There, he recalled the death of his aunt and the dreadful prospect of having to rely on the charity of relatives, which he calls "bitterer than captivity's lot," clearly implying that his life was less than carefree after his parents died; while he succeeded in acquiring a decent education, security remained elusive.[117]

Ennodius' fictional families offer us a different perspective on relationships because of the thematic choices Ennodius made. We find them scattered about the corpus, both among the smaller occasional pieces and in the academic *dictiones,* whose relationship to reality we considered in chapter 2 and whose relevance to the construction of the family will soon be evident.

Reconciliation between parent and offspring is the subject of one epigram, entitled "verses about one who committed theft so that he might reconcile son to mother."[118] Nothing in the text of the poem indicates what the misdeed was, but the first-person speaker endorses "holy deceptions which supply good issue" by sowing the seeds of peace with hatreds; the teleological approach to resolving personal differences resembles a certain Wodehouse story.[119] Aware of the moral paradox inherent in using wrong to bring about right, Ennodius still finds peace in the bosom of the family preferable to war.

Neither poem nor speech, the curious piece inscribed "a sister to a brother" offers a theoretical alternative to the sibling relationship played out in the dossier to Euprepia; the vagueness of its references, coupled with abundant observations on how affection and duty should ideally coordinate, contrasts with the conclusion's legal formulas.[120] This so-called letter depicts an unidentified sister justifying her strictness toward her son and

---

117. #438.21; see chapter 1.

118. #131: *versus de eo qui ut filium matri reconciliaret furtum fecit.*

119. #131, v. 2: *amplector sanctas quae dant bona semina fraudes;* 4–5: *qui natum matris per culpam reddit amori, / hunc odiis constat missurum semina pacis.* Cf. P. G. Wodehouse, "Pearls Mean Tears," in *The Inimitable Jeeves* (1924).

120. #120 (Jan.–Oct. 505): *exemplar epistulae quam ipse dictavit. fratri soror.* Magani, *Ennodio* 3, 356 (a letter somehow germane to Ennodius' ministry); Léglise, *Oeuvres* 1, 40–41 (a will in epistolary form).

her extraordinary love for her brother with an argument reinforced by the dichotomy between words and things. The sister defends her conduct by criticizing the laxity of others: "when the name 'son' is believed to have more value than filial obedience . . . he who disdains severity in the case of his offspring signifies that the idea of it pleases him more than its worth."[121] Her central pronouncement, "for it is right that the ever-faithful community of the sibling relationship be preferred even to one's progeny," corresponds closely with the idiom of Ennodius' direct addresses to Euprepia, suggesting that this document may represent affirmations of sisterly devotion that Ennodius wished to receive from his Euprepia's pen, rehearsed at a safe remove from their imagined authoress.[122]

Turning to the 15 academic *dictiones,* we encounter relationships of an unquestionably fictional type. We have already seen in chapter 2 that certain declamations display awareness of social realities, testifying to Ennodius' predilection for clothing domestic dramas in the pretext of public order. What the characters and crises of these fifteen items say about families in the Christianized sixth century now takes center stage. Virgins of various sorts appear in three of the ten *controversiae* (as Sirmond called them); all except one of the remaining seven, however, involve violations of the parent-child relationship, with the one apparent exception indicting an envoy who had betrayed the fatherland, in other words an issue of political infidelity.[123] Dealing with adult situations from the pre-Christian past, the five discourses on epic themes (Sirmond's *ethicae*) fall into three types: expositions by Diomedes, Menelaus, and Dido on the consequences of sexual infidelity, whose possible relevance to the contemporary scene I explored in chapter 2, Thetis' maternal lament for her son's inevitable death, and a prediction of Hercules' fate by Juno, his divine anti-mother.[124] Whether they originate in traditional tale or legal fiction, we can resolve practically all the characters in these *dictiones* into fathers, mothers, and sons. My point is not merely that these declamations turn on aberrant, cheerless situations—all declamations and most serious works of literature do—but that these situations predominantly involve defective family relationships rather than points of political or religious legislation,

121. #120.1–2: *quando plus creditur fili vocabulum valere quam obsequium . . . qui in prole censuram neglegit conceptum magis designat sibi placere quam meritum.*

122. #120.2: *fas enim est germanitatis semper fidele consortium etiam partubus anteferri;* cf. Constable, "Forged Letters," 20–26.

123. Virgins: #223, #278, #380. Parents and children: #222 (stepmother against stepson and husband), #239, #243, #261, #363, #467. Legate: #221.

124. #208, #414, #466 (infidelity); #220 (Thetis' sorrow); #436 (Juno's prediction).

and that Ennodius speaks for the prosecution far more often than for the defense. We could regard even the treasonous legate as a son who has mortally wounded the *pietas* he owes the land that bore him, as I suspect Ennodius was thinking in that *dictio* about the schism that had not yet ceased to harrow his alternative family of the Italian Church.[125]

A good place for us to begin examining the predicaments in which Ennodius' characters find themselves, the fundamental moral issues they imply, and the ways in which Ennodius chooses to resolve these issues is his oration defending a son once held captive by pirates who refuses to provide for his now-destitute father. This piece is the longest and most fully developed of his *dictiones,* boasting all the divisions of a complete textbook speech along with a theme taken directly from one of the Quintilianic *Major Declamations.*[126]

Entitled "The Ransomed Invalid," the Quintilianic declamation took the part of a wretched, grief-stricken father. Forced to decide which of his two sons he wanted released, the father chose the ailing spendthrift, who proceeded to die on the way home. The bereaved parent argues with an abundance of contrary-to-fact conditions that the surviving son, who succeeded in escaping from the pirates' clutches by his own exertions, should nevertheless support him out of filial piety and gratitude. He contends that he loved both his sons but pitied the sick one more, hurling several variations on the theme "insolent youth" at his adversary and disparaging him for his ungrateful rudeness and pride.[127] The father's utterances have considerable recourse to pathos, with a touching vignette of the ailing son in chains, who is alleged to have thanked his "best brother" with failing breath and said, "I would be supporting Father if he had ransomed you."[128] The old man's own sad prospects dominate the finale as self-pity mounts. "I would not live long even if you were both supporting me," he whimpers, alleging concern for his son's reputation and piety but ultimately stating "I will go begging; you will support me."[129]

Whatever modern scholars think about its actual authorship, this decla-

---

125. *patria* occurs five times in #221, *pietas* twice, and the last three paragraphs (5–7) employ metaphors of injury and health. The procreative *patria:* #2.1 (*genitale solum*).

126. #363 (late summer 509; no title in the MS) in eight sections; cf. [Quint.] *Decl. Maj.* 5, *Aeger redemptus.*

127. The son is often addressed as *iuvenis,* usually without modifiers; cf. *Decl. Maj.* 5.2, 4, 13, and 21.

128. *Decl. Maj.* 5.21.

129. *Decl. Maj.* 5.22–23; cf. Saller, *Patriarchy, Property and Death,* 114, 125–27; Parkin, "Out of Sight, Out of Mind," 131–34.

mation's Quintilianic attribution gave it considerable authority in the eyes of Ennodius and his well-schooled contemporaries, so his treatment of the topic begins with modest reticence, inquiring, "Is it right to speak against Quintilian unless it is on behalf of the truth, or does eagerness for speaking make the one dispensing words of justice forgetful of himself?"[130] In good rhetorical fashion, Ennodius replies to his own queries with the same opposition of deceitful sophistication and honest artlessness he invokes in crises of friendship and truth, modestly declaring "let simplicity fortified by the favor of the heavenly powers proceed against a man most eloquent."[131] What follows, however, is a bravura display of verbal and conceptual diversification, more ornate both in structure and detail than its second-century predecessor. The imagined audience, for example, whom the earlier declaimer addressed merely as "gentlemen of the jury," Ennodius addresses as "men of leadership," "most honorable judges," and "most scrupulous judges."[132]

Enhanced by a wealth of color and variation, Ennodius previews his defense of the escaped son as the speech proper opens, setting temporal legislation against transcendent rights: "Vainly do you implore sustenance from the bounty of the law, who by your acts have abrogated the laws of nature: the law decrees that victuals be accorded to fathers, but that obligation exists only so much in a name."[133] When a father decides that a dying, wastrel son is more worth saving than a healthy, responsible one, says Ennodius, he shows his complete disregard for decency and indeed life itself, so that the survivor declares, "it is clear that even the wastrel's ashes were preferred to me."[134] As Ennodius tells the audience, this is the speech of a good son who passed his youth in frugal anticipation of his majority, watching what he had refused to squander spent by his father on his sibling's extravagances; since this son has had to endure the torments

---

130. As many as four different authors may have composed the *Major Declamations:* Steinmetz, *Untersuchungen zur römischen Literatur,* 188–90. #363.2: *numquid fas est adversus Quintilianum nisi pro veritate dicere, aut inmemorem sui loquendi facit aviditas qui tribuit verba iustitiae?*

131. #363.2: *fallentes decet urbanitas . . . sine solacio oratoriae artis aequitas adseratur . . . procedat contra eloquentissimum virum caelestium favore munita simplicitas.* Cf. #49.1–2; #317.

132. #363.4 and 18 (colorless *iudices*); cf. #363.3 (*principes viri*), 4 (*cognitores amplissimi*), 33 (*sanctissimi cognitores*).

133. #363.4–5: *frustra pastum beneficio legis inploras qui factis tuis naturae iura solvisti: exhiberi victum patribus ius decernit, non est tantummodo sacramentum istud in nomine.*

134. #363.6: *clarum est me et cineribus vitiosi fuisse postpositum.*

both of piratical captivity and of paternal indifference, he suggests virtue is more of a punishment that its own reward. Against the father's claim of insufficient money to ransom both brothers, the son disconsolately recollects his father's partiality, unmistakable even before the other brother was chosen, and allows that man to take no credit for his son's successful escape "with the gods as guides."[135]

When Ennodius turns the speech to the fundamental idea that the earth's produce should sustain everyone, which he links to proper family feeling, he accords great importance to the power of the will. In the Quintilianic declamation the father presented a case heavily dependent on the weight of the law that emphasized the son's quasi-contractual obligation to support him. Ennodius, however, chooses to affirm a positive role for the affections in which exemplary behavior, not arbitrary commands, cause someone to do the right thing. Since compassion is voluntary in nature, he asks, "is there a place for mercy when domination presses?"[136] Devotion cannot be ordered, so the father has betrayed himself: "he proclaims what he deserves from a son, who supposes the latter does not respond to the duties of nature unless he is forced."[137] A father, Ennodius says, must conduct himself as a genuinely loving parent before he can expect filial piety from his offspring. Faithful to good declamatory practice yet pursuing his own agenda, Ennodius renegotiates the eternal crisis of filial obligation, with Aeneas and Scipio, paradigms of sonship from myth and history, reinforcing his contention that for both parents and offspring, goodwill is by nature voluntary and good deeds reciprocal, moved by external stimuli and inward desire.[138]

The Quintilianic defender of the father's legal rights found it expedient to represent the son as an offensively intemperate juvenile. In contrast, Ennodius' young man is compelled by fate to speak more in sorrow than in anger, stating, "the hardships of native soil and foreign lands are one and the same thing, as far as I can see, and homecomers and captives feel equal bitterness."[139] Two years later, as we have seen, Ennodius chose sim-

---

135. #363.12–16: *dis ducibus;* Reboul, *La rhétorique,* 25.

136. #363.19: *numquid misericordiae locus est ubi instat imperium?*

137. #363.23: *pronuntiat quid de filio mereatur qui eum ad officia naturae nisi coactum aestimat non venire.*

138. #363.21–23, 27–28; Beard, "Looking (Harder)," 61–62; Saller, *Patriarchy, Property and Death,* 108–11.

139. #363.24: *una est, quantum video, genitalis soli et peregrinationis adversitas nec dispar amaritudo redeuntibus et captivis.* Cf. #438.21 and #2.1; Ahl, "Art of Safe Criticism."

ilar words to render his own distress; either both occurrences are empty
clichés, or both express his perception of the relative merits of barbarian
captivity and toxic family life. Go figure. Harrowed by piratical privations
and tortures, the son of Ennodius' *dictio* has returned home only to suffer
further at the hands of a heartless father. Even one of the barbarous
pirates had tried to console him, saying, "fear nothing, sigh not over this
affliction; if your parent lives, you will be separated only a little while from
the harbor of freedom."[140] The son believed his captors not "inhumane
masters: they were the sort who could be softened also by entreaty," and
tears would have made up for lack of gold had his father truly wanted to
bring both sons home.[141] In conclusion he declares that, prematurely
debilitated by his ordeal, he is physically and mentally indisposed to fulfill
demands enemies would shrink from making and trusts his father will find
his imminent decease as pleasing as that of his brother.[142]

The stance and argumentation of this particular *dictio* indicate an intellectual environment conspicuously different from that of Quintilian's
emulators of the high Empire. That barbarians could on occasion be more
humane than so-called civilized folk would not have been utterly surprising to Ennodius' hearers and readers, who would have had experience of
enough genuine barbarians to form their own opinion about people who
would once have been the "Scythians" of literary convention, but the sympathetic pirate must yield the prize for novelty to the disillusioned son.
While traditional Roman notions about the behavior expected of fathers
and sons were still nominally in place, their images refurbished from time
to time by poets and legislators, Christianity had already begun by the end
of the fourth century to alter how seriously people took them.[143] In the old
days fathers were sometimes misunderstood or embattled, but never altogether wrong or wicked. The tendency of the pre-Ennodian Latin declamations shows that sons spurned fathers only at considerable moral and
financial risk; although it was rhetorically feasible to claim otherwise,
speakers might entertain only so much irreverence toward the Roman
father, like Mom, the Flag, and apple pie today. With Christianity's fundamental, if often disregarded, rejection of the natural family in favor of

---

140. #363.30: *nil metuas, nil de hac adflictione suspires; si creator tuus superest, parum a
libertatis statione seiungeris.*

141. #363.31: *non habuimus, iudices, dominos inhumanos; fuerunt qui potuissent et prece
molliri.*

142. #363.35: *qui gravaris de vivaci praesentia desideriorum summam capias de sepulchris.*

143. See Evans Grubbs, "Constantine and Imperial Legislation on the Family"; and
Hunt, "Christianising the Roman Empire."

kinship with God, it became morally and emotionally possible to talk about how the ideal father-son relationship, finally revealed in the incarnation of Jesus Christ, corresponded with reality and departed from it.

Ennodius was familiar with the parable of the prodigal son, to whom he compares his own erring self.[144] We can regard the *dictio* examined here as an oratorically formulated meditation on the feelings of the other son, the good, dutiful son who worked hard, never left home, and became understandably irritated to discover his father was celebrating the wastrel brother's return. Unlike the Quintilianic father, the father of the parable took the trouble to allay his son's anger by reaffirming their common cause and justifying his joy with the words, "you are always with me, and all my things are yours: it was, however, proper to feast and rejoice, because your brother here was dead, and lives again; he had been lost, and is found."[145] The topical vitality of Ennodius' rebuttal of the rhetor known to him as "Quintilian" is undeniable once we realize that its backdrop is the sharing, giving celebration of life contained in the closing words of the parable of the prodigal son. The traditional Roman paradigm of father-son relations expressed through a static legal mythology is here superseded by a Christian model founded on the belief that exemplary action conduces more to good than domineering words. Only by virtue of this model can complementarity of will and action within and between individuals exist, be it in the Trinity or between mortal fathers and sons.

Long thought the acme of affectation, the *dictiones* originating in epic scenarios in fact afford more opportunities to observe Ennodius' creative treatment of traditional family units. A learned audience would have been well acquainted with the story of the subterfuges Thetis adopted in the effort to avert the fate awaiting her son Achilles; the failure of her ploys offered rhetoricians an obvious opportunity to meditate on futility. The words Ennodius chose to put into Thetis's mouth, however, reveal his particular outlook. Alluding to the familiar episodes from Achilles' life, she speaks as an immortal subject to grief, who can perceive the future but change neither it nor her son's mortal nature, and asks, "who would believe a provision that both goddess and mother devised was ineffective?"[146] Some pages ago we noted Ennodius' epigrammatic celebration of a successful mother-son conciliatory gambit. Despite divine prescience,

---

144. #438.15; cf. Eph. 3.14–15.

145. Luke 15.31–32 (my translation from the Vulgate text).

146. #220.1: *quis credat inefficacem fuisse provisionem quam et dea et mater invenit?* Sources, structure analyzed: Schetter, "Die Thetisdeklamation des Ennodius."

Thetis's protective deceptions are doomed to failure; he allows this fictional mother scant comfort, only the undying glory of Achilles dead and her own decorous silence.

Some years later Ennodius chose the figure of Juno, another goddess, to convey reflections on death and glory in a *dictio* sparked by Hercules' defeat of Antaeus. Properly speaking, Juno was mother to neither, but her partisanship of Antaeus and antipathy to Hercules, her husband Jupiter's bastard son, mark her as a kind of evil stepmother. Her claim that Antaeus, her champion, "stands great by his own strength, but will be the greatest through his downfall" (by coming into contact with the earth that bore him), is unintentionally valid for Hercules too, in view of his eventual death and apotheosis.[147] Ennodius makes Juno's protest, "if misfortune flatters our enemy, we attain to laurels," betray the irony of her situation, glorified by an enemy who from birth has resisted her every attempt to crush him and whose elevation to the gods will spring from the most grievous affliction.[148] Her final words seek to rebut the notion that Hercules' invincibility is assured: "who would not believe he has nothing left to accomplish, beholding his enemy sprawled on the ground? On the contrary, our side's resolve will revive from its swoon and the incident endured, luckily for the foe, will furnish a reason to increase our strength."[149] An audience conversant with the symbolic and euhemeristic readings of Hercules current in Late Antiquity would have had no difficulty grasping this scene's figurative implications.[150] Precisely because Juno tries and fails to prevent her husband's son from fulfilling his destiny, her malevolence the antithesis of maternal nurture, Ennodius requires her to testify to Hercules' immortal virtue just as her champion is overthrown.

One of Ennodius' *controversiae,* however, contains a clear portrayal of the stereotypical fiend Juno only approximates: an evil stepmother who, unable to convince her husband to hate his son from a previous marriage, poisoned both of them.[151] Assuming the prosecutorial role, Ennodius des-

---

147. #436.1 (summer 511): *stat propriis magnus viribus, sed erit maximus per ruinam.* Cf. #13.1–2 (early 502); Luc. 4.589–660.

148. #436.1: *si hosti nostro blanditur adversitas, nos ad laureas pervenimus.*

149. #436.3: *quis non credat nihil superesse quod peragat, cum humi fusus hostis aspicitur? at nostrae partis intentio de oppressione suscitabitur et augmentandi roboris causam feliciter pro inimico perfuncta res suggeret. oppressio* and *suscitare* have medical connotations, cf. #438 (esp. 9–14).

150. Cf. Fulg. *Myth.* 2.2–4; Isid. *Etym.* 1.3, 3.71, 8.11; Kennell, "Hercules' Invisible Basilica," 167–71.

151. #222 (Jan.–Sept. 506).

ignates the stepmother's primary target with unaccustomed precision, using the technical term for stepson (*privignus*) rather than any sort of artful circumlocution. He portrays this woman's enmity toward her stepson as so great that it drove out all affection for her husband: "where in the world was the spirit of conjugal kindness, where the sacrament of the marital tie? The thought of the stepson had more effect than that of the marriage bed."[152] Poisoning both the spouse and his son thus constitutes twofold infidelity, betraying the vows of marriage and the dictates of motherhood. This speech distinguishes nicely between dramatic topoi and real life, observing that stepmothers are a useful invention and indeed often anything but wicked, for "under this name, a woman attends more warily to another's offspring, the more scrupulously she wants to avoid a tragic reputation."[153] Ennodius makes no further effort to balance his portrayal, however, by highlighting the situation's ambiguities; this fictional woman remains utterly abhorrent, the antithesis of the virtuous wives and virgins enshrined in his sepulchral epigrams.[154]

Permutations on the theme of parricide take center stage in three *dictiones* in which Ennodius also speaks as a prosecutor. The earliest deals with what is now termed "elder abuse," specifically a son's withholding food from his aged father so as to cause death. Taking a moral position consistent with his other utterances, Ennodius gives vent to an initial burst of horrified aporia, then denounces the son for devising an unheard-of means of eliminating unwanted parents: "most glaring is the invention of your wickedness, neither to banish your own creator's demise, as a devoted son, nor to inflict it, as befits a cruel one."[155] The crime offers opportunities for pathetic paradox: the perpetrator feeds on the wasting away of his victim, and a faltering, wrinkled father vainly envisions his grown son, a strapping young man, as the sustenance of his last days. Ennodius also introduces examples from the field of natural history rather than his customary literature or technology. These last Ennodius deploys just before the perora-

---

152. #222.4: *ubinam gentium fuit animus coniugalis diligentiae? ubi maritalis sacramentum copulae? plus egit privigni quam tori recordatio.*

153. #222.7–8: *saepe tamen sub hoc vocabulo mater accedit eo cautior circa germen alienum quo sollicitius nomen tragicum vult vitare.* Cf. Dixon, *Roman Family,* 147, and "Conflict in the Roman Family," 152–53.

154. It may involve Ennodius' alternative family, the Church: the antiheretical #464 contains the closest verbal parallels to the characterization of this crime and its condemnation.

155. #239.2 (Jan.–Sept. 506): *prima est malorum tuorum adinventio, creatoris proprii exitium nec removere ut pium filium nec ut crudelem decet inferre.* Then and now, the theme is far from imaginary.

tion in order to prove that this son is guilty not only of offending against human law but also of violating the law of nature that orders the behavior of wild animals. Since, so he believes, even fierce eagles and ravaging wolves receive food from their young, he can ask "what sort of disposition is ignorant of how to imitate winged creatures in respect to affection for their own?"[156] Although Ennodius proposes no specific punishment, this evil deed must not spread.

The second *dictio* focuses on the classic parricide, with a political twist. In this permutation of the theme, Ennodius assails a tyrant for honoring a son who slew his father. Twin wrongs provoke his indignation: the glorification of a "father-destroyer" (*patris extinctor*) as a public hero, and the usurpation of authority by the individual granting the honor.[157] The speaker pauses momentarily, contemplating the political outrage of conferring a statue on so unworthy a recipient—"caught among the cliffs of your virtues, venerable leader, I know not whether I should accuse you because you are a tyrant, or because you honor parricides with a reward"—before he pronounces both tyrant and parricide "worthy of crosses and to be expelled from the present life in sacks."[158] Ennodius' allusion to the peculiarly grotesque fate reserved for those who kill their parents develops into a wholesale indictment of the tyrant's regime; he demonstrates, point by point, how the usurper's crimes correspond to the parricide's, with the logical conclusion that he should suffer the identical punishment. In their respective domains, both usurpation and parricide are terrifying acts that menace the foundations of human society, rendering the personal and the political, the public and the private, completely interchangeable: "this thing you do in regard to the fatherland is what this man inflicted on his parent . . . nothing remains that either a prostrate fatherland or a destroyed father would trust."[159]

Ennodius' third *dictio* on the subject of parricide occurs very late in the corpus and is much briefer than the rest, but contains the greatest number

---

156. #239.7: *quale est ingenium, quod circa diligentiam suorum alites nescit imitari? transeo multiplicibus exemplis luporum rapacitates.* Cf. Cassiod. *Var.* 2.14; Parkin, "Out of Sight, Out of Mind," 124–26.

157. #243.3–4 (Oct.–Dec. 506).

158. #243.4: *inter virtutum tuarum, venerande princeps, deprehensus abrupta nescio, utrum accusem quod tyrannus es an quod honoras praemio parricidas; utrique digni crucibus et de praesenti vita culleis effugandi.*

159. #243.7–9: *hoc tu circa patriam geris quod intulit hic parenti, in eo fortasse crudelior tu credendus . . . nihil est quod residuum aut adflicta credat patria aut pater extinctus.* Cf. Cic. *Rosc. Am.* 24–26 (66–73); Kennell, "Herodes Atticus."

of dead relatives.[160] The son in this piece, evidently disowned for good reason, first slew his father, then disposed of his mother to forestall dissent, finally tricking and killing his younger brother. The prosecution's speech begins here, presenting an open-and-shut case adorned with appropriate circumstantial details: a broken-down wall, a dagger, a lethal projectile. The plot against his brother has already nullified the murderer's exculpatory assertions when his accuser's voice informs him, "you lost your hope of defense when you sketched your mother's limbs with steel."[161] Ennodius' choice of theme and persona show his awareness of rhetoric's limits: he prosecutes because no cleverness could excuse killing one's parents and junior sibling, even figuratively.

Not all Ennodius' invented sons are murderers; one manages to afflict his family after their death, as the *dictio* assailing a dice-player illustrates. This offender had already squandered the fortune bequeathed him by the frugality of past generations when he staked the field that held the tombs of his ancestors (his last remaining property) and lost. Ennodius' role in this speech is to insist that the duty of observing the final wishes of one's ancestors transcends any sort of transient financial exigency. Consequently, he tells the dissolute son that alienating the final resting place of his family would have been unacceptable even to redeem a child taken hostage by the enemy, let alone for the sake of a game. "Reverence for the deceased is common to all people and, respecting piety, all humanity demands a care worthy of the final lot of its founders," he thunders and ends by exhorting the audience sitting in judgment to envisage all of this sacrilegious man's ancestors present to claim the amends justly due them.[162] Ennodius could have denounced impiety of this sort in patently Christian terms but in this *dictio,* as in his other rhetorical indictments of crimes against the family, he argues in the traditional mode; while he and his audience undoubtedly held to the principles of Christian morality, the genre enabled him to make observations about moral behavior without mentioning Christianity.

Ennodius' thematic preoccupations sometimes produce amusing collocations of subject and audience, particularly in the three *dictiones* com-

---

160. #467 (sometime in 513), with no MS title.

161. #467.3: *perdidisti spem defensionis, cum genetricis ferro membra describeres.* Cf. Dixon, *Roman Family,* 147–48, and "Conflict in the Roman Family," 153–66.

162. #261.7: *communis est universis defunctorum reverentia et circa religionem sorte ultima conditorum dignam poscit humanitas universa culturam.* It was written for Ambrosius, Faustinus' son (*PLRE* 2, 69); cf. #424–26.

posed with Arator in mind.[163] The last of them, which argued against letting a captured city's priests and virgins go free, I discussed in chapter 2
because of its relevance to the contrasting vocations of Arator, the future
subdeacon, and Maximus, for whom Ennodius wrote an epithalamium.
The first two, however, are among the items concerned with parricide. As
Arator was an orphan with a persistent yet postponed calling to the religious life, Ennodius' choice of subject appears somewhat strange unless we
take its relationship to the ideal family of Christian theology into account.
When Arator later decided to elaborate on the sacramental implications
contained in the prose text of the Acts of the Apostles, he chose heroic
verse.[164]

Despite its title, the *dictio* "against a legate who betrayed his fatherland
to the enemy" cited earlier in this chapter has less to do with secular affairs
of state than with family loyalties. The family here is not Ennodius' natural kin, I suggest, but the elective family of the Church clad in the idioms
of old Roman political discourse. Ennodius' preoccupation with simultaneous incompatibilities dominates the *dictio*'s first sentence, which seeks to
distinguish between the punishment a traitor deserves and the sacred office
of envoy.[165] Since the *sacramentum* in question can denote both a secular
oath of office and the sacrament of holy orders, treason just as easily takes
schism's place in this speech. Ennodius asserts that the legate's crime lies in
the utter thoroughness with which he used his office to betray his people:
"our counsels bore a way for you, so that you might emerge more pernicious to the fatherland; we managed, while seeking a champion, for you to
appear a more powerful enemy of the state."[166] By so abusing a position of
trust, the traitor is compared to a malign physician; in chapter 5 we will
find Ennodius using medical imagery in explicitly ecclesiastical contexts.[167]
The piece concludes by demanding the offender be punished without
regard for his status, so as to serve the cause of common probity and
pietas, the duty of sons and patriots. Why did Ennodius pursue this line of
reasoning? Lexically speaking, without fathers there would be no fatherland, and contemporary events do lend weight to the *dictio*'s dramatic sit-

---

163. #239, #243, #380.

164. Hillier, *Arator,* esp. 17–19.

165. #221.1 (Jan.–Sept. 506): *et proditoris meritum et sacramentum legati.*

166. #221.3: *ut nocentior contra patriam existeres, viam tibi consilia nostra pepererunt; nos
egimus ut fortior hostis, dum propugnatorem quaerimus, adpareres.* The envoy's cunning:
#221.4 (*quantis colorum varietatibus et urbanitate letali*); cf. #49.65 and #317.1.

167. #221.6. Cf. #49.21–23, 121; #464.6.

uation. The time range for this piece's composition (the first nine months of 506) coincides with the period leading up to Pope Symmachus' reception of a deacon named Johannes. A partisan of the antipope Laurentius for several years, this deacon left a letter in which, repenting of his discordant views, he anathematized those who had tried to supplant Symmachus.[168] Ennodius may have been less than happy with how the reconciliation of the former Laurentians to Symmachus was proceeding and so worked out some of his disagreements in this *dictio.*

Given the problems that could arise from particular human beings and their likenesses, Ennodius sometimes found abstractions an apt way of reflecting on issues of physical and spiritual parentage. This mannerism is quite apparent in the range of metaphorical expression in two items, a pedagogical *dictio* of 505 and the larger tract for Ambrosius and Beatus composed late in the collection. When he introduces the son of a certain departed Eusebius to liberal studies, Ennodius reviews the occupations that require practice and calls persistence "the mother of arts," whereas negligence is "the stepmother of erudition."[169] This identification of positive and negative qualities occurs elsewhere, with good and bad female roles from the repertory of close kinship usually expressed through abstract nouns of feminine gender, though limited largely to educational and oratorical settings.[170] The late tract (Sirmond's *Paraenesis Didascalica*) exhibits this practice to the highest degree, exhorting the two young men to "love modesty, the mother of all good works," and to integrate chastity with decency, its philological and ethical cognate, before they encounter Purity herself, who precedes Faith.[171] Appearing in a genealogical progression, these virtues subsequently acquire an attendant when they reach the threshold of liberal studies, "Grammar, the nursemaid, as it were, of all the rest."[172] Not really one of the family in respect to essential merit, grammar nonetheless retains her place as a trusted servant who prepares the immature soul for higher knowledge. Grammar reminds her explicitly Christian audience "that bygone age said we were the best parents / because we count with approval as our offspring / what a belly

---

168. Wirbelauer, *Zwei Päpste,* 24–25, 34–38; Moorhead, *Theoderic,* 124–26.

169. #124.3: *sicut artium . . . invenitur mater instantia, ita noverca eruditionis est neglegentia.* Eusebius: *PLRE* 2, 422.

170. E.g., #3.7; #240.8, 31; #263.80; #314.1; #414.2; #455.2.

171. #452.1–9, at 5: *matrem bonorum operum amate verecundiam; Castitas* appears in 7, *Fides* in 9. Cf. #80.10, #85.5, #98.10.

172. #452.11: *quasi nutricem ceterarum anteponunt grammaticam.*

swelling with the seed of learning has brought forth, / nor has wantonness enslaved the rights of a noble heart."[173] She and Rhetoric, her successor, represent patterns of thought and language essential to virility and Romanity; though insufficient for salvation, they lay the foundation for a future edifice of Christian virtue built by the demeanor of exemplary men rather than the precepts of the lecture hall.

Ennodius' enveloping vision of the family is not his alone. Other Gallic writers operating under similar constraints share his claustrophobic realization that families are the actual and metaphorical sources of nurture as well as obligation. Exemplary is Eucherius of Lyon's hortatory letter, a cautionary essay on the blandishments of worldly prestige and knowledge that threaten to seduce his kinsman Valerianus away from true Christianity. Introducing his discourse with a motto—"well fastened by the bond of blood are those who are united by the bond of love"—Eucherius explains that he and Valerianus should rejoice in the conjunction of charity and propinquity as a gift of God, as the two necessary modes of relating (the flesh of natural generation and the individual immortal mind) interact to produce a single sentiment.[174] Crass carnality, however, is the least of Valerianus' temptations. Because he regards Valerianus as heavenly leadership material, Eucherius challenges him to disregard the affections and obligations of fleshly parentage in favor of his duty "to recognize and accept his own creator and to devote his life, a divine gift, that is, to divine service and worship."[175] He contrasts the anxieties of obtaining earthly advancement, for instance through adoption by some wealthy and estimable man, with the incomparably more exalting invitation to become a son of God. Eucherius speaks of fathers and sons, not masters and slaves, and of belonging to an ideal family whose members work together for heavenly rewards rather than competing for the world's vain prizes.

Although an individual's identity still centers on the natural family, Eucherius warns against the family's power to distract and impede impressionable souls, preferring saints like Gregory, Basil, and Paulinus of Nola, who rejected the fleeting rhetorical and philosophical attainments beloved of their ancestors to embrace salvation, the eternal and incorruptible

---

173. #452.13: *nos parentes dixit aetas illa maior optimos, / quod favore conputamus esse nostra pignora / quae dedit venter tumescens litterati seminis, / nec libido subiugavit iura clari pectoris.*

174. The so-called *Epistola Paraenetica, PL* 50.711–26 (711: *bene alligantur vinculo sanguinis, qui vinculo consociantur amoris*); cf. Wes, "Crisis and Conversion," 253–57.

175. *PL* 50.713–15 (713: *proprium cognoscere auctorem cognitumque suscipere, vitamque, id est divinum donum, in divinum officium conferre*).

good. In the letter's closing paragraphs, Eucherius keeps urging Valerianus not to seek the things of this world but, in a shift of metaphor, to look about and steer away from his "sea of troubles" into the calm harbor of the religious life.[176]

When the ambition of individuals and families raised storms of ill feeling, however, the ideal family of the Church could not afford complete emotional protection to its members. When bishop of Clermont-Ferrand, Sidonius Apollinaris had to supervise an episcopal election in the neighboring see of Bourges; he preserved his sermon for the occasion in a subsequent letter.[177] Sidonius' animadversions concerning the congregation's attitude suggest a calling to religious office could provoke accusations of favoritism based on the candidate's background, character, and education. Whoever the nominee—a monk renowned for holiness, one of the diocesan clergy, a civil servant—he will inevitably be criticized by someone, though Sidonius is careful to repeat such remarks only as preface to his exposition of the merits of the actual bishop-to-be. When Laurentius of Milan died and Ennodius was passed over for preferment, let us remember that it was his kinsman Avienus who received Ennodius' disgruntled confidences; thanks to Sidonius, we have some idea of what may have been in other people's minds at the time.

Ennodius' own relationships with individuals like Avienus, Arator, Messala, and Aurelianus thus witness to the ways the elective affinities of the Church could collide with natural family relationships. Arator's ascetic disapproval of marriage, particularly in Maximus' case, earned him a lecture from Ennodius about society and civility, while Messala's own marriage estranged him from Ennodius the celibate deacon. In contrasting circumstances, the waning of another friendship became evident in the last letter to Aurelianus. After his promotion to bishop, Aurelianus communicated so infrequently that Ennodius had to acquire what news he could from second- or third-hand reports.[178]

Ennodius' response to the new bishop's inconsiderateness is anticipated in a letter of the fifth-century Gallic churchman Salvian, who reacted to the effect of ecclesiastical preferment on intimacy with similar displeasure. Eucherius of Lyon did notify old friends when he became a bishop, but by

---

176. *PL* 50.723–26 (*de pelago negotiorum tuorum velut in quemdam professionis nostrae portum prospice proramque converte*), a metaphor familiar to Ennodius.

177. Sid. Apoll. *Epist.* 7.9, to Perpetuus of Tours; cf. *Carm.* 16, vv. 71–128, a thanksgiving to Faustus of Riez.

178. Aurelianus: #455.

means of a servant rather than in person. Salvian found the maneuver so off-putting that he wrote Eucherius to let him know. Because he considered an oral message transmitted by a slave inferior to a real letter from Eucherius himself, Salvian reproved his correspondent for a lack of love and hoped for improved relations if negligence, rather than egotism, caused the lapse. Although he did not think the new bishop suffered from arrogance, Salvian wanted Eucherius to reply for the sake of his former regard "lest, if in certain of your obligations your practice differs, something may seem permitted to new honors in your case."[179] Salvian simply wanted their old relationship to continue; bishops, however, were bound by a more stringent discipline, which necessitated a higher degree of separation from both laymen and subordinate clergy, as Gallic councils reiterate. The social repercussions are painfully evident in the correspondence of Salvian and Ennodius, but spiritual compensations remained. Pious women like Camella, who sent Ennodius her son to be educated at Milan, might offer prayers for him, and one of them, Apodemia, went so far as to present him with a monastic hooded cloak, which Ennodius perhaps saw as a sign of his life to come.[180]

Laden with reflections on the nature of family relationships, both concretely and in the abstract, we can read Magnus Felix Ennodius' literary remains as a representation of the author as a seemingly self-contained creation. Compared with the celebrations of family life found in the works of Sidonius Apollinaris and especially of Ausonius, whose *Parentalia* engross social historians with their loving technicalities, Ennodius has given scholars looking beyond his authorial personae little to work with.[181] We know with certainty only the names of his father (Firminus, by indirection), one of his sisters (Euprepia, with whom he had a quasi-public epistolary relationship), and two nephews (Lupicinus and Parthenius). All the rest of his family members are either nameless, most notably his mother, or names without precise designations. Some of those names belong to people for whom Ennodius has a great liking—Olybrius, Faustus, Avienus, Messala, Laurentius—but that liking owes more to common literary and ecclesiastical interests than to simple consanguinity. Further-

---

179. Salvian *Ep.* 2 , to Eucherius (late 420s or early 430s): *ne, si in quibusdam officiorum tuorum mos discreparit, aliquid in te novis honoribus licuisse videatur.* Lagarrigue (*Salvien* 1, 17) called this subject a "traditional school theme," developed "avec une ardeur innocente."

180. Camella (#431.3); cf. Domnica (#285), possibly identical with Domnina (#302), Arcotamia (#291, #319), Firmina (#305; #165, #229). Apodemia (#441) sent the *cuculla* in the last third of 511.

181. Cf. now Lolli, *D.M. Ausonius,* 19–25, 43–44.

more, we have seen that Ennodius locates far more of what he has to say about families, most of them thoroughly dysfunctional, in fictional contexts such as *dictiones* than in his own personal correspondence. Through the hardships of his early life, the reversals of fortune that attended his youth, and the timely interventions of clergymen like Epifanius and Laurentius, Ennodius came to realize that his real home was the Church, where the relationships he formed were voluntary, lasting affinities of choice (*Wahlverwandtschaften*) rather than frail accidents of birth.

Ennodius' consciousness of the conjunctions and conflicts that spring from the double bonds of blood and vocation is by no means unique but, as we have seen, it finds its most voluble and characteristic expression in writings in which religious and educational concerns intersect. Both the natural family and the family of those dedicated to God made demands that bred dilemmas in their turn, yet, through the interplay of these two forces, an individual might also gain greater freedom. The religious life offered an alternative to the traditional power of the natural family, fostering *Wahlverwandtschaften* that made it easier for Ennodius to relate to family, friends, and fellow churchmen. As his concerns with money and property demonstrate, his poverty was relative rather than absolute. He could keep body and soul together in a canonically approved manner as well as assist his bishop but his resources fell far short of the wealth required to compete socially with men like Faustus and Boethius. Such great men and their piously erudite womenfolk found it more congenial to associate with a well-placed deacon, supported intellectually, emotionally, and socially by his religious vocation, than with someone's poor cousin. While Ennodius did not, of course, act as his own hagiographer, the way his writings distance him from his birth family and draw him closer to the fellowship of exemplary Christians foreshadows the day when others would regard him as a saint.[182]

---

182. Ennodius' success in divorcing himself from his natural family finds parallels in Merovingian hagiography: see Theis, "Saints sans famille?"

CHAPTER 5

Speaking Out for the Faith

This book's title calls Ennodius a gentleman of the Church, but up to now we have been looking at aspects of Ennodius' life and work that were not necessarily concerned with his responsibilities as a Christian and, more strictly, as a member of the Catholic clergy. In light of his religious profession the traditional mythological motifs that appear in writings for Christian audiences, like the *dictio* for Epifanius' episcopal anniversary, have been diagnosed as "pagan intrusions," but we could just as easily label the Scriptural or patristic allusions he embeds in secular literary occasions such as satirical epigrams or social letters "Christian intrusions."[1] In this chapter we will at last consider what Ennodius wrote in his professional capacity as a Catholic clergyman. Among the documents connected with his official assignments are letters of several kinds, *dictiones* for bishops, two saints' lives, blessings of the Paschal candle, a few prayers, and the polemical works defending Pope Symmachus (the *Libellus*) and attacking Eastern schismatics (the *in Christi nomine*).

On certain occasions, Ennodius mixes secular forms and sacred content, but Christian values prevail. In one of the collection's earliest items, a *dictio* from early 503 celebrating his return from the ecclesiastical hurly-burly of Rome, Ennodius gives voice to his literary enthusiasms in a traditionally oratorical manner; at the same time, he never forgets that he is also speaking in his quality as deacon.[2] The prose preface of this piece is replete with Vergilian allusions and a vigorous appreciation of rhetorical expertise, while the elegiac verses that follow transcend their genre as Ennodius modulates his song from a windblown maritime narrative reminis-

---

1. Christian: #192, #213, and #406. "Pagan": #43, #260. Cf. Fontaine, "Ennodius," 417; Vessey, "Patristics and Literary History"; and "Literacy and *Letteratura*."

2. #2.2 plus 20 elegiac couplets (see vv. 1–2, 37–40). Lebek, "Deklamation und Dichtung," offers little but faulty emendations.

cent of Ovid into an Ambrosian hymn to the saving grace of the Incarnation. A year or so later, gracefully entrusting his nephew Lupicinus to the
grammaticus and rhetor Deuterius for instruction in the art of civilized discourse appropriate to a future senator, Ennodius observes that a successful student can amplify the renown of his teachers; he carefully distinguishes "your Maro" from "our Jerome," conscious of the ideological
divide separating Deuterius' profession from his own.[3] In early 512, late in
the works, Ennodius treated the youthful Ambrosius and Beatus to a sam-
pling of the amenities still offered by traditional education, which could
happily coexist with the Christian virtues of modesty, purity, and faith.
The close of his exposition features a list of individuals whose lives exem-
plify the principles of moral and intellectual virtue already enunciated; the
roll call culminates in Stefania, the sister of Faustus, whom Ennodius
characterizes as "the Catholic Church's most shining light."[4]

A certain number of the pieces copied into the register of Ennodius'
compositions did not necessarily circulate under his own name. The earliest of these is a directive that all priests and deacons should live with at
least one approved person as a companion so as to prevent scandal.[5]
Another is a letter directed to a group of exiled churchmen from Vandal-
ruled North Africa, which counsels the "little flock" to be of good cheer in
spite of its tribulations; the message's character is evident in the reference
it makes to a previous letter that the Africans had sent to a deacon requesting "the benediction of the blessed martyrs Nazarius and Romanus."[6]
That deacon would either have been Pope Symmachus' right-hand man
Hormisdas or Ennodius himself; the martyrs are the key to his identity.
Romanus was a martyr of Antioch celebrated by the poet Prudentius and
venerated in Milan, but Nazarius was peculiarly Milanese, as his remains
had been rediscovered by St. Ambrose himself.[7] If these Africans desired a
true relic of St. Nazarius, they would have had to apply to Laurentius of
Milan, the highest-ranking bishop to support Pope Symmachus, so even if
the addressees had appealed to Rome, the deacon must be Ennodius him-

---

3. #69.14: *Maro vester . . . Hieronymus noster.* Cf. #23.3 (to Avienus); Kaster, *Guardians,*
61; Klingshirn, *Caesarius,* 73–74.

4. #452.25 (widow of Asterius). Cf. #394.3; *PLRE* 2, 173–74, 1028. "Christian pedagogy": Magani, *Ennodio* 3, 49, 245–53; Rallo Freni, *La Paraenesis didascalica,* 30–32.

5. #8 (early 501), *praeceptum quando iussi sunt omnes episcopi cellulanos habere.*

6. #51 (summer 503), quoting Luke 12.32 (*nolite timere, pusillus grex*). Caspar, *Geschichte*
2, 128; Sardella, *Società chiesa e stato,* 162–63.

7. #51.5; Lanzoni, *Le Diocesi* 2, 1101; Prudentius, *Perist.* 10. Nazarius: Paulinus, *Vita
Ambrosii* 32, 2–4; Ennodius' hymn (#349).

self. He finally assures them God will restore calm to the churches when He pleases, as a kind of spiritual tax remission, "so that the grief which adversity imposed is consoled by the sweetness of peace."[8] With the disorders besetting the Church in Italy, Africa, and the East, both writer and readers could approve of this sentiment.

The implicit presence of Symmachus in the letter to the Africans, together with the works composed especially for the bishop of Rome, which comprised at least the *Libellus* and the *in Christi nomine,* show Ennodius working behind the scenes as a ghostwriter on at least three occasions.[9] Such compositions for Symmachus were by no means unusual, since Jerome, Prosper, and Gelasius had done likewise for the popes whom they served. The vagaries of the manuscript tradition, however, make it more difficult to ascertain how much ghostwriting Ennodius may have done, for the most recent edition of the *Clavis Patrum Latinorum* calls only two of the items in Sirmond's text of Ennodius spurious and shifts the question to the entry for Symmachus, which says Ennodius drew up ten to twelve of that pope's letters, but offers few points of comparison.[10] As far as we can see, Ennodius' works were composed and circulated in different ways—he sent some items to friends for comment and emendation and prepared other pieces on behalf of ecclesiastical superiors—but preserved uniformly as an archive by being copied into a register and selectively transmitted after his death, all of which indicates his style of production and publication was more medieval than classical.[11]

The letter to Constantius on free will testifies to another aspect of Ennodius' responsibilities as a churchman: dispensing theological advice in the form of personal correspondence. Here, Ennodius enters the swirling waters of the controversy over the role of the human will in salvation vis-à-vis divine grace, which Westerners found as unsettling as Easterners did

---

8. #51.5: *dabit deus, cum ipsi placuerit, reducem ecclesiis quietem, ut maerorem quem indixit adversitas pacis dulcedine consoletur.*

9. #49 and #464. On #464, see Townsend and Wyatt, "Ennodius and Pope Symmachus." Ertl, "Diktatoren," 66–67, cites only these two items.

10. Dekkers, *Clavis,* 486–89 (Ennodius, nos. 1487–1503) and 546–47 (Symmachus, no. 1678). Spuria: #1 (the *dictio* for Laurentius), beginning at *usu rerum venit inter homines;* #247 (to Parthenius, so B), a supposed "letter to Venantius," whose alternative addressees are Avitus (the recipient of the item following, so VLT) and Avienus (C; cf. Vogel's apparatus for Venantius). Cf. #464, discussed later.

11. Ertl, "Diktatoren," 57–66; cf. 67–71; Norberg, "Style personnel et style administratif"; *S. Gregorii Magni Registrum* (*CCSL* 140), v–viii; Markus, *Gregory,* 14–16; Constable, *Letters and Letter-Collections,* 42–52, 56–62, and "Forged Letters," 26–37.

the relationship of Christ's divine and human natures. Constantius had apparently encountered someone "asserting, about freedom of the will, that the license to choose has been given to man only in one respect, which is the worse"; Ennodius declares the proposition a trial of the faithful and hardly short of blasphemy.[12] He insists that God could hardly be just if He required human beings incapable even of desiring what is good to strive toward it, then balances the human-divine equation by paraphrasing St. Paul's letter to the Romans: "what else is there except to say, I know how to choose the right way, but unless grace from on high aids me as I begin, I will tire."[13] Taking pains to affirm grace's necessary role in preparing for and guiding good behavior, he nonetheless maintains, within the field of reference characteristic of his views on a well-ordered universe, that "unless both our will, which is free, and our effort render allegiance to such admonitions, we plunge down to peril and hell not at some command, but on our own."[14] For Ennodius the very words in which the Scriptures phrase God's injunctions indicate the potentiality to do or be otherwise: "what does the so-frequent 'don't' in the heavenly reproof look back to, if willing something else was not allowed?"[15] The responsibility for making the initial choice between good and evil rests with the individual, for all that divine grace must fulfill the promise of that choice.

Like Vincent of Lérins and Faustus of Riez before him, Ennodius did not find Augustine's magisterial interpretation of the relationship between grace and free will congenial, let alone written in stone, and sharply observes how "the Libyan disease's poisons" have spread.[16] What troubled him about the Augustinian view was its insistence on one hand that God can save people without any effort on their part and on the other that lost souls are individuals whom divine grace is unwilling to liberate. In a society in which most people were finally being raised as Christians and

---

12. (Fall 503) #56.6–7: *inventus est homo . . . adserens de arbitrii libertate homini in una tantum parte quae deterior est eligendi datam esse licentiam? o scismaticam propositionem quae . . . habet in fronte blasfemias.*

13. #56.9: *quid est aliud nisi dicere, novi dextrum iter eligere, sed nisi ingredientem iuverit gratia superna lassabo;* cf. Rom. 7.18–25.

14. #56.10: *sed nisi talibus monitis et voluntas nostra quae libera est et labor praestet obsequium, ad periculum et gehennam non imperio aliquo sed sponte devolvimur.*

15. #56.12: *totiens 'noli' in superna admonitione quo respicit, si aliud velle non licuit?* See also 56.15, on Eccles. 15.17, a passage cited both by Pelagians and Augustine himself; Brown, *Augustine,* 345–75.

16. #56.16: *video quo se toxica Libycae pestis extendant.* Cf. Weaver, *Divine Grace and Human Agency,* 157–60, 168–75; Brown, *Augustine,* 398–407.

many aspired to greater devotion, Augustine's model did not always appear the most suitable for encouraging moral behavior, since the alternative it presented to unsolicited salvation was damnation in spite of oneself. All commit sins from time to time despite the best of intentions; if grace is denied and we lack even the conception of goodness, why bother to try at all? Those contemplating the mystery of God's merciful omnipotence could find the question slightly otiose; nonetheless, it exposes the twin dangers of presumption and despair inherent in the view of human will Ennodius assailed for Constantius' edification. A little-known document of the struggle to define the operations of divine grace, this letter of instruction indicates some Italian interest in the question in the early sixth century, during the interval between the writings of Faustus of Riez and Fulgentius of Ruspe.[17] We might fault Ennodius for his confidence in the human capacity to make moral choices, but he made a real effort to address the concerns of a thoughtful adult perhaps unmollified by Gospel images of sheep and infants.

From time to time Ennodius' handling of this contentious theme has aroused suspicions that he might have been tolerant of Pelagianism, especially considering his patent distaste for the stringent Augustinian doctrine that would become the Western standard; the "Semi-Pelagian" label is unmerited, however, as many orthodox fifth- and sixth-century Gallic churchmen harbored reservations about the bishop of Hippo's teaching on the operation of grace.[18] There is nothing to suggest that Ennodius' Italian and Gallic contemporaries (who included Symmachus, Hormisdas, and Avitus) lodged any complaints, nor do his writings smack of the imperturbable self-sufficiency commonly imputed to Pelagians. Among Ennodius' more modern readers, neither Sirmond in the seventeenth century nor Léglise in the early twentieth found fault with the Constantius letter; Sirmond even drew on it to support his own refutation of the Jansenist doctrine of predestination.[19] While Ennodius' subsequent request to Constantius to "remove my trifles from public scrutiny" does suggest trepidation of a sort, fear of broad criticism of a brief study meant for private con-

---

17. Unknown to Weaver, *Divine Grace and Human Agency;* cf. Avitus, *Ep.* 4 (*MGH AA* 6.2.29–32).

18. Léglise's inference (*Oeuvres* 1, 167, 537–42), derived from Dupin, *Nouvelle bibliothèque* 4, 26–27. But cf. de Labriolle, *Histoire de l'église* 4, 397–419; Hauschild, "Gnade IV," 480–85; Markus, "Legacy of Pelagius."

19. Magani, *Ennodio* 3, 32–38; Léglise, *Oeuvres,* 167; Sirmond, *Historia Praedestinatiana,* chap. 10 (= *Opera Varia* 4, 287–89).

sumption on "a matter shadowy and unsettled," not of the specific charge of heterodoxy, is meant.[20] This work is confined to the simple statement of a unitary position concerning the human will for a private correspondent, so Ennodius' argument dispenses with the byways of circumstantial detail. In contrast, in another item of limited circulation, the confessional letter that records his own spiritual progress (#438), Ennodius is quite voluble about his constant need to be prodded toward goodness by God's grace, dispelling any suspicion that he regards salvation as a do-it-yourself affair.

Though it is not strictly a professional communication, we will now briefly examine a letter to a man named Servilio because it has some relevance to Ennodius' spiritual development. Léglise, while casting the addressee in the role of Ennodius' "master in the sacred sciences," did not analyze its tendency as a devotional, doctrinal communication.[21] Opening with a general premise, that pupils are more confident of success when their instructor is present, which narrows to the specific expectation of Servilio's advent, Ennodius declines to boast of his own expertise. He nevertheless hopes that his holy visitor will not think he "has entrusted the Church's progeny to a degenerate son," for, even if his memory cannot return fruit a hundredfold, it can still give the cultivator a good yield: "come therefore, so that you, like a good farmer, may behold your crop spread before you."[22] Further agricultural motifs, in the form of plows, scions, fruitfulness, and stormy blasts, show this letter's kinship with Ennodius' patently educational writings, although Servilio is distinguished by instructing his charges in spiritual matters instead of verbal technique; what clarifies the relationships Ennodius hints at from the letter's start is the disclaimer, "I do not want to burden Your Sanctity's conscience with the prejudice of praise: you will examine the things which are declared by the testimony of letters."[23] Servilio once taught Ennodius, presumably while he was still in Ticinum, but this letter concerns an unnamed youth ("the Church's progeny") whom Servilio entrusted to the deacon of Milan. Now the old teacher, his judgment unclouded by flattering messages, comes to see for himself what has become of his charge. Who might he be?

---

20. #57.1: *nugas meas a publico rigore subducite . . . pagina nostra res crepera atque anceps est.* Cf. #224.5: *a publico rigore me subtrahe,* of his verses about Aponus.

21. #236 (Aug.–Sept. 506); Léglise, *Oeuvres* 1, 303, cf. 20.

22. #236.2: *ne degeneri te credas ecclesiasticum germen filio conmisisse . . . veni ergo ut coram positus segetem tuam boni agricolae vice respicias.*

23. #236.3: *nolo praeiudicio laudis sanctitatis tuae gravare conscientiam; inspicies quae litterarum testimonio declarantur;* see chapter 2 for horticultural vocabulary in pedagogical contexts.

Since Ennodius' nephew Parthenius had recently gone to Rome to study, he cannot be Servilio's former pupil, whereas two of the three items immediately following this letter were intended for Arator, an orphan under the Church's protection; he is clearly the person Ennodius and Servilio have in mind.[24]

Turning from the upright but shadowy Servilio to Ennodius' professional relationships with the famously holy, we have a single letter to Caesarius of Arles, written after that eminent bishop had visited Italy to defend himself against charges of treason at Ravenna and to receive privileges from Pope Symmachus.[25] Replying to Caesarius, who had already written to satisfy his request to maintain contact after safely reaching home, Ennodius first reminisces how persuasively Caesarius' episcopal accoutrements and personal humility had worked upon King Theoderic to secure his acquittal: "when has a prince's purple despised either the hair shirt or the pallium?"[26] Claiming only to have supported and celebrated Caesarius' virtues, he gives no indication of any outstanding service he may have rendered the metropolitan of Arles, whom he envisions among the venerable martyrs menaced by tyrants of old. A miniature encomium of the addressee takes up half the letter, fusing the ideal qualities of a good bishop with those actually possessed by Caesarius. Ennodius' remarks about the good churchman's upbringing, appearance, and chaste manner of life are broadly diagnostic for bishops, as is the standard tribute, "you teach both by admonitions and examples," but Caesarius' oratorical and literary gifts command his greatest admiration.[27] "Who would not wish, when you are speaking, to read so as to know more?" Ennodius asks, overwhelmed that his Gallic kinsmen have sent someone who, "while reconciling his own talent to books through repetition, shapes even the teachers."[28] Expounding the Scriptures is one of a

---

24. #236.3. Arator: #237 and #239, contemporary with #236 (#85.17–18: his orphanhood, care by the Church). Parthenius to Rome: #225–#228.

25. #461 (early 513). See *V. Caes. Arel.* 1.24–30; Klingshirn, *Caesarius,* 124–32; Moorhead, *Theoderic,* 189–90; Wolfram, *History,* 313. Caesarius may also have been the recipient of #458: Sundwall, *Abhandlungen,* 69.

26. #461.2: *quando principalis purpura aut cilicia despexit aut pallium?* Confirmed by the *Vita Caesarii* and echoed in #80 (Epifanius' influence on various rulers); Caspar, *Geschichte* 2, 124–28; Ensslin, *Theoderich,* 291–94.

27. #461.5: *et monitis doceas et exemplis;* see Klingshirn, *Caesarius,* 146–51.

28. #461.5: *quis non optet te loquente ut sciat plura non legere? tu dum libris genium relatione concilias et magistros informas.* On the utility of oral repetition and its implications for reading: Horsfall, "Statistics or States of Mind?" 73–75.

bishop's principal duties, but the grace with which Caesarius fulfills both the oral and textual elements of his pedagogical responsibilities evokes an amazement no less genuine for being appropriate to the situation. Such complimentary language does not, however, signal the letter's end; a bit of business must be taken care of. Beyond desiring to be kept abreast of goings-on in Caesarius' part of the world, Ennodius wants to prevent Caesarius from acceding to the entreaty of a certain Rusticus who, "as far as I hear, is clothing his promiscuity with the name of wives and thinks a criminal matter can be excused by legal jargon."[29] As with his kinswoman Aetheria a few years earlier, Ennodius attempts to stop a sexual miscreant outside his territory because physical distance must not be permitted to weaken the Church's moral law. This quick finale, which trusts Caesarius will reply to the problem, reminds us the best kind of business letter is one that contains the least business possible, as the bearer would attend to the unsightly particulars.[30]

All the *dictiones* Ennodius composed for various bishops have implications for his view of the episcopate in action, though that fact has formerly been ill-appreciated.[31] Only those possessing overt historical relevance, like the first item in the corpus (a speech from 503 on the anniversary of Laurentius of Milan's consecration) and the celebration of Epifanius of Ticinum's thirtieth year as a bishop in 496/7 (which Ennodius drew upon and revised when he composed the *Life* of Epifanius) have drawn much notice.[32]

As part of the encomium of Laurentius' person and actions contained in that first work in the corpus, Ennodius presented a brief history of the trying tumults Laurentius of Milan survived to attain the venerable prominence signified by the epithet "star of the churches." The election and consecration of Ennodius' superior coincided with the onset of hostilities between Theoderic and Odoacer, making his early years as bishop a harsh learning experience: "while your new steps still sank beneath the dignity laid upon you, the adversity of inevitable time caught you up, and wars that struck against freedom rendered the pontificate's novice a very well-

---

29. #461.7: *qui, quantum audio, fornicationes suas nomine vestit uxorum et vocabulo legis putat excusari posse rem criminis;* not in *PLRE* 2.

30. Constable, *Letters and Letter-Collections,* 53–55.

31. E.g., Schanz-Hosius, 141–42; Bardy, "Saint Ennodius de Pavie," 254–56; Fontaine, "Ennodius," 403; Wermelinger, "Ennodius," 656; Olivar, *La predicación,* 306–7.

32. #1 (Laurentius' anniversary) and #43 (Epifanius' 30th anniversary as a bishop). See Lanzoni, *Le diocesi,* 988, 1021–22; Cesa, *Ennodio,* 26; Moorhead, *Theoderic,* 30–31.

seasoned soldier."[33] Despite such misfortunes, he always put his flock first. Ennodius stresses Laurentius' upright selflessness and courage, dealing with hostile barbarians and refuge-seeking Italians in the face of brutality and blandishments. For both speaker and audience at this commemoration, most important was that the bishop persevered in goodness, hoping for peace yet "remembering the atrocities, lest they pass away unpunished through forgetfulness."[34]

Ennodius presently remarks that the next section of the narrative, which concentrates on the captive Laurentius' personal and vicarious sufferings on behalf of his faithful congregation, is better suited to the proleptically hagiographical context. Though claiming, "I do not want to linger on sad things, I do not want to open up the tragedy of an evil time . . . lest by the telling I force you to relive what you suffered," he affirms that the worthy bishop did endure torture, hunger, cold, and disease.[35] Then the tribulations of Milan and its bishop come to an end: Laurentius, the good shepherd, restores his people to their former well-being, comforting them, assisting them materially, and encouraging by example; moreover, he has the city's buildings repaired.

At this point in the *dictio,* with Milan's moral and physical restoration effected, Ennodius might have ended the narration of Laurentius' life and work, but he needed to address a more pressing matter. First alluding to it as "the contest of your life, the eminence of highest purpose," he portrays his bishop's response to the "captivity" that has arisen in the Roman Church as his crowning endeavor.[36] Faced with the calamity of two bishops contending for the see of Rome, Laurentius of Milan did battle for the Church once again. Ennodius, his deacon, dwells impressively on Laurentius' tireless labors in guiding the deliberations of the synod that absolved Symmachus of wrongdoing. Although professing himself at a loss for detail, Ennodius says the gathering comprised "as many varieties of opinions as sorts of people," but those with "a taste for spiritual discernment" held to Laurentius "like a general" on the main issues as he subdued bul-

---

33. #1.12: *novellis te adhuc inpositae dignitatis labantem vestigiis ineluctati temporis suscepit adversitas et tironem pontificii exercitatissimum militem adversus libertatem inpacta bella reddiderunt;* 25. He withstood Rugi, Burgundians, and Goths: Mochi Onory, *Vescovi e città,* 196–97, 232, 241.

34. #1.13: *detestabilia retinens, ne per oblivionem inpune transirent.*

35. #1.15: *nolo diutius tristibus inmorari, nolo tragoediam maligni temporis aperire . . . ne te narrando cogam denuo sustinere quae passus es.*

36. #1.20: *ad agonem vitae tuae, ad summi celebritatem propositi perventurus . . . nata est in ecclesia Romana captivitas.*

lies with blandishments, smashed the proud-hearted with humility, and solidified wavering opinions with counsel.[37] He goes on to assert that anyone who through "raw obstinacy" disagreed with Laurentius "seethes in the billows of lamentation" with only his tears for comfort, though he must admit that partisan zeal still sparked hostilities.[38] In conclusion, Ennodius lists Laurentius' accomplishments: "to you, therefore, the protection of the venerable canons is owed; to you what occurs without a blot on the episcopacy is owed, whatever wickedness rages at present; to you what accusers concealed from others with surreptitious deceit was obvious; with you was it certified that hatreds must not be satisfied whenever faith forsakes anyone causing outrage."[39]

These anaphoric allusions indicate the limits of the political success Ennodius could gracefully claim for his bishop by 503; as the *Libellus* and other documents relating to the woes of Symmachus indicate, the battle to influence public opinion continued for years.[40] The last paragraph boasts a fanfare of imperatives affirming Laurentius' admirable qualities, which are likened to those of Abraham. Echoing the earlier section on the bishop's leadership of the Milanese, Ennodius proclaims Laurentius' active virtues. He exhorts him to manifest his personal piety as an inspiring example to the faithful, to show proper severity in correcting wrongdoers, and to "abide without stain in testimony to the highest glory."[41] A final resolution of the Roman Church's discords had to wait.

Ennodius' earliest preserved work is a *dictio* he composed for Epifanius of Ticinum's thirtieth anniversary as a bishop in 496. Consisting of a prose preface and 170 hexameter verses, this piece is far shorter and more emphatically literary than the *Life of Epifanius* written eight years later, but no less an expression of Christian faith.[42] In the preface the author represents himself as somewhat anxious about people who talk to themselves, for when a man in holy orders appeals to a crowd with florid ora-

---

37. #1.21: *quot hominum genera, tot sententiarum varietates . . . sed quibus inerat spiritalis sapor intellegentiae, quasi ducem te principalis deliberationis caritate tenuerunt.*

38. #1.22: *coquitur lamentationis aestibus qui a te cruda obstinatione descivit.*

39. #1.24: *tibi ergo debetur venerabilium custodia canonum, tibi quod sine episcopali nota contigit quidquid in praesentia saevit inprobitas, tibi patuit quod aliis accusantes clandestina fraude texerunt, apud te conpertum fuit non satisfaciendum odiis quotiens fide deseritur qui lacessit.*

40. #1.25; Wirbelauer, *Zwei Päpste*, 66–154.

41. #1.25: *in testimonio summae gloriae sine labe perdura.*

42. #43 has five sections: overture (vv. 1–35), election (vv. 36–87), infancy and entry into clergy (vv. 88–122), episcopal labors (vv. 123–61), finale (vv. 162–70). Cf. Pavlovskis, "From Statius to Ennodius," 559–60.

tory more appropriate to youth, their silences become rather noisy, asking "now why should he recite publicly, whom public praise neither befits nor pleases?"[43] This *dictio* was clearly among the first official assignments of a rather junior Ennodius in 496. Even if we set aside chapter 1's deliberations about his birth and put it back to 473, he could have been no more than twenty-four.[44] Moreover, in spite of the exception constituted by Epifanius himself, the ecclesiastical establishment's gerontocratic nature and concern for decorum promised a naturally fussy group of auditors. Although the clamorous silences of holiness seem to contradict the notion of public oratory, Ennodius maintains the merits of his subject deserve the greatest praise—"if an account must be rendered for useless speech, it must no less for useless silence"—and so proceeds, encouraged by the prayers of his mentor and inspiration, to distance himself from the "bilge of ballads" in order to utter true praise.[45] Although his preface asserts the irreproachability of both theme and medium, Ennodius nevertheless essays a *captatio benevolentiae:* "now favor with your mind one about to recite what is sure; in this work, if I do not say lesser things because of my slender talent, I will not make up greater ones for the sake of boasting."[46]

When he begins to praise Epifanius in hexameter verse, Ennodius takes nearly a fifth of the poem to explain his artistic situation. The first sixteen lines evoke the polytheistic, error-filled productions of the seer-poets of old, when "depraved divinities fabricated restraints of morals with deceptive song," particularly Phoebus and "the thrice-three sisters" at the Oracle of Delphi.[47] The truth-telling poetry of contemporary Christians surpasses it, Ennodius contends. First, he enjoins Faith to spurn "the lyre's tongue" and invokes "that Spirit, / in whose inexhaustible year always revives / whatever the earth produces, the sea brings forth, the air delivers," controlling too all things fluid and solid, animal and vegetable, then "the Son, the most high Lord God Christ, at whom all things tremble," in

---

43. #43.2–3: *nunc cur recitet publice, quem laus nec decet publica nec delectat?*

44. Sundwall, *Abhandlungen,* 13–14, 73 (495/6); Cesa, *Ennodio,* 14, 211 (497); Lanzoni, *Le diocesi,* 988 (495).

45. #43.3: *si reddenda est de otioso sermone ratio, non minus de otioso silentio . . . absit a me sentina carminum.*

46. #43.5: *nunc favete mentibus certa dicturo; in quo opere si minora pro ingenii exiguitate non dixero, pro iactantia maiora non fingam.*

47. #43, vv. 10–12: *retinacula morum / numina fallaci finxerunt sordida cantu: / Phoebum et ter ternas dixerunt esse sorores.* Oracular responses were in dactylic hexameters (e.g., Hdt. 1.47, 55, 65, and 85).

a *tour de force* of noun-laden lines.[48] Having addressed the second and third persons of the Trinity, Ennodius now prays that another be present in his utterances, "who, when he entered the ancient seer's breast, aided the prophet as he was about to speak with slender voice in King Pharaoh's time."[49] As these words allude to Joseph interpreting Pharaoh's dreams in the Book of Genesis, Joseph's inspiration comes from God the Father, thus completing an invocation to the Trinity. Furthermore, Ennodius' characterization of the seer Joseph—"filling the prince's ears with influential speech, a tone of discretion, a proper integrity"—modulates from introductory preamble to consideration of the honorand by noting some of Epifanius' own qualities.[50]

Ennodius then invites his audience to give well-deserved thanks as they celebrate Epifanius' thirtieth year as a bishop. "Behold the day we all embrace as holy, on which heavenly brightness willed to impart itself to earth / more readily and to animate souls with kindred rays, / in whom the world rejoices though its joys are not of the world," he proclaims, indicating the universal reverence for Epifanius, identified with a word (*vates*) he has already applied both to deceitful poets of Greco-Roman antiquity and to Joseph, true prophet of God and prefiguration of Christ.[51] The next fifty lines feature Epifanius' election as the central event of the piece, with the bishop's virtues at center stage. Ennodius shines a highly becoming light upon the laity and clergy of Ticinum as well, telling Epifanius that "a free crowd, to be praised for its compliance, made you its permanent master"; then "for everyone there was the same spirit, for all crowds a single voice," confirmed when "the crowd of priests and the court venerated by the ages elected, wanted, deserved, accepted, and loved" their new bishop.[52]

---

48. #43, vv. 17–20: *nunc linguam citharae quae cantat pollicis ore, / sperne, fides: magis ille veni nunc spiritus, oro, / cuius inexhausto reviviscit semper in anno / quidquid terra creat gignit mare parturit aether;* 24–29: *quem cuncta tremescunt: / fons via dextra lapis vitulus leo lucifer agnus / ianua spes virtus verbum sapientia vatis / hostia virgultum pastor mons rete columba / flamma gigans aquila sponsus patientia vermis / filius excelsus dominus deus omnia Christus.*

49. #43, vv. 30–32: *nunc precor ut dictis adsit qui pectora prisci / vatis ut ingressus Pharaonis tempore regis / adiuvit gracili locuturum voce profetam,* perfecting the doxology.

50. #43, vv. 34–35: *conplentem principis aures / pondere voce sono sensu probitate pudore.* Cf. Gen. 41; Pizarro, *Writing Ravenna,* 32. Epifanius' own virtues: vv. 74–79, 130–34, and #80.17, 62–66, 152–53.

51. #43, vv. 38–40: *ecce diem voluit quo se iubar indere terris / promptius et radiis animas animare propinquis / quo gaudet mundus cum non sint gaudia mundi.* Epifanius *vatis* (v. 42, MSS orthography); cf. vv. 1 (*vatibus antiquis*), 30–31 (*prisci vatis*).

52. #43, vv. 55–56: *libera te dominum posuit sibi turba perennem, / servitio laudanda suo;* 58: *omnibus idem animus, turbis vox omnibus una;* 86–87: *turba sacerdotum venerandaque curia saeclis / elegit voluit meruit suscepit amavit.* Discordant *turbae:* #1.10 and 21; #49.65.

Once Epifanius is elected, Ennodius shifts time and place to "something else, new and wondrous for all to tell," namely the miracle that marked the infant Epifanius as dedicated to God.[53] Even before he relates that marvelous event, Ennodius explains how the holy infant was weaned from the breast with herbal elixirs, "so that the son might not know how to recognize the mother by taste," lending a nice touch of asceticism.[54] When the wonder itself occurs, light suffuses Epifanius' cradle and the aether manifests its obedience just as with Elijah's chariot of fire: "no differently, then, does the flame running through enclose, illuminate, venerate, esteem, and encompass the boy."[55] Seeing this phenomenon, Epifanius' father (the *Life* calls him Maurus) realizes the child must be given to God as a gift of honor, whereupon Bishop Crispinus of Ticinum appears and takes Epifanius into his care, an edifying Elijah to Epifanius' Elisha.[56]

The remainder of the poem celebrates the mature Epifanius, hailed as "holy parent" and true heir of Crispinus. In a play upon the Gospel parable of the talents, his recovery of the captives snatched away to Gaul by the Burgundians constitutes special proof of his good stewardship.[57] That Epifanius could secure the prisoners' return to Liguria by overcoming an armed king with his prayers proves the power of speech mightier than weapons: "thus the martial tongue blunts swords with its stroke, / thus the brave blade of words subdues the sword."[58] This adage about the efficacy of Epifanius' verbal skills in restoring abducted Ligurian farmers leads into the final part of the narrative, which represents the bishop as the overseer of God's estate.[59] Making extensive use of agricultural imagery, Ennodius depicts Epifanius as a cultivator of souls, a farmhand in humanity's vineyards and fields who toils while awaiting his master's return; thus, he associates the bishop specifically with his Christian flock, whose calling is to heaven, and with education in a more general sense. After an allusion to

---

53. #43, vv. 88–89: *ecce aliud dictuque novum mirabile cunctis / transieram.*

54. #43, vv. 93–95: *callida mentitum genetrix cum forte saporem / herbarum querulis infundit dura labellis, / nesciat ut natus gustu cognoscere matrem,* contrasting with vv. 121–22. The episode does not recur in #80.

55. #43, vv. 105–6: *prospera non aliter puerum tunc flamma pererrans / circuit inlustrat veneratur suspicit ambit.* Elijah's *currus igneus:* 2 Kings 2.11. Literary antecedents of the miracle: Cesa, *Ennodio,* 125.

56. #43, vv. 107–20. Cf. #80.175; Barnish, "Ennodius' Lives," 16.

57. #43, vv. 123–27.

58. #43, vv. 132–33: *sic pugnax gladios obtundit verbere lingua, / sic ferrum expugnat verborum lammina fortis;* cf. #1.11, describing Laurentius.

59. #43, vv. 134–62. Captives: #80.138–41.

the parable of the barren fig tree, which I discussed in chapter 2, Ennodius at last turns to the man whose life's work he honors and addresses him directly: "receive now with favor, golden light of our life, / the joys which a modest song affords you."[60] Promising better work next time, he seeks indulgence for his present effort, determined that "a tricky syllable should by no means waver," and so returns to his artistic starting point.[61]

This *dictio* for the living Epifanius, in comparison to the prose *Life* of that bishop, does not cater to the desire for straight narrative history. Its structure is certainly "less linear" than that of the *Life,* but the observation that it is "a bravura piece in which the desire to praise the saint with a show of rhetorical ability and learned quotations has led to loss of expository clarity and of content" misses the point somewhat.[62] The *dictio* for Epifanius' anniversary is indeed a work for show, but its rhetoric is no "empty" exhibition at its subject's expense. Ennodius intended it to be a masterpiece of the traditional art of epideictic oratory for those who could still appreciate it. In effect, he created a hagiographical pageant with words, designing its tableaux of momentous events in the holy bishop's life as a mythic cycle for present and future devotees.

Ennodius' views of what bishops should be and do also emerge in the less personal *dictiones,* destined for bishops whom he did not directly serve. As we saw in chapter 3, he shows Honoratus of Novara, praised for his "basilica of the Apostles," as an educator of a special kind, who teaches by means of sturdy buildings, not feeble words.[63] By turning a temple where the old gods were once worshiped into a place dedicated to Peter and Paul, foremost among the apostles, the bishop of Novara provides physical confirmation of Christianity's triumphant truth to all beholders, whether believers or not.

Ennodius composed another ecclesiastical *dictio* so that the *vicarius* Stefanius might praise Bishop Maximus of Ticinum for the exemplary conduct and character that carried him from secular office to the leadership of his church. Its culminating observation, "you, polished and shaped by these favors of heaven, will train up the people more by doing than by talk-

---

60. #43, vv. 163–64: *suscipe nunc dexter, vitae lux aurea nostrae, / gaudia quae* [CPb; *quem* B] *faciunt modicum tibi promere carmen.*

61. #43, v. 170: *usquam ne fallax nutaret syllaba; dixi;* cf. #438.6–7.

62. Cesa, *Ennodio,* 26. Vogel noted quotations from Vergil, Sidonius Apollinaris, and others.

63. #98.

ing," places a premium on action, not speech, in stimulating goodness and discouraging sin.[64] Ennodius closes the speech by having Stefanius declare, "I have dedicated these things to Your Beatitude summarily, as it were, for the sake of commending my tongue. If, by your prayers, success smiles on my life, I will consecrate myself by fully reporting your deeds, so that what is known to all may be saved in letters that will endure for posterity, as long as the subsequent age rejoices."[65] These words are as indicative of Ennodius' own convictions as of the man who delivered them or the worthy bishop they honored: though a worthy honorand more easily justifies its exercise, writing's power prevails.

A few years later, Ennodius wrote another celebratory *dictio* for Maximus of Ticinum when he consecrated a church to John the Baptist.[66] Ennodius found this saint a singularly inspiring subject, as we will see, and quickly approached the heart of the matter: "who, on the subject of blessed John, prophet and apostle . . . may doubt that even mute mouths are loosened?"[67] His mother's fertility and the dumbness of his father Zacharias, whose power of speech was restored only when John was named, foretold the prophetic character of John's life as the Forerunner of the Word of God, "before the entrance of the Light," at "the threshold of this life."[68] Because Zacharias recovers his voice through the act of uttering his son's name, his predicament illuminates the nature of divine and human communication. Accordingly, Ennodius has the speaker affirm, "by all is it rightly believed that the apostle John is the key of words," providing a Christian foundation for verbal praxis.[69] After this homage to Christ's forerunner as the patron of the church being dedicated comes news of John's companions: "in his entourage Antoninus, hero of an ancient age, and the united brilliance of the most blessed Cassian make a mystery out of a building, a heavenly institution out of an earthly habitation, what cannot be defiled by old age out of the work of human

---

64. #214.8: *tu his eruditus et formatus caeli benificiis plus agendo plebem instituens quam loquendo.* Cf. *PLRE* 2, 1031 (Stephanus 18).

65. #214.9: *haec beatitudini tuae quasi strictim pro linguae meae conmendatione dedicavi. si precibus tuis vitae successus adriserit, gestorum tuorum plena me relatione consecrabo, ut quae universis nota sunt mansuris in posterum litteris quatenus gaudeat aetas secutura serventur.*

66. #277 (first third of 508). Laurentius of Milan, addressing Maximus as *frater sanctissime* (#277.7), likely gave the speech (cf. #314). Bullough, "Urban Change," does not list this building among Pavia's pre-924 churches.

67. #277.4: *deinde quis in beati Iohannis prophetae et apostoli . . . vel muta dubitet ora laxari?*

68. #277.4: *ante lucis ingressum. . . limen vitae huius.* Cf. Luke 1.5–25, 57–80; John 1.6–18.

69. #277.5: *ab universis iure creditur Iohannes apostolus clavis esse verborum.*

hands."[70] These holy colleagues of John complete the new church's features, and the discourse concludes, exhorting Maximus to trust in his good intentions, for ruin will never threaten an offering validated by Christ. In this *dictio* occasion (the dedication of a church) and message (the divine Word's validation of human discourse) neatly coincide with Ennodius' own preoccupations.

From Epifanius to Caesarius, living bishops elicited paradigmatic statements about episcopal virtue, but Ennodius articulated his conception of sanctity at greater length in the *Lives* of Epifanius of Ticinum and Antonius of Lérins. In chapter 3 we considered what these hagiographical works say about the natural world; let us now look at the evidence they offer for the role of bishops and holy men. Whereas the *Panegyric* of King Theoderic dwells on those aspects of Theoderic's character Ennodius considered most valuable for preserving earthly civilization as he knew it, the *Life* of Epifanius focuses on the qualities and events that show the foundation and growth of an individual life in Christ, in other words, the formation of a saint. The heroic virtues Ennodius credited to Epifanius present him as a most civilized saint, who even in youth understood how to behave properly before God, as any holy person should do, as well as with fellow humans of all types and conditions. Ennodius describes this gift in terms that would easily have suited a member of the ruling classes at the Roman Empire's height: "he would receive old men with dignity, young men courteously and, already at that time, he would boldly curb scoundrels; he was submissive to the most important, obedient to superiors enjoining holy things, pleasant and obliging to equals, affable in pure charity to his subordinates."[71] Such qualities stood Epifanius in good stead throughout his life, whether enduring an assault by the reprehensible Burco, attempting to reconcile Ricimer and Anthemius, pacifying the ferocious Rugi who had settled in Ticinum, or prevailing upon the king of the Burgundians to release the farmers of Liguria. Like Cassiodorus, Ennodius also endows Theoderic with a sense of *civilitas* for the sake of estab-

---

70. #277.5: *in huius comitatu Antonius, vetusti heroa saeculi, et beatissimi Cassiani iuncta claritudo faciunt de aede sacramentum, de terrena habitatione caeleste collegium, de manu factis quod nulla possit senectute violari;* cf. #101. Antoninus is probably the fourth-century Syrian martyr (Apamea) and Cassian the martyred schoolmaster of Forum Cornelii (modern Imola); cf. Prudent. *Perist.* 9.

71. #80.11: *accipiebat senes graviter iuvenes comiter et cohercebat iam tunc facinorosos audacter. erat primis subiectus, prioribus sancta iniungentibus obsecundans, aequalibus blandus atque officiosus, sequentibus mera caritate communis.* Cf. Cesa, *Ennodio,* 129; Barnish, "Ennodius' Lives," 14–16.

lishing the king's cultural and political credentials, but the hagiographical context of Epifanius' characterization shows certain traditional social values being transformed into certifiably Christian ones.[72]

While Epifanius never sought positions of influence, he did not shun them either, in sharp contrast to Antonius of Lérins, the subject of Ennodius' other essay in hagiography.[73] For most of his life Antonius tried to escape human society, fleeing holy orders and all companionship as snares for the soul. Wrestling with his own fallen nature, he was bothered by bears and, still more, by people attracted by the rumor of his sanctity. He finally had to remove himself to the island monastery of Lérins, where he discovered his religious colleagues were spiritual reinforcements in the battle for salvation. Antonius' life incarnates a development already adumbrated by the middle of the fifth century when, in Markus's words, "the charisma of the representative holy man was passing to the holy community."[74] As spiritual home and societal resource, the haven of Lérins was more powerful than a lone hermit.

Earlier I noted the paucity of miracles in both these *Lives*. Ennodius describes the cradle wonder in Epifanius' anniversary *dictio,* which the *Life* dispatches in one sentence, and the fiery column that Antonius beholds as the elderly hermit's soul is taken up into heaven tersely and in remarkably similar terms.[75] Beyond the image of the holy man striving to become more acceptable to God stand his interactions with those around him. Ennodius presents Epifanius' superbly appropriate relations with diverse kinds and conditions of human beings, usually influencing their behavior for the better, as both a dynamic revelation of one man's character and a solid statement of how sanctity should be manifested in society. He shows even the solitary Antonius occasionally communicating with other creatures in order to reform them, because love of one's neighbor is as essential to Christian life as individual devotion.

One document later in the corpus may represent Ennodius' own thoughts on the meaning of episcopal ordination. Composed for "a bishop starting out," it invokes God's grace in strengthening and tempering a new leader of his flock, reiterating the axiom, "let reality, not utterance, bear witness to the pontiff's splendor; the renown of this office shines more

---

72. Theoderic: #263.11–12 and 15–18. Epifanius: #80.17–26, 51–75, 118–19, 151–77. Cf. Cassiod. *Var.* 1.11, 27, 30, 32, 44; 2.24; 3.24; 4.17.
73. #240.
74. Markus, *End of Ancient Christianity,* 193 (on Cassian, *Conl.* 24).
75. #80.8 and #240.2; cf. Van Uytfanghe, "La controverse biblique," 212–17.

brightly with the sign of truth than of talk."[76] The ideal bishop must be the gardener of his own soul and his flock's shepherd; Ennodius' choice of imagery affirms that intellectual cultivation and spiritual advancement are consecutive, not antithetical. Near the end of the address he exalts one episcopal attribute above all: "we know how much more humble than his servants he who is called to religious authority will be; he who is about to assume such a command must yield even to persons of meanest condition."[77] Ennodius' portrayal of the blessed Epifanius was founded upon the Apostle Paul's words, "I am become all things to all men in order to gain all"; the same words justify these normative statements.

In addition to the ideals represented in the *dictiones* and *Lives* for ecclesiastical audiences, Ennodius' conception of active, adaptable sanctity emerges in his dealings with a second group, larger and more diverse, consisting of friends and professional acquaintances to whom he wrote about his relationship with God. The letter to Arcotamia, the Gallic relative whose son was a monk at Lérins, epitomizes his outlook: "if your piety believes me, it is a bigger thing to overcome the world in the line of battle than to avoid it."[78] Far from being incompatible with the love of God, living one's life in the world, interacting socially with other human beings, could be a way to holiness for lay people and diocesan clergy alike. When they obtruded, temporal exigencies were not to be taken as opportunities for incivility, though Ennodius occasionally fell short of his own ideal, as we saw in the literary-critical exchange with Beatus.[79] The letters in which he tried to obtain repayment of a loan made to Pope Symmachus are models of tactful forbearance; when his friend Maximus marries, polite behavior is the subject of his letter to Arator.[80] Through reassurance instead of stinging rebuke, by nurturing emotional proximity through little kindnesses, with admissions of weakness that entail pleas for prayer and mutual aid—this is how Ennodius discharges the obligations of friendship, even when business is also involved. His letters show a cluster of voluntary relationships—the *Wahlverwandtschaften* of chapter 4—predominantly ecclesiastical in origin and cultivated within a life in Christ. Christian love

---

76. #336.4: *splendorem pontificis res non lingua testetur; plus lucet claritas huius officii veritatis indicio quam loquelae* (autumn 508).

77. #336.6: *scimus quantum erit humilior famulantibus qui ad religiosum vocatur imperium; necesse est ut etiam extremae condicionis personis obtemperet cui inminet sic iubere.* Then quotes 1 Cor. 9.22.

78. #319.4: *si mihi credit pietas tua, plus est in acie vicisse saeculum quam vitasse.*

79. E.g., #405–7.

80. #77, #139, #283, #300 (Symmachus); #387 (Arator).

of neighbor informed the traditional epistolary rituals of friendship, freed from the compulsions of fleshly *parentelae.*

As outlined in chapter 1, Ennodius appears in subsequent tradition as papal diplomat, builder of churches, poet-hagiographer, and founder of choirs, developments we will examine in the postscript.[81] Many details are confused and resist verification, but it is no accident that he was remembered for much the same things he celebrated in the saintly bishops personally known to him: teaching, works of charity and construction, eloquence, fortitude, discretion. The paradigm presented by the *Vita Epifani* anticipates a model episcopate noted for administrative and doctrinal expertise rather than its glorious martyrs and confessors.

The high points of Ennodius' production on behalf of the Church of Rome are unquestionably the early *Libellus adversus eos qui contra synodum scribere praesumpserunt* defending Pope Symmachus, and the late *in Christi nomine,* directed against eastern Christological errors.[82] In these two pieces, composed ten years apart, Ennodius articulated the official Roman line on contested matters of discipline and doctrine with such epigrammatic authority that pious posterity preserved his name.

The *Libellus'* full title translates as "An Indictment against Those Who Have Presumed to Write against the Synod." Its place in the annals of ecclesiastical controversy and, more precisely, its value to the papacy derive from the fact that the participants in the synod in question (late 502) had set a crucial precedent: having declared themselves incompetent to judge the Successor of Peter, they absolved Pope Symmachus from all charges of wrongdoing. That gathering had convened to judge the bishop of Rome because of the Symmachan schism, which erupted in 498. According to the *Liber Pontificalis* (in its now canonical pro-Symmachan recension), Anastasius III "was struck down by the divine will" after less than two years as pope while secretly pursuing a resolution of the Acacian schism.[83] His death precipitated the rival elections and consecrations of Symmachus, a deacon popular with the majority of Romans, and Laurentius, an ascetic priest favored by many senators. The Acacian schism had itself been precipitated by the Emperor Zeno's attempt in 482 to promulgate a document of reconciliation known as the *Henotikon,* which

---

81. *LP* 54; *CIL* 5.2, 6464; Gianani, *Opicino de Canistris,* 116.

82. #49 (early 503), *in nomine patris et filii et spiritus sancti. libellus adversus eos qui contra synodum scribere praesumserunt;* #464.

83. Events of November 498: *LP* 52 (*nutu divino percussus est*). The *LP*'s authorship: Wirbelauer, *Zwei Päpste,* 142–47, after Duchesne.

advanced a politic alternative to the Christological definitions of the Council of Chalcedon (with much help from Pope Leo the Great's *Tomus*) without the Bishop of Rome's approval.[84] When Felix, the then-pope, found out about the *Henotikon,* he rejected the document summarily, excommunicating Zeno and the document's actual author, Acacius, Patriarch of Constantinople; the names of Zeno, Acacius, and their successors were struck from the Roman Church's prayers. In the next fifteen years, the political leadership of both Byzantium and Italy changed but without improvement in East-West ecclesiastical relations.

Since the double election of 498, Symmachus, Laurentius, and their supporters endured considerable legal and personal stress; all parties appealed to Theoderic to resolve the matter. A triumphant Symmachus confirmed his position through a synod in 499 and dispatched Laurentius to a bishopric in Campania, but Laurentius' supporters continued to fight Symmachus and his people both in court and in the streets, accusing Symmachus of administrative and sexual misconduct.[85] A series of interventions by king Theoderic (at the height of the troubles, he even sent another bishop, Peter of Altinum, as apostolic visitor to the Roman Church, so displeasing everyone) resulted in four more synods in the years 501–2; it was the last of them, mindful of the weakness of their own position relative to the Roman see's authority and Symmachus' personal popularity, which cleared Symmachus of all charges lodged against him by the pro-Laurentians.[86] But that was not the end of the matter, as we have seen Ennodius obliged to concede when praising his own bishop Laurentius of Milan. Displeased with the synod's decision, the anti-Symmachan forces renewed hostilities by publishing a pamphlet (now lost) linked to Roman senatorial circles that raised a variety of accusations. These charges can be reconstructed from Ennodius' criticisms of the pamphlet, which was entitled "Against the Synod of the Unseemly Absolution" (*adversus synodum absolutionis incongruae*), and its authors.[87]

84. Schwartz, *Publizistische Sammlungen,* 197; cf. de Labriolle, *Histoire de l'église* 4, 295–97; Meyendorff, *Imperial Unity and Christian Divisions,* 194–206; Noble, "Theodoric and the Papacy," 399–400. The schism also underlies #464.

85. The complaints included making free with the Church's property, changing the date of Easter, and consorting with loose women: Caspar, *Geschichte* 2, 89; Wirbelauer, *Zwei Päpste,* 9–21; Noble, "Theodoric and the Papacy," 405–9.

86. Synods: *MGH AA* 12 (Mommsen) 393–455, esp. 430–32. Moorhead, *Theoderic,* 114–39; Wirbelauer, *Zwei Päpste,* 21–34; Noble, "Theodoric and the Papacy," 404–8; Sardella, *Società chiesa e stato,* 70–96.

87. #49.7. See Wirbelauer, *Zwei Päpste,* 34–37, 147–49; cf. Moorhead, *Theoderic,* 121–22; Hope, *Leonine Sacramentary,* 69–77.

In the *Libellus* Ennodius shows himself righteously partisan, for he must have believed his stance in confronting and overcoming the allegations of Symmachus' pro-Laurentian foes completely justified. As well, he evidently took considerable pleasure in vanquishing those same foes as literary rivals on the field of discourse. These two factors, plus the numerous issues he had to address, entail greater length: this composition is second only to the *Life* of Epifanius in size. Although first and foremost a polemic against the enemies of the Successor of Peter, its mandate to persuade embraces both blame and praise for greatest effect in presentation. Accordingly, Ennodius devotes at least as much care to the imagery and tactics of argumentation as to substantive fact; his treatment of the subject and audience makes it clear that his chosen strategy holds literary values fully equal to legal advocacy.

Structurally, the *Libellus* breaks down into four main sections. First comes the introduction (sec. 1–6), followed by a point-by-point refutation of the seven main allegations put forth by the opposition, interspersed with supplementary observations (sec. 7–71).[88] The opposition's main charges were: (1) the synod's absolution of Symmachus was unseemly; (2) the selection of judges was defective; (3) the bishops summoned were old and feeble; (4) Symmachus refused to obey the synod's summons, barricading himself in St. Peter's; (5) to clear himself, Symmachus called a synod without precedent; (6) crowds of women upheld the beleaguered Symmachus; (7) Symmachus failed to fulfill his episcopal duties. Following the refutation are additional declarations of principle (sec. 72–97). Three speeches by Peter, Paul, and Rome, personages symbolic of Church and City, form the conclusion (sec. 98–139); the Eternal City has the last word.

Ennodius undertakes his task with prefatory protestations of unworthiness, as topos-hunters would expect, but quickly shifts to a programmatic characterization of his never-named opponents:

Customarily, fervor in speaking demands a liking for many things. If a spirit is greedy for praise and desires to purchase favor with sweat, or ignores the torture of narrative from blandishments of glory, or, bound by profit's shackles, sells the allegiance of his tongue and,

---

88. Dupin, *Nouvelle bibliothèque* 6, 28–31; Magani, *Ennodio* 2, 82–84 (14 allegations); Caspar, *Geschichte* 2, 89–103; Wirbelauer, *Zwei Päpste,* 150–52.

with his mind dominated by the urge to possess, already takes his endowment for granted, he is thus incapable of fearing the hazards that beset him in the exercise of the pen. Or, constrained by need, he brings forth an utterance deplorable, without any polishing whatsoever, and shows the public a countenance unconscious of shame, so that while he is slave to his charge he forswears attention to ornament, because the accoutrements of speaking are not a matter of business but of repose, and embellished words belong not to active service but to retirement.[89]

Ennodius' aphorisms propose that utilitarian urges produce nothing but verbal mediocrity and that his highly cultivated senatorial opponents are in reality slaves to a materialistic desire for praise and profit that morally and stylistically vitiates their every utterance. The charge that Pope Symmachus' foes are neither spiritual nor eloquent forms the real leitmotiv of the *Libellus,* which Ennodius calls "a discourse compelled by the barking of the wicked," an oratorical ministry dedicated to elders "against whom the poisons of hissing tongues have been poured forth."[90] He therefore strives to demonstrate the baseness of the pope's enemies not with theological argument, but by drawing attention to their aesthetic and moral shortcomings. He disparages the opposition's technique and personal qualities in zoological and literary-critical modes, assimilating hostile utterances to animal behavior, appealing to piety, and making forceful use of Scripture, radiantly confident his cause will prevail.

The chief topics at issue range from formal challenges to questions about the validity of the synod that exonerated Symmachus, the legitimacy of Theoderic's actions throughout the controversy, and of course Symmachus' conduct generally. The first point Ennodius makes about the anti-Symmachan, pro-Laurentian pamphlet concerns its name ("Against

---

89. #49.1–2: *solet dicendi affectum multarum rerum ardor exigere, si aut avarus laudis est animus et favorem desiderat sudore mercari, aut per blandimenta gloriae crucem narrantis ignorat, aut lucri adstrictus conpedibus linguae vendit obsequium et dum animus habendi cupidine subiugatus praesumptum aestimat iam tenere conpendium, sic ingruentia per stili exercitium nescit timere discrimina aut necessitate conclusus profert eloquium sine quacumque lima captivum et nesciam pudoris frontem monstrat in medium ut dum intentioni famulatur diligentiam decoris abiuret quia dicendi ornamenta non sunt negotii sed quietis, nec militiae sunt picta verba sed otii.*

90. #49.3–4: *coactam vocem pravorum latratu religiosis mentibus commendo . . . oris ergo ministerium pro ingenii valitudine sacerdotibus dedo, adversus quos sibilantium effusa sunt venena linguarum.*

the Synod of the Unseemly Absolution"). He dismisses the men responsible for its composition as "straying, sore-filled sheep . . . able to provoke
a great flock of shepherds," who advertise their schismatic ineptitude by
choosing a foolish title and publishing information reprobates would normally conceal.[91] On the second point, he seizes the weapons of literary criticism and gives his argument a satirical turn, linking perspiration and
inspiration (or lack of it) to transform anti-Symmachan objections to
synod organization into "a serious and respectable proposition, not only
brought forth from an armpit, but reeking."[92] Ennodius then takes his
opponents' claim not to be enemies of the pope as further proof of their
stilted unspirituality, calling them "men smoothed with every file of
artifice and purified in smiths' forges, who have found sweated-out testimony to confirm their statements."[93]

The third serious point Ennodius tackles is the charge that "the citizen
body of Rome is witness as to whether all bishops convened were elderly
and feeble."[94] He disposes of this assertion, which he finds laughably
deficient in oratorical flair, by reminding his audience that the bishops
themselves had stated they were "vigorous in age and weak in body."[95]
Ennodius even says that Symmachus' adversaries deserve a scolding for
claiming that the king's intervention accomplished little: the innocence
they cultivate in words, they slight with deeds, and what cultivation their
speech possesses merely plows through the byways, sowing darnel and
harvesting "chaff, with which hell's fire will quicken" to destroy them.[96]
Familiar from the educational writings, this agricultural metaphor gains
intensity from its new context: eternal punishment and reward raise the
stakes far above worldly edification.

---

91. #49.8: *estne aliquis praeter vos sic inter oves ulcerosas deputandus et erraticas, qui magnum gregem potuisset lacessire pastorum?* Cf. Caspar, *Geschichte* 2, 101–3.

92. #49.9: *sed redeamus ad gravem et venerabilem non solum ex ala productam sed
mefiticam propositionem.*

93. #49.11: *o homines omni artis lima conpositos et caminis fabrilibus excoctos, qui ad stip-
ulationem dictorum desudata invenere testimonia.* As Theoderic's documents did not call them
"Symmachus' enemies," they thought themselves safe.

94. #49.12–13: *testis est Romana civitas, si omnes episcopi senes et debiles convenerunt.* The
anti-Symmachans construed the bishops' age as an admission of incompetence before the
king.

95. #49.12: *se aetate valentes et corpore inbecillos esse dixerunt.* The reading is problematic; cf. *MGH AA* 12.426.

96. #49.15: *si tamen cultus est in loquella vestra quam scabro vomere velut agentes per
devium aratra proscinditis, marcenti solo lolia conmendantes, recepturi pro tali inpendio paleas
quibus gehennae in perniciem vestram ignis animetur.* Cf. *Dig.* 9.2.27.14 and 1.3.4–5; Kerr,
"Matthew 13:25. Sowing *Zizania.*"

Ennodius derides his opponents, who alleged that the Roman pontiff's attackers received no hearing, as "mindful of heaven's mandate" in having "elevated their party from adulterous association," an allusion to their own sexual slanders against Symmachus.[97] Against further charges that Symmachus had contravened the king's commands by asserting his own right to call a synod, Ennodius hurls words like *sacrilege* and *insanity,* opining that his foes cannot distinguish between hatred and truth.[98] Ridiculing the opposition's literary aspirations, he then attacks their attempt to sway the synod against Symmachus with metaphors of sickness and healing.[99] Wondering whether their queries—"because he is held to be the vicar of blessed Peter the apostle, do you forbid the chief physician to administer a remedy to his body? How do you refuse to confer healing on his soul?"—are "a great joke or a very great lament," Ennodius ironically applauds his opponents' selfless concern, then invokes Isaiah against those bothersome to men and God.[100] In quoting Scripture in the body of the *Libellus,* Ennodius applies Isaiah's words with special force.[101]

Augmented by the muck and bulk of the barnyard's larger denizens, the zoo of schismatics grows again when Ennodius brings on the cows. Countering the opposition's question of why Symmachus met with a king unqualified to judge his case, he retorts, "does the murk of sin or divine dread so bog you down in bovine stupor that your mind either deceitfully passes over a modest excuse or, oppressed by the dullness of beasts, does not recognize it?"[102] If we find fault with Ennodius' colorful manner of expression, we should remember that in the *Libellus* he has calibrated the relationships between a given subject and its audience, genre, and occasion with the same care as in all his other writings. He observed the thoroughly traditional axiom that an orator had to balance the demands of subject,

97. #49.16: *qui caelestis mandati memores partem suam a consortio adulteri subduxerunt.*
98. #49.19–20; cf. #1.23.
99. #49.21: *divinum subdidistis exemplum quod ita quadratis constat alloquiis ut ipsum in eo Crispum tenere lineam putes.* Cf. #452.14; Quint. *Inst.* 2.5.9, 9.4.60 and 69; Cassiod. *Var.* 2.7.
100. #49.21–22: *quia beati Petri apostoli vicarius aestimatur, prohibetis archiatrum eius corpori adferre medicinam? quomodo vos animae eius curationem exhibere rennuitis? magnum per divina ridiculum an maxima lamenta sint nescio;* Luke 4.23. Featured: Isa. 7.13, 8.12, and 10.1; Prov. 18.3. Ennodius' Bible: Dubois, *La latinité,* 70–71; Petitmengin, "Les plus anciens manuscrits"; Gribomont, "Cassiodore et la transmission."
101. Isaiah appears frequently, in at least seven clusters of quotations. The selection may indicate a set of views current in hostile senatorial circles: Wirbelauer, *Zwei Päpste,* 153–54.
102. #49.27: *sic vos in stuporem pecualem peccati nebula aut divinus horror oblimat, ut verecundam excusationem aut fraude mens vestra transeat aut beluarum pressa hebetudine non agnoscat?*

occasion, genre, and audience, not simply describe something and his feelings about it. Ennodius designed this pamphlet for a specific, highly cultivated senatorial audience whose only shortcoming, consistent with its support of Laurentius, was an antipathy to the person and policies of
Symmachus.[103] The tone and technique of this document indicate that its
audience could handle a greater stylistic and affective range than the mum-
bling obfuscations of modern bureaucracy.

The anti-Symmachans' use of various Scriptural and historical
examples to further their argument is a recurring object of Ennodius'
attacks, both moral and literary-critical. "By words or bayings," he
says, Symmachus' opponents claimed the role of Esau for their bishop,
making Symmachus into a wily Jacob through his more recent episcopal consecration.[104] This analogy was patently ill-conceived: Symmachus, a deacon who had served his episcopal "father" more faithfully
than the priest Laurentius, could justly claim to be Esau, while Jacob
was after all the chosen of God. Ennodius consequently asks his foes
some questions about their own birthright-snatching behavior and
dereliction toward the parental figure of blind Isaac, who lived to bless
the morally appropriate son.[105] He again makes the intellectual compe-
tence of Symmachus' adversaries an issue, observing "believe me, the
things you propose are not suitable for attack and are inimical to
peace," because the ambiguities in the story of Esau rendered it not so
much a real weapon as a tool of provocation.[106] Ennodius later produces more dubious examples from the opposition in the persons of
Samuel and Athanasius; as with Esau and Jacob, he deftly seizes upon
their ambiguities and turns them back on their authors. Admitting that
Athanasius (an orthodox bishop who suffered great tribulations and
was eventually exonerated) has something in common with Symmachus—"although the situation shows that blessed Athanasius is
unequal to the Roman bishop, as far as knowledge is granted, they are
in fact still comparable in troubles"—Ennodius vigorously expands the
thought of the bishop of Alexandria into a rebuke of Symmachus'
opponents for "Cynical prattling" (*canina loquacitate*), telling them,
"the poison of the new serpent hisses more craftily in you than in the

---

103. Cf. Moorhead, *Theoderic,* 121; Wirbelauer, *Zwei Päpste,* 152; Reydellet, "Ennodio,"
691–92. Sardella (*Società chiesa e stato,* 47–50, 145) denies any lay/clerical split.
104. #49.29: *Esau mentionem . . . nescio verbis an latratibus indidistis.*
105. #49.29–31; cf. Schwartz, *Publizistische Sammlungen,* 230.
106. #49.31: *credite mihi, pacis inimica sunt, impugnationi non sunt idonea quae profertis.*

adversaries of Athanasius."[107] Schism and heresy turn their perpetrators into detestable beasts, Ennodius repeatedly suggests.[108]

Literary criticism, more Isaiah, and an adroit use of canons attend Ennodius' declaration of renewed resolve to prosecute the matter to the fullest. Alluding to his opponents, he states the current position of his oratorical dory: "having entered the open sea of Ciceronian profundity, they transport our little boat along uncertain coasts with gusts of questions; in it, with Christ holding the tiller, I will nevertheless make port and disperse all of your whirlwinds one by one."[109] In addition to literary elements and citations from the book of Isaiah, Ennodius supplies "canons, in whose sight it is a crime to overstep the hoary definitions of the fathers," which state that no credence must be given to accusers coming from the house of the enemy; his contemporaries may not have been convinced, but clerics three hundred years later found his selection of authoritative bon mots useful.[110]

The fourth accusation against Symmachus was that he had disregarded "imperial authority," meaning Theoderic's summons, by making his stand "in the Apostolic See, as if in a sort of fortress."[111] According to Ennodius, this contention betrays his adversaries' feigned ignorance of what derives from "the serpent's knowledge" (i.e., death). He asserts that it was they who cunningly drove Symmachus, "arrayed with such defenses against your ranks and in witness to his innocence denouncing the world's weapons, away from the judges' very chambers, providing that he should neither live guiltless and unattacked nor, driven from the judges' untainted investigation, have solace."[112] Ennodius then lands more facetious blows

---

107. #49.47: *sed quamvis beatum Athanasium Romano antistiti, quantum nosse datur, inparem locus ostendat, facto tamen in negotiis conparantur* [MSS; *conparantor* Vogel]; 50: *sed astutius in vobis quam in Athanasii adversariis novelli virus serpentis insibilat.* Cf. Sardella, *Società chiesa e stato,* 51; a demonstration follows.

108. Cf. #49.53–59 (more scabby sheep, twisted snakes); 97 and 105 (defenseless sheep beset by rapacious wolves).

109. #49.31: *Tullianae enim profunditatis pelagus ingressi cumbulam nostram quaestionum flatibus per litorum incerta transmittunt, in qua tamen Christo clavum tenente portum ingrediar et singillatim de turbinibus vestris universa discutiam;* cf. Isa. 10.15, 14.4–5, 19.14, 21.2, 28.14; Verg. *Aen.* 7.378–405. Other nautical imagery: #49.51–52, 72–75, 86–91.

110. #49.34: *canones, apud quos nefas est cana patrum definita transcendere;* 40. Both cite Carthage (419), can. 4, can. 2. Ninth-century use: Fuhrmann, *Einfluß und Verbreitung* 1, 148–50.

111. #49.36: *imperialis auctoritas . . . in sede apostolica quasi in quadam arce consistit.*

112. #49.37: *quid illam quae ex viperina scientia descendit ignorantiam fingitis? . . . istam laetitiae faciem ex iudiciorum censura venientem vafra provisione sacerdotis vestri oculis abstulistis, ut eum talibus adversus acies vestras instructum munitionibus et innocentiae in testimonio orbis tela deferentem ab ipsis iudiciorum adytis pelleretis, providentes ut nec sine inpugnatione insons viveret nec haberet solacium de incorrupta iudicum inquisitione pulsatus;* cf. Wisd. of Sol. 9.5 and 10, Prov. 15.32 and 10.21; Moorhead, *Theoderic,* 115; *LP* 53.3–5.

against his opponents, juxtaposing their vaunted moral and literary perfection with the servility of their witnesses, meanwhile upholding Symmachus' supporters as truly freeborn servants of God under attack by
rapacious wolves.[113] Giving allegiance to more venerable principles, he
expresses dislike of the opposition's novelties and condemns their publicistic efforts as obfuscation: even if "a pale seeker of gold" probed their work
for signs of understanding or "a miner let light into the unaccustomed
crannies of their speeches," they would still be forcing change and doing
violence to tradition.[114]

The last three accusations were aimed directly at Symmachus. Referring
to the question of why the pope called an unprecedented synod to deal
with his crimes as falsehood, Ennodius prays for divine aid to find his way
through this labyrinth fit for snakes, reminding his adversaries of canons
that apply to all clerics who abscond before sentences are rendered. At this
point he resurrects the image of diseased sheep: "it behooved that a troop
devoted to the service of this matter arrive as an army of physicians to treat
the ulcers of a lost and depraved flock."[115] As well, he compliments his
foes on the "brilliant penmanship" and "words painted with the brush of
deception" they used to condemn Symmachus' absence from the synodal
assemblies, recalling that it was anxiety that kept the pope in hiding and
his supporters out on the streets.[116]

Ennodius was still obliged to deal with the most notorious of the accusations against Symmachus, that "crowds of women assembled with the
aforementioned (sc. Symmachus) for the rulings."[117] This is the only time
Ennodius allows explicit mention of sex, and he discredits the accusation,
which he terms a piece of "sophisticated circumstantiality" put forth by
the "most blasphemous of men," with a shot of Cicero and another flash
of Isaiah.[118]

---

113. #49.42–43, with Isa. 37.29 and 41.11.

114. #49.52: *non si auri pallidus inquisitor occurrat, in sensibus vestris latentium venarum
motus inveniat et insuetis lucem latebris sermonum fossor admittat.* Cf. #105, v. 7; Luc. 4.298.
Ridicule demolishes the question of why the pope called the synod without a precedent.

115. #49.57: *ad huius rei ministerium devotum deo oportuit agmen occurrere, ut perditi et
profligati gregis ulceribus medicorum exercitus subveniret;* Noble, "Theoderic and the
Papacy," 408–9.

116. #49.60: *stilo splendidissimo . . . fallaciae peniculo depicta verba.*

117. #49.65: *mulierum turbas . . . cum praefato ad iudicia convenisse.*

118. #49.65–66: *urbanis coloribus . . . illa vestra subtilitate . . . profanissimi hominum;* cf.
Cic. *Cael.* 3.6 plus Isa. 30.12–13, 49.25, 51.7, and 57.3–4. On Symmachus and scandal, see
#7; Caspar, *Geschichte* 2, 91–92, and 112. Allusions to adultery are few and figurative (16, 98,
125), while ecclesiastical controversy assimilated spiritual and sexual fidelity; cf. Aug. *Serm.*
24. 1 and 6 (Dolbeau).

The last point follows closely: had Symmachus been derelict in his episcopal duty and made free with the Church's property? Ennodius replies
with a countercharge of obstructionism against his adversaries, alleging
that Symmachus' difficulties in fulfilling his episcopal responsibilities,
especially toward the needier members of his flock, were caused by the
obstructiveness of others. He insists it was "through (the opposition's)
suggestion that the Church's property, which had long been the food of
the hungry, was taken away," to the detriment of the poor.[119] Ennodius is
unwilling to allow his adversaries to absolve themselves from endangering
the Church's ministry, but concedes that dragging everyone through the
mud will not mend matters.

After treating several minor issues raised by the anti-Symmachans during his rebuttal of the major accusations, Ennodius focuses on two objec-
tives. The first is to defend Symmachus in his quality as the Successor of
Peter, the bishop of Rome; this was the document's immediate goal as well
as what ensured its popularity in the medieval period. The second is to persuade his opponents, for the most part prominent Roman laymen such as
Festus, Boethius, and Q. Aurelius Symmachus, who had supported Laurentius since his election. If we recollect the letters Ennodius usually wrote
and the correspondents for whom he intended them, the reason why this
document's vocabulary more closely approximates literary criticism than
theology becomes clearer: defending Symmachus required an essentially
antisenatorial stance.[120]

In keeping with the peace extolled in the work's preface, Ennodius
deplores the combativeness of his opponents just before he embarks on
another excursus, this time in elaborately metaphorical praise of
Theoderic's piloting of the ship of state. The king's excellence inspires a
plea for union on earth and in heaven that pronounces the unspiritual
opposition "slaves of the belly and the body."[121] Calling their disordered
contentions about provincial synods and apostolic visitors to a "knotless
snare," Ennodius accuses his adversaries of obstructing the path of discourse with a tangle of "thorn bushes" and "brambles of eloquence"; he

---

119. #49.68: *iam per suggestionem vestram sublatis ecclesiae opibus qui diu fuerat cibus
esurientium famis mancipium videretur effectus.* Wirbelauer, *Zwei Päpste,* 84–85; Noble,
"Theoderic and the Papacy," 402.

120. He stresses the moral and intellectual faults of Symmachus' opponents. Boethius' *De
Fide Catholica* and *Contra Eutychen et Nestorium* present a more analytical rendering of truth
and error. Cf. Caspar, *Geschichte* 2, 114–17.

121. #49.72–75 (ship of state); 79: *vos servos ventris et corporis . . . mancipia vos esse terrena.*

likens their faults to the nuisances of harvest, in contrast to Theoderic's cooperativeness and devotion to St. Peter.[122] The literary-critical tone intensifies when he inveighs against the darkness of pretended new illumination as a brazen deception proposed by "an opinion-maker" then tries another approach: "I am not belittling you people who write things down, by whose good offices it results that the deeds of our forebears are conveyed to us embellished, but I shall not be silent about God's blessings, because our ruler surpasses the seemliness of speech with deeds."[123] The "writers" he alludes to are now obscure, but Q. Aurelius Memmius Symmachus, the father-in-law of Boethius and author of a lost *Roman History,* must have been among those targeted. The reappearance of King Theoderic at this precise point in the work is noteworthy. Ennodius characterizes him as a "venerable weigher of causes," who has attended personally to religion's needs and the enemy's desires with a single document and, in selecting the judges, "himself thrust the accusers out of their place and himself brought the accused back to hope."[124] To bedevil an opposition composed of theologically adept aristocrats, praising an Arian Germanic king for his protection of the Catholic bishop of Rome, a man well loved by his flock, left little to be desired.

For the final third of the work Ennodius elevates the tone of Symmachus' defense by arguing from his cosmic status. "God willed that the successors of blessed Peter the Apostle owe their innocence only to heaven and display an inviolate conscience to the most cunning examiner's investigation."[125] Intending that the mere mention of this condi-

---

122. #49.81–82: *ecce enode est, quod ad laqueum praeparastis . . . callis ante pervius dumetis novella interclusione vestitur . . . nos eloquii vepribus dum gradimur per plana retinetis;* Wirbelauer, *Zwei Päpste,* 151.

123. #49.85–86: *opinionis fabricator . . . non derogo vobis descriptoribus quorum beneficio contigit ornata ad nos maiorum gesta perduci; sed dei beneficia non tacebo, quia princeps noster rebus superat decora sermonum.* The keyword is *descriptor;* cf. Jord. *Get.* 16 and 28. Whatever its relationship to Jordanes (see Croke, "A.D. 476: The Manufacture of a Turning Point," 91–110), Symmachus' work makes chronological sense here (Markus, pers. comm., 17 Sept. 1997).

124. #49.86–87: *venerabilis causarum trutinator . . . in electione venerandorum iudicum ipse accusantes extra ordinem reppulit, ipse ad spem retulit accusatum.* Ennodius avoids naming Laurentius, calling him the tool of evil (i.e., senatorial) forces; many Romans were unhappy with the Goths: Moorhead, *Theoderic,* 129–33, 166–72.

125. #49.93: *deus . . . voluit beati Petri apostoli successores caelo tantum debere innocentiam et subtilissimi discussoris indagini inviolatam exhibere conscientiam.* Anything else is a "term of falsity" (92: *titulo falsitatis . . . mendaciis adhaerentia verba*); cf. #49.24–26. See Caspar, *Geschichte* 2, 105–6; Sardella, *Società chiesa e stato,* 147–53.

tion put a stop to all caviling at potential accusations and judgments on earth, he reinforces the idea by quoting the essential Gospel verse. "You are Peter, and upon this rock will I build my Church, and whatsoever you loose upon earth shall be loosed also in heaven"; if all acknowledge Peter's see as the foundation of the Church, no excuse exists for mortifying its incumbent, Isaiah's words then tell the audience.[126] At that favored major prophet's reappearance Ennodius modulates into the first and longest of the three closing speeches with a "what if?" Admitting he is no Isaiah, he imagines that St. Peter, "if you were to hear him, would say the following things."[127]

Peter's speech differs from the foregoing debate not so much in the instruments of its argumentation—charges, countercharges, metaphors, models—as in the candid tone with which the figure of the first bishop of Rome infuses the whole proceeding, primarily through use of the question-and-answer format. Unlike Ennodius, Peter can appeal directly to the audience's emotions by asking, "why . . . by the ripping apart of the Church's flock, do you subject me to new sufferings even after those of the flesh? It is an unheard-of kind of sacrilege that you gloss over with the honor of counterfeit religion."[128] The same charges of fornication, adultery, and debauchery that Ennodius aimed at Symmachus' opponents now issue from the lips of Peter, as do images of the scales of judgment, peasants, sheep and wolves, and spiritual parenthood; against the other side's many claims, he states, "few are the things which I have asserted."[129] In addition, since the paradigmatic fisherman of souls delivers the speech, Peter's stated preference for nautical and piscatorial metaphors rather than "syllogisms . . . and figures of speech" comes across as a dig at Boethius.[130] When Peter tells his adversarial audience to "look back at Rome," he illustrates the process of the city's conversion mainly by the fate of Rome's temples and statues: when the thundering Jupiter of obsolete superstition is being transformed into new vessels, the opposition's vexation of the Church amounts to fat sacrifices for

126. #49.95; cf. Mt. 16.18–19, Isa. 10.3.

127. #49.96: *quem si audiretis, haec diceret.* The full speech: 97–120.

128. #49.97: *quid . . . divulsione ecclesiastici gregis novis me et post carnem passionibus subiugatis? inauditum sacrilegii genus est, quod mentitae religionis honore coloratis.*

129. #49.106: *pauca sunt quae adserui, sed quanta ex his pendeant aestimate;* cf. 77.

130. #49.104: *syllogismos a me sermonum et schemata non quaeratis;* cf. 31, meant for an audience conversant with all the synonyms.

the Devil.[131] Neither other schisms nor hostile attacks on present conditions signify anything, for regardless of slashing attacks, "the tongue of the Pontiffs remains the interpreter between God and men."[132]

Through his patronage of the new, Christianized Rome, Ennodius' Peter can allude to "the heavenly Curia," enriched by Roman senatorial benefactions, contrasting it with people who calumniate others with the Gospels and endanger both souls and bodies, their "heart smothered with thick brambles" while blaming others for their failings.[133] Such is Peter's civilized Romanity that the simple fisherman makes a typically conciliar utterance on procedure: "about a discrepancy of the books I make no complaint."[134] After displaying reluctance to indulge in quibbling, he lectures the opposition about appropriately contrite behavior, which happens to resemble that of Symmachus' anxious, sorrowing partisans, and dismisses lingering criticisms as best left unspoken, unpublicized, and unremembered.[135] With the clergy disgraced by the schism and "windy elocution" (*elocutio ventosa*) about religion yielding no harvest, Peter concludes by telling his hearers "that Rome, head of the world, is laid low through your exertions, and the see that is the nursemaid of the pontificate is despised as if it were the last seat."[136]

Ennodius used Peter's deluge of questions to represent the grief-stricken voice of authority; he has Paul take a firmer line: "with that freedom of speech which he has always used, he thundered forth, berating the chief of the Apostles for his lenience" as an affectionate parent reluctant to send his diseased children under the surgeon's knife.[137] He intends the collegial disagreement and elaborate medical metaphor as a momentary diversion for his erudite audience as well as a reminder that the schism's remnants must be ruthlessly eradicated. Just as an individual's decaying

---

131. #49.107–8: *Romam respicite . . . dum de veteri tonante nova merito vascula praeparantur,* anticipating #98; cf. Juv. 10.61–64.

132. #49.111: *cur laceratis sententiam . . . et inter deum atque homines interpres extitit lingua pontificum.*

133. #49.112–16: *illa enim caeli curia variarum dotibus aucta curulium . . . densis cor vestrum vepribus suffocatur,* addressing Symmachus' adversaries.

134. #49.116: *de codicum diversitate nil conqueror,* quotes 1 John 1.8. Cf. *Gesta Conl. Carth.* xi–xiii, 160, 171 (1.222–23; 2.53) (*CCSL* 149a).

135. #49.117–20, cf. 61–64.

136. #49.118–20: *plura levitas dehonestat . . . mundi caput Romam per vestras intentiones esse prostratam et nutricem pontificii cathedram quasi ultimum videre sedile despectam,* citing 2 Tim. 2.23; cf. 62.

137. #49.121: *illa qua semper usus est eloquii intonuit libertate, apostolorum principem lenitatis incessens;* cf. #464.6.

flesh presages death, Paul states, so also does the Body of Christ's corruption. The pitiless tone of the introduction carries over into the speech proper, which Paul begins with two pronouncements on judging and being judged taken from his Epistle to the Romans, Ennodius' almost exclusive source of Pauline Scriptural texts for the *Libellus*.[138] The questions he asks, while less frequent than Peter's, come mostly from his own letter to the Christians of Rome and serve to point out the number of villainous hypocrites currently at large. Emblematic is this splendid catalogue: "full of iniquity, fornication, avarice, worthlessness, envy, murders, condemnation, guile, malignity, you impute malice; proud, puffed-up discoverers of wickedness, not obeying your parent, imprudent, disordered, without goodwill, without mercy."[139] Forbearing to cite additional vices, Ennodius assumes the take-no-prisoners persona of Paul to attack a target he has heretofore avoided naming: Symmachus' rival Laurentius. Pointing the finger at the holier-than-thou hypocrisy of men he calls "the followers or escorts of adulterous Laurentius," Paul asks the audience how, "after that beguiling communion's stain and plague detestable to the whole world," they could cast blame on God's innocent priests; he then alludes to his life and death, saying "you follow a man . . . transfixed not with a pen, let me say, but with the whole sword of the Church's entitlement."[140] Like Peter's, the address ends with an outburst of strong feeling.

If the audience fails to find Paul's speech therapeutic, Ennodius commands them to "look at your city, the world's parent; she approaches you in grief, behind her defenders the Apostles."[141] Peter's speech had briefly alluded to the city's passage from the old religion to Christianity, but Rome herself emphasizes the world capital's human element. She starts with great men of antiquity like the Curii, Fabii, and Decii, who represent both standard literary-historical references and senatorial ancestors. The now Catholic city, however, disowns those worthies of a bygone age, "whom the Church did not regenerate," just as mercilessly as Peter and

---

138. #49.122 (citing Rom. 2.1–2, 14.22, appropriately). Exceptions: 2 Tim. 3.8 and 4–5.

139. #49.125: *accusatis malitiam, repleti iniquitate fornicatione avaritia nequitia invidia homicidiis condemnatione dolo malignitate, superbi elati inventores malorum, parenti non oboedientes, insipientes incompositi sine adfectione sine misericordia.*

140. #49.125–26: *docetis fornicantibus neminem esse miscendum, adulteri Laurenti aut sequaces aut praevii . . . post illam inlecebrosae communionis maculam et pestem toto orbe exsecrabilem sacerdotes dei quasi obsoleta conparatos communione culpatis . . . et sectamini hominem toto ecclesiasticae inscriptionis non dicam stilo sed ense perfossum.*

141. #49.128: *saltim orbis parentem urbem vestram respicite. ipsa vos post defensores suos apostolos maerens adgreditur.*

Paul rejected present-day schismatics and heretics; "innocence without faith is prodigal of works: joined with the guilty is the one most observant of justice, Scipio, because he knew not Christ," she declares.[142] Though his thought often seems medieval in temper, Ennodius was near enough to pre-Christian antiquity to find virtuous pagans inconceivable, unlike the safely distanced Dante. Rome's status as cultural capital empowers her to make further allusions to literature and its production. As Ennodius himself does on other occasions, she speaks of writing, reading, and rereading, and admonishes her erring hearers with a panoply of synonyms and periphrases appropriate for members of the senatorial class and consuls past and present, among them "crown of honors," "flower of Rome," "possessors of robes and curule chairs."[143] Rejoicing that Christian consuls now do homage to the Successor of Peter "with the old infidelity set aside," Rome repeatedly asks her auditors who (*quis*) is responsible for intruding on her happiness to destroy it, for she does "not recognize an illustrious stock in such a business."[144] Appealing to the opposition's sense of their own personal superiority, she states that the real members of the senatorial elite are distinguished by their actions: they take no part in others' misdeeds, nor direct the behavior of sinners.[145] Her final censure falls on those she calls "scions of the crossroads," whose degenerate habits and clandestine vices she now claims to recognize.[146] Commanding their return to "amicable obscurity" while the sun yet shines, Rome bids Symmachus' adversaries "provide harmony for the Church either by absence or by emendation"; she will know "from the amendment of their deeds" whether they want "to be numbered among the resplendent bloodlines."[147]

From the preface's professed aversion to distraught writers grasping at profit and prestige to Rome's delicate distinction between the conventionally well-bred and the contentious children of the streets, the *Libellus* is

---

142. #49.130–31: *quos ecclesia non regeneravit et reliquos misi plurimae prolis infecunda mater ad tartarum . . . profligata est operum sine fide innocentia; criminosis iunctus est aequi observantissimus quia Christum ignoravit Scipio;* Moorhead, *Theoderic,* 122 and n. 32. Cf. Dante, *Paradiso,* cantos 19–20.

143. #49.132–33: *ecce honorum corona orbis genius flos Romanus . . . multos trabearum et curulium possessores supremus regnator sine dispendio cultus aut dignitatis amplectitur.*

144. #49.134–36: *veteri infidelitate deposita . . . generosam in tali negotio prosapiem non agnosco.*

145. #49.137: *splendor sanguinis, etsi communionem criminum incurrit, nescit tamen ducem se praebere peccantibus.*

146. #49.138: *vos potius video, triviorum germina, vos agnosco.*

147. #49.139: *redite potius ad amicam caecitatem, nobis serenam et diurnam lucem relinquite: concordiam ecclesiae aut absentia aut correctione praestate. si tamen vultis vos numerari inter splendidas prosapies, actuum emendatione cognoscam.*

fiercely intent on exposing and exploiting social contrasts for partisan religious ends. As we have seen from his letters, the men Ennodius faced were highly articulate members of the senatorial class whom he would normally have gratified with pleasing sentiments and images. On this occasion, however, they happened to be Symmachus' adversaries, so Ennodius disregards their elite status to subdue them and affirm the Bishop of Rome above reproach as the Successor of Peter. Citing Scripture and tradition, he addresses his senatorial adversaries with robust self-assertion rather than obsequious deference. His attention to the niceties of literary style shows the ancient equation of aesthetic value with moral virtue still retained some influence, but his confidence in denouncing their alleged facts and tendentious interpretations testifies to Christianity's introduction of two new factors, the sanctity of the humble and revealed truth; the well-bred and well-spoken no longer enjoyed a monopoly on truth and goodness. The post-Imperial political situation also fortified Ennodius. The real foci of power in this piece are the Apostolic See, Theoderic and his Goths, and God himself. The Senate, on the other hand, is ever reminded of its marginalization, intellectual (through numerous proofs that its members are less clever than they suppose), political (by copious praise of Theoderic's prudence and piety), religious (with attention to the schism's causes and consequences), and economic (by noting the See of Peter's enrichment by generations of senatorial benefactions). Although Ennodius observes the subtleties of confrontational Latin, his apparently traditional language, studded with references to the Classical past, masks a fundamental change in sensibility. Like Augustine, he converted forms and figures from oratory, satire, and epic to the service of a new aesthetic founded on Christian truth, not traditional, likelihood-based persuasion. Aware that people like Boethius and his father-in-law valued good Latinity, Ennodius chose his phrases carefully, but the moral rightness of his cause gave him leave to transcend aesthetic niceties. The prosopopoeiae of Peter, Paul, and Rome with which the *Libellus* ends mark the limits of reasoned, human-sized argument. When both Apostles, the re-founders of *Roma Christiana,* and the city herself speak on Symmachus' behalf, they embody the logic of a magnificent deus (rather, *dea*) ex machina, part Late Antique literary taste, part inexorable authority.[148]

---

148. Claud. *Cons. Prob. et Olyb.* 205–65 (Tiber); *Bell. Gild.* 1.17–200 (Rome; Africa); *M. Theod.* 132–340 (Virgo/Iustitia; Urania, Muses); *Cons. Stil.* 2.228–407 (Spain, Gaul; Britain, Africa, Italy; Rome); *VI Cons. Hon.* 146–200 (Eridanus et al.). Sid. Apoll. *Carm.* 2.318–521 (Oenotria, Tiber; Rome, Aurora); 5.13–367 (Rome; Africa; Rome); 7.45–598 (Rome; Jupiter). Boeth. *Cons.* 1.1–3, 5–6; 2.1–4; 3.1; 4.4. Cf. Wirbelauer, *Zwei Päpste,* 152–54.

In comparison to the *Libellus,* the *in Christi nomine* is a far more concise work concerning the Acacian schism that we may consider a preliminary exercise for the missions to Constantinople Ennodius would undertake for his old friend, the deacon Hormisdas, who became Bishop of Rome in 514. Sirmond classed this piece as a *dictio;* it certainly assumes an oratorical stance, but it also bears a strong resemblance to a letter credited to Symmachus and addressed to Eastern ecclesiastics.[149] To complete our survey of Ennodius' activities as a spokesman for Roman orthodoxy, we shall first consider this document for what it tells about Ennodius' strategy for attacking heresy, then consider its implications for early sixth-century papal chancery practice.

Indicative of this work's late position in the corpus and the urgency of its subject, namely the continuing rift with the East, is the alacrity with which Ennodius gets down to business. Invoking the rational necessity of speech at this juncture, he declares that "with faith's encouragement, we sally forth into the duty of discourse."[150] Even without the recognized parallels in the papal letter that Vogel cites in his *apparatus criticus,* it is immediately evident that Ennodius is composing not for his own use, but for Pope Symmachus, as he treats friends and colleagues rather differently. Whereas in the *Libellus* his address began in the first-person singular, thereafter alternating between singular and plural depending on the situation, this work uses the first person plural throughout, characterized by the opening affirmation, "for us particularly, whom the weight of obedience proffered by others encourages, it is fitting either to raise up those doing good or to repress evildoers."[151] The speaker implies the audience is well disposed but inferior in status and takes credit for their good behavior, optimistically remarking that to instruct them is like spurring on a running horse.

Then comes his reason for writing: "you are aware how much Nestorius and Eutyches, twin prodigies of diabolical conception, have corrupted the long-chaste discipline of the Eastern churches by the fornication of faithlessness" by rejecting truth and spreading error.[152] Though slightly remi-

---

149. #464 (early 513); Thiel, *Epistolae pontificum romanorum,* 717 (= *PL* 62.61–64, 8 Oct. 512). Cf. *LP* 54.1–4; Caspar, *Geschichte* 2, 118–23.

150. #464.1 (*fide hortante in officium sermonis erumpimus*), alluding to 1 Cor. 9.16 and Eccles. 3.7; the latter is this work's only non-Pauline citation.

151. #464.2: *nos praecipue quos praelati ceteris hortatur pondus obsequii decet aut bona facientes elevare aut mala comprimere.*

152. #464.3: *stat apud conscientias vestras quanta Nestorius et Eutyches, gemina diabolicae informationis ostenta, diu castam ecclesiarum orientalium disciplinam perfidiae fornicatione corruperint.*

niscent of his *dictiones* on mythological adulteries, the phraseology Ennodius adopts here is firmly rooted in the traditions of heresiological polemic, which transforms doctrinal differences into acts of utter depravity, usually sexual.[153] After mentioning the names of Nestorius and Eutyches, each responsible for a different error in defining the relationship between God the Son (the Second Person of the Trinity) and the human being Jesus Christ, Ennodius reviews the history of faulty Christology for his audience, whose veneration for the council of Chalcedon he takes for granted. The main cause of the current Acacian schism remained widespread Eastern resistance to the definition of Christ's nature as fully divine and fully human promulgated in 451 at Chalcedon, where Pope Leo the Great's formulations had enjoyed Imperial patronage. Recollecting the punishment of Dioscorus of Alexandria, Chalcedon's leading opponent, and the translation of the orthodox bishop Flavianus' remains to Constantinople, the speaker expresses outrage about those who suffered exile or death in the factional violence provoked by the enforcement of Chalcedon's decrees. He asks his hearers: "Where in the world is Timotheus unknown, who because of Proterius' murder—to be recalled with suspicion—did not shrink from becoming more than a parricide? For by his accursed persecution of a pontiff he surpasses both the categories and titles of crimes."[154] Working with a historic incident, the slaughter and physical annihilation of a bishop of Alexandria, Ennodius gains access to the declaimer's traditional repertory through an extended conception of paternity and thereby portrays the event as a case of horrific parricide. He further develops the metaphor of familial relationships by stating that those who tried to aid the discredited Dioscorus met the same sinister fate: "from their superior, these men obtained an inheritance both of enthusiasms and of ruin."[155] Thus, he establishes a pattern: spreading false doctrines contrary to authority is tantamount to sexual promiscuity, insubordinate disloyalty equals killing one's father, and those who sympathize with condemned heretics inherit their destructive enthusiasms.

---

153. #464.2–3. Cf. #208, #414; Cameron, "Texts as Weapons."

154. #464.4–5: *ubi gentium Timotheus ignoratur, qui propter suspiciendae recordationis Proteri caedem fieri plus quam parricida non horruit? nam sacri persecutione pontificis et genera criminum vicit et nomina;* cf. #239.2. Events of 449–57: de Labriolle, *Histoire de l'église* 4, 271–80; Caspar, *Geschichte* 2, 166; Chadwick, *Early Church,* 201–5.

155. #464.5: *hi de praecessore suo et studiorum hereditatem adepti sunt et ruinae;* cf. Luke 22.26. He names the guilty parties *Petrus et Cyrus et Timotheus:* the first and third are the Alexandrian bishops Petrus Mongus and Timotheus Aelurus, but the second may, through a confusion of Eastern prelates, be the Syrian Theodoret of Cyrrhus; see the relevant section of Symmachus' letter (*PL* 62.62).

At this point Ennodius confronts his audience with copious memorials of the evils since Chalcedon and exhorts, "accordingly, brothers, hold to the fathers' judgment abiding on high and sticking close to blessed Peter, because we wish the unity of a pure Church, and one not having stain."[156] This is the only occurrence of the imperative in the entire document, used for bidding other bishops to conform to Roman (i.e., Chalcedonian) doctrine. What has thus far seemed a simple proposal for ecclesiastical unity grows more complicated in the balance of the piece (over a third of the text), which presents several programmatic assertions interspersed with suggestive questions. The illusion of collegiality conjured up by the mention of "brothers" vanishes when Ennodius says, "we cannot bear patiently those who burp empty and blasphemous things against our Christ" and "we know that he who does not use the knife's remedy on gangrenous limbs gives his allegiance to creeping ills."[157] Appropriated by a true believer, the Church as Christ's body becomes the subject of a medical parable: the patient needs surgery, for the disease will spread unless the rotting parts (heretics) are amputated.

Of course, this is a peaceful confrontation, Ennodius insists; with immortal souls at risk, who could let fear impede him or the powers of this world overrule a higher authority? In a crushing array of interlocked clauses he holds the proximate cause of the crisis's latest phase up for censure:

What of Acacius who, moved from his judgement by the devil's fell command, blushed that he had so long been a champion of truth and, abandoning the trappings of a brilliant contest, overcame the triumph which he had earned by pious effort under Basiliscus; who alone resents his rewards almost at the time he obtains them, cutting off the hope of good fruit with the sickle of perfidy![158]

---

156. #464.6: *proinde, fratres, manentem in supernis patrum et adhaerentem beato Petro tenete sententiam, quia nos mundae ecclesiae et non habentis maculam optamus unitatem.*

157. #464.6: *patienter ferre non possumus vana in Christum nostrum et blasfema ructantes. scimus quia qui in putribus membris non utitur ferri medicina, serpentibus morbis praestat obsequia, nam nisi secentur tabefacta contaminant;* cf. #49.121.

158. #464.8: *quid Acacius, qui diro diaboli a sententia sua motus imperio erubuit diu propugnatorem se fuisse veritatis et clari deserens ornamenta certaminis triumfum suum, quem sub Basilisco pio sudore meruerat debellavit; qui solus praemiis suis pene tempore adeptionis invidet, spem bonorum fructuum perfidiae falce succidens.* Originally opposing the usurper Basiliscus' anti-Chalcedonian policy (475–76), Acacius later made concessions unacceptable to Rome: de Labriolle, *Histoire de l'église* 4, 284–90; Caspar, *Geschichte* 2, 15–41.

Acacius' worst crime, according to this indictment, was that he knew better but rejected it; of course, it was the devil who caused his change of heart
and turned him into an evil farmhand. Given Ennodius' metaphorical tendencies, which fuse agriculture and education of every sort, this image
evokes the very antithesis of model bishop Epifanius, teacher and cultivator of souls. The matter is closed: "no defense remains to a man who
returns to the death-dealing poisons of schisms after the sweet taste of
righteousness."[159] Referring to recent sad events in Constantinople, to
which this document responds, Ennodius ends by professing silent grief
without compromising on doctrinal issues: "those who do not submit to
the remedies offered have deservedly had no comfort at a time when they
are hard pressed."[160]

The seriousness of the subject precluded sentiments we might otherwise
expect in a collegial exhortation, such as solicitude, approbation, or
encouragement. When Ennodius assumed the character of the bishop of
Rome addressing his fellow churchmen with a message of guidance, there
was no time for epistolary small talk, since deviation from authority in
respect to doctrine and discipline equaled death. Envisioning the situation
as a moment in the epic struggle between good and evil, Ennodius struc-
tured his discourse in the form of an address instead of the letter that the
actual occasion required and that appears in the collection attributed to
Symmachus. On the basis of numerous correspondences with Ennodius'
dictio, that letter was thought to have been adapted from it by Ennodius
himself, keeping much of the *dictio*'s "rhetorical quality" while substituting a loftier spirit of papal authority for its supposedly greater rationality
and legalism.[161] I am less sure.

Without a full rereading of the Symmachan epistle, the preceding
analysis of *in Christi nomine* should make it clear that, having already said
all there was to say about the bishop of Rome's unimpeachably magisterial qualities in the *Libellus,* Ennodius could easily speak in the voice of
authority when he wanted to. The letter of Symmachus is distinguished by
directness in addressing the audience, blend of admonition and sympathy,

---

159. #464.8: *nihil defensionis superest homini post dulcem iustitiae saporem ad mortifera
scismatum venena redeunti.*

160. #464.9: *qui enim oblatis remediis non oboediunt, merito nihil consolationis tempore quo
premuntur habuerunt.* Poison *dictio:* #222. Macedonius, bishop of Constantinople, was
deposed and exiled in August 511 after refusing to hand over the original acts of Chalcedon:
Marcell. Com. *Chron.* a. 511 (*MGH AA* 11.97); de Labriolle, *Histoire de l'église* 4, 311–12.

161. Wyatt ("Ennodius and Pope Symmachus, Part II," 290–91) believed Ennodius composed both #464 (as the rough draft) and Symmachus' letter.

more plentiful citation of incidents, ungainly transitions from one idea to another, and wider use of Scripture; points of contact with Ennodius' piece are observable but not necessarily in the same order.[162] That Ennodius helped draft the document that became Symmachus' letter to the Easterners is patent in the wording and imagery the letter and *dictio* share. Pondering the dissimilarities of form, content, and chronology, however, I believe Ennodius drafted something for the pope on the Eastern problem—a letter or perhaps something more oratorical—which through a process of group discussions and multiple revisions became two separate pieces, the papal letter and his own declamatory work.[163] With his mastery of epistolary tone and form Ennodius would not have composed a peremptory harangue of unyielding authority when Symmachus needed a more diplomatically fraternal though no less assertive letter. What he initially provided and what we may suppose he revised for Symmachus was likely a letter, but I suggest that he may have received enough collegial suggestions for improving the Symmachan document to prefer his own portfolio contain this imperious *dictio*.

For treating problems of heresy and schism in the East, Ennodius adopted an unusually strident tone; is it, however, indicative of a generally unfavorable attitude toward Greeks?[164] Disparaging characterizations of politics and religious dissent in Greek areas do occur in some other works, yet they are few in number and do not reflect mindless Latin bigotry on Ennodius' part; we will see that he intended them to function as specific references for specific audiences. Horrid events since Nestorius did occur in Greek territory, but, in the document we have just examined, Ennodius does not portray them as manifestations peculiar to diseased Greek minds; the perpetrators are evil men, not corrupt Greeks or bad Syrians. In displaying the See of Peter as the doctrinal authority all should follow, Ennodius does not impute any concomitant superiority to Latin-speaking Westerners.

When Ennodius reviews secular political events in his *Life* of Epifanius and the *Panegyric* for King Theoderic and the subject of the Greek east arises, he likewise treats it in a completely nuanced manner. Among the more prominent episodes in his narrative of Epifanius' life, vividly illustrating the holy bishop's diplomatic gifts, is the quarrel Epifanius resolves

---

162. *PL* 62.62–64: allusions to *Antiochiae mala* and the groans of Apamea and Tyre; recipients requested to consider whether reason demands preservation of the holy fathers' *dogmata* and to keep the faith; perils of disregarding the Apostolic See's admonition; those forsaking heretical poisons welcomed. The clumsiness indicates the work of a committee.

163. #464 comes from early 513, the Symmachus letter is dated 8 October 512.

164. Fontaine ("Ennodius," 406–7) thought so.

between the *magister militum* Ricimer, long established as the real power in Italy with the title of *patricius,* and Anthemius, an emperor whom the Eastern government had sent out in 467 to rally the West.[165] The *Life's* exposition includes several speeches by the relevant individuals. The disgruntled Ricimer speaks first. Residing at Milan, he is approached by a group of Ligurian aristocrats who beseech him to make his peace with Anthemius. He yields to their pleas, initially asking who should lead the delegation: "who is there who could restrain an agitated Galatian, and a ruler too?"[166] So far as Anthemius' origins are concerned, Ricimer's utterance makes no claim to factual accuracy; in an unsympathetic context, it merely applies a colorful synonym to someone from Asia Minor.[167] We have no reason to suppose that Ennodius' audience expected accurate geographical information about the eastern Mediterranean and should be conscious of the *Life's* dual nature. Within the work Ricimer addresses Ligurians; outside it Ennodius addresses an Italian readership.

The Ligurian nobles respond to Ricimer's queries by proposing the new bishop of Ticinum, already renowned for his ability to tame even crazed beasts. With "a countenance like his way of life," Epifanius is a man "whom anybody, if Catholic and Roman, could certainly revere, and even a little Greek could love him, if he were worthy of seeing him."[168] This allusion to Anthemius sounds rather rude; it was meant to. Ennodius illustrates the power of Epifanius' virtue through a juxtaposition of good Italian Catholics with an alien emperor of uncertain beliefs contained within a speech given by prominent Ligurians to a barbarian general who had been doing very well without any emperor whatsoever. Thus, we can see that Ennodius speaks here not in his own voice, but in the character of two parties equally critical of the ruler from the East. Although the events he depicts took place before he was born, Ennodius had enough experience of prominent Ligurians to fashion a plausible likeness of the cultural tolerance they would have exhibited in such a case.[169]

---

165. Ricimer had been in Roman service since the early 450s; Anthemius arrived in 467. The rift probably dates to early 471: Cesa, *Ennodio,* 148–50.

166. #80.53: *quis est qui Galatam concitatum revocare possit et principem?* Cf. Jones, *Later Rom. Emp.,* 243.

167. Cesa, *Ennodio,* 152–53; cf. Claud. *In Eutr.* 1.59.

168. #80.54: *cui est vultus vitae similis, quem venerari possit quicumque, si est catholicus et Romanus, amare certe si videre mereatur, et Graeculus.* Cesa, *Ennodio,* 153, cites Sid. Apoll. *Ep.* 1.7.5; cf. Dubuisson, "*Graecus, Graeculus, Graecari,*" 322–29.

169. For Pietri ("Aristocratie et société cléricale," 438) it showed Ennodius was ignorant of Hellenic culture and equated it with paganism, but the Latin-speaking view of Hellenophone heretical tendencies and *Graeculus's* pedigree as a categorical insult render the phrase neither deliberate nor personal; see Dubuisson, "*Graecus, Graeculus, Graecari,*" 329.

Another characterization of Greece that has caused distress occurs in
the narrative section of the *Panegyric* for King Theoderic, when Ennodius
recounts the momentous events in Illyricum, when the Goths wrested Sir-
mium and its neighboring territory from Byzantine control by obtaining
the allegiance of their Gepid allies, led by a certain Mundo. "Through the
meddling of the federate Mundo, Greece registered discord," as Ennodius
tells it: once Mundo and his men went over to the Gothic side, Theoderic's
army had to confront and defeat a hostile Byzantine force of Bulgars.[170]
Alluding to a period of deteriorating relations between the Imperial and
royal courts, this is the panegyrist's exalted way of saying that Eastern
troops commenced overt hostilities on a certain occasion rather than, in
Fontaine's version, that "Greece has chosen disunity as her profession."[171]

The only point at which Ennodius disparages anything connected with
Greece is when he extols Theoderic's achievements by belittling those of
Alexander the Great. Poets celebrated the latter's deeds, robed in antiquity, so their authenticity remains suspect; furthermore, the "leader from
Pella" (*Pelleus ductor*) could never have been mistaken for even a virtuous
pagan, which makes him fair game in Ennodius' quest to praise "the merits of our king," raised as a Christian from infancy.[172] Otherwise, Greek
culture elicits far more compliments than derision from Ennodius, who
acclaims both Theoderic's education in Hellenic Constantinople and the
polished bilingualism of Pomerius and Boethius.[173] On the basis of his preserved utterances, examined in context, we cannot say that Ennodius
labored under a burden of chronic suspicion and wholesale enmity toward
Greeks either historical or contemporary; politically or theologically awk-
ward individuals were another matter.

Having looked at the evidence for Ennodius' attitude toward Greece
and Greeks, we should also consider his views on other non-Catholics.
Concerning the barbarians resident in Italy, Ennodius is eminently prag-

---

170. #263.63: *per foederati Mundonis adtrectationem Graecia est professa discordiam.*
Croke, "Mundo the Gepid," 129; Moorhead, *Theoderic,* 174–75 (poor relations between
Ravenna and Constantinople).

171. Fontaine, "Ennodius," 406–7, arbitrarily states these words epitomize Ennodius'
mistrust toward the contemporary East, whereas references to Greek antiquity are merely
"some *clichés*" lodged in his memory.

172. #263.78–80: *regis nostri merita . . . illum verae religionis ignarum obtinuit erroris
mater inscitia; te summi dei cultorem ab ipso lucis limine instructio vitalis instituit.* Alexander's
dubious personal behavior outweighs his military exploits.

173. Theoderic in Greece: #263.11, with contextually typical flower-fruit imagery.
Pomerius and Boethius: #39.2, #370.4. Greek culture: Garzya, "Cassiodoro e la grecità";
Kirkby, "Scholar and His Public."

matic: he never mentions that Theoderic was a heretical Arian, nor does he make derogatory generalizations about Goths. As a man of the Church, however, he does have something to say about the Jews, who were neither schismatics nor heretics, but infidels wholly beyond the pale of Christianity. The *benedictiones cerei,* two lengthy prayers Ennodius composed for the blessing of the Paschal candle on Holy Saturday, contain distinctly anti-Jewish elements.[174] The first blessing is taken up largely by thanksgiving and praise in the form of a wide-ranging thematic development elaborating on the holiness of the night before the Resurrection. Ennodius introduces two figures to provide contrast: the incense-burning Panchean of the mysterious East, accompanied by sundry animal-sacrificers, and the "Judaic butcher, who is wont by the scarring of groins to count as many souls acquired for himself as he wounds."[175] Though slightly more concise on the subject of becoming a "citizen of heaven" through purification and rebirth, the second blessing comes to a similar point: "it is the time when our bodies and souls are dedicated to Christ the redeemer with an unused sword, when salvation is not sought through wounds, when the priest's right hand abjures the butcher's work."[176]

How much of the anti-Semitic content in these two prayers derives from the context of Christian apologetic and exegetical writing, in which the tradition of anti-Semitic defamation was already inveterate, and how much can we attribute to Ennodius' personal convictions? The only other indication of his attitude toward Jews is the hymn to St. Stephen, the protomartyr stoned to death by an angry crowd of Jews, which first apostrophizes the saint's foes as "slaughter's agent, bestowing life from death" then calls them "impious," maddened yet innocent because of their victim's prayers.[177] Ennodius' characterization is consistent with the narrative of Acts, in which Stephen says extremely provocative things to his

---

174. #14 (Easter 502) and #81 (Easter 504), the oldest datable documentation for this liturgical usage (*hoc cereum lumen:* #14.6 and 10; #81.9); cf. Duchesne, *Liber Pontificalis* 1, 225 (on *LP* 43). As poetic liturgical prose: Fontaine, *Études sur la poésie latine tardive,* 200–205.

175. #14.7: *non enim hic turicremis Pancheus adoletur ignis altaribus . . . procul hinc lanista Iudaicus qui per cicatrices inguinum animas sibi adquisitas tot solet numerare quot vulnerat.* Cf. Verg. *G.* 2.139, 4.378; Claud. *Epith. Hon.* 94–95.

176. #81.5–7: *de parente limo caeli civis effectus . . . tempus est quo corpora nostra vel animae redemptori Christo feriato mucrone dedicentur, quo salus per vulnera non quaeratur, quo sacerdotis dextera lanistae opus abiuret.*

177. #345, vv. 7–8: *necis minister, aspice, / de morte vitam conferens;* 22: *dum saxa ferrent impii;* 25–28: *orabat ex fide loquens, / ne nescientes noxios / caelestis ira perderet. / insons erat vesania, / reum furor provexerat.*

Jewish auditors before they turn on him; it does not increase the denigration inherent in an already biased account, though the very person of Stephen had become a type of anti-Semitic totem.[178]

Since Constantine, Christian emperors had continued to erode the legal status of Jews; they were expressly prohibited from converting their slaves to Judaism from Christianity (which would involve circumcision), entering the civil service, and building new synagogues.[179] Christian discourse conferred a still worse ethical status upon Jews. From the earliest days of the Church, followers of Christ had built the edifice of their religion upon the beliefs and practices of Judaism, reinterpreting the latter to demonstrate its relative error and impiety.[180] Circumcision exerted a peculiar fascination; the Fathers contrasted its worthlessness with baptism and the Resurrection, so Ennodius may have considered some reference to this characteristic practice desirable in a formal pre-Easter blessing.[181] As for immediate contacts, Jewish communities existed in Rome and throughout northern Italy, in cities such as Milan, Genoa, and Aquileia, so Ennodius probably encountered them while attending to official or personal business.[182] We have seen that he had abundant opportunities, particularly among the satirical epigrams but also in other more private, personal works, to show individuals in a bad light, but none of them are recognizably Jewish. The two blessings and the hymn, all of which operate within the domain of Christian ritual hostility to Jews, represent the sum of Ennodius' glaringly anti-Semitic utterances. Though we cannot be certain, the available evidence suggests that Ennodius preferred to coexist peacefully with diverse persons for the sake of mutual benefit and kept ideology for special occasions.[183]

The documents we have examined thus far were all prompted by special occasions during the period of Ennodius' diaconate or earlier. To find out

---

178. Acts 6–7. Ruether, *Faith and Fratricide*, 76–77, 92–94. The arrival of Stephen's relics on Minorca led to the forced conversion of the island's Jewish community in 418 (*PL* 41.821–33; see now Bradbury, *Severus of Minorca*): Hunt, *Holy Land Pilgrimage*, 213–14.

179. *Cod. Theod.* 16.8 and 9, and *Nov. Theod.* 3 (1 Jan. 438); cf. Ruether, *Faith and Fratricide*, 184–95.

180. Ruether, *Faith and Fratricide*, 64–182.

181. Ruether, *Faith and Fratricide*, 152–55, 161–63, 172. At #14.8 (cf. Exod. 14, 1 Cor. 10.1–2), another *Hebreus* is exhorted to cross the saving Red Sea of baptism while the Egyptian founders and only sin is shipwrecked. See Hillier, *Arator*, 151–79.

182. See Ruggini, "Ebrei e Orientali," 192–213, 245–49; Lizzi, *Vescovi e strutture*, 164–65. Ennodius knew Triggua, a Goth with Jewish connections: #445; *An. Val.* 82; Moorhead, *Theoderic*, 73–74, 228; Amory, *People and Identity*, 423–24 (as Triwila *saio*).

183. Caution would have been needed: Vence (461/491), can. 12 (*CCSL* 148).

what became of him as man and churchman, we need to look elsewhere. In 513, he reached his fortieth year, turning point for Greco-Roman traditionalists and Christians alike; although we do not see Ennodius dwelling on the subject of advancing age in the mawkish modern style, he must have thought about it.[184] The more philosophical but no less literary Synesius, bishop of Ptolemaïs in Cyrenaica, was similarly allusive about age around the same time in his life.[185]

The passage of time, failing health, and the loss of lay friends through marriage or death kept reminding Ennodius of the significance of his religious vocation. In 508 he wrote a letter to Avienus about his disappointment: a hoped-for promotion had gone to another, and the preferred person's unworthiness made Ennodius feel that he looked still worse. This missive's subject points toward the direction indicated by a slightly later item, the *dictio* for a new bishop, which attests to a growing thoughtfulness on Ennodius' part about the duties of bishops, as it even includes prayers for use during the Mass.[186] As both letter and *dictio* were drafted within the same interval, the consecration of Eustorgius, who succeeded Laurentius of Milan at around this time, quite likely prompted the latter's composition. As it bears no sign of having been intended for Eustorgius himself, I prefer to think the *dictio* represents Ennodius' vision of how he would fill the episcopal office if providence favored him. The address's final sentence, "just now, let the beneficence of divinity be present for its duty and him whom it does not find worthy of so great an eminence let it render so," implies misgivings similar to those Ennodius shared with Avienus while praying for celestial deliverance from his disappointment.[187]

The *dictio* on being a bishop is itself embedded within the correspondence with Maximus, whose devotion to a life of chastity first drew approval but whose subsequent wedding arrangements caused an adjustment of expectations.[188] Ennodius' air of distress, both physical and spiritual, intensifies markedly. Ailing and slightly cantankerous in late summer 509, he reproaches Maximus for a thirty days' absence ostensibly caused by uxoriousness: "nevertheless, having accepted the honor of a greeting, a

---

184. Galen, *Anim. pass.* 1.10; Gaudemet, *L'église,* 124–26.

185. Cameron, "Synesius and Late Roman Cyrenaica," 421–22.

186. Letter: #314.1; *dictio* (fall 508): #336 (7–9, preface; 10–11, collect). See Jungmann, *Missarum Solemnia* 1, 478–99; 2, 145–61.

187. #336.6: *modo divinitatis operatio adsit muneri suo et quem dignum apice tanto non invenit efficiat.* Cf. Cassiod. *Var.* 1.9; 2.29.

188. See chapters 2 (chastity) and 3 (epithalamium).

taste of the droplets, as a brother should from a brother, receive what has been sent; blush, you, because you neither ask after a sick man nor dispatch wedding delicacies that could allay the tedium."[189] His way of coping with Avienus and Messala's matrimonial plans also bears on the question of his eventual fate. Since certain canons regulating the behavior of deacons and other higher clergy expressly forbade their presence at nuptials and other festive occasions, Ennodius' polite apology to Avienus for being unable to attend his wedding may mask real unease.[190]

With the deepening of Ennodius' commitment to the demands of the religious life, we find toward the end of the collection a counterweight to the estimable young men whose company Ennodius has cultivated since his first known writings. Beginning in 508 with Domnica and Arcotamia and ending with Apodemia and Agnella four years later are thirteen letters to female correspondents.[191] Chronologically speaking, these letters start halfway through the corpus, but their profile is higher because the span 508 to 513 contains fewer items. In comparison, only three women appear as correspondents prior to 508—Speciosa, Euprepia, and Helisaea—accounting for ten items in all. All are closely connected to Ennodius, and the first two happen to be his ex-wife and sister.[192] The increased number of female correspondents is hardly overwhelming but does suggest the circle of Ennodius' friendships, once confined almost entirely to socially prominent younger men, had expanded to embrace the friendship of pious matrons.[193] His letter to Agnella in early 512, the latest of the group, illustrates the ideals and motives that underlie this part of the correspondence. "It is just that a freeborn man of religious intention venerate a widow holy and well-born," he declares, "you have done well, lady Agnella, to reject this world's blandishments"; he further praises her for "seeking not only pardon but a crown."[194] Parodying the way sick people rejoice in reme-

189. #356.2: *tamen honore salutationis accepto, gustum de guttulis ut fratrem decet a fratre, directa suscipite. erubesce tu, quia nec aegrum requiris nec de nuptialibus deliciis quae possent fastidium relevare transmittis.*

190. Esp. #459.5. Cf. Ferrandi Breviatio Canonum (523/546), can. 113 (*CCSL* 149; = Laodicea, tit. 52); Vence (461/491), can. 11 (*CCSL* 148; = Agde, can. 39).

191. Domnica, or Domnina, (#285, #302); Arcotamia (#291, #319); Firmina (#305; cf. #165, #229); Barbara (#393, #404); Stefania (#394, #439, #442); Camella (#431; cf. #457); Apodemia (#441); Agnella (#449).

192. See chapter 4. Speciosa: #35, #36; Euprepia: #52, #84, #109, #219, #268, #293, #313; Helisaea: #177.

193. Cf. #332, on Viola.

194. #449.1–2: *iustum est ut religiosi homo propositi sanctam viduam et nobilem veneretur ingenuus . . . bene fecisti, domna Agnella, mundi istius blandimenta respuere, et dum celsiora sequeris, etiam quae potuerunt venire a legitimis remediis non habere; scisti non solum veniam quaerere sed coronam.*

dies, Ennodius asks his correspondent for therapeutic action: "that for me, a friend and your relative, you do not cease to make supplication at the threshold of the Apostles, so that I may deserve to honor what I preach and what I extol in others not neglect myself."[195]

Less than a year had passed since he finished writing the confessional letter to God; a long road to holiness still lay ahead. Ennodius needed all the prayers his devoted friends could offer before he became a bishop, let alone a saint.

---

195. #449.2–3: *gaudeant de medicina languentes . . . rogo ut pro me amico et parente tuo apostolorum liminibus non desinas subplicare ut merear servare quod praedico et quod in aliis extollo ipse non neglegam.*

Postscript: Silence and Sainthood

Reckoning from 474, as we have already seen, Ennodius would have been in his fortieth year by late 513, an age fully compatible with the canons regarding the age at which men could be made bishops. No work in the corpus can plausibly be dated later than this, and by 514 he must have been firmly established as bishop of Ticinum, since the pope dispatched him to Constantinople the next year. On the evidence of the labors of other Late Antique prelates such as Sidonius Apollinaris at Clermont-Ferrand, Laurentius of Milan, Caesarius of Arles, and the bishops of Rome, we are entitled to assume that, at Ticinum and abroad, Ennodius continued drafting letters, addresses, and prayers until his death in July 521, for his episcopal duties would have included supervising the diocese's affairs and preaching to congregations, even if he could no longer permit himself to compose enigmatic *dictiones* and satirical epigrams.[1] But that later oeuvre from his years as a bishop is lost. In this concluding postscript, we will survey the evidence for Ennodius' episcopacy and posthumous reputation.

The question of why we have so much documentation, official and private, from Ennodius' diaconate while his episcopal papers went altogether missing cannot be easily answered. But surely it had something to do with having been kept in two different, separate locations. His writings as bishop of Ticinum would have been deposited in the cathedral chancery, whereas the registers of his diaconate in Milan might have been left in that city or brought along to Ticinum, where Ennodius could have stored them at his residence or entrusted them to someone else for safekeeping. The next half-millennium was to prove less than placid for Ennodius' see. A Gothic center that had endured Justinian's wars, the city was captured by

---

1. Lanzoni, *Le diocesi,* 989; Jungmann, *Missarum Solemnia* 2, 148–51; Moreton, *Eighth-Century Gelasian Sacramentary,* 20–21.

the Lombards in 572 and became their capital under the new name of Pavia, then came under Frankish control in 774, finally suffering the ravages of a Magyar sack in 924.[2] Milan's lot was similarly troubled. Though nowhere was wholly secure, Ennodius' earlier works turned out to be in a safer place, or someone thought them more worth saving.

In the corpus we have a good deal of Ennodius' correspondence while deacon at Milan, but it is completely one-sided: he did not preserve his correspondents' letters, so their perspective is utterly lost. This fate befalls Ennodius himself after 513. The *Collectio Avellana,* a compilation of imperial, papal, and sundry other communications, which constitutes the bulk of the evidence for Ennodius' participation as the senior legate in two missions to the East, contains nothing from Ennodius' own hand.[3] Furthermore, to construct a narrative account of his diplomatic activities—in contrast to the commands, reproaches, and counsels contained in the *Collectio*—we need to consult the chapter on Pope Hormisdas' episcopate in the *Liber Pontificalis.*

This chronicle of the popes limits mention of Ennodius to the tale of how Hormisdas, "showing the Apostolic See's compassion" for the anathematized Greeks, dispatched the bishop of Ticinum and several other clerics to the Emperor Anastasius, with whom "they achieved nothing."[4] On a second occasion Ennodius was sent with another set of colleagues to carry letters and other documents, to which the emperor again refused to assent, attempting instead to bribe the legates. They resisted, so "the furious Emperor threw them out by the back door and put them on a dangerous ship," charging officials to keep them away from urban centers; Ennodius and his colleagues nevertheless managed secretly, "through the hands of orthodox monks," to circulate letters validating Rome's stand throughout the cities of the East.[5] The chronicler notes that some bishops compliant with the imperial will promptly sent their copies of the seditious letters off to the capital, which goaded Anastasius to further transports of rage at the pope's interventions; the old emperor died in July 518. By then Ennodius was out of the diplomatic picture; he did not participate in the third delegation that met successfully with Justin, the new emperor.[6]

---

2. Wickham, *Early Medieval Italy,* 24–47; Bullough, "Urban Change," 94–99.

3. Cited as *Coll. Avell. (Epistulae Imperatorum Pontificum . . . Avellana quae dicitur collectio. CSEL* 35.2); Mochi Onory, *Vescovi e città,* 237; Caspar, *Geschichte* 2, 133–48.

4. *LP* 54.2; Ennodius is also named first in 54.3. Cf. Davis, *Book of Pontiffs,* 47, 102–3.

5. *LP* 54.3–4.

6. *LP* 54.5–8; Caspar, *Geschichte* 2, 153–66; de Labriolle, *Histoire de l'église* 4, 319–20.

Turning from the synopsis to the details, the *Collectio* offers several sets of interrelated messages for the period 515–17, all of which are concerned with the problem of heresy and discipline in the East. There are letters from Pope Hormisdas to various Eastern and Western bishops and their associates and to the Emperor Anastasius himself, together with replies and queries from these people.[7] Among them we find letters to and about Ennodius and his colleagues, several identifying them as the bearers of letters to third parties; the lists of their names, inscribed immediately after the sender and the addressee, always put Ennodius' first, trusted representative of Catholic pope and Arian king.[8]

Other pieces in the collection were intended to provide the legates with information and advice for handling various individuals and situations; one notable document from 515 contains prodigiously detailed instructions.[9] "With the assistance of God and the prayers of the Apostles," it begins, "as you are coming into Greek territories, if bishops want to meet you, receive them with the veneration which is fitting," then warns the legates against accepting dinner invitations or food, save under certain conditions.[10] Their arrival in Constantinople prompted another set of conditions, concerned mostly with deflecting visitors until the audience with the emperor has taken place. The directions for that imperial audience, certainly the most important part of the whole endeavor, occupy the bulk of the document, specifying what Ennodius and his colleagues had to ensure the emperor knew of and ratified. The items they had to attend to included the letters brought by Hormisdas' emissaries, the exact nature of Christ, the proper conduct of previous emperors, the writings of Pope Leo and the fathers of Chalcedon pertaining to the heretics Nestorius, Eutyches, and Dioscorus, and the fate of Constantinople's deposed bishop;

---

7. To bishops and other ecclesiastics: *Coll. Avell.* 106 (Apr. 515); 118, 120, 121, 122 (Nov. 516); 123 (Apr. 517); 124 (Mar. 517); 128, 129, 130, 131, 132, 133 (Apr. 517); 137 (Feb. 517); 139 (end 517). From bishops, etc.: *Coll. Avell.* 105 (Jan. 515); 117, 119 (Oct. 516); 136 (516–Jan. 517). To Anastasius: *Coll. Avell.* 108 (Apr. 515); 110 (July 515); 112, 114 (Sept.? 516); 115 (Aug. 515); 126, 127 (Apr. 517). From Anastasius: *Coll. Avell.* 107 (Jan. 515), 109 (Dec. 514–May 515); 111, 113 (July 516); 125 (winter 515); 138 (July 517).

8. *Coll. Avell.* 115.1 and 12 (Aug. 515); 125 (winter 515); 126.1 and 16 (Apr. 517); 127 (Apr. 517); 119.1 and 2 (Oct. 516). Cf. Ensslin, *Theoderich,* 298, 303–13; Moorhead, *Theoderic,* 195–96.

9. *Coll. Avell.* 116, 116a, 116b (Aug. 515) give directions for the first embassy. See Caspar, *Geschichte* 2, 134–36; Schwartz, *Publizistische Sammlungen,* 251. *Coll. Avell.* 134 and 135 (Apr. 517) tell Ennodius and a colleague how to deal with the church of Nicopolis (in Epirus Vetus).

10. *Coll. Avell.* 116.1.

an appendix demands that the emperor officially anathematize all heretics since Nestorius, with particular emphasis on Acacius.[11]

This material is presented in a manner that contrasts strongly with the simple "if . . . , then do . . ." of the earlier sections; here the questions that Eastern clerics and the emperor were supposed to ask, as well as what Ennodius and his colleagues were to say in reply, are given in virtual dialogue form. In the earliest exchange the legates are told to "use these words" to have the documents accepted, so that Anastasius was supposed to ask, "What is in the documents?" then be told, "They contain greetings to Your Piety and he (sc. Hormisdas) gives thanks to God because he recognizes you are concerned about the Church's unity; read, and you comprehend."[12] The plan was evidently meant to ensure that the faith-defining letters of Hormisdas became documents of record before more difficult matters were broached.

This protracted question-and-answer format is typified by small, simple queries from the emperor and large, authoritative replies by the legates, interspersed with performance cues such as "give thanks and kiss the breast of His Clemency," if Anastasius said he welcomed the Council of Chalcedon and Pope Leo's letters, and "to these words, add entreaties and tears," before asking the emperor to contemplate God's judgment.[13] The combination of obsessive stage management, absolute certitude, and quasi-Socratic method is formidable. Whether intended primarily to curb improvisation or merely to preclude ambiguities, the scheme can only have cramped Ennodius' style and was in any event ineffective in winning the emperor over. Still, this document could have been the ideal script for a dramatic reconciliation of the churches of East and West—had Anastasius been less certain of his position and his clergy more tractable in the face of Hormisdas' vehement refusal to consider further deliberations.

Anastasius' actual reaction signally failed to coincide with Hormisdas' intentions. Returning to Italy in the winter of 515/16, Ennodius and his colleagues carried a courteous letter from the emperor to the pope that in many respects seemed to settle the religious controversies separating Constantinople from Rome. Its Christological affirmations appeared sound, and it rousingly anathematized Nestorius and Eutyches. Then the emperor posed a question of his own: "we wonder, however, for what reason you wished to write some things to us about the most blessed fathers who gath-

---

11. *Coll. Avell.* 116.5–22 (appendix: 116b).
12. *Coll. Avell.* 116.6.
13. *Coll. Avell.* 116.12 and 15.

ered at Chalcedon," since their decisions had been repeatedly ratified by his predecessors and defended as a true expression of the Nicene faith.[14] Since Leo the Great, no bishop of Rome could bear hearing that Chalcedon's decrees were just another version of Nicaea's definitions, so Hormisdas was bound to be displeased. Many Easterners, however, found the Chalcedonian definitions unreasonably and divisively definite. This view underlay Anastasius' subsequent avowal that he had expended "no little zeal" in trying to bring about ecclesiastical unity, even writing to the troublesome Alexandrians on several occasions, and motivated his appeal, "now, weigh carefully all the things that must be done, because Our Clemency judges it a grave thing, respecting the venerable Church, that living men be cast out on account of dead ones, and we know that what you write on this subject cannot be ordained without much outpouring of human blood."[15] There is no mention of Acacius, the person responsible for the document at the center of the current dispute.

On his next visit to the emperor, Ennodius brought Hormisdas' two-installment reply, composed in the spring of 517; the tone and content of both letters make the second mission's failure no surprise. The first letter opens with a justification of the pope's delay in replying, which involved some defensive remarks concerning pastoral exertions, then rises to its obligatory theme. Condemning Nestorius and Eutyches is all very well, "but it is a matter of truth, Lord Son, and of Catholic discipline that you should hate even the followers and comrades of those whose leaders you judge must be condemned."[16] The emperor's letter touched upon many points, but Hormisdas chose to disregard the appeal to compassion and fix on the omission of Acacius, whose infamies he now recounted and castigated, expansively blaming him for everything currently wrong with the Eastern churches.[17] He instructed Anastasius that his duty was to heal the Church by smiting and terrorizing the infidels; to reinforce this injunction, the pope mentioned that a delegation of Gallic bishops had inquired about the unity issue before he introduced his envoys.[18] The second letter is much shorter and less elaborate, complaining that a conspiracy existed against the Chalcedonian bishop of Nicopolis and the emperor should come to his

---

14. *Coll. Avell.* 125.7.

15. *Coll. Avell.* 125.11.

16. *Coll. Avell.* 126.6.

17. *Coll. Avell.* 126.7–14, alleging among other things that before Acacius, *perfidia* sullied only Alexandria.

18. *Coll. Avell.* 126.14–16, featuring more tearful entreaty; cf. 136, 137 (Avitus of Vienne).

aid. By marveling "that the obstinacy of the plotters is disturbed neither by God's attention nor your own," Hormisdas broadly implied that Anastasius was in some way involved in the intrigue; the evaporation of decorum coincided with the outbreak of a propaganda war, as Ennodius also carried several other letters for bishops and monks of varying degrees of orthodoxy.[19]

Anastasius' answer of July 517 went directly to the point. Opposing Hormisdas' excuses for silence with references to Scripture and affirming the teachings of Christ, the emperor continued to insist on a message of mercy, despite the efforts of certain people to prove differently. Anastasius would go no further. The letter ends thus: "We do not think that those who have learned mercy are unmerciful, but from the present time we are withholding our request with taciturnity, judging it unreasonable to apply the goodness of prayers to those who, in obstinate refusal, are unwilling to be queried, for we can bear to be injured and nullified; we cannot be commanded."[20]

For this emperor matters would remain at a standstill as long as the pope continued to demand complete acquiescence to the Roman definition of orthodoxy at the expense of mere human considerations such as political stability and public order. Ennodius and his colleagues, conspicuously forbidden any exercise of individual discretion in their dealings, would have found their mission to the imperial court effectively over even before they were expelled in the manner the *Liber Pontificalis* recounts. Neither it nor the *Collectio Avellana* contains anything confidential about Ennodius' activities as a papal emissary, but his reliance on a network of orthodox monks to disseminate the letters with which Hormisdas had entrusted him is consistent with tactics employed by both sides of the controversy since the Council of Ephesus.[21] Anastasius' alleged use of an unsafe ship to dispose of the envoys clearly contributes to the myth of perfidious despotism propagated by his enemies, as it recalls the Emperor Nero's murderous artifice for killing his mother.[22] The tale that Ennodius braved the wrath of an impious and tyrannical ruler conforms to the ancient tradition of plain-

---

19. *Coll. Avell.* 127.3; cf. 128–33, 138.

20. *Coll. Avell.* 138.1–5. *LP* 54.4 imputes similar sentiments to the emperor; his reaction was hardly unforeseen: Schwartz, *Publizistische Sammlungen,* 254–55; Caspar, *Geschichte* 2, 147–48.

21. *Coll. Avell.* 139, cf. 130, 132; Bacht, "Die Rolle des orientalischen Mönchtums."

22. Suet. *Ner.* 34.2: *solutilem navem.* The *LP* has two versions: *in navem periculosam* (full text); *in nave sub periculo mortis* (Felician epitome).

speaking philosophers and holy men, enhancing the bishop of Ticinum's luster as a dauntless confessor of the faith.[23]

One piece of material evidence survives from the sixth century that pertains to Ennodius' service as bishop of Ticinum: his epitaph. Inscribed on a marble panel, it takes the form of nine elegiac couplets plus a line recording the date of his decease (17 July 521). The inscription today occupies a niche in the south wall of the main apse of the twelfth-century Romanesque sandstone church of S. Michele Maggiore in Pavia.[24] Although its language shows traces of Ennodian influence, the epitaph's orthography and content leave the question of Ennodius' role in its composition unsettled; the third line, "brilliant indeed in his offspring, himself more noble than his kinsmen," is especially ambiguous.[25] The poem refers to his distinguished family in a manner more typical of the funerary epigrams of Gallic bishops than of Italians, blithely credits Ennodius with restoring orthodoxy in the Eastern churches, and characterizes him as a mighty speaker on doctrinal matters, furthermore proclaiming him a generous, prudent benefactor and a builder of splendid churches adorned "with hymns and gold."[26]

The current resting place of Ennodius and his epitaph is obviously not a church that he founded. To find out about that church, his first resting place, we need to consult a later source, a fourteenth-century encomium of Pavia whose author was for centuries called the Anonymus Ticinensis but is now known to be the Pavian Opicino de Canistris.[27] Opicino's praise of his native city contains a catalogue of churches, with a section on the extramural church "of St. Victor the martyr, which blessed Ennodius, bishop of Pavia and doctor of the Greeks, founded, and there he first lay; in it, he appointed that the divine office be done by one choir in the Greek tongue, with responses by another in the Latin tongue."[28] That Ennodius

---

23. Cf. Brown, *Power and Persuasion,* 61–70, 117, 135.

24. Next to the choir stalls, evidently moved more than once (autopsy, 11.5.94). Merkel, "L'epitafio di Ennodio," 83; Vogel, lviii; Mommsen, *CIL* 5.2, 6464 (= Dessau, *ILS* 2952).

25. *CIL* 5.2, 6464, v. 3: *clarus prole quidem, generosior ipse propinquis.* Merkel, "L'epitafio," 139–40, supposed its author might have been a cleric, possibly related to Ennodius; Heinzelmann, *Bischofsherrschaft,* 64, suggested Ennodius himself.

26. *CIL* 5.2, 6464, vv. 3–8 (family/personal), 9–14 (doctrinal work), 15–16 (benefactions); 17–18: *templa deo faciens ymnis decoravit et auro / et paries functi dogmata nunc loquitur.* See Heinzelmann, *Bischofsherrschaft,* 236–42; Scheibelreiter, *Der Bischof in merowingischer Zeit,* 9–50.

27. Gianani, *Opicino de Canistris.*

28. Gianani, *Opicino de Canistris,* 87: *Ecclesia sancti Victoris martiris, quam condidit beatus Enodius episcopus papiensis doctor Grecorum, et ibi primo iacuit. In qua ordinavit fieri officium divinum ab uno choro in lingua greca, ab alio in lingua latina responderi;* cf. 116.

dedicated a church to Victor, the saint to whom he attributed his miraculous recovery, should not surprise us, nor that it was located outside the city walls, as space for construction in the center of town would have been scarce. The antiphonal choirs and bilingual chanting, however, are an intriguing feature explainable by Ennodius' missions to the East and esteem for Greek culture; a similar institution is ascribed to his contemporary and episcopal colleague Caesarius of Arles.[29] Opicino compensates for his lateness as a source by corroborating his statement. He explains that the custom with the choirs continued, "just as it is observed today in the church of S. Michele Maggiore on the feast of the same Saint Ennodius who now lies there."[30] Some centuries before Opicino, therefore, both choirs and body had been moved into the city proper to the church of S. Michele; Ennodius is still there, though his choirs are not.

Once Ennodius had laid his writing aside and the report of his deeds in the East had been disseminated in clerical circles, who continued to know or care about him and his works? An Italian abbot named Florianus, who appears to be one of Ennodius' early correspondents, wrote a letter to bishop Nicetius of Trier referring to his mentor in highly complimentary terms as a hammer of heretics and upholder of truth.[31] Early readers of Ennodius' *Life* of Epifanius may have included Eugippius, the Campanian abbot who composed the *Life* of Severinus of Noricum, and the anonymous author of a Gallic hagiographical work.[32] Fontaine proposed that Venantius Fortunatus, who was originally from Ravenna, was so influenced by Ennodius' writings as to generate a tradition in Francia of reading him, but, with nearly two undocumented centuries separating the poet-bishop of Poitiers from the bishop of Ticinum's Carolingian readers, more evidence would be desirable.[33]

In the later eighth century the Lombard historian Paul the Deacon went into exile in Francia after northern Italy fell to the Franks. Schooled at

---

29. *V. Caes. Arel.* 1.19 (*MGH SRM* 3, 463–64) rationalized chanting as a means of preventing idle gossip; cf. Klingshirn, *Caesarius*, 93. Greek was traditional in certain contexts: Brou, "Les chants en langue grecque," 171–72, 176–78, and "Les chants . . . premier Supplément"; Cattaneo, *Terra di Sant'Ambrogio*, 90–91.

30. Gianani, *Opicino de Canistris,* 87: *sicut hodie servatur in ecclesia sancti Michaeli maioris in festo eiusdem sancti Enodii, qui nunc ibi iacet.* His church to St. Victor was extramural: Bullough, "Urban Change," 91 n. 31.

31. Florianus' letter, c. 550: Vogel, lix–lx (= *Epistulae Austrasiacae,* 5, *MGH Epp.* 3, 116–17). He was also Ennodius' godson: #20, #21; Ruggini, "Ticinum," 305.

32. See Cesa, *Ennodio,* 33–35, for Eugippius' connections, the author of the *Vita Bibiani,* and Po Valley hagiographers / local historians.

33. Fontaine, "Ennodius," 420. Paulus Diaconus was the first medieval writer to show Ennodian borrowings: Vogel, xxvi–xxvii; Lapidge, "The Authorship," 272.

Pavia, he is the most likely person to have rediscovered Ennodius' works and brought them over the Alps to the court of Charlemagne, for a number of verse epistles circulated among Paul's friends there show a peculiarly Ennodian interplay of form and content.[34] Northeastern Francia, by an interesting coincidence, is also where the earliest surviving manuscripts of Ennodius' works appear to have been copied; if we credit Paul with carrying the archetype from Lombardy to Francia, it helps put that manuscript in the right place at the right time.[35] This hypothesis possesses the added charm of having Ennodius' works arrive in northern Europe and be appreciated as works of literary art several decades before the compilers and inventors of canon law discovered and exploited them as a source of authority.

These creative Carolingian canonists were among Ennodius' most assiduous medieval readers; going under names like Isidorus Mercator (or Peccator), they selected items from the corpus and turned them to new uses.[36] Their excerpts betray a conception of utility that would have been unimaginable to Ennodius, for whom content and context were inseparably united. For instance, they attributed the authorship of one of his letters to Olybrius (examined in chap. 4 in connection with Ennodius' family ties) to Pope Liberius, who was bishop of Rome some 150 years before Ennodius' own work for the See of Peter.[37] For the sake of what they perceived this letter to say about the business of being a bishop, these men could overlook its distinctively personal elements, unmistakable when viewed in the context of the whole Ennodian oeuvre. Likewise, out of Ennodius' four letters concerning the episcopal election at Aquileia, the canonists selected only the one addressed to Liberius the patrician for repackaging as a decretal of Pope Symmachus, presumably because it contained exemplary utterances concerning the merits of Marcellinus, Aquileia's new bishop.[38] These same reader-users also transformed the *dictio* Ennodius

---

34. Lapidge, "The Authorship," 253–60 (the meter's invention, use in Late Antiquity; Ennodius' contribution emphasized: #26 to Faustus); Goffart, *Narrators,* 329–47.

35. Bruxellensis 9845–9848, copied for Lorsch in northeastern Francia, and Vaticanus Latinus 3803, written at Corbie: Bischoff, *Die Abtei Lorsch,* 48, 75. Paul and Ennodius: Goffart, *Narrators,* 358–71.

36. Isidorus, also known as I. Peccator, is implicated in the "Capitula Angilramni" and the writings of Benedictus Levita: Fuhrmann, *Einfluß und Verbreitung* 1, 137–94.

37. #48 (from 503). On the forger Isidorus Mercator, see Vogel, xlv, lii–liii; Fuhrmann, *Einfluß und Verbreitung.*

38. #174, *Ennodius Liberio Patricio* (early 506) becomes *Symmachus episcopus ecclesiae catholicae urbis Romae Liberio patricio salutem* despite Ennodius' typical protestations about brevity (#174.3). Cf. #168, #177, #178, to Avitus, Helisaea, and Avitus, respectively. The old bishop, Marcellianus, had been an anti-Symmachan: Moorhead, *Theoderic,* 120–21; O'Donnell, "Liberius the Patrician," 41–42; Lanzoni, *Le diocesi,* 891.

wrote for delivery by the *vicarius Italiae* Stefanius before Maximus, bishop of Ticinum, into a letter of Pope Symmachus to Laurentius of Milan by supplying a new title and a salutatory formula.[39] Formally, the piece remains a work of oratory, but the canonists clearly thought minimal relabeling was sufficient to give it decretal status.

Thus reprocessed and repackaged into digestible, doctrine-rich portions, Ennodius' works seem to have found their way back to Italy by the middle of the ninth century, with Nicolaus I the first medieval pope to show demonstrable knowledge both of Pseudo-Isidore and of Ennodius.[40] From that point on, Ennodius became the possession of letter-writers, poets, and, most of all, astute churchmen.[41] In the tenth century one bishop, Otwinus of Hildesheim, found the *Life* of Epifanius so affecting a work of hagiography that he absconded with the remains of Epifanius and Speciosa—was it mere proximity, or had he read Ennodius' letters?—to take back to his see in Saxony.[42] The French monastic reformer Abbo of Fleury seems to have borrowed at least one Ennodian turn of phrase for his *Life* of St. Edmund.[43] Sprung from the schools of Late Antiquity, Ennodius' synthesis of grammar and morals foreshadows the world Alan of Lille constructed in his *Lament of Nature,* and the epistolary technique that so repels modern scholars commended him to the practitioners of the *ars dictaminis,* the high medieval discipline of letter writing.[44]

The rediscovery of Ennodius' works in the modern period must be credited not to Grynaeus' slapdash *editio princeps* but to Jacques Sirmond, whose philological and historical knowledge of Late Antiquity and the early Middle Ages is still paradigmatic for all students of the text. We still rely on Sirmond's insights, his detailed elucidations of a body of writings he was the first to make intelligible, and justly so. His masterful refashioning of the works' outward form, however, means that what we see we perceive through the packaging of a late Renaissance–early Baroque aesthetic as far removed from Ennodius' Late Antique sensibility as we are from the

---

39. #214 (early 506); cf. Lanzoni, *Le diocesi,* 988; Cesa, *Ennodio,* 27.

40. Ps.-Isidore: Fuhrmann, *Einfluß und Verbreitung* 2, 241–72. Nicolaus I (858–67): Vogel, xxvii (*PL* 119.942). See also Ullmann, "*Romanus Pontifex.*" Hostile: Arnulf of Lisieux, c. 1160 (Vogel, lx–lxi).

41. *Acta Sanctorum, Iulii 4 (dies XV–XIX),* 275–76: Ennodius (17 July) a doctrinally solid, long-venerated *episcopus* and *confessor.*

42. Geary, *Furta Sacra,* 141, 185; cf. Picard, *Le souvenir,* 648–49.

43. Abbo, *Life of St. Edmund,* 10 (in *Three Lives of English Saints*): *rex et martyr intravit senatum curiae caelestis;* cf. #1.21.

44. See Ziolkowski, *Alan of Lille's Grammar of Sex,* 143–44 (extreme views on grammatical rules); Rouse and Rouse, "Ennodius in the Middle Ages."

worldview of the First Crusade. The fact that Sirmond reworked Ennodius' writings according to his temporally conditioned perception of each
item's inward genre has obscured the variety, craftsmanship, and still
more the immediacy the works can communicate when we read them
chronologically and in relation to their audiences. Although in approaching Ennodius we ourselves cannot pretend to be unencumbered by intellectual baggage, we can at least hang Sirmond's overcoat out of the way so
as to have a clearer look at the substance of Ennodius' works, remote yet
vivid.

Concordance of Opus Numbers

In the following list, the numbers on the left represent the numbering of Ennodius' works in Vogel's edition, those on the right Sirmond's categories and numeration.

#1 = *Dict.* 1

#2 = *Carm.* 1,6

#3 = *Dict.* 7

#4 = *Epist.* 1,1

#5 = *Epist.* 1,2

#6 = *Epist.* 1,3

#7 = *Epist.* 1,4

#8 = *Opusc.* 7

#9 = *Epist.* 1,5

#10 = *Epist.* 1,6

#11 = *Epist.* 1,7

#12 = *Epist.* 1,8

#13 = *Epist.* 1,9

#14 = *Opusc.* 9

#15 = *Epist.* 1,10

#16 = *Epist.* 1,11

#17 = *Epist.* 1,12

#18 = *Epist.* 1,13

#19 = *Epist.* 1,14

#20 = *Epist.* 1,15

#21 = *Epist.* 1,16

#22 = *Epist.* 1,17

#23 = *Epist.* 1,18

#24 = *Epist.* 1,19

#25 = *Epist.* 1,20

#26 = *Carm.* 1,7

#27 = *Carm.* 1,8

#28 = *Epist.* 1,21

#29 = *Epist.* 1,22

#30 = *Epist.* 1,23

#31 = *Epist.* 1,24

#32 = *Epist.* 1,25

#33 = *Epist.* 1,26

#34 = *Epist.* 2,1

#35 = *Epist.* 2,2

#36 = *Epist.* 2,3

#37 = *Epist.* 2,4

#38 = *Epist.* 2,5

#39 = *Epist.* 2,6

#40 = *Epist.* 2,7

#41 = *Epist.* 2,8

#42 = *Epist.* 2,9

#43 = *Carm.* 1,9

#44 = *Epist.* 2,10

#45 = *Epist.* 2,11

#46 = *Carm.* 2,1

#47 = *Epist.* 2,12

#48 = *Epist.* 2,13

#49 = *Opusc.* 2

#50 = *Carm.* 2,2

#51 = *Epist.* 2,14

#52 = *Epist.* 2,15

#53 = *Epist.* 2,16

#54 = *Epist.* 2,17

#55 = *Epist.* 2,18

#56 = *Epist.* 2,19

#57 = *Epist.* 2,20

#58 = *Epist.* 2,21

#59 = *Epist.* 2,22

#60 = *Epist.* 2,23

#61 = *Epist.* 2,24

#62 = *Epist.* 2,25

#63 = *Epist.* 2,26

#64 = *Epist.* 2,27

#65 = *Epist.* 2,28

#66 = *Epist.* 3,1

#67 = *Epist.* 3,2

#68 = *Epist.* 3,3

#69 = *Dict.* 8

#70 = *Carm.* 2,3	#109 = *Epist.* 3,28	#144 = *Epist.* 4,14
#71 = *Epist.* 3,4	#110 = *Epist.* 3,29	#145 = *Epist.* 4,15
#72 = *Epist.* 3,5	#111 = *Epist.* 3,30	#146 = *Epist.* 4,16
#73 = *Epist.* 3,6	#112 = *Carm.* 2,17	#147 = *Carm.* 2,34
#74 = *Epist.* 3,7	#113 = *Epist.* 3,31	#148 = *Carm.* 2,35
#75 = *Epist.* 3,8	#114 = *Epist.* 3,32	#149 = *Epist.* 4,17
#76 = *Epist.* 3,9	#115 = *Epist.* 3,33	#150 = *Epist.* 4,18
#77 = *Epist.* 3,10	#116 = *Epist.* 3,34	#151 = *Epist.* 4,19
#78 = *Epist.* 3,11	#117 = *Epist.* 4,1	#152 = *Epist.* 4,20
#79 = *Epist.* 3,12	#118 = *Epist.* 4,2	#153 = *Epist.* 4,21
#80 = *Opusc.* 3	#119 = *Epist.* 4,3	#154 = *Epist.* 4,22
#81 = *Opusc.* 10	#120 = *Epist.* 4,4	#155 = *Epist.* 4,23
#82 = *Epist.* 3,13	#121 = *Epist.* 4,5	#156 = *Carm.* 2,36
#83 = *Epist.* 3,14	#122 = *Epist.* 4,6	#157 = *Epist.* 4,24
#84 = *Epist.* 3,15	#123 = *Opusc.* 8	#158 = *Epist.* 4,25
#85 = *Dict.* 9	#124 = *Dict.* 11	#159 = *Epist.* 4,26
#86 = *Epist.* 3,16	#125 = *Epist.* 4,7	#160 = *Epist.* 4,27
#87 = *Epist.* 3,17	#126 = *Carm.* 2,18	#161 = *Epist.* 4,28
#88 = *Epist.* 3,18	#127 = *Carm.* 2,19	#162 = *Carm.* 2,37
#89 = *Epist.* 3,19	#128 = *Carm.* 2,20	#162a = *Carm.* 2,38
#90 = *Epist.* 3,20	#129 = *Carm.* 2,21	#162b = *Carm.* 2,39
#91 = *Epist.* 3,21	#130 = *Carm.* 2,22	#162c = *Carm.* 2,40
#92 = *Epist.* 3,22	#131 = *Carm.* 2,23	#162d = *Carm.* 2,41
#93 = *Epist.* 3,23	#132 = *Carm.* 2,24	#162e = *Carm.* 2,42
#94 = *Dict.* 10	#133 = *Carm.* 2,25	#162f = *Carm.* 2,43
#95 = *Epist.* 3,24	#134 = *Carm.* 2,26	#163 = *Carm.* 2,44
#96 = *Carm.* 2,8	#134a = *Carm.* 2,27	#164 = *Carm.* 2,45
#97 = *Carm.* 2,9	#134b = *Carm.* 2,28	#165 = *Carm.* 2,46
#98 = *Dict.* 2	#135 = *Epist.* 4,8	#165a = *Carm.* 2,47
#99 = *Carm.* 2,10	#136 = *Carm.* 2,29	#165b = *Carm.* 2,48
#100 = *Carm.* 2,11	#136a = *Carm.* 2,30	#165c = *Carm.* 2,49
#101 = *Carm.* 2,12	#136b = *Carm.* 2,31	#166 = *Epist.* 4,29
#102 = *Carm.* 2,13	#137 = *Epist.* 4,9	#167 = *Epist.* 4,30
#103 = *Carm.* 2,14	#138 = *Epist.* 4,10	#168 = *Epist.* 4,31
#104 = *Carm.* 2,15	#139 = *Epist.* 4,11	#169 = *Carm.* 2,50
#105 = *Carm.* 2,16	#140 = *Carm.* 2,32	#170 = *Epist.* 4,32
#106 = *Epist.* 3,25	#141 = *Epist.* 4,12	#171 = *Epist.* 4,33
#107 = *Epist.* 3,26	#142 = *Epist.* 4,13	#172 = *Epist.* 4,34
#108 = *Epist.* 3,27	#143 = *Carm.* 2,33	#173 = *Epist.* 4,35

#174 = *Epist.* 5,1

#175 = *Epist.* 5,2

#176 = *Epist.* 5,3

#177 = *Epist.* 5,4

#178 = *Epist.* 5,5

#179 = *Carm.* 2,51

#180 = *Carm.* 2,52

#180a = *Carm.* 2,53

#180b = *Carm.* 2,54

#180c = *Carm.* 2,55

#181 = *Carm.* 2,56

#182 = *Carm.* 2,57

#182a = *Carm.* 2,58

#182b = *Carm.* 2,59

#183 = *Carm.* 2,60

#184 = *Carm.* 2,61

#184a = *Carm.* 2,62

#184b = *Carm.* 2,63

#185 = *Carm.* 2,64

#186 = *Carm.* 2,65

#187 = *Carm.* 2,66

#188 = *Carm.* 2,67

#189 = *Carm.* 2,68

#190 = *Carm.* 2,69

#190a = *Carm.* 2,70

#190b = *Carm.* 2,71

#190c = *Carm.* 2,72

#191 = *Carm.* 2,73

#192 = *Carm.* 2,74

#193 = *Carm.* 2,75

#194 = *Carm.* 2,76

#195 = *Carm.* 2,77

#196 = *Carm.* 2,78

#197 = *Carm.* 2,79

#198 = *Carm.* 2,80

#199 = *Carm.* 2,81

#200 = *Carm.* 2,82

#201 = *Carm.* 2,83

#202 = *Carm.* 2,84

#203 = *Carm.* 2,85

#204 = *Carm.* 2,86

#205 = *Carm.* 2,87

#206 = *Carm.* 2,88

#207 = *Carm.* 2,89

#208 = *Dict.* 24,
   Carm. 2,90

#209 = *Carm.* 2,91

#210 = *Carm.* 2,92

#211 = *Carm.* 2,93

#212 = *Carm.* 2,94

#213 = *Carm.* 1,2

#214 = *Dict.* 3

#215 = *Carm.* 2,95

#216 = *Carm.* 2,96

#217 = *Carm.* 2,97

#218 = *Epist.* 5,6

#219 = *Epist.* 5,7

#220 = *Dict.* 25

#221 = *Dict.* 14

#222 = *Dict.* 15

#223 = *Dict.* 16

#224 = *Epist.* 5,8

#225 = *Epist.* 5,9

#226 = *Epist.* 5,10

#227 = *Epist.* 5,11

#228 = *Epist.* 5,12

#229 = *Carm.* 2,98

#230 = *Carm.* 2,99

#231 = *Carm.* 2,100

#232 = *Carm.* 2,101

#232a = *Carm.* 2,102

#233 = *Carm.* 2,103

#234 = *Carm.* 2,104

#235 = *Epist.* 5,13

#236 = *Epist.* 5,14

#237 = *Carm.* 2,105

#238 = *Carm.* 2,106

#239 = *Dict.* 17

#240 = *Opusc.* 4

#241 = *Epist.* 5,15

#242 = *Epist.* 5,16

#243 = *Dict.* 18

#244 = *Epist.* 5,17

#245 = *Carm.* 1,1

#246 = *Epist.* 5,18

#247 = *Epist.* 5,19

#248 = *Epist.* 5,20

#249 = *Epist.* 5,21

#250 = *Epist.* 5,22

#251 = *Epist.* 5,23

#252 = *Epist.* 5,24

#253 = *Epist.* 5,25

#254 = *Epist.* 5,26

#255 = *Epist.* 5,27

#256 = *Carm.* 2,107

#257 = *Carm.* 2,108–9

#258 = *Epist.* 6,1

#259 = *Epist.* 6,2

#260 = *Carm.* 2,110

#261 = *Dict.* 19

#262 = *Carm.* 1,3

#263 = *Opusc.* 1

#264 = *Carm.* 2,111

#265 = *Carm.* 2,112

#266 = *Carm.* 2,113

#267 = *Carm.* 2,114

#267a = *Carm.* 2,115

#267b = *Carm.* 2,116

#268 = *Epist.* 6,3

#269 = *Epist.* 6,4

#270 = *Epist.* 6,5

#271 = *Epist.* 6,6

#272 = *Epist.* 6,7

#273 = *Epist.* 6,8

#274 = *Epist.* 6,9

#275 = *Epist.* 6,10

#276 = *Epist.* 6,11

#277 = *Dict.* 4

#278 = *Dict.* 20

#279 = *Epist.* 6,12

#280 = *Epist.* 6,13

#281 = *Epist.* 6,14

#282 = *Epist.* 6,15

#283 = *Epist.* 6,16

#284 = *Epist.* 6,17

#285 = *Epist.* 6,18

#286 = *Epist.* 6,19

#287 = *Epist.* 6,20

#288 = *Epist.* 6,21

#289 = *Epist.* 6,22

#290 = *Epist.* 6,23

#291 = *Epist.* 6,24

#292 = *Epist.* 6,25

#293 = *Epist.* 6,26

#294 = *Epist.* 6,27

#295 = *Epist.* 6,28

#296 = *Epist.* 6,29

#297 = *Epist.* 6,30

#298 = *Epist.* 6,31

#299 = *Epist.* 6,32

#300 = *Epist.* 6,33

#301 = *Epist.* 6,34

#302 = *Epist.* 6,35

#303 = *Epist.* 6,36

#304 = *Epist.* 6,37

#305 = *Epist.* 6,38

#306 = *Epist.* 7,1

#307 = *Epist.* 7,2

#308 = *Epist.* 7,3

#309 = *Epist.* 7,4

#310 = *Epist.* 7,5

#311 = *Epist.* 7,6

#312 = *Epist.* 7,7

#313 = *Epist.* 7,8

#314 = *Epist.* 7,9

#315 = *Epist.* 7,10

#316 = *Epist.* 7,11

#317 = *Epist.* 7,12

#318 = *Epist.* 7,13

#319 = *Epist.* 7,14

#320 = *Dict.* 12

#321 = *Epist.* 7,15

#322 = *Epist.* 7,16

#323 = *Epist.* 7,17

#324 = *Epist.* 7,18

#325 = *Carm.* 2,117

#326 = *Carm.* 2,118

#326a = *Carm.* 2,119

#326b = *Carm.* 2,120

#326c = *Carm.* 2,121

#326d = *Carm.* 2,122

#327 = *Carm.* 2,123

#328 = *Carm.* 2,124

#329 = *Carm.* 2,125

#329a = *Carm.* 2,126

#329b,c = *Carm.* 2,127

#330 = *Carm.* 2,128

#331 = *Epist.* 7,19

#332 = *Carm.* 2,129

#333 = *Carm.* 2,130

#334 = *Epist.* 7,20

#335 = *Epist.* 7,21

#336 = *Dict.* 5

#337 = *Epist.* 7,22

#338 = *Carm.* 2,131

#339 = *Carm.* 2,132

#340 = *Carm.* 2,133

#341 = *Carm.* 1,10

#342 = *Carm.* 1,11

#343 = *Carm.* 1,12

#344 = *Carm.* 1,13

#345 = *Carm.* 1,14

#346 = *Carm.* 1,15

#347 = *Carm.* 1,16

#348 = *Carm.* 1,17

#349 = *Carm.* 1,18

#350 = *Carm.* 1,19

#351 = *Carm.* 1,20

#352 = *Carm.* 1,21

#353 = *Carm.* 2,134

#354 = *Carm.* 2,135

#355 = *Carm.* 2,136

#356 = *Epist.* 7,23

#357 = *Epist.* 7,24

#358 = *Epist.* 7,25

#359 = *Epist.* 7,26

#360 = *Epist.* 7,27

#361 = *Epist.* 7,28

#362 = *Epist.* 7,29

#363 = *Dict.* 21

#364 = *Carm.* 2,137

#364a = *Carm.* 2,138

#364b = *Carm.* 2,139

#364c = *Carm.* 2,140

#365 = *Carm.* 2,141

#366 = *Carm.* 2,142

#367 = *Carm.* 2,143

#368 = *Epist.* 7,30

#369 = *Epist.* 7,31

#370 = *Epist.* 8,1

#371 = *Carm.* 2,144

#372 = *Carm.* 2,145

#373 = *Carm.* 2,146

#374 = *Carm.* 2,147

#375 = *Carm.* 2,148

#376 = *Epist.* 8,2

#377 = *Epist.* 8,3

#378 = *Epist.* 8,4

#379 = *Carm.* 2,149

#380 = *Dict.* 22

#381 = *Epist.* 8,5

#382 = *Epist.* 8,6

#383 = *Epist.* 8,7

#384 = *Epist.* 8,8
#385 = *Epist.* 8,9
#386 = *Epist.* 8,10
#387 = *Epist.* 8,11
#388 = *Carm.* 1,4
#389 = *Epist.* 8,12
#390 = *Epist.* 8,13
#391 = *Epist.* 8,14
#392 = *Epist.* 8,15
#393 = *Epist.* 8,16
#394 = *Epist.* 8,17
#395 = *Epist.* 8,18
#396 = *Epist.* 8,19
#397 = *Epist.* 8,20
#398 = *Epist.* 8,21
#399 = *Epist.* 8,22
#400 = *Epist.* 8,23
#401 = *Epist.* 8,24
#402 = *Epist.* 8,25
#403 = *Epist.* 8,26
#404 = *Epist.* 8,27
#405 = *Epist.* 8,28
#406 = *Epist.* 8,29
#407 = *Epist.* 8,30
#408 = *Epist.* 8,31
#409 = *Epist.* 8,32
#410 = *Epist.* 8,33
#411 = *Epist.* 8,34
#412 = *Epist.* 8,35

#413 = *Epist.* 8,36
#414 = *Dict.* 26
#415 = *Epist.* 8,37
#416 = *Epist.* 8,38
#417 = *Epist.* 8,39
#418 = *Epist.* 8,40
#419 = *Epist.* 8,41
#420 = *Epist.* 8,42
#421 = *Epist.* 8,43
#422 = *Epist.* 9,1
#423 = *Carm.* 1,5
#424 = *Epist.* 9,2
#425 = *Epist.* 9,3
#426 = *Epist.* 9,4
#427 = *Epist.* 9,5
#428 = *Epist.* 9,6
#429 = *Epist.* 9,7
#430 = *Epist.* 9,8
#431 = *Epist.* 9,9
#432 = *Epist.* 9,10
#433 = *Epist.* 9,11
#434 = *Epist.* 9,12
#435 = *Epist.* 9,13
#436 = *Dict.* 27
#437 = *Epist.* 9,14
#438 = *Opusc.* 5
#439 = *Epist.* 9,15
#440 = *Epist.* 9,16
#441 = *Epist.* 9,17

#442 = *Epist.* 9,18
#443 = *Epist.* 9,19
#444 = *Epist.* 9,20
#445 = *Epist.* 9,21
#446 = *Epist.* 9,22
#447 = *Epist.* 9,23
#448 = *Epist.* 9,24
#449 = *Epist.* 9,25
#450, #451 = *Carm.*
  2,150, *Dict.* 13
#452 = *Opusc.* 6
#453 = *Carm.* 2,151
#454 = *Epist.* 9,26
#455 = *Epist.* 9,27
#456 = *Epist.* 9,28
#457 = *Epist.* 9,29
#458 = *Epist.* 9,30
#459 = *Epist.* 9,31
#460 = *Epist.* 9,32
#461 = *Epist.* 9,33
#462 = *Carm.* 2,5
#463 = *Epist.* 9,34
#464 = *Dict.* 6
#465 = *Carm.* 2,6
#466 = *Dict.* 28
#467 = *Dict.* 23
#468 = *Epist.* 9,35
#469 = *Carm.* 2,4
#470 = *Carm.* 2,7

Bibliography

Editions of Ennodius

The *editio princeps: Monumenta S. Patrum Orthodoxographa*, ed. J. J. Grynaeus. *pars altera*, 269–480. Basel, 1569.

Ennodi Carmina, ed. A. Schottus. Milan, 1610.

Beati Ennodii Ticinensis Episcopi Opera, ed. A. Schottus. Tournai, 1611.

Magni Felicis Ennodii Episcopi Ticinensis Opera, ed. J. Sirmond. Paris, 1611. Reprint. *Opera Varia* 1. Paris, 1696 = Venice, 1728.

Magni Felicis Ennodii Opera, ed. G. Hartel. *CSEL* 6. Vienna, 1882.

Magni Felicis Ennodi Opera, ed. F. Vogel. *MGH AA* 7. Berlin, 1885.

Other Premodern Texts

Acta Sanctorum, Iulii 4 (dies XV–XIX), ed. J. Bollandus, G. Henschenius, and J. Carnandet. Paris, 1868.

Acta Synhodorum Habitarum Romae, ed. T. Mommsen. *MGH AA* 12:393–455. Berlin, 1894.

Alcimi Ecdicii Aviti opera quae supersunt, ed. R. Peiper. *MGH AA* 6.2. Berlin, 1883.

Anthologia Latina, ed. A. Riese and F. Bücheler. Leipzig, 1869–1926.

Aratoris de actibus apostolorum, ed. A. P. McKinlay. *CSEL* 72. Vienna, 1951.

The Works of Ausonius, ed. R. P. H. Green. Oxford, 1991.

Calpurnius Flaccus. Declamationes, ed. L. Håkanson. Stuttgart, 1978.

Cassiodori Senatoris Variae, ed. T. Mommsen. *MGH AA* 12. Berlin, 1894.

Césaire d'Arles. Sermons au peuple. 1, ed. M.-J. Deléage. *Sources Chrétiennes* 175. Paris, 1971.

Theodosiani Libri XVI cum Constitutionibus Sirmondianis, ed. T. Mommsen and P. M. Meyer. 2 vols. in 3. 3d ed. Berlin, 1962.

Concilia Africae, A. 345–A. 525, ed. C. Munier. *CCSL* 149. Turnholt, 1974.

Concilia Galliae, A. 314–A. 506, ed. C. Munier. *CCSL* 148. Turnholt, 1963.

Concilia Galliae, A. 511–A. 695, ed. C. de Clercq. *CCSL* 148A. Turnholt, 1963.

Declamationes XIX maiores Quintiliano falso ascriptae, ed. L. Håkanson. Stuttgart, 1982.

Epistulae Austrasiacae, ed. W. Gundlach. *CCSL* 117. Turnholt, 1957.

Epistulae Imperatorum Pontificum aliorum inde ab a. CCCLXVII usque ad a. DLIII datae, Avellana quae dicitur collectio, ed. O. Guenther. *CSEL* 35.2. Vienna, 1898.

Epistolae Romanorum Pontificum genuinae, ed. A. Thiel. Braunsberg, 1867–68. Reprint. Hildesheim, 1974.

Gesta Conlationis Carthaginiensis anno 411, ed. S. Lancel. *CCSL* 149A. Turnholt, 1974.

S. Gregorii Magni Registrum Epistularum, ed. D. Norberg. *CCSL* 140–140A. Turnholt, 1982.

Liber Pontificalis, pars prior, ed. T. Mommsen. *MGH Gesta Pontificum Romanorum* 1.1. Berlin, 1898.

M. Valerii Martialis Epigrammaton Libri, ed. W. Heraeus and J. Borovskii. Leipzig, 1976.

Maximi Taurinensis Sermones, ed. A. Mutzenbecher. *CCSL* 23. Turnholt, 1962.

Opicino de Canistris, L'"Anonimo Ticinese" (Cod. Vat. Pal. Lat. 1993), ed. F. Gianani. Pavia, 1927 [= *Anonymus Ticinensis commentarius seu de laudibus Papiae,* ed. L. A. Muratori, *Rerum Italicarum Scriptores* 11. Milan, 1727].

Die nichtliterarischen lateinischen Papyri Italiens aus der Zeit 445–700, ed., trans. J.-O. Tjäder. 1: Papyri 1–28. 2: Papyri 29–59. Skrifter Utgivna av Svenska Institutet i Rom, 4°, XIX.1–2 [text], XIX.3 [plates]. Lund, 1954–55 (XIX.1 and 3); Stockholm, 1982 (XIX:2).

Vita Caesarii Arelatensis. In *Passiones Vitaeque Sanctorum Aevi Merovingici et Antiquiorum Aliquot,* ed. B. Krusch. *MGH SRM* 3. Hannover, 1896.

M. Fabii Quintiliani Declamationes Minores, ed. D. R. Shackleton Bailey. Stuttgart, 1989.

Salvien de Marseille. Oeuvres, vol. 1, ed. G. Lagarrigue. *Sources Chrétiennes* 176. Paris, 1971.

L. Annaeus Seneca Maior. Oratorum et Rhetorum Sententiae, Divisiones, Colores, ed. L. Håkanson. Leipzig, 1989.

Sidonius. Poems and Letters, ed. and trans. W. B. Anderson. 2 vols. Cambridge, MA, and London, 1936–65.

Three Lives of English Saints, ed. M. Winterbottom. Toronto, 1972.

Secondary Works

Actes du XIe congrès international d'archéologie chrétienne. Lyon, Vienne, Grenoble, Genève et Aoste (21–28 Septembre 1986). 3 vols. Collection de l'École Française de Rome 123. Rome, 1989.

Ahl, F. "The Art of Safe Criticism in Greece and Rome." *AJP* 105 (1984): 174–208.

Altaner, B., and A. Stuiber. *Patrologie.* 8th ed. Freiburg, 1978.

Amory, P. *People and Identity in Ostrogothic Italy, 489–554.* Cambridge, 1997.

Anastasi, R. "Dati biografici su Aratore in Ennodio." *Miscellanea di studi di letteratura cristiana antica* 1 (1947): 141–52.

Angenot, M., J. Bessière, D. Foukkema, and E. Kushner, eds. *Théorie littéraire: Problèmes et perspectives.* Paris, 1989.

Arjava, A. *Women and Law in Late Antiquity.* Oxford, 1996.

Bacht, H. "Die Rolle des orientalischen Mönchtums in die kirchenpolitischen Auseinandersetzungen um Chalkedon (431–519)." In *Entscheidung um Chalkedon,* vol. 2 of *Das Konzil von Chalkedon. Geschichte und Gegenwart,* ed. A. Grillmeier and H. Bacht, 193–314. Würzburg, 1954.

Bagnall, R. S., A. Cameron, and S. R. Schwartz. *Consuls of the Later Roman Empire.* Atlanta, 1987.

Banniard, M. *Viva Voce. Communication écrite et communication orale du IVᵉ au IXᵉ siècle en Occident latin.* Paris, 1992.

Bardy, G. "Saint Ennode de Pavie." In *Le Christianisme et l'Occident barbare,* ed. J. R. Palanque, 229–64. Paris, 1945.

Barnes, T. D. "Augustine, Symmachus, and Ambrose." In McWilliam, *Augustine,* 7–13.

———. "Late Roman Prosopography: Between Theodosius and Justinian." *Phoenix* 37 (1983): 248–70.

Barnish, S. J. B. "Maximian, Cassiodorus, Boethius, Theodahad: Literature, Philosophy and Politics in Ostrogothic Italy." *Nottingham Medieval Studies* 34 (1990): 18–32.

———. "Ennodius' Lives of Epiphanius and Antony: Two Models for the Christian Gentleman." *Studia Patristica* 24 (1993): 13–19.

———. trans. and comm. *The Variae of Magnus Aurelius Cassiodorus Senator.* Liverpool, 1992.

Barnwell, P. *Emperor, Prefects, and Kings. The Roman West, 395–565.* Chapel Hill, 1992.

Beagon, M. "Nature and Views of Her Landscapes in Pliny the Elder." In Shipley and Salmon, *Human Landscapes,* 284–309.

———. *Roman Nature: The Thought of Pliny the Elder.* Oxford, 1992.

Beard, M. "Looking (Harder) for Roman Myth: Dumézil, Declamation and the Problems of Definition." In *Mythos in mythenloser Gesellschaft: das Paradigma Roms,* ed. F. Graf, 44–64. Stuttgart, 1993.

Benjamin, C. "Ennodius." *RE* 5.2 (1903): 2629–33.

Binns, J. W., ed. *Latin Literature of the Fourth Century.* London, 1974.

Birt, T. *Das antike Buchwesen.* Berlin, 1882. Reprint. Aalen, 1959.

Bischoff, B. *Die Abtei Lorsch im Spiegel ihrer Handschriften.* 2d ed. Lorsch, 1989.

Blaise, A. *Dictionnaire latin-français des auteurs chrétiens.* Turnholt, 1967.

Bloomer, W. M. *Latinity and Literary Society at Rome.* Philadelphia, 1997.

Blumenthal, U.-R. "Fälschungen bei Kanonisten der Kirchenreform das 11. Jahrhunderts." In *Fälschungen im Mittelalter* 2, 241–62.

Bognetti, G. P. "Il vescovo Lorenzo e la collaborazione con Teodorico." In *Dall'invasione dei barbari all'apogeo del governo vescovile (493–1002).* Vol. 2 of *Storia di Milano,* 3–24. Milan, 1954.

Bonner, S. F. *Roman Declamation in the Late Republic and Early Empire.* Liverpool, 1949.

Bowersock, G. W. "From Emperor to Bishop: The Self-Conscious Transformation of Political Power in the Fourth Century A.D." *CP* 81 (1986): 298–307.

———. *Hellenism in Late Antiquity.* Ann Arbor, 1990.

Bowman, A. K., and G. Woolf, eds. *Literacy and Power in the Ancient World.* Cambridge, 1994.

Bradbury, S., ed. *Severus of Minorca. Letter on the Conversion of the Jews.* Oxford, 1996.

Bréhier, L. "Les colonies d'orientaux en occident au commencement du moyen-âge." *BZ* 12 (1903): 1–39.

Brou, L. "Les chants en langue grecque dans les liturgies latines." *Sacris Erudiri* 1 (1949): 165–80.

———. "Les chants en langue grecque dans les liturgies latines: premier supplément." *Sacris Erudiri* 4 (1952): 226–38.

Brown, P. R. L. *Augustine of Hippo.* Berkeley, 1969.

———. *The Body and Society. Men, Women and Sexual Renunciation in Early Christianity.* New York, 1988.

———. *The Cult of the Saints.* Chicago, 1981.

———. *Power and Persuasion in Late Antiquity: Towards a Christian Empire.* Madison, WI, 1992.

Bruggisser, P. *Symmaque ou le rituel épistolaire de l'amitié littéraire. Recherches sur le premier livre de la correspondance.* Fribourg, 1993.

Brunhölzl, F. *Geschichte der lateinischen Literatur des Mittelalters 1. Von Cassiodor bis zum Ausklang der karolingischen Erneurerung.* Munich, 1975.

Bullough, D. A. "Urban Change in Early Medieval Italy: The Example of Pavia." *PBSR* 34 (1966): 82–130.

Butler, R. *Choiseul.* Vol. 1 of *Father and Son, 1719–1754.* Oxford, 1980.

Cabrol, F. "Huile." *DACL* 6.2 (1925): 2777–91.

Cameron, A. "Synesius and Late Roman Cyrenaica." *JRA* 5 (1992): 419–30.

Cameron, Av. *Christianity and the Rhetoric of Empire.* Sather Classical Lectures 55. Berkeley, 1991.

———. "Texts as Weapons: Polemic in the Byzantine Dark Ages." In Bowman and Woolf, *Literacy and Power,* 198–215.

Carini, M. "*L'itinerarium brigantionis castelli* di Ennodio: una nota preliminare." *Atene e Roma* 33 (1988): 158–65.

Caspar, E. *Geschichte des Papsttums von den Anfängen bis zur Höhe der Weltherrschaft.* 2 vols. Tübingen, 1930–33.

Cattaneo, E. *Terra di Sant'Ambrogio. La chiesa milanese nel primo millenio.* Milan, 1989.

Cesa, M. *Ennodio. Vita del beatissimo Epifanio.* Biblioteca di Athenaeum 6. Pavia, 1988.

———. "Integrazioni prosopografiche tardo-imperiali." *Athenaeum* 64 (1986): 236–40.

Chadwick, H. *Boethius. The Consolations of Music, Logic, Theology, and Philosophy.* Oxford, 1981.

———. *The Early Church.* Harmondsworth, 1967.

Chastagnol, A. "Le formulaire de l'épigraphie latine officielle dans l'antiquité tardive." In Donati, *La terza età dell'epigrafia,* 11–65.

Chevallier, R. *La romanisation de la celtique du Pô.* BEFAR 249. Paris, 1983.

Christie, N. "Barren Fields? Landscapes and Settlements in Late Roman and Post-Roman Italy." In Shipley and Salmon, *Human Landscapes,* 254–83.

Clark, G. *Women in Late Antiquity: Pagan and Christian Life-Styles.* Oxford, 1993.

Clarke, M. L. *Rhetoric at Rome. A Historical Survey.* 3d ed. London, 1996.

Combet-Farnoux, M. "Sixte II." *DACL* 15.1 (1950): 1501–15.

Constable, G. *Letters and Letter-Collections.* Typologie des sources du moyen-âge occidental, Fasc. 17. Turnholt, 1976.

———. "Forged Letters in the Middle Ages." In *Fälschungen im Mittelalter,* 5:11–37.

Corbier, M. "L'écriture en quête de lecteurs." In *Literacy in the Roman World,* 99–118.

Corn, J. J. "Object Lessons / Object Myths? What Historians of Technology Learn from Things." In Kingery, *Learning from Things,* 35–54.

Courcelle, P. *Les lettres grecques en occident de Macrobe à Cassiodore.* Paris, 1943.

———. *Les Confessions de Saint Augustin dans la tradition littéraire.* Paris, 1963.

Croke, B. "A.D. 476: The Manufacture of a Turning Point." *Chiron* 13 (1983): 81–119.

———. "Cassiodorus and the *Getica* of Jordanes." *CP* 82 (1987): 117–34.

———. "Mundo the Gepid: From Freebooter to Roman General." *Chiron* 12 (1982): 125–35.

Culler, J. "La littérarité." In Angenot and Bessière, *Théorie littéraire,* 31–43.

Curtius, E. R. *European Literature and the Latin Middle Ages.* Bollingen Series 36. Princeton, 1953.

Cutler, A. "Five Lessons in Late Roman Ivory." *JRA* 6 (1993): 167–92.

D'Angelo, E. "Tematiche omosessuali nella letteratura di età teodericiana. Il caso Ennodio." In *Teoderico il Grande,* 645–54.

Davis, R., trans. and intro. *The Book of Pontiffs (Liber Pontificalis).* Liverpool, 1989.

Dekkers, E., and A. Gaar. *Clavis Patrum Latinorum.* 3d ed. Steenbrugge, 1995.

de Labriolle, P., G. Bardy, L. Bréhier, and G. de Plinval. *De la mort de Théodose à l'election de Grégoire le Grand.* Vol. 4 of *Histoire de l'Église.* Paris, 1948.

Delbrueck, R. *Die Consulardiptychen und verwandte Denkmäler.* Berlin and Leipzig, 1929.

Di Berardino, A., ed. *Encyclopedia of the Early Church.* Cambridge, 1992.

Dixon, S. "Conflict in the Roman Family." In Rawson and Weaver, *Roman Family,* 149–67.

———. "Continuity and Change in Roman Social History: Retrieving 'Family Feeling(s)' from Roman Law and Literature." In *Inventing Ancient Culture: Historicism, Periodization and the Ancient World,* ed. M. Golden and P. Toohey, 79–90. London, 1997.

———. *The Roman Family.* Baltimore, 1992.

Donati, A., ed. *La terza età dell'epigrafia. Colloquio internazionale AIEGL 1986 Bologna.* Faenza, 1988.

Döpp, S. "Cyllarus und andere Rosse in römischem Herrscherlob." *Hermes* 124 (1996): 321–32.

Drinkwater, J., and H. Elton, eds. *Fifth-Century Gaul: A Crisis of Identity?* Cambridge, 1992.

Dubois, A. *La latinité d'Ennodius.* Paris, 1903.

Dubuisson, M. "*Graecus, Graeculus, Graecari:* l'emploi péjoratif du nom des Grecs en Latin." In *ΕΛΛΗΝΙΣΜΟΣ: quelques jalons pour un histoire de l'identité grecque,* ed. S. Saïd, 315–35. Leiden, 1991.

Duchesne, L., ed. *Liber Pontificalis.* 2 vols. Paris, 1955.

Dupin, L. E. *Nouvelle bibliothèque des auteurs ecclesiastiques.* Vol. 4. 2d ed. Paris, 1703. Reprint. Westmead, 1970.

Ellis, S. P. "Late-Antique Dining: Architecture, Furnishings and Behaviour." In Laurence and Wallace-Hadrill, *Domestic Space,* 41–51.

Ensslin, W. *Theoderich der Grosse.* Munich, 1947.

Ernout, A. "*Dictare,* dicter, allemand *dichten.*" *REL* 29 (1951): 155–61.

Ertl, N. "Diktatoren frühmitteralterlicher Papstbriefe." *Archiv für Urkundenforschung* 15 (1938): 56–132.

Evans Grubbs, J. "Constantine and Imperial Legislation on the Family." In Harries and Wood, *Theodosian Code,* 120–42.

Faivre, A. *Naissance d'une hiérarchie. Les premières étapes du cursus clérical.* Paris, 1977.

Fälschungen im Mittelalter. Internationaler Kongreß der Monumenta Germaniae Historica, München, 16.–19. September 1986. Schriften der Monumenta Germaniae Historica, 33.1–5. Hannover, 1988.

Fantham, E. *Roman Literary Culture: from Cicero to Apuleius.* Baltimore, 1996.

Ferguson, E., ed. *Encyclopedia of Early Christianity.* 2 vols. 2d ed. New York, 1997.

Ferrai, L. A. "Il matrimonio di Ennodio." *Archivio Storico Lombardo,* 2d ser., 20 (1893): 948–57.

Fertig, M. *Magnus Felix Ennodius und seine Zeit.* Vol. 1. Passau, 1855.

Fini, C. "Le fonti delle *dictiones* di Ennodio." *Acta Antiqua Academiae Scientiarum Hungaricae* 30 (1982–84): 387–93.

Fontaine, J. "Ennodius." *RAC* 5 (1962): 398–421.

———. *Études sur la poésie latine tardive d'Ausone a Prudence.* Paris, 1980.

Fontaine, J., and C. Pietri, eds. *Le monde latin antique et la Bible.* Bible de Tous les Temps 2. Paris, 1985.

Fougnies, A. *Een Studie over de clausulen bij Ennodius.* Brussels, 1951.

Fuhrmann, H. *Einfluß und Verbreitung der pseudoisidorischen Fälschungen. Von ihrem Auftauchen bis in die neuere Zeit.* Schriften der Monumenta Germaniae Historica, 24.1–3. Stuttgart, 1972–74.

Fuhrmann, M. *Rom in der Spätantike. Porträt einer Epoche.* Munich, 1994.

Galbiati, E., A. Poma, and L. Alfonsi. *Magno Felice Ennodio (474–521). Contributi nel XV centenario della nascità.* Pavia, 1975.

Garnsey, P. *Ideas of Slavery from Aristotle to Augustine.* Cambridge, 1996.

———. "Sons, Slaves — and Christians." In Rawson and Weaver, *Roman Family,* 101–21.

Garzya, A. "Cassiodoro e la grecità." In *Atti della settimana di studi Flavio Magno Aurelio Cassiodoro (Cosenza-Squillace 19–24 settembre 1983)*, ed. S. Leanza, 118–34. Soveria Mannelli, 1986.

Gaudemet, J. *L'église dans l'empire romain.* Paris, 1958.

Geary, P. *Furta Sacra. Thefts of Relics in the Central Middle Ages.* Princeton, 1978.

Gessel, W. M. "Reform am Haupt. Die Pastoralregel Gregors des Großen und die Besetzung von Bischofsstühlen." In *Papsttum und Kirchenreform. Historische Beiträge. Festschrift für Georg Schwaiger zum 65. Geburtstag,* ed. M. Weitlauff and K. Hausberger, 11–36. St. Ottilien, 1990.

Gignac, F. T. *A Grammar of the Greek Papyri of the Roman and Byzantine Periods.* Vol. 1. *Phonology.* Testi e documenti per lo studio dell'antichità, no. 55. Milan, 1976.

Głowinski, M. "Les genres littéraires." In Angenot and Bessière, *Théorie littéraire,* 81–94.

Goffart, W. *The Narrators of Barbarian History (A.D. 550–800).* Princeton, 1988.

Goodman, M. *Mission and Conversion: Proselytizing in the Religious History of the Roman Empire.* Oxford, 1994.

Grabar, A. *L'empereur dans l'art byzantin.* Paris, 1936.

Gribomont, J. "Cassiodore et la transmission de l'héritage biblique antique." In Fontaine and Pietri, *Le monde antique latin,* 143–55.

Grundmann, H. "*Litteratus-illitteratus.* Der Wandel einer Bildungsnorm vom Altertum zum Mittelalter." *Archiv für Kulturgeschichte* 40 (1958): 1–65.

Gurevich, A. *Historical Anthropology of the Middle Ages,* ed. J. Howlett. Cambridge, 1992.

Gusso, M. "Sull'imperatore Glycerio (473–74 D.C.)." *SDHI* 58 (1992): 168–93.

Haarhoff, T. J. *Schools of Gaul. A Study of Pagan and Christian Education in the Last Century of the Roman Empire.* Oxford, 1920.

Halsall, G. "The Origins of the *Reihengräberzivilisation:* Forty Years On." In Drinkwater and Elton, *Fifth-Century Gaul,* 196–207.

Harries, J. and I. Wood, eds. *The Theodosian Code.* Ithaca, 1993.

Hasenstab, B. *Studien zu Ennodius.* Munich, 1890.

Hauschild, W.-D. "Gnade IV." *TRE* 13 (1984): 476–95.

Heather, P. *The Goths.* Oxford, 1996.

———. "The Historical Culture of Ostrogothic Italy." In *Teoderico il Grande,* 317–53.

———. "Literacy and Power in the Migration Period." In Bowman and Woolf, *Literacy and Power,* 177–97.

Heinzelmann, M. *Bischofsherrschaft in Gallien. Zur Kontinuität römischer Führungsschichten vom 4. bis 7. Jahrhundert. Soziale, prosopographische u. bildungsgeschichtliche Aspekte. Francia* Beiheft 5. Munich, 1976.

Helm, R. "Heidnisches und christliches bei spätlateinischen Dichtern." In *Natalicium Johannes Geffcken zum 70. Geburtstag,* 1–46. Heidelberg, 1931.

Herescu, N. I. "Le mode de composition des écrivains (*dictare*)." *REL* 34 (1956): 132–46.

Hill, B. T. "Constantinopolis." In *Gold Jewelry. Craft, Style and Meaning from Mycenae to Constantinopolis,* ed. T. Hackens and R. Winkes, 141–47. Publications d'Histoire de l'Art et d'Archéologie de l'Université Catholique de Louvain 36. Louvain-la-neuve, 1983.

Hillier, R. *Arator on the Acts of the Apostles. A Baptismal Commentary.* Oxford, 1993.

Hope, D. *The Leonine Sacramentary. A Reassessment of its Nature and Purpose.* Oxford, 1971.

Hopkins, K. "Conquest by Book." In *Literacy in the Roman World,* 133–58.

Horsfall, N. "Statistics or States of Mind?" In *Literacy in the Roman World,* 59–76.

Hunt, E. D. "Christianising the Roman Empire: The Evidence of the Code." In Harries and Wood, *Theodosian Code,* 143–58.

———. *Holy Land Pilgrimage in the Later Roman Empire, AD 312–460.* Oxford, 1982.

Jaffé, P. *Regesta Pontificum Romanorum.* 2d ed. Leipzig, 1885.

Johnson, M. J. "Toward a History of Theoderic's Building Program." *DOP* 42 (1988): 72–96.

Jones, A. H. M. *The Later Roman Empire, 284–602.* Oxford, 1964.

Jones, C. "Women, Death, and the Law during the Christian Persecutions." In *Studies in Church History* 30, ed. D. Wood, 121–34. Oxford, 1993.

Jullian, C. *Histoire de la Gaule.* Vol. 5. Paris, 1920.

Jungmann, J. A. *Missarum Solemnia. Eine genetische Erklärung der römischen Messe.* 2 vols. 4th ed. Vienna, 1958.

Kaster, R. A. *Guardians of Language: The Grammarian and Society in Late Antiquity.* Berkeley, 1988.

Kennell, N. M. "Herodes Atticus and the Rhetoric of Tyranny." *CP* 92 (1997): 346–62.

Kennell, S. A. H. "Ennodius and his Editors." *C&M* 51 (late 2000).

———. "Ennodius and the Pagan Gods." *Athenaeum* 80 (1992): 236–42.

———. "Hercules' Invisible Basilica (Cassiodorus, *Variae* I, 6)." *Latomus* 53 (1994): 159–75.

———. "Aponus and his Admirers." In *In altum: Seventy-five years of Classical Studies in Newfoundland,* ed. M. Joyal. Calgary, 2000.

———. "Sex, Money, Death." Forthcoming.

Kent, J. P. C., and K. S. Painter, eds. *Wealth of the Roman World, A.D. 300–700.* London, 1977.

Kerr, A. J. "Matthew 13:25. Sowing *Zizania* among Another's Wheat: Realistic or Artificial?" *JTS* 48.1 (1997): 108–9.

Kibedi Varga, A. "Rhétorique et production du texte." In Angenot and Bessière, *Théorie littéraire,* 219–34.

Killick, D. "Optical and Electron Microscopy in Material Culture Studies." In Kingery, *Learning from Things,* 204–50.

Kingery, W. D., ed. *Learning from Things: Method and Theory of Material Culture Studies.* Washington, DC, 1996.

———. "Materials Science and Material Culture." In Kingery, *Learning from Things,* 181–203.

Kinney, D. "The Evidence for the Dating of S. Lorenzo in Milan." *Journal of the Society of Architectural Historians* 31 (1972): 92–107.

Kirkby, H. "The Scholar and His Public." In *Boethius. His Life, Thought, and Influence,* ed. M. Gibson, 44–69. Oxford, 1981.

Kitzinger, E. *Byzantine Art in the Making.* Cambridge, MA, 1980.

Klauser, Th. "Diakon." *RAC* 3 (1957): 897–909.

Klingshirn, W. E. *Caesarius of Arles: The Making of a Christian Community in Late Antique Gaul.* Cambridge, 1994.

Krautheimer, R. *Rome. Profile of a City, 312–1308.* Princeton, 1980.

———. *Three Christian Capitals: Topography and Politics.* Berkeley, 1983.

Kushner, E. "Articulation historique de la littérature." In Angenot and Bessière, *Théorie littéraire,* 111–25.

Laistner, M. L. W. "The Influence during the Middle Ages of the Treatise 'De Vita Contemplativa' and Its Surviving Manuscripts." In *Miscellanea Giovanni Mercati,* 2:344–58. Studi e Testi 122. Vatican City, 1946.

Lanzoni, F. *Le diocesi d'Italia dalle origini al principio del secolo VII (an. 604).* Studi e Testi 35, 1–2. Faenza, 1927.

Lapidge, M. "The Authorship of the Adonic Verses 'ad Fidolium' Attributed to Columbanus." *Studi Medievali,* 3d ser., 18.2 (1977): 249–314.

Laurence, R., and A. Wallace-Hadrill, eds. *Domestic Space in the Roman World: Pompeii and Beyond. JRA* Supplementary Series 22. Portsmouth, RI, 1997.

Lausberg, M. *Das Einzeldistichon. Studien zum antiken Epigramm.* Munich, 1982.

Lazard, S. "Les byzantinismes lexicaux de l'Exarchat de Ravenne et de la Pentapole." *Byzantion* 56 (1986): 354–426.

Lazzaro, L. *Fons Aponi. Abano e Montegrotto nell'Antichità.* Padua, 1981.

Leary, T. J. *Martial Book XIV. The Apophoreta.* London, 1996.

Lebek, W. D. "Deklamation und Dichtung in der *Dictio Ennodi diaconi quando de Roma rediit.*" In *Philanthropia kai Eusebeia. Festschrift für Albrecht Dihle zum 70. Geburtstag,* ed. G. W. Most, H. Petersmann, and A. M. Ritter, 264–99. Göttingen, 1993.

Leclercq, H. "Disque." *DACL* 4.1 (1920): 1173–91.

———. "Milan." *DACL* 11.1 (1933): 983–1102.

———. "Notaire." *DACL* 12.2 (1936): 1623–40.

Léglise, S. "Saint Ennodius et la haute éducation littéraire dans le monde romain au commencement du VIᵉ siècle." *L'Université Catholique* 5 (1890): 209–28, 375–97, 568–90.

———. *Oeuvres complètes de Saint Ennodius, évêque de Pavie.* Vol. 1, *Lettres.* Paris, 1906.

Literacy in the Roman World. JRA Supplementary Series 3. Ann Arbor, 1991.

Lizzi, R. *Vescovi e strutture ecclesiastiche nella città tardoantica (L'Italia Annonaria nel IV–V secolo d.C.).* Como, 1989.

Lolli, M., ed. *D. M. Ausonius Parentalia.* Collection Latomus 232. Brussels, 1997.

Lotter, F. "Antonius von Lérins und der Untergang Ufernorikums." *Historische Zeitschrift* 212 (1971): 265–315.

Lubar, S. "Learning from Technological Things." In Kingery, *Learning from Things,* 31–34.

Luiselli, B. "Note sulla perduta 'Historia Romana' di Q. Aurelio Memmio Simmaco." *Studi Urbinati* 49.1 (1975): 529–35.

Lumpe, A. "Ennodiana." *Byzantinische Forschungen* 1 (1966): 200–210.

———. "Die konziliengeschichtliche Bedeutung des Ennodius." *Annuarium Historiae Conciliorum* 1 (1969): 15–36.

Lynch, J. H. *"Spiritale Vinculum:* The Vocabulary of Kinship in early Medieval Europe." In *Religion, Culture, and Society in the Early Middle Ages. Studies in Honor of Richard E. Sullivan,* ed. T. F. X. Noble and J. J. Contreni, 181–204. Studies in Medieval Culture 23. Kalamazoo, 1987.

Macadam, A., ed. *Blue Guide: Northern Italy.* 9th ed. London, 1991.

MacCormack, S. *Art and Ceremony in Late Antiquity.* Berkeley, 1981.

———. "Latin Prose Panegyrics." In *Empire and Aftermath: Silver Latin II,* ed. T. A. Dorey, 143–205. London, 1975.

Magani, F. *Ennodio.* 3 vols. Pavia, 1886.

Magistretti, M. *La liturgia della chiesa milanese nel secolo IV.* Milan, 1899.

Maguire, H. *Art and Eloquence in Byzantium.* Princeton, 1981.

Markus, R. A. *The End of Ancient Christianity.* Cambridge, 1990.

———. *Gregory the Great and His World.* Cambridge, 1997.

———. "The Legacy of Pelagius: Orthodoxy, Heresy, and Conciliation." In *The Making of Orthodoxy: Essays in Honour of Henry Chadwick,* ed. R. Williams, 214–34. Cambridge, 1989.

———. "Paganism, Christianity and the Latin Classics in the Fourth Century." In Binns, *Latin Literature of the Fourth Century,* 1–21.

Marotta Mannino, B. "La 'Vita Antoni' di Ennodio fra tradizione classica e cristiana." *Orpheus* 10 (1989): 335–57.

Marrou, H.-I. *A History of Education in Antiquity.* Paris, 1948. Trans., Madison, WI, 1982.

Martindale, J. R. *The Prosopography of the Later Roman Empire.* Vols. 2–3. Cambridge, 1980–92.

Mathisen, R. W. "Epistolography, Literary Circles and Family Ties in Late Roman Gaul." *TAPA* 111 (1981): 95–109.

———. *Roman Aristocrats in Barbarian Gaul: Strategies for Survival in an Age of Transition.* Austin, 1993.

Matthews, J. F. "The Letters of Symmachus." In Binns, *Latin Literature of the Fourth Century,* 58–99.

McCormick, M. *Eternal Victory: Triumphal Rulership in Late Antiquity, Byzantium, and the Early Medieval West.* Cambridge, 1986.

McHugh, M. P. "Ennodius." In Ferguson, *Encyclopedia of Early Christianity,* 371.

McKitterick, R. *The Carolingians and the Written Word.* Cambridge, 1989.

———, ed. *The Uses of Literacy in Early Mediaeval Europe.* Cambridge, 1990.

McLynn, N. B. *Ambrose of Milan: Church and Court in a Christian Capital.* Berkeley, 1994.

McWilliam, J., ed. *Augustine: From Rhetor to Theologian.* Waterloo, 1992.

Merkel, C. "L'epitafio di Ennodio e la basilica di S. Michele in Pavia." *Reale Accademia dei Lincei, Classe di Scienze Morali: Memorie* 3, ser. 5, pt. 1 (1896): 83–219.

Meyendorff, J. *Imperial Unity and Christian Divisions.* Crestwood, NY, 1989.

Milano capitale del impero romano 286–402 d.c. Milan, 1990.

Mirabella Roberti, M. *Milano Romana.* Milan, 1984.

Misch, G. *Das Altertum.* Vol. 1 of *Geschichte der Autobiographie,* 2d ed. Leipzig, 1931.

Mochi Onory, S. *Vescovi e città (sec. IV–VI).* Bologna, 1933.

Momigliano, A. "Gli Anicii e la storiografia latina del VI secolo." In *Secondo contributo alla storia degli classici,* 231–53. Rome, 1960.

Mommaerts, T. S., and D. H. Kelley. "The Anicii of Gaul and Rome." In Drinkwater and Elton, *Fifth-Century Gaul,* 111–21.

Monachino, V. S. *Ambrogio e la cura pastorale a Milano nel secolo IV,* 2d ed. Milan, 1973.

Moorhead, J. *Theoderic in Italy.* Oxford, 1992.

Morabito, S. *Paganesimo e cristianesimo nella poesia di Ennodio.* Catania, 1947.

Moreton, B. *The Eighth-Century Gelasian Sacramentary.* Oxford, 1976.

Munier, C. *Les Statuta ecclesiae antiqua.* Bibliothèque de l'Institut de Droit Canonique de l'Université de Strasbourg 5. Paris, 1960.

Murga, J. L. "Tres leyes de Honorio sobre el modo de vestir los Romanos." *SDHI* 39 (1973): 129–86.

Näf, B. "Fulgentius von Ruspe, Caesarius von Arles und die Versammlungen der römischen Senatoren." *Klio* 74 (1992): 431–46.

———. *Senatorisches Standesbewusstsein in spätrömischer Zeit.* Freiburg, 1995.

———. "Das Zeitbewußtsein des Ennodius und der Untergang Roms." *Historia* 39 (1990): 100–123.

Navarra, L. "Le componenti letterarie e concettuali delle 'Dictiones' di Ennodio." *Augustinianum* 12 (1972): 465–78.

———. "Contributo storico di Ennodio." *Augustinianum* 14 (1974): 317–42.

———. *Ennodio e la "facies" storico-culturale del suo tempo.* Cassino, 1974.

———. "Ennodius." In Di Berardino, *Encyclopedia of the Early Church,* 272–73.

Neunheuser, B. "Oil." In Di Berardino, *Encyclopedia of the Early Church,* 611.

Nevett, L. "Perceptions of Domestic Space in Roman Italy." In Rawson and Weaver, *Roman Family,* 281–98.

Nichols, F. M., and E. Gardiner, eds. *The Marvels of Rome; Mirabilia Urbis Romae,* 2d ed. New York, 1986.

Noble, T. F. X. "Theodoric and the Papacy." In *Teoderico il Grande,* 395–423.

Noethlichs, K. L. "Materialien zum Bischofsbild aus den spätantiken Rechtsquellen." *Jahrbuch für Antike und Christentum* 16 (1973): 28–59.

Norberg, D. "Style personnel et style administratif dans le registrum epistularum de Saint Grégoire le Grand." In *Grégoire le Grand,* ed. J. Fontaine, R. Gillet, and S. Pellistrandi, 489–96. Paris, 1986.

Norden, E. *Die antike Kunstprosa.* 2 vols. 5th ed. Stuttgart, 1958.

O'Donnell, J. J. "Liberius the Patrician." *Traditio* 37 (1981): 31–72.

Olivar, A. *La predicación cristiana antigua.* Barcelona, 1991.

O'Meara, J. J. "Augustine's *Confessions:* Elements of Fiction." In McWilliam, *Augustine,* 77–95.

Painter, K. "Late-Roman silver plate: a reply to Alan Cameron." *JRA* 6 (1993): 109–15.

Parezo, N. "The Formation of Anthropological Archival Records." In Kingery, *Learning from Things*, 145–72.

Parkin, T. "Out of Sight, Out of Mind: Elderly Members of the Roman Family." In Rawson and Weaver, *Roman Family*, 123–48.

Pascal, C. B. *The Cults of Cisalpine Gaul.* Coll. Latomus, vol. 75. Brussels, 1964.

Pavlovskis, Z. "From Statius to Ennodius: A Brief History of Prose Prefaces." *Rendiconti Istituto Lombardo, Classe di Lettere e Scienze Morali* 101 (1967): 535–67.

Pecere, O. "La cultura greco-romana in età gota tra adattamento e trasformazione." In *Teoderico il Grande*, 355–94.

Petersen, J. M. "Did Gregory the Great Know Greek?" In *Studies in Church History* 13, ed. D. Baker, 121–34. Oxford, 1976.

Petitmengin, P. "Les plus anciens manuscrits de la Bible latine." In Fontaine and Pietri, *Le monde latin antique*, 89–117.

Picard, J.-C. "Ce que les textes nous apprennent sur les équipements et le mobilier liturgique nécessaires pour le baptême dans le Sud de la Gaule et l'Italie du Nord." In *Actes du XIe congrès international d'archéologie chrétienne* 2:451–68.

———. *Le souvenir des évêques. Sépultures, listes épiscopales et culte des évêques en Italie du Nord des origines au Xe siècle.* BEFAR 268. Paris, 1988.

Pietri, C. *Roma Christiana. Recherches sur l'Église de Rome, son organisations, sa politique, son idéologie de Miltiade à Sixte III.* BEFAR 224. 2 vols. Rome, 1976.

———. "Aristocratie et société cléricale dans l'Italie chrétienne au temps d'Odoacre et de Théodoric." *MEFRA* 93 (1981): 417–67.

———. "Le sénat, le peuple chrétien et les partis du cirque à Rome sous le pape Symmaque (498–514)." *MEFRA* 78 (1966): 123–39.

Pietri, L. "*Pagina in pariete reserata:* épigraphie et architecture religieuse." In Donati, *La terza età dell' epigrafia*, 137–57.

Pizarro, J. M. *Writing Ravenna: The Liber Pontificalis of Andreas Agnellus.* Ann Arbor, 1995.

Polara, G. "I distici di Ennodio." In *La poesia cristiana latina in distici elegiaci. Atti del convegno internazionale Assisi, 20–22 marzo 1992,* ed. G. Catanzaro and F. Santucci, 217–39. Assisi, 1993.

Posner, E. *Archives in the Ancient World.* Cambridge, MA, 1972.

Prown, J. D. "Material/Culture: Can the Farmer and the Cowman Still Be Friends?" In Kingery, *Learning from Things*, 19–27.

Raby, F. J. E., ed. *The Oxford Book of Medieval Latin Verse.* Oxford, 1959.

Rallo Freni, R. A. *La Paraenesis didascalica di Magno Felice Ennodio con il testo latino e la traduzione.* Messina and Florence, 1981.

Rawson, B., and P. Weaver, eds. *The Roman Family in Italy: Status, Sentiment, Space.* Canberra and Oxford, 1997.

Reboul, O. *La rhétorique.* 4th ed. Paris, 1993.

Relihan, J. C. *Ancient Menippean Satire.* Baltimore, 1993.

Reydellet, M. "La Bible miroir des princes, du IVe au VIIe siècle." In Fontaine and Pietri, *Le monde latin antique*, 431–53.

———. *La royauté dans la littérature latine de Sidoine Apollinaire à Isidore de Séville.* BEFAR 243. Rome, 1981.

———. "Ennodio, Magno Felice." *Dizionario Biografico degli Italiani* 42 (1993): 689–95.

Riché, P. *Education and Culture in the Barbarian West, Sixth through Eighth Centuries.* Columbia, SC, 1976.

Robert, L. *Hellenica XI–XII.* Paris, 1960.

Roberts, M. *Biblical Epic and Rhetorical Paraphrase in Late Antiquity.* ARCA 16. Liverpool, 1985.

———. *The Jeweled Style.* Ithaca, 1989.

———. "The Use of Myth in Latin Epithalamia from Statius to Venantius Fortunatus." *TAPA* 119 (1989): 321–48.

Roger, M. *L'enseignement des lettres classiques d'Ausone à Alcuin. Introduction à l'histoire des écoles carolingiennes.* Paris, 1905.

Rohr, C. *Der Theoderich-Panegyricus des Ennodius.* MGH Studien und Texte Bd. 12. Hannover, 1995.

Rouse, R. H., and M. A. Rouse. "Ennodius in the Middle Ages: Adonics, Pseudo-Isidore, Cistercians, and the Schools." In *Popes, Teachers, and Canon Law in the Middle Ages,* ed. J. R. Sweeney and S. Chodorow, 91–113. Ithaca, 1989.

Ruether, R. R. *Faith and Fratricide: The Theological Roots of Anti-Semitism.* New York, 1979.

Ruggini, L. C. "Ebrei e orientali nell'Italia settentrionale fra il IV e il VI secolo d.Chr." *SDHI* 25 (1959): 186–308.

———. *Economia e società nell' "Italia Annonaria."* Milan, 1961.

———. "Ticinum: dal 476 d.C. alla fine del Regno Gotico." In *L'età antica,* Vol. 1 of *Storia di Pavia,* 271–312, Pavia, 1984.

Saller, R. P. *Patriarchy, Property and Death in the Roman Family.* Cambridge, 1994.

Salway, B. "What's in a Name? A Survey of Roman Onomastic Practice from c. 700 B.C. to A.D. 700." *JRS* 84 (1994): 124–45.

Sardella, T. *Società chiesa e stato nell'età di Teoderico. Papa Simmaco e lo scismo laurenziano.* Soveria Mannelli, 1996.

Schanz, M., C. Hosius, and G. Krüger. *Die Literatur des fünften und sechsten Jahrhunderts.* Vol. 4.2 of *Geschichte der römischen Literatur bis zum Gesetzgebungswerk des Kaisers Justinian.* Munich, 1920.

Scheibelreiter, G. *Der Bischof in merowingischer Zeit.* Vienna, 1983.

Schetter, W. "Die Thetisdeklamation des Ennodius." In *Bonner Festgabe Johannes Straub,* ed. A. Lippold and N. Himmelmann, 395–412. Bonn, 1977.

———. "Zu Ennodius *Carm.* 2,1 Hartel." *Hermes* 114 (1986): 500–502.

Schramm, P. E. *Herrschaftszeichen und Staatssymbolik.* Schriften der Monumenta Germaniae Historica, 13.1. Stuttgart, 1954.

Schröder, B.-J. *Titel und Text. Zur Entwicklung lateinischer Gedichtüberschriften. Mit Untersuchungen zu lateinischen Buchtiteln, Inhaltsverzeichnissen und anderen Gliederungsmitteln.* Berlin, 1999.

Schwartz, E. *Publizistische Sammlungen zum Acacianischen Schisma. Abhandlungen der Bayerischen Akademie der Wissenschaften,* phil.-hist. Abt. N.F. 10. Munich, 1934.

———. "Der sechste nicaenische Kanon auf der Synode von Chalkedon."

Sitzungsberichte der Preussischen Akademie der Wissenschaften, phil.-hist. Abt. (1930): 611–40.

Schwind, J. *Arator-Studien*. Hypomnemata 94. Göttingen, 1990.

Scott, J. "From Literal Self-Sacrifice to Literary Self-Sacrifice: Augustine's Confessions and the Rhetoric of Testimony." In McWilliam, *Augustine,* 31–49.

Scott, S. "The Power of Images in the Late-Roman House." In Laurence and Wallace-Hadrill, *Domestic Space,* 53–67.

Settia, A. A. "Le fortificazioni dei Goti in Italia." In *Teoderico il Grande,* 101–31.

Shanzer, D. "Ennodius, Boethius, and the Date and Interpretation of Maximilianus' Elegia III." *RFIC* 111 (1983): 183–95.

Shelton, K. J. *The Esquiline Treasure.* London, 1981.

Shipley, G., and J. Salmon, eds. *Human Landscapes in Classical Antiquity: Environment and Culture.* London, 1996.

Sirmond, J. *Ep. ad Nicolaum Fabrum.* In *Ennodi Opera.* Paris, 1611. Reprint. *Opera Varia,* vol. 1.

———. *Historia Praedestinatiana.* Paris, 1643. Reprint. *Opera Varia,* vol. 4.

Smith, C. D. "Where Was the 'Wilderness' in Roman Times?" In Shipley and Salmon, *Human Landscapes,* 154–79.

Solignac, A. "Julien Pomère." *Dictionnaire de Spiritualité* 8 (1974): 1594–1600.

Stein, E. *Histoire du Bas-Empire.* 2 vols. Brussels, 1949–59.

Steinhauser, K. B. "The Literary Unity of the Confessions." In McWilliam, *Augustine,* 15–30.

Steinmetz, P. *Untersuchungen zur römischen Literatur des zweiten Jahrhunderts nach Christi Geburt.* Wiesbaden, 1982.

Stock, B. *Augustine the Reader.* Cambridge, MA, 1996.

———. *Listening for the Text.* Baltimore, 1990.

Straw, C. *Gregory the Great. Perfection in Imperfection.* Berkeley, 1988.

Stroheker, K. F. *Der senatorische Adel im spätantiken Gallien.* Tübingen, 1948.

Strong, D. E. *Greek and Roman Silver Plate.* London, 1966.

Sumner, G. V. "Germanicus and Drusus Caesar." *Latomus* 26 (1967): 413–35.

Sundwall, J. *Abhandlungen zur Geschichte des ausgehenden Römertums.* Helsinki, 1919. Reprint. New York, 1975.

Tanzi, C. "La cronologia degli scritti di Magno Felice Ennodio." *Archeografo Triestino,* n.s. 15 (1890): 339–412.

Teitler, H. C. *Notarii and Exceptores.* Dutch Monographs on Ancient History and Archaeology 1. Amsterdam, 1985.

Teoderico il Grande e i Goti d'Italia. Atti del XIII congresso internazionale di studi sull'Alto Medioevo (Milano, 2–6 novembre 1992). 2 vols. Spoleto, 1993.

Theis, L. "Saints sans famille? Quelques remarques sur la famille dans le monde franc à travers les sources hagiographiques." *Revue Historique* 255 (1976): 3–20.

Thomas, E., and C. Witschel. "Constructing Reconstruction: Claim and Reality of Roman Rebuilding Inscriptions from the Latin West." *PBSR* 60 (1992): 135–77.

Thraede, K. *Grundzüge griechisch-römischer Brieftopik.* Zetemata 48. Göttingen, 1970.

Tilley, C., ed. *Reading Material Culture. Structuralism, Hermeneutics, and Post-Structuralism.* Oxford, 1990.

Toynbee, J. M. C., and K. S. Painter. "Silver Picture Plates of Late Antiquity: A.D. 300 to 700." *Archaeologia* 108 (1986): 15–65.

Townsend, W. T., and W. F. Wyatt. "Ennodius and Pope Symmachus." In *Studies in Honor of E. K. Rand,* ed. L. W. Jones, 277–91. New York, 1938.

Ullmann, W. "*Romanus pontifex indubitanter efficitur sanctus:* Dictatus Papae 23 in Retrospect and Prospect." *Studi Gregoriani* 6 (1959–61): 229–64.

Usener, H. *Anecdoton Holderi.* Bonn, 1877. Reprint. Hildesheim, 1969.

Vaes, J. "*Nova construere sed amplius vetusta servare:* la réutilisation chrétienne d'édifices antiques." In *Actes du XIᵉ congrès international d'archéologie chrétienne* 1:299–319.

Van Uytfanghe, M. "La controverse biblique et patristique autour du miracle, et ses répercussions sur l'hagiographie dans l'Antiquité tardive et le haut Moyen Âge latin." In *Hagiographie, cultures et sociétés, IVᵉ–XIIᵉ siècles,* 205–31. Paris, 1981.

Vessey, M. "Literacy and *Litteratura,* A.D. 200–800." *Studies in Medieval and Renaissance History* 13 (1992): 139–60.

———. "Patristics and Literary History." *Literature and Theology* 5.4 (1991): 341–54.

Vismara, G. "Le *Causae Liberales* nel tribunale di Agostino vescovo di Ippona." *SDHI* 61 (1995): 365–72.

Vollenweider, M.-L. *Deliciae Leonis. Antike geschnittene Steine u. Ringe aus einer Privatsammlung.* Mainz, 1984.

Ward-Perkins, B. *From Classical Antiquity to the Middle Ages: Urban Public Building in Northern and Central Italy, AD 300–850.* Oxford, 1984.

Watson, A. "Religious and Gender Discrimination: St. Ambrose and the Valentiniani." *SDHI* 61 (1995): 313–26.

Weaver, R. H. *Divine Grace and Human Agency: A Study of the Semi-Pelagian Controversy.* Macon, GA, 1996.

———. "Semipelagianism." In Ferguson, *Encyclopedia of Early Christianity,* 1046–47.

Wermelinger, O. "Ennodius." *TRE* 9.5 (1982): 654–57.

Wes, M. A. "Crisis and Conversion in Fifth-Century Gaul: Aristocrats and Ascetics between 'Horizontality' and 'Verticality.'" In Drinkwater and Elton, *Fifth-Century Gaul,* 252–63.

Wharton, A. J. *Refiguring the Post Classical City: Dura Europos, Jerash, Jerusalem and Ravenna.* Cambridge, 1995.

Whitby, Mary, ed. *The Propaganda of Power: The Role of Panegyric in Late Antiquity.* Mnemosyne Supp. 183. Leiden, 1998.

Wickham, C. *Early Medieval Italy. Central Power and Local Society 400–1000.* Ann Arbor, 1989.

Wirbelauer, E. *Zwei Päpste in Rom. Der Konflikt zwischen Laurentius und Symmachus (498–514).* Studien und Texte. Quellen und Forschungen zur Antiken Welt 16. Munich, 1993.

Wojtowytsch, M. *Papsttum und Konzile von den Anfängen bis zu Leo I (440–461)*. Päpste und Papsttum 17. Stuttgart, 1981.

Wolfram, H. *History of the Goths*. Berkeley, 1988.

Wood, I. "Administration, Law and Culture in Merovingian Gaul." In McKitterick, *Uses of Literacy*, 63–81.

―――. *The Merovingian Kingdoms, 450–751*. London, 1994.

Zelzer, K. "Das Mönchtum in Italien zur Zeit der Goten." In *Teoderico il Grande*, 425–49.

Zelzer, M. "Die Briefbücher des hl. Ambrosius und die Briefe extra collectionem." *Anzeiger der Österreichischen Akademie der Wissenschaften*, phil.-hist. Klasse 112 (1975): 7–23.

Zetzel, J. E. G. *Latin Textual Criticism in Antiquity*. Salem, NH, 1984.

Ziolkowski, J. M. *Alan of Lille's Grammar of Sex: The Meaning of Grammar to a Twelfth-Century Intellectual*. Speculum anniversary monographs, 10. Cambridge, MA, 1985.

Index